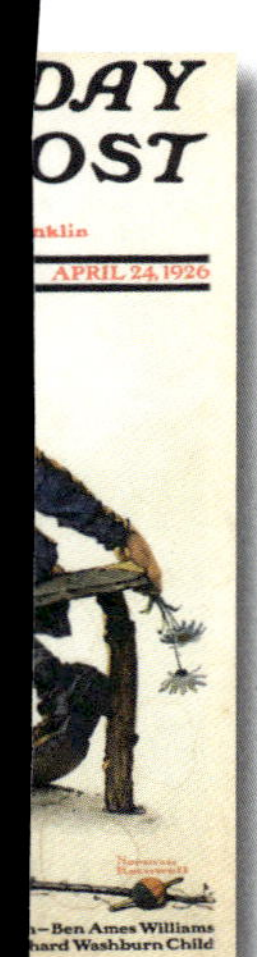
APRIL 24, 1926

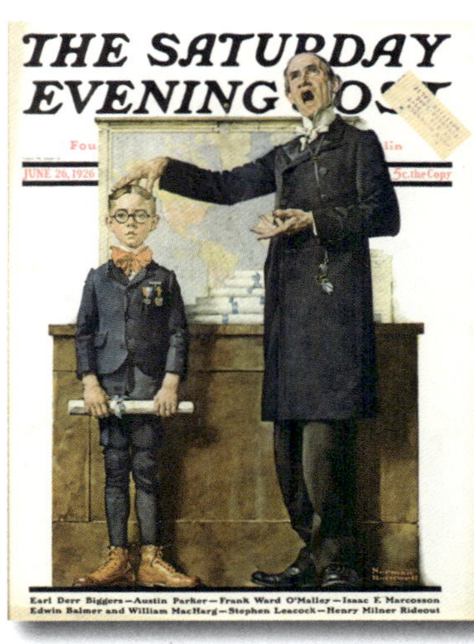
THE SATURDAY
EVENING
JUNE 26, 1926
Earl Derr Biggers—Austin Parker—Frank Ward O'Malley—Isaac F. Marcosson
Edwin Balmer and William MacHarg—Stephen Leacock—Henry Milner Rideout

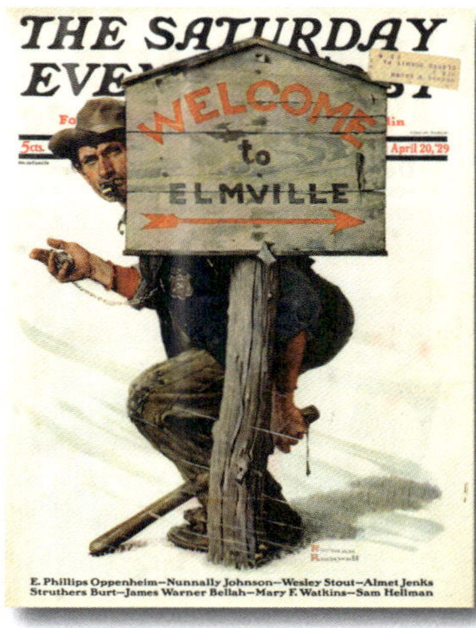
THE SATURDAY
WELCOME to ELMVILLE
April 20,'29
E. Phillips Oppenheim—Nunnally Johnson—Wesley Stout—Almet Jenks
Struthers Burt—James Warner Bellah—Mary F. Watkins—Sam Hellman

AF477849
Susan Ertz—Christian Gauss—Charles Brackett—Dwight Mitchell Wiley
Courtney Ryley Cooper—Thomas Beer—Nunnally Johnson—Henry Ford

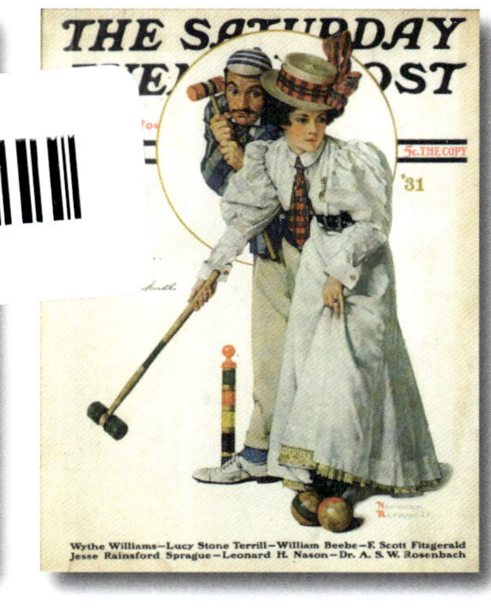
THE SATURDAY
'31
Wythe Williams—Lucy Stone Terrill—William Beebe—F. Scott Fitzgerald
Jesse Rainsford Sprague—Leonard H. Nason—Dr. A. S. W. Rosenbach

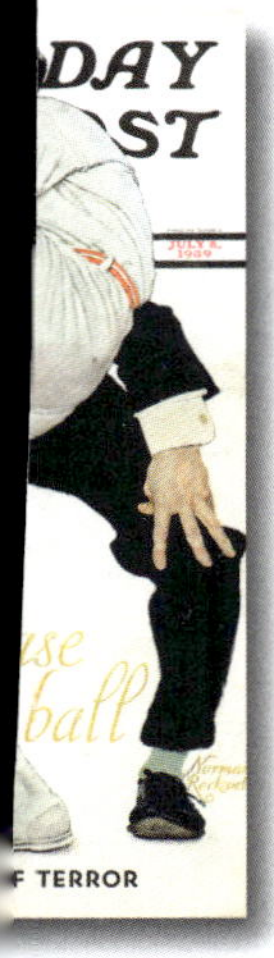

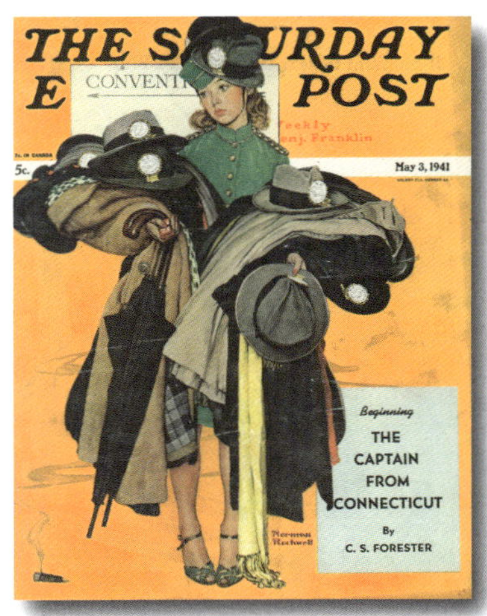
POST
May 3, 1941
Beginning
THE CAPTAIN FROM CONNECTICUT
By C. S. FORESTER

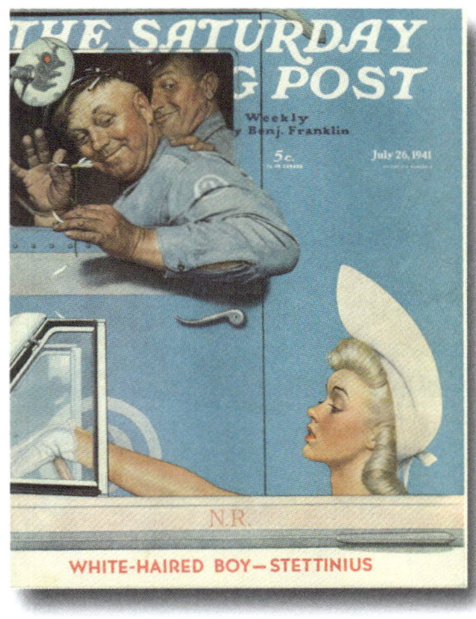
POST
July 26, 1941
WHITE-HAIRED BOY—STETTINIUS

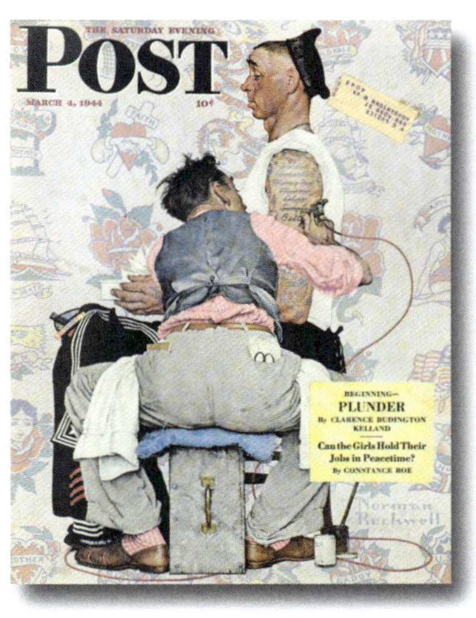
THE SATURDAY EVENING
POST
MARCH 4, 1944
10¢
BEGINNING—
PLUNDER
By CLARENCE BUDINGTON KELLAND
Can the Girls Hold Their Jobs in Peacetime?
By CONSTANCE ROE

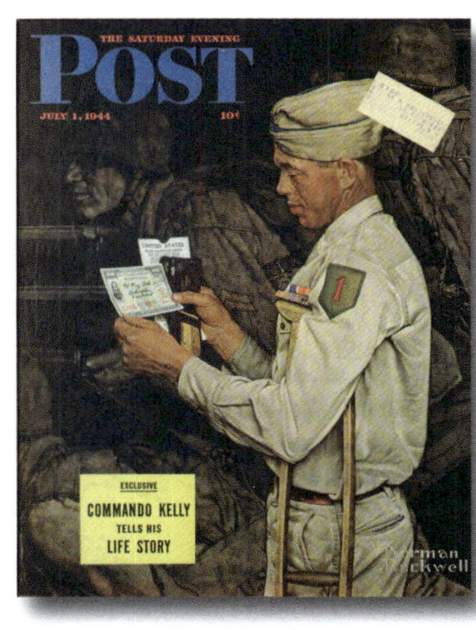
THE SATURDAY EVENING
POST
JULY 1, 1944
10¢
EXCLUSIVE
COMMANDO KELLY
TELLS HIS
LIFE STORY

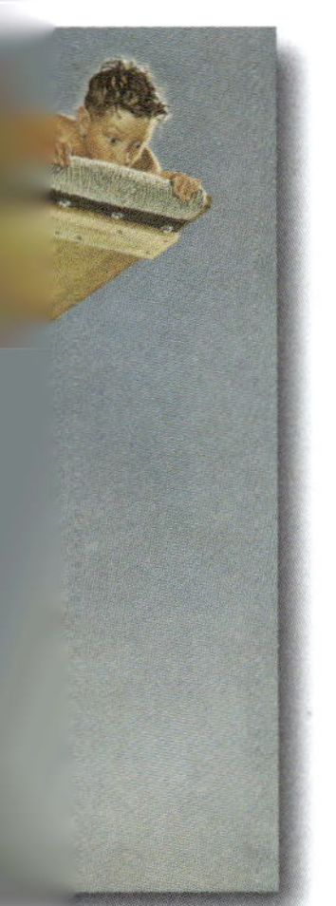

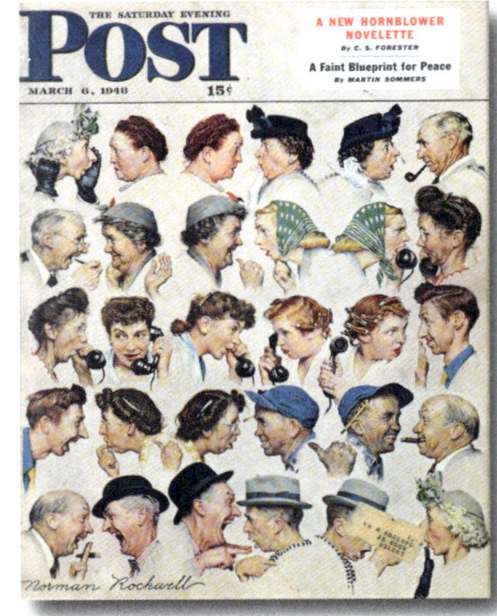
THE SATURDAY EVENING
POST
MARCH 6, 1948
15¢
A NEW HORNBLOWER NOVELETTE
By C. S. FORESTER
A Faint Blueprint for Peace
By MARTIN SOMMERS
Norman Rockwell

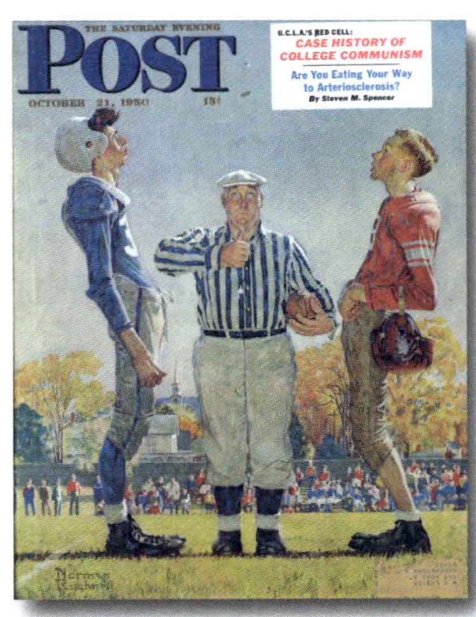
POST
OCTOBER 21, 1950
15¢
U.C.L.A.'S RED CELL:
CASE HISTORY OF COLLEGE COMMUNISM
Are You Eating Your Way to Arteriosclerosis?
By Steven M. Spencer

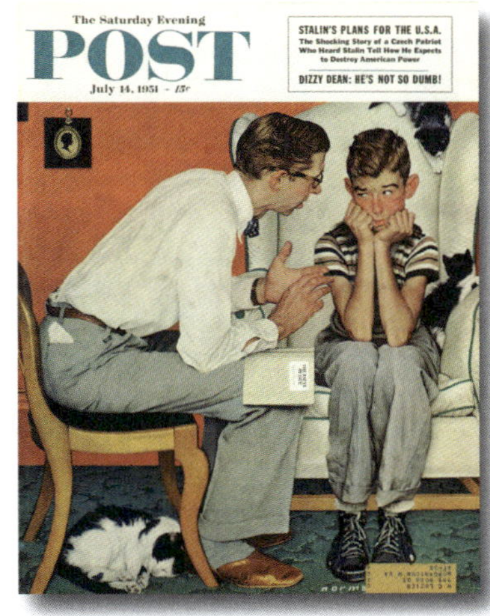
The Saturday Evening
POST
July 14, 1951 — 15¢
STALIN'S PLANS FOR THE U.S.A.
DIZZY DEAN: HE'S NOT SO DUMB!

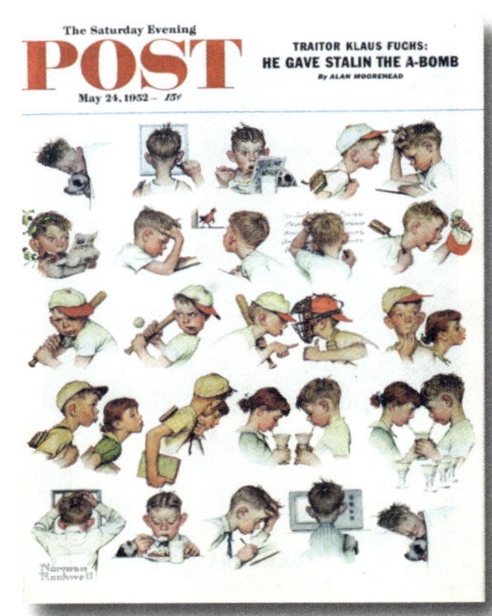
The Saturday Evening
POST
May 24, 1952 — 15¢
TRAITOR KLAUS FUCHS:
HE GAVE STALIN THE A-BOMB
By ALAN MOOREHEAD

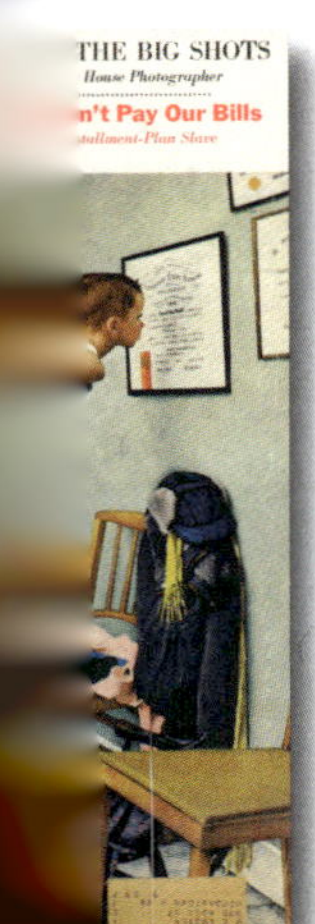
THE BIG SHOTS

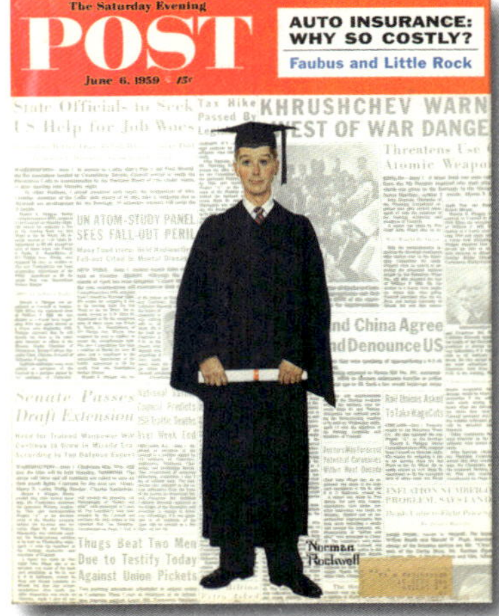
The Saturday Evening
POST
June 6, 1959 — 15¢
AUTO INSURANCE:
WHY SO COSTLY?
Faubus and Little Rock

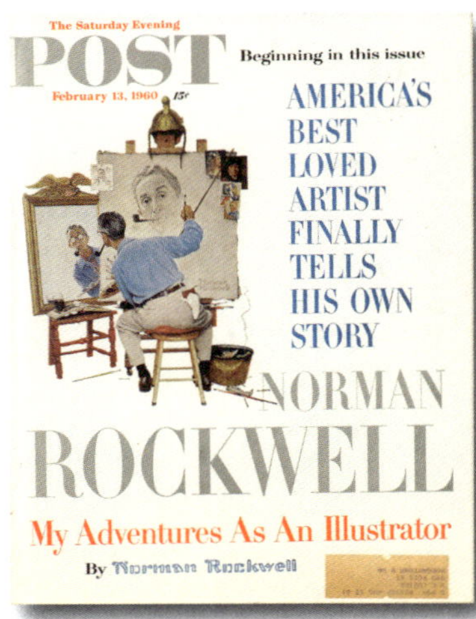
The Saturday Evening
POST
February 13, 1960 — 15¢
Beginning in this issue
AMERICA'S
BEST
LOVED
ARTIST
FINALLY
TELLS
HIS OWN
STORY
NORMAN
ROCKWELL
My Adventures As An Illustrator
By Norman Rockwell

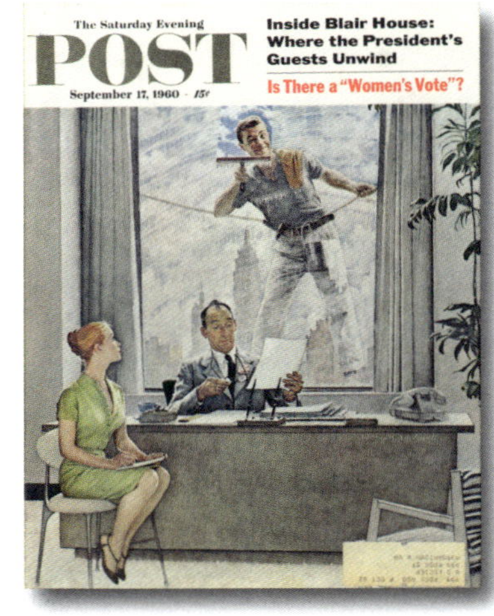
The Saturday Evening
POST
September 17, 1960 — 15¢
Inside Blair House:
Where the President's
Guests Unwind
Is There a "Women's Vote"?

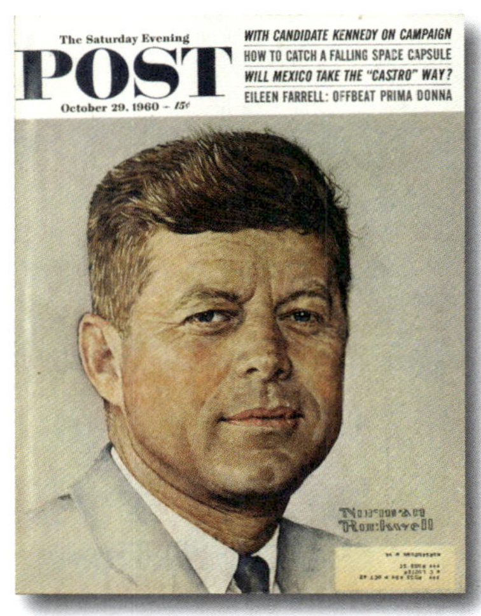
The Saturday Evening
POST
October 29, 1960 — 15¢
WITH CANDIDATE KENNEDY ON CAMPAIGN
HOW TO CATCH A FALLING SPACE CAPSULE
WILL MEXICO TAKE THE "CASTRO" WAY?
EILEEN FARRELL: OFFBEAT PRIMA DONNA

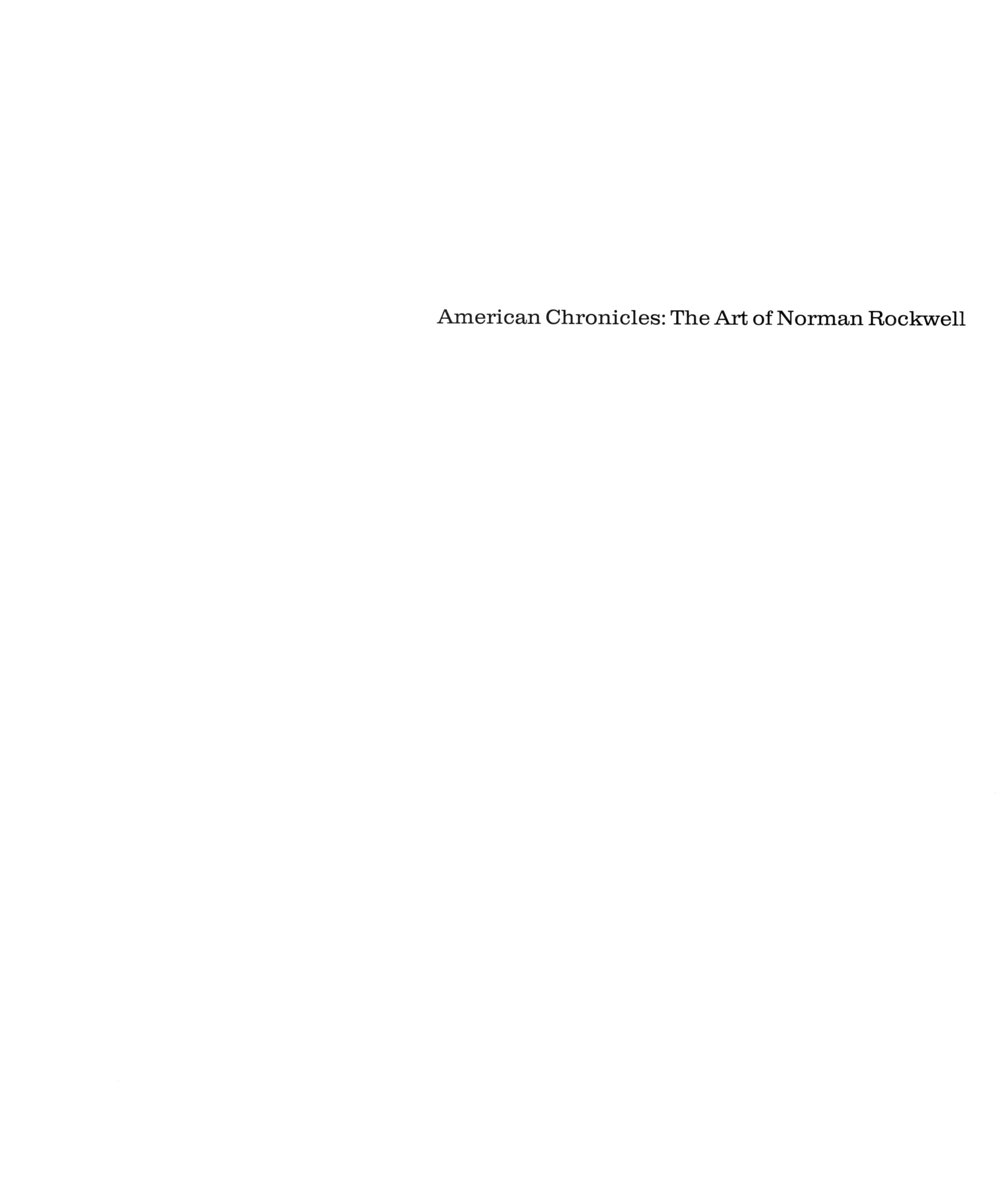

American Chronicles: The Art of Norman Rockwell

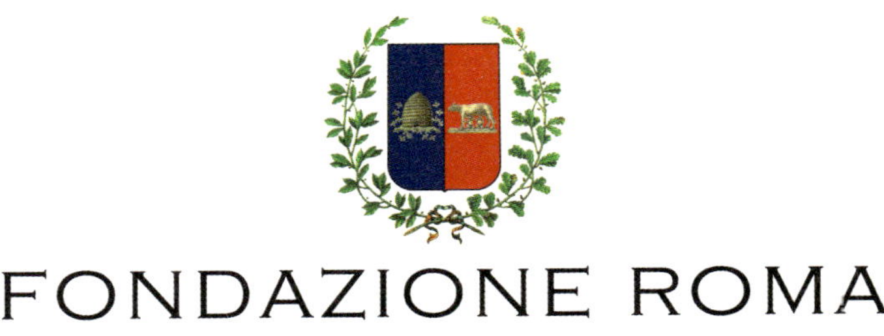
FONDAZIONE ROMA

American Chronicles: The Art of

Norman Rockwell

edited by
Danilo Eccher and Stephanie Haboush Plunkett

exhibition organized by
Norman Rockwell Museum,
Stockbridge, Massachusetts, USA
and
Fondazione Roma-Arte-Musei

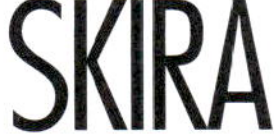

Cover
The Runaway, 1958
Painting for *The Saturday Evening Post* cover, September 20, 1958
Oil on canvas, 35.75 x 33.5 inches
Norman Rockwell Museum Collection, NRM.1973.18
1958 © SEPS. Licensed by Curtis Licensing, Indianapolis, IN, USA

Back cover
Triple Self-Portrait, 1960
Painting for *The Saturday Evening Post* cover, February 13, 1960
Oil on canvas, 44.5 x 34.75 inches
Norman Rockwell Art Collection Trust, NRACT.1973.19
1960 © SEPS. Licensed by Curtis Licensing, Indianapolis, IN, USA

Front and back endpapers
Saturday Evening Post covers
© SEPS. Licensed by Curtis Licensing, Indianapolis, IN, USA

Art Director
Marcello Francone

Design
Luigi Fiore

Editorial Coordination
Eva Vanzella

Editing
Timothy Stroud

Layout
Antonio Carminati

Translations
Paul Metcalfe and Simon Turner for *Scriptum*, Rome

Iconographical Research
Paola Lamanna

First published in Italy in 2014 by
Skira Editore S.p.A.
Palazzo Casati Stampa
via Torino 61
20123 Milano
Italy
www.skira.net

Printed and bound in Italy. First edition

ISBN: 978-88-572-2576-0
(hard cover)
ISBN: 978-88-572-2681-1
(soft cover)

Distributed in USA, Canada, Central & South America by Rizzoli International Publications, Inc., 300 Park Avenue South, New York, NY 10010, USA.
Distributed elsewhere in the world by Thames and Hudson Ltd., 181A High Holborn, London WC1V 7QX, United Kingdom.

American Chronicles: The Art of Norman Rockwell

Rome, Fondazione Roma Museo
Palazzo Sciarra
November 11, 2014 – February 8, 2015

Exhibition promoted by

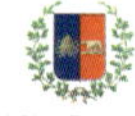

FONDAZIONE ROMA

President
Emmanuele Francesco Maria Emanuele
Director General
Franco Parasassi

Organized by
Norman Rockwell Museum, Stockbridge, Massachusetts, USA
Director / CEO
Laurie Norton Moffatt

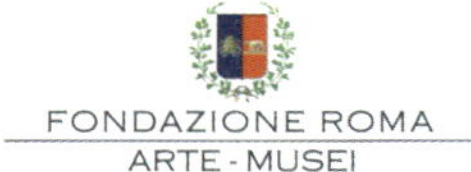

Secretary General
Tatyana Kasyanenko

In collaboration with

laFondazioneNY

Chairman
Riccardo Viale

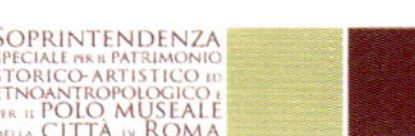

Superintendent
Daniela Porro

Exhibition curated by
Danilo Eccher
Stephanie Haboush Plunkett

Production

Exhibition Design
Baldessari e Baldessari architetti e designers

Staging Coordination
AFPGEO

Staging
Gamma Eventi

Lighting Designer
Giuseppe Mestrangelo
Iskra Mestrangelo
Light Studio - Milan

Graphic Design
Francesca Pavese
Stefania Conchiglia

Graphics
Gruppo Fallani

Preservation Control
Laura Cibrario
Fabiola Jatta

Transportation
Arterìa

Insurance
Willis Italia

Security
Sipro - Sicurezza Professionale

Lighting System
GPCR

Security System
Metrovox

CSE / Security Coordination
Angelo Giuseppe Amodeo

Microclimate System
Silvestrini Impianti

Translations
Susan M. Aulton

Communications and Media
Roncaglia & Wijkander

Web Communications and Social Media
cittàinnternet

Video Production
Logica Video

Groups and Booking Office
Civita Cultura

Educational Services
Senza titolo

Audioguides
Antenna International

Video Post-production
Zenit Arti Audiovisive - Torino

Catalogue edited by
Danilo Eccher
Stephanie Haboush Plunkett

Essays by
Danilo Eccher
Stephanie Haboush Plunkett
Laurie Norton Moffatt
Linda Szekely Pero

Entries by
Linda Szekely Pero

Special thanks to

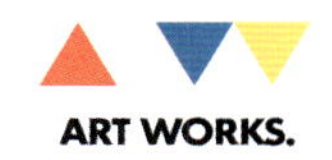

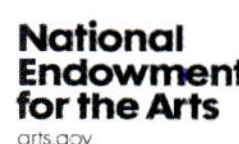

The Henry Luce Foundation
Curtis Licensing, a division of *The Saturday Evening Post*
Norman Rockwell Family Agency
Stockman Family Foundation

Thanks also to
Sara d'Alessandro

Through its operative branch, the Fondazione Roma-Arte-Musei, the Fondazione Roma now opens the autumn season of the Museo Fondazione Roma-Palazzo Sciarra with a new artistic and cultural event devoted to Norman Rockwell (New York, 1894 – Stockbridge, 1978), one of the most enchanting figures in 20th-century American art. The opening comes fifteen years after the inauguration of the museum's first exhibition, which took place in 1999 with the presentation of the masterpieces of the Fondazione Roma Collection to the general public. On that occasion I pointed out that culture, our form of "clean energy", plays a key part in the development of society by making it possible, through the dissemination of knowledge, to reduce differences and social strife but also to revitalize, through the discovery of beauty, an impetus that leads to individual and collective enhancement and ultimately to the improvement of society as a whole. Culture is therefore, in my view, also a tool involved in the country's economic recovery. In this sense therefore, the Fondazione Roma Museo, created in accordance with my wishes both as a home for the works of the vast collection and as an exhibition venue, is not so much simply a container of individual events as it is a proactive centre of initiatives with a significant scholarly and popularizing dimension, one that is capable of contributing to the cultural development of Rome by means of a sensitivity to the osmosis between different cultures that lays the foundations for dialogue, concord and the development of peoples.

The criteria adopted in planning the museum's exhibitions, in accordance with my precise instructions, have a twofold thrust. On the one hand, Rome's contribution to culture over the centuries, masterfully represented by ground-breaking events such as *The Fifteenth Century in Rome, The Renaissance of the Arts from Donatello to Perugino, The Renaissance in Rome. Inspired by Michelangelo and Raphael, The Rome of Piranesi. The Eighteenth-Century City in the Great Vedute, Rome and Antiquity. Reality and Vision in the 18th Century* and *The Roman Countryside from Hackert to Balla*, continuing all the way up to contemporary art with *The Unrepeatable Nineteen Sixties. A Dialogue between Rome and Milan.* On the other, the relationship between Rome and the international art scene, from which we have drawn significant stimuli, as epitomized by exhibitions on the art of China, Japan and Russia (*Masterpieces from the Forbidden City. Qianlong and His Court, Hiroshige. The Master of Nature* and *Kazimir Malevich. Beyond Figuration, Beyond Abstraction*) as well as the United States, with Edward Hopper, Georgia O'Keeffe, Louise Nevelson and now Rockwell, a man of great interpretive and communicative talent capable of encapsulating the content of a whole story in the space of a single image.

An acute observer, Rockwell used the powerful medium of the cover illustration—of which he produced over 300 between 1916 and 1963 for *The Saturday Evening Post*—to address the events, problems, intangible values, feelings, festivities and ways of life of an America that strikes us as truly infectious. Precursors of the modern snapshot, his works also focus on social issues, such as the fight against poverty and the battle for civil rights.

As a chronicler of his time, which covers practically the whole of the 20th century, Rockwell managed to maintain a delicate balance between idealism and reality. The works born out of his intuitive reasoning and feelings are like windows open on old America, from which he loved to lean in order to observe, reflect or simply find amusement. Rockwell captures gestures, feelings and status symbols with extraordinary talent on the surface of his support, drawing on the everyday life of ordinary people, a micro-history narrated through the effectiveness of drawings full of humor and sentimentality. The magical "painting," generated by reflection on a photograph used as a starting point, sometimes becomes nostalgic, enveloped in an almost fairytale realism adorned with carefree colour in a noontime glow that conveys the sense of optimism and confidence in the future typical of his time.

In short, in the era of the popularizing illustration, Rockwell expressed pride and sorrow with an always uncritical and objective eye, as well as delicate—and sometimes uproarious—irony that gives way to deep love for what he perceives as virtues. I refer in particular to tolerance and respect for values, secular and religious, which are transformed in Rockwell's imagination into precious occasions to address, for example, the dramas of life, conflicts and contradictions, racial hatred and social injustices. Emblematic in this connection is the *Four Freedoms* series of paintings, on show here, inspired by President Roosevelt's famous speech and published in *The Saturday Evening Post* before being exhibited in numerous American cities to raise funds for the war.

Promoted by the Fondazione Roma and jointly organized by the Norman Rockwell Museum of Stockbridge, Massachusetts, and the Fondazione Roma-Arte-Musei, the show will make Rockwell's importance in the field of illustration clear to everyone. A dynamic array of paintings, posters and photographs will provide the visitor with insight into the work of an artist loved by the countless multitudes of people he reached through the medium of printed reproduction.

In conclusion, I wish to thank the Norman Rockwell Museum in the person of its director Laurie Norton Moffatt and the exhibition's curators—Stephanie Haboush Plunkett, chief curator of Norman Rockwell Museum, and Danilo Eccher, director of the Galleria Civica d'Arte Moderna e Contemporanea in Turin—as well as Riccardo Viale, chairman of La Fondazione NY, who contributed so much to the conception and development of the project.

Emmanuele Francesco Maria Emanuele
President, Fondazione Roma

On visiting the Robert Kennedy Center's *Freedom Fighters* exhibition a few months ago, I came across an image of Norman Rockwell's painting *The Problem We All Live With* (1964) in the midst of the violent, brutal photographs of segregation and racism in America. It shows the young African-American girl Ruby Bridges escorted to school by federal marshals past a wall daubed with racist graffiti, like a passage from hell to poetry. This sweet, helpless child, fragile and dignified, flanked and protected by federal officers, the symbol of governmental authority, to enable her to exercise a right denied her, has more impact on our faculty of empathetic identification than a thousand realistic photographs. The child walks with an unnatural stride to keep in step with her bodyguards, like a prisoner. Her attitude is not one of resignation, however, but of marching towards a new horizon. Many years later, as a mature woman, Bridges was in fact to see this painting of her exhibited in the White House in 2011 in the company of an African-American president.

Norman Rockwell has a rare gift for a painter: the ability to astonish with normality, to make the viewer identify without expressive overstatement, to tell us more with a few strokes than a tome of sociology. We understand this gift on looking at the *Four Freedoms* series (1943) and above all the painting *Freedom of Speech*. The figure of a standing worker, looking upwards with a resolute expression of hope and dignity, suggests that his message to an audience of tranquil representatives of the American middle class will succeed in overcoming reservations and skepticism. The strength of the liberal ideal and the many social and political problems and obstacles to its achievement are masterfully expressed in this simple painting of iconic and universal value.

The unique genius of this painter, chronicler and illustrator of 20th-century American reality explains the interest manifested against the prevailing trend by Prof. Emmanuele F.M. Emanuele, whose well-known determination and farsightedness have resulted in the splendid event now held by the Fondazione Roma in its exhibition centre. Together with the Norman Rockwell Museum and the Fondazione Roma-Arte-Musei, joint organizers of the exhibition, La Fondazione NY has helped to make the initiative a reality through its head of cultural projects Renata Rosati. This is yet another example of successful transatlantic collaboration between Italy and the United States.

Riccardo Viale
Chairman, La Fondazione NY

Contents

Danilo Eccher

Norman Rockwell

It is hard to think of Norman Rockwell's work without being plunged into the flow of American society. It draws us into the dreams, desires, fears and ethical values of a community that, in the "short" twentieth century, witnessed the transformation of a nation on the fringes of a still Eurocentric world and its conquest of the supremacy that America still enjoys today. This historic journey is narrated by Norman Rockwell, and his images are the faces, landscapes, homes, and stories of this society. He portrays an era of dramas and tragedies, as well as amazing rebirths, and one that experienced the darkest fears and the most radiant freedoms. What makes Rockwell so significant is that he was able to witness this history, and that he himself tells the tale by choosing characters and stories, illustrating hopes, and giving voices and faces to the common people's most intimate and authentic feelings. The remarkable vantage point offered by magazine covers of the time enabled him to build up the incredible iconographic vocabulary with which he portrayed the world around him. But what makes Rockwell's art so outstanding is not its documentary aspect—it is not simply the way it rapidly responds to and captures the mood of his day. In his artistic research there is a degree of conceptual intricacy and linguistic sophistication that allows him to introduce a number of different levels of interpretation into his work. This adds a more attentive and sophisticated artistic composition, which draws on more refined notions, and the iconographic narrative that is so adored by the public. In other words, there are connections and allusions, skills and affinities with the history of art which open up surprising and innovative critical prospects.

Already in the early work *Slim Finnegan* of 1916, which Rockwell made for *The Saturday Evening Post* when he was 22 years old, the construction is open to a number of areas of critical interpretation that overshadow the immediate narrative realism. On a symbolic level, it shows a nation that is still young but absolutely determined, courageous and enterprising: even the dog in the foreground points to the cohesion of a society which by now is well aware of its dominant position. The risk of descending into rhetoric is avoided by the children's play, which shifts the symbolism towards the more reassuring field of innocent fun. Here we can already see early signs of caricature, which Rockwell was to maintain for most of his career, allowing him to create the visual interaction he needed to soften the literary burden. Rockwell was to use this device many times and indeed two years later, in 1918, it had become firmly established in his *Cousin Reginald Spells Peloponnesus*, painted for *Country Gentleman*. Against an abstract background split between the black of the blackboard and the white of the wall, we see the boys pulling faces, red-cheeked, and the contrast between the immobility of their bodies and rich expressiveness of their faces. Once again, the world of young people reveals the traits of a society undergoing a profound transformation, suggesting behavioral interpretations and ethical attitudes on which the future would be modeled. Chromatically impeccable, all made up of shades of white, black and red against a flat background, with stiff postures and starched clothes, the work affords space solely to the recital of the faces, to three states of mind, and to three aspects of an increasingly complex reality and of a truth that lies elsewhere. The element of caricature undoubtedly softens the asperity of the symbolism, as Andy Warhol was to do forty years later with his serial repetition. However, in Rockwell it also acts as an amused citation and a kleptomaniac foray, as in the case of *Christmas Trio* of 1923.

In this work, the figure of the violinist with a top hat recalls Lyonel Feininger's gangly characters in *White Man.* These ideal figures, with their excessive bodies, are deformed by the song and the cold, and volumes and lines overlap and mingle together in their diversity with the landscape we see beyond the panoramic circular window.

This visual grammar appears with even greater composure in two works like *If Your Wisdom Teeth Could Talk They'd Say, Use Colgate's* of 1924 and *The Stay-at-Homes* of 1927, where, beyond the actual context of their creation—an advertisement and a women's magazine—the formal structure tends to bring together the purely illustrative and the more artistic aspects. They achieve this through the definition of detail and the refinement of the individual elements. In the painting of the interior, with its glimpse through to the adjoining room, the perspective of the fireplace, the belt on the chair and the striped carpet, and in the landscape, with the bricks of the chimney, the handkerchief dangling beneath the old man's jacket and the stripes of the little sailor, every element helps create a realistic narrative. Each picture is based on the order of a reality that is certain, reliable and absolute. A reality free from any doubt, a tangible, secure image to which the eye can be entrusted in all simplicity, with unguarded curiosity. What we see in these works is not so much the atmosphere of American realism of the previous century as the sophisticated and cultured ambiguity of Jacques-Louis David's Napoleonic rhetoric. In these works by Rockwell we find *The Death of Marat*, and *Napoleon Crossing the Alps* and an extraordinarily skilful

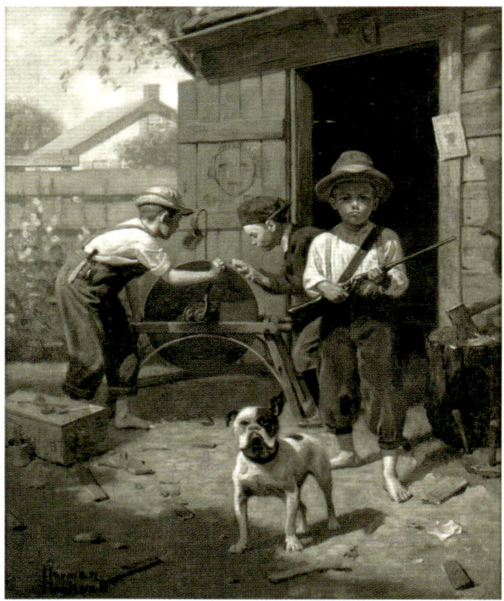

Norman Rockwell
Slim Finnegan (We did everything we could to get ready not to be stabbed), 1916
Painting for *The Saturday Evening Post* story illustration, July 8, 1916
Oil on canvas *en grisaille*, 24 x 22 inches
Norman Rockwell Museum Collection, NRM.1987.2

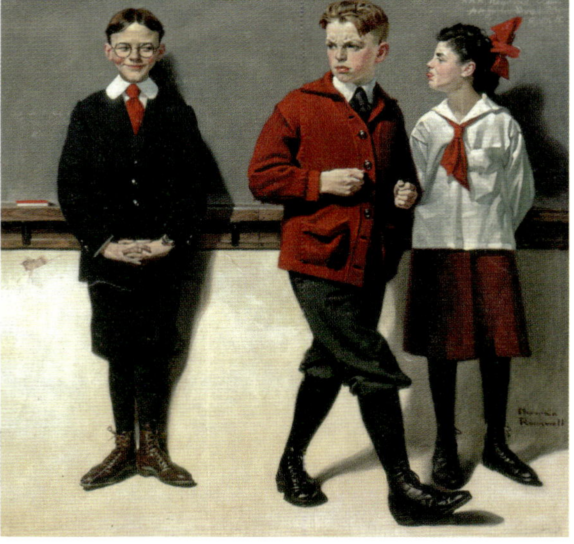

Norman Rockwell
Cousin Reginald Spells Peloponnesus, 1918
Painting for the *Country Gentleman* cover, February 9, 1918
Oil on canvas, 30 x 30 inches
Norman Rockwell Museum Collection, NRM.1978.11

use of a precise literary realism that protects and helps convey the more subtle symbolic function. In these elegant, formal allusions, we can see the great cultural stature of Rockwell, and his desire to delve deep into the body of the illustration, imposing much closer attention, freeing the description from its decorative setting and taking it into the more ethereal atmosphere of cultured conceptuality. This process does not cast aside its popular nature, nor does it attempt to abandon the simplicity of a familiar story and the delicacy of a wish. Here we see how the great effort of realism comes straight back to us in the details, coming to life in the backgrounds, evaporating in the mastery of color and then re-emerging in the theatricality of the chiaroscuro.

This study and refinement of visual language appears in many of his works of the early 1940s and more so in works such as *A Scout Is Helpful* of 1939 and, even more forcefully, in *Mine America's Coal* of 1944. In these works, emotional involvement and narrative power are combined with the drama of light and with the obsessive realism of the detail. In these almost Caravaggesque compositions, the characters emerge from the darkness of the background, igniting a cinematic luminosity that emphasizes the importance of the detail, attracting our interest to the fragment. It is clear how the dramatic, theatrical element is essential to the structure of the illustration, and how the carefully arranged figures, the light distributed on the subjects, and the details apparently abandoned on the stage all contribute to a stage-setting that certainly responds to the needs of illustration but that also suggests a cultured mannerist legacy.

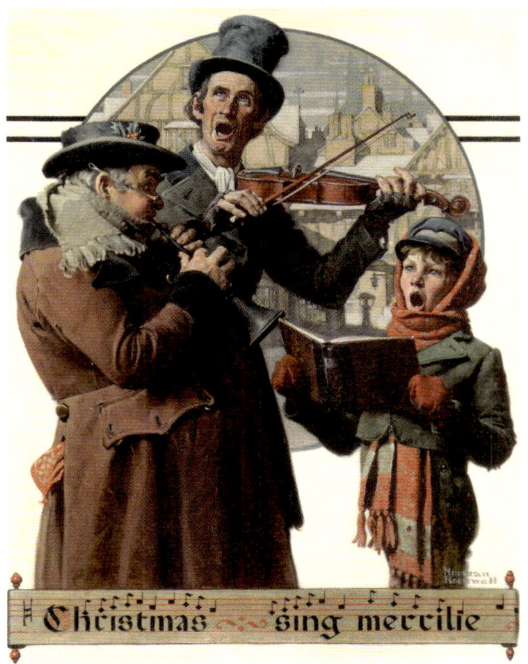

Norman Rockwell
Christmas Trio, 1923
Painting for *The Saturday Evening Post* cover, December 8, 1923
Oil on canvas, 28.25 x 21.5 inches
Norman Rockwell Art Collection Trust, NRACT.1973.2

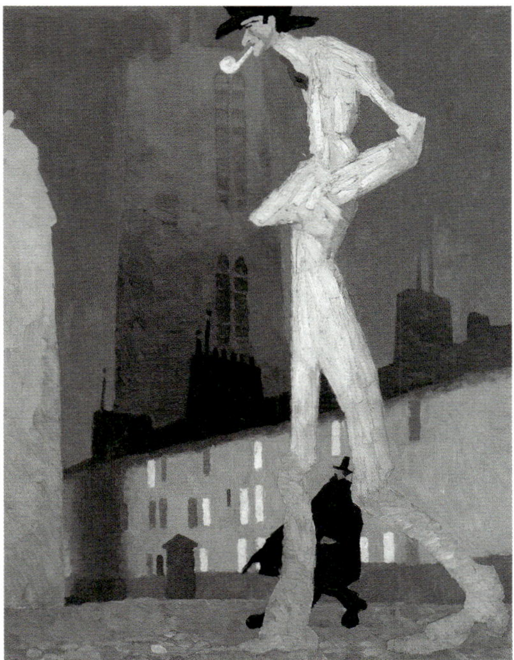

Lyonel Feininger
The White Man, 1907
Oil on canvas, 26.9 x 20.6 inches
Madrid, Carmen Thyssen-Bornemisza Collection – Museo Thyssen-Bornemisza

Rockwell constantly wavers between popular story-telling, which ensures an immediate emotional involvement, and erudite visual expressions that capture the atmospheres of classical art, literature and sophisticated symbolism.

As such, it is easy to reconstruct the poetic process that makes the figure of the child so central. Works like *Going and Coming* of 1947 and *Girl at Mirror* in 1954, but especially *Day in the Life of a Little Girl* of 1952, are exemplary works of an expressive complexity of rare impact. In these cases, and right from his very earliest works, children are not just the metaphorical face of a young society that is growing up and dealing with minor mistakes, but one with great dreams. It is also a surprising stylistic model that, on the formal level, accepts any pictorial risk and any experiment. The irony of pulling a face is more effective on children, for theirs is a fertile ground for pictorial games and their world is extreme, excessive, and perfectly cinematic and literary. But it is precisely this cinematic use of the image, right from the framing of the figures, that allows Rockwell to convey the broadest, profoundest values of the American Dream also through the figure of the child. Puritan ethics, Irish character and Anglo-Saxon determination are all mixed into the pigment in works such as *Freedom from Want* and *Freedom from Fear*. It is no coincidence that these both date from 1943, when the tragedy of the war in Europe led to the recognition and celebration of family values, the need for protection and the burden of responsibility. Here too, although inevitably exasperated by the war years and by the journalistic context, Rockwell does

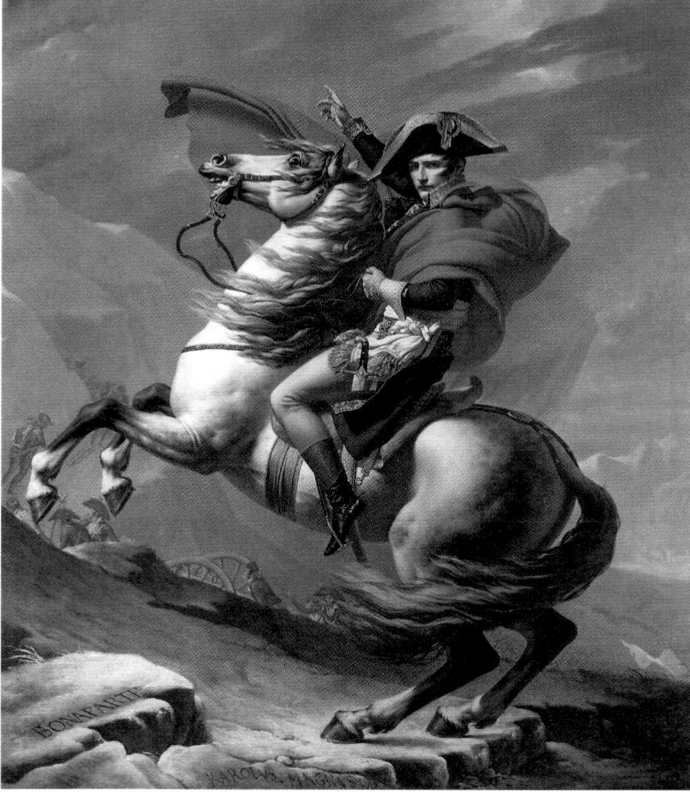

Jacques-Louis David
Napoleon Crossing the Alps, 1801–02
Oil on canvas, 126.4 x 96.9 inches
Vienna, Kunsthistorisches Museum

not fall into the trap of banal rhetoric, but adopts the forms of classical art. By playing on the wallpaper, on the reflections on the dishes, and on the 'bombing... horror' on the folded newspaper in the father's hands, the scene explodes into countless themes, adding greater mystery and poetry to the main subject. The American Dream is explicit but Rockwell's art shows it through painting, igniting the flames of emotion and poetry. It is this artistic outburst, this pictorial grammar, that sets Norman Rockwell's art apart from mere illustration, though without ever betraying its public and popular intent. More than three hundred covers of the *Saturday Evening Post* made Rockwell the most important American illustrator and his school made the history of illustration. The need to portray the most intimate, secret aspects of American society once a week undoubtedly constituted an exceptional platform and a special window from which to look out, and through which to show himself, in an ongoing dialogue with his public and his own society. In works such as *The Runaway* of 1958, this extremely close relationship with reality and the mediation of painting is particularly illustrative: a child running away from home is shown in the setting of an American diner, in a family atmosphere, with the good-natured, understanding police officer, the smiling owner, with spaghetti on the menu and a radio that is no longer a threat: everything can be worked out, everything overcome. Rockwell's painting does not recount reality but interprets and paraphrases it, observing its infinite nuances and opening it up to multiple interpretations.

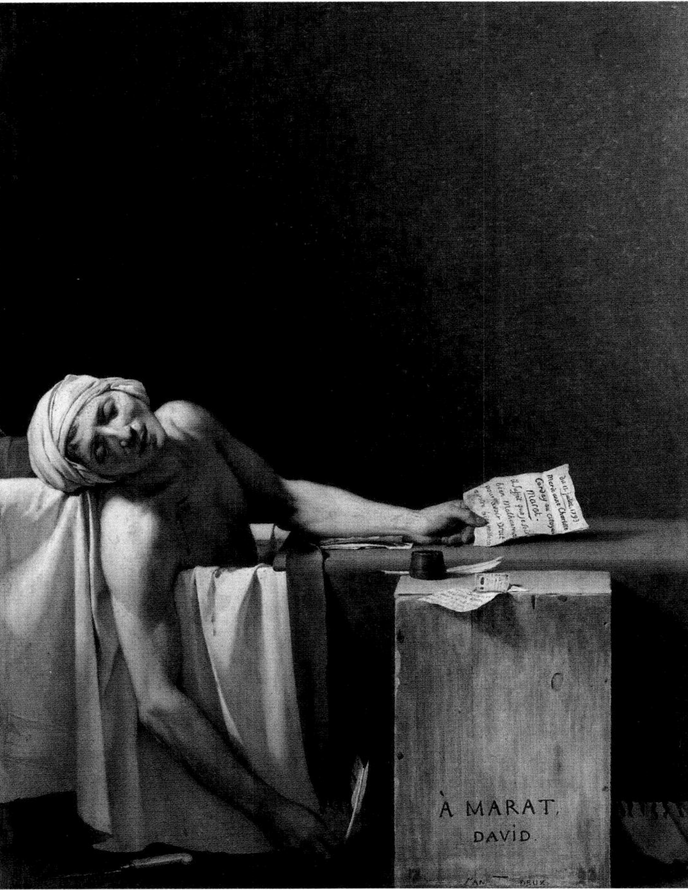

Jacques-Louis David
The Death of Marat, 1793
Oil on canvas, 65 x 50.5 inches
Brussels, Royal Museums of Fine Arts of Belgium

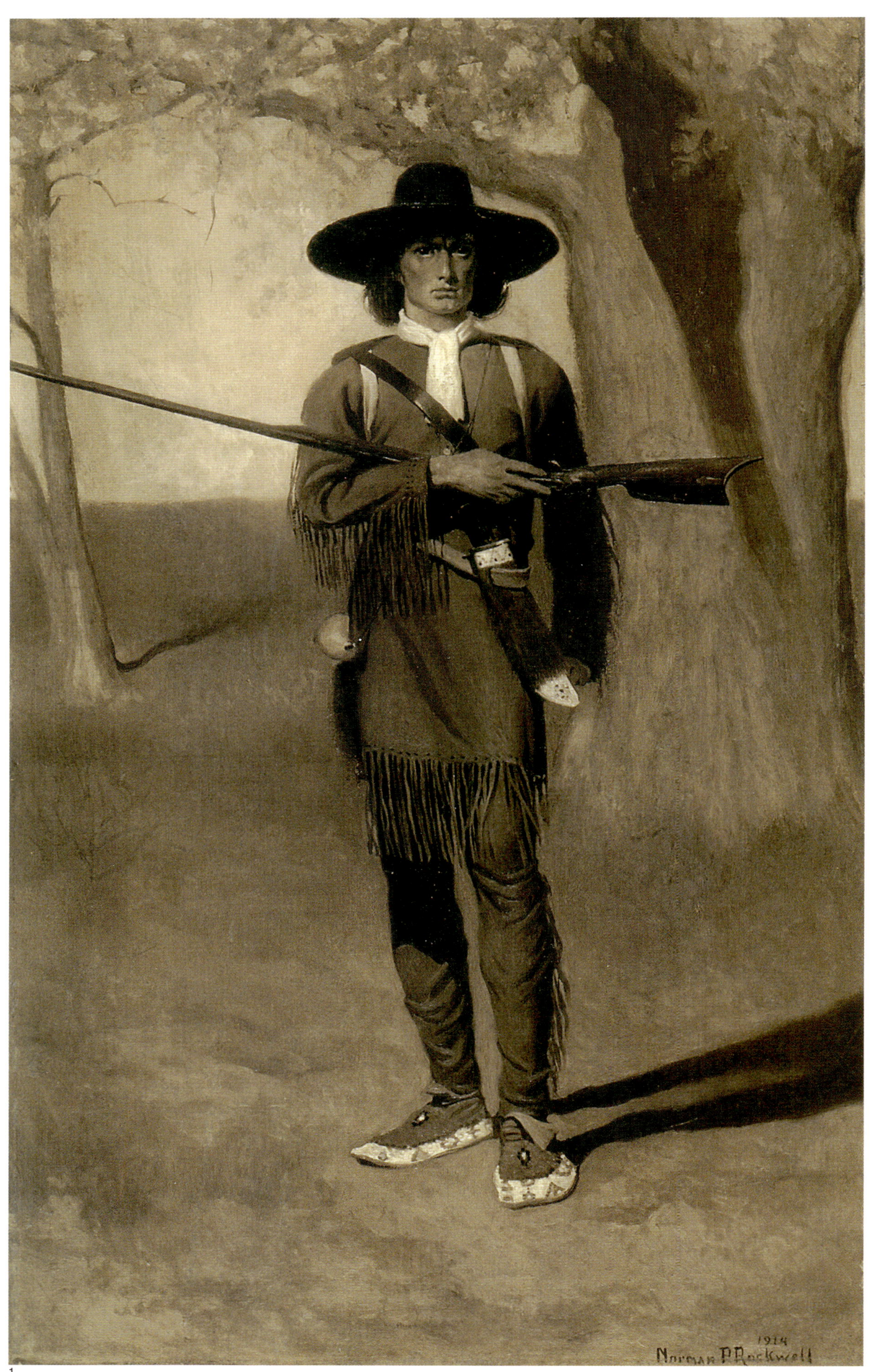

1

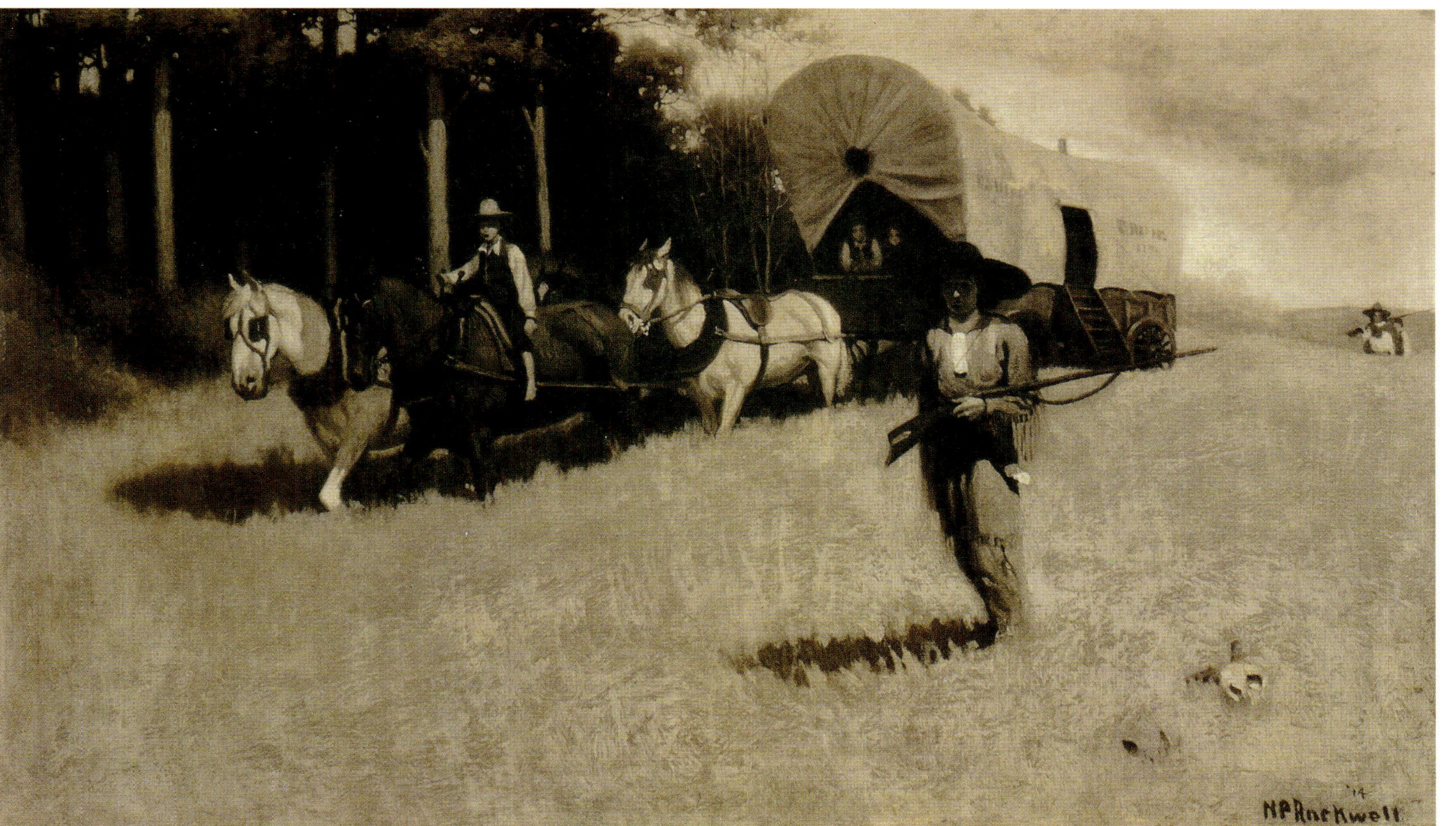

2

1. *Daniel Boone, Pioneer Scout*, 1914
Painting for *Boys' Life* story illustration, July 1914
Oil on canvas, 20 x 12.5 inches
Norman Rockwell Museum Collection, NRM.1989.1

2. *The Road Led Through the Passes of the Hills*, 1914
Painting for *Boys' Life* story illustration, September 1914
Oil on canvas, 17.125 x 28 inches
Norman Rockwell Museum Collection, Gift of the Estate of Samuel and Lillian Whinston, NRM.1995.9

In 1912, after illustrating the new *Boy Scout Hikebook* for the Boy Scouts of America, Rockwell was offered a permanent job on their new monthly, *Boys' Life*. After just six months, he was promoted to art director at a salary of $50 per month, and was responsible for producing cover art, illustrating one story per issue, and hiring and editing all additional artwork for the magazine. In 1914, Rockwell produced nineteen paintings and drawings to illustrate Everett T. Tomlinson's *Scouting With Daniel Boone* in eight installments of the magazine. In Tomlinson's story, set in 1773, Boone is hired by Virginia's Governor Dunmore to lead five families from Yadkin, North Carolina, through the wilderness hunting grounds of the Shawnee Indians to a settlement in Clinch, Virginia.
Daniel Boone, Pioneer Scout and *The Road Led Through the Passes of the Hills* illustrated the story's second and fourth installments.
In the first, *Daniel Boone, Pioneer Scout*, Rockwell shows Boone as he is described by the text–"a tall man, quiet in his bearing, lean almost to thinness, in the prime of middle life and with every indication of self-control as well as of strength stamped upon his face and form." Later in the story, Boone escorts a band of twenty-seven men, hired to clear a road from the settlement in Clinch to a region in Kentucky. *The Road Led Through the Passes of the Hills* depicts Boone as sentry during their journey. Both illustrations are painted *en grisaille*, French for "in gray."
When illustrators knew their work would be printed in black and white, they often painted in tones of a single color, usually gray, brown, or blue, enabling them to better judge how the illustration would look in print. Rockwell used either brown (sometimes called sepia) or gray for his *en grisaille* paintings.

Odds & Ends
To encourage faithful readership of the eight monthly issues containing the Daniel Boone series, *Boys' Life* offered $300 in prizes in an essay contest. Writer of the best essay on "the qualities of Daniel Boone, which made him a good Scout and a valuable citizen, and why those qualities are important in life today," won a grand prize of $50. 56 runners-up won prizes from $1 to $25.

But the life of a newspaper is also one of domestic news, which can at times be tough and hard to make palatable. It requires decisions and stances to be adopted, a courage that Rockwell did not lack and that led him to create a work like *The Problem We All Live With* of 1964. This is based on a prominent news item from New Orleans, where every morning deputy marshals accompanied the first colored child to the public state school to protect her from the insults and threats of the whites. The illustration, which appeared in *Look* in January 1964, conveys a clearly political message, and the dignity of the child's steps also gives it a powerful ethical value, but it is its pictorial construction that deserves special attention. As in many other works, Rockwell uses a cinematic form of framing, narrating the fragile fragments of the story—the girl's star-spangled exercise book, the wedding rings on the marshals' fingers and the fact that they are probably fathers, the document poking out of the pocket, the tomato splattered against the wall. Above all, he divides the scene into three bands of grey: the road, the step and the wall. The three intensities of colour spread across lines of tones, as in the drapes behind sixteenth-century Madonnas, isolating the scene and heightening the emotional intensity of the subject. Similarly, the child enhances the chromatic contrast between the white dress and her black skin, imposing her image, while forgoing the centrality of the picture to make room for the shapeless mess of the tomato.

It was this civic sensibility that, just a few years later, in 1965, led Rockwell to create his *Murder in Mississippi*. Here he tackles the classic theme of compassion in a

3. *No Swimming*, 1921
Painting for *The Saturday Evening Post* cover, June 4, 1921
Oil on canvas, 25.25 x 22.25 inches
Norman Rockwell Art Collection Trust, NRACT. 1973.15

Norman Rockwell might have been thinking of his boyhood summer vacations in upstate New York as he captured a simple joy of country life in *No Swimming*. Rockwell was branded as an illustrator of children during his early career, which was dominated by his association with *Boys' Life* magazine and another children's magazine, *St. Nicholas*. He perfected the art of painting from the point of view of boys and girls in genre scenes such as this one, capturing slices of life as a camera might have.
But such images, just a click away for photographers, were a challenge for artists. Before Rockwell began using photography to aid his painting process, his models had to hold their poses for lengthy stretches, sometimes with limbs propped up by stacks of books or held with ropes and pulleys. Rockwell kept a pile of nickels on a table next to his easel. "Every twenty-five minutes," he recorded, "I'd transfer five of the nickels to the other side of the table, saying, 'Now that's your pile.'"

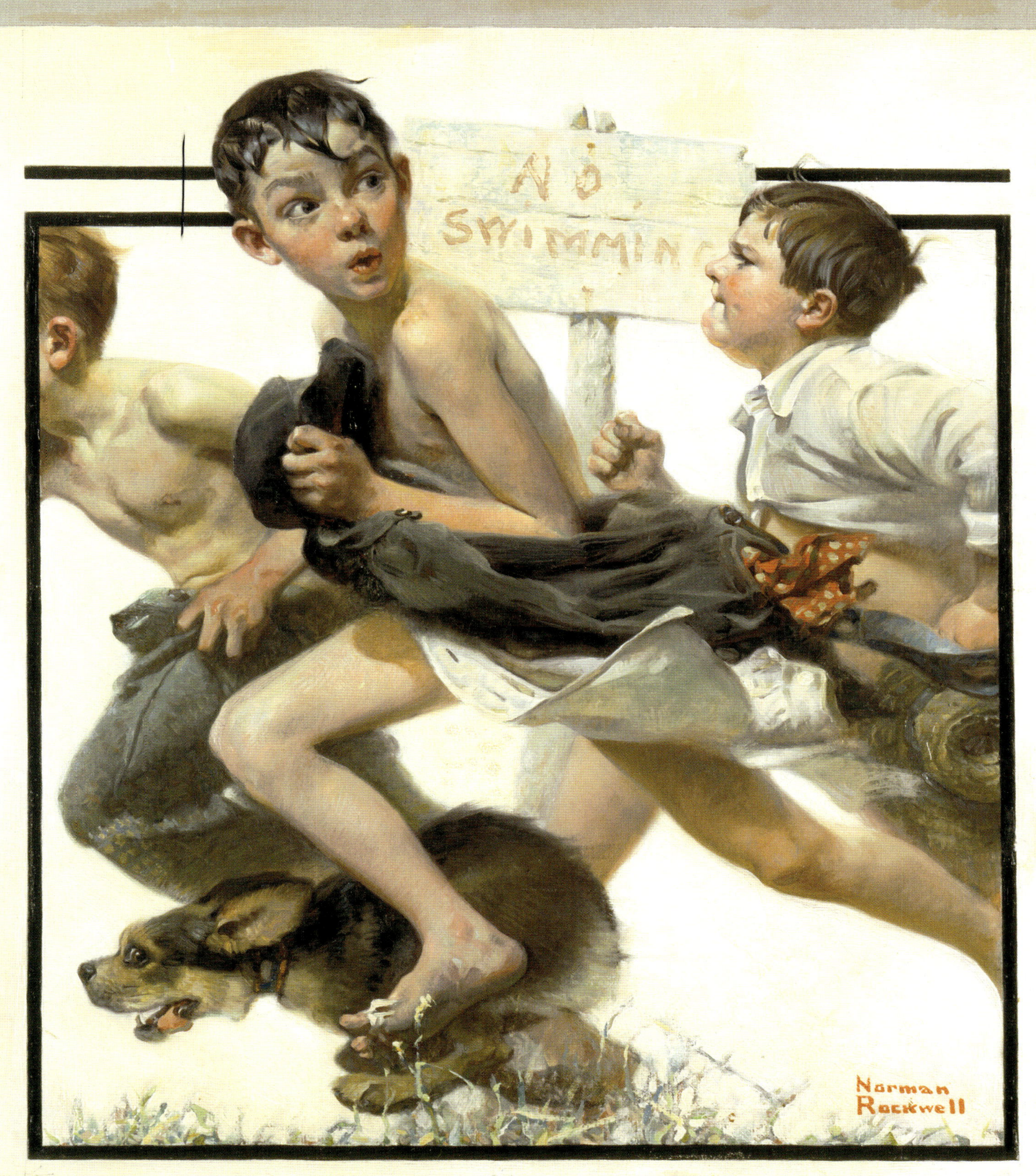

3

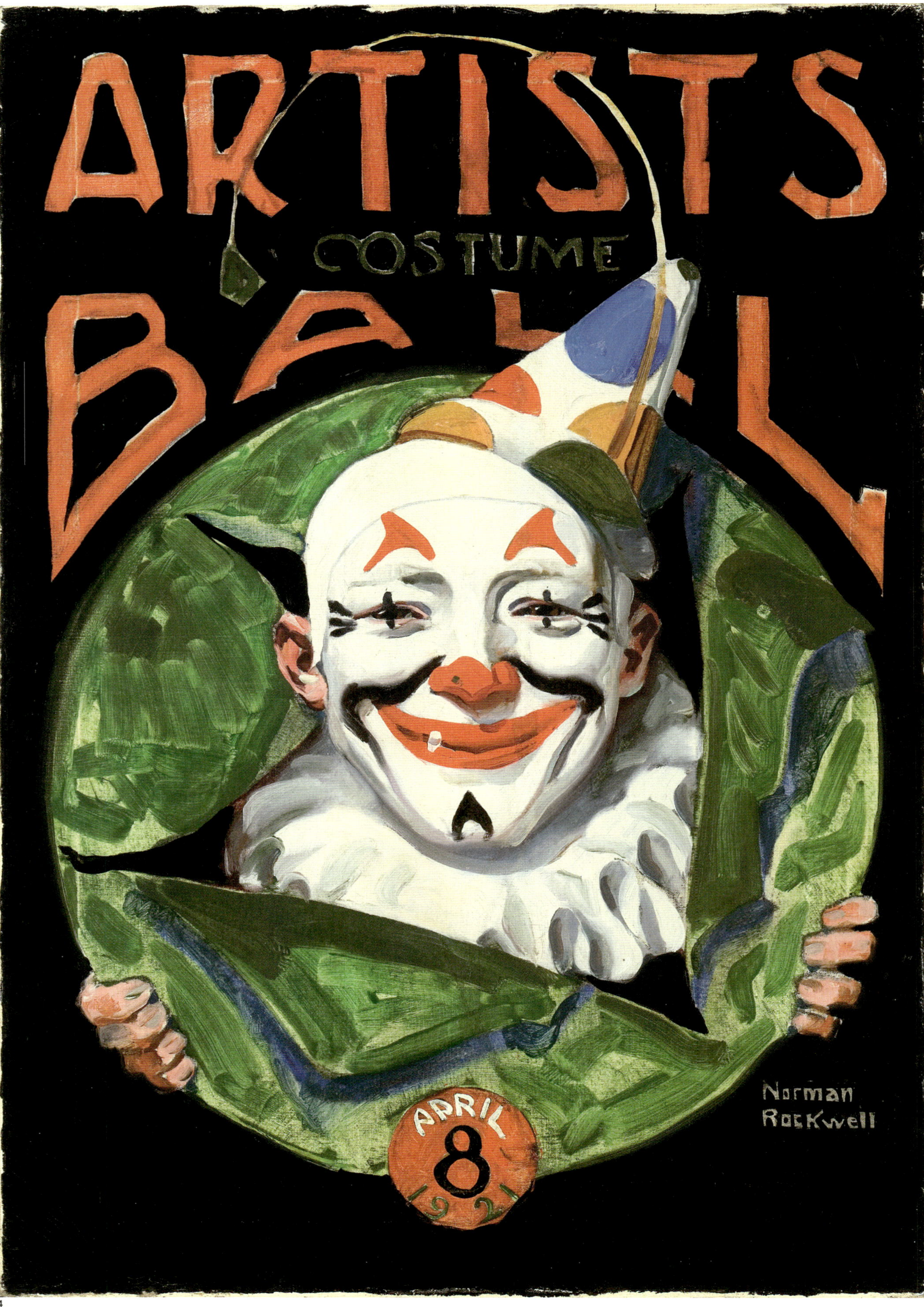

4

work that has an almost academic structure. We can see the contemporary quality of a construction that comes from a thorough documentation of the news and from considerable photographic research. In other words, there is a clear, particularly precise and disciplined methodology that relies not only on poetic sensibility, which is assisted by amazing technical skill, but also knows that it must work on a meticulous study of historical facts, on the poses of the figures, and on details that are documentary rather than imaginary. The countless photographic trials, already used for many other works, such as *Runaway*, reveal the manic obsessiveness of a formal research that left nothing to chance, and the protracted, complex process that led from photographic experimentation and scenic drama to the painted picture. It is this long, painstaking path that ultimately turns the image into a seemingly simple and straightforward story, and an acute pictorial grammar that creates a bright, fluent visual language.

Norman Rockwell's art thus runs along two parallel lines: one, more alluring and engaging, is the process of illustration, which captures the eyes with the simplicity of a poetic and emotional image; the other, tinged with erudite classicism, is found deep in the spirals of his mind, in the rigid discipline of his studies, and in the risks of artistic experimentation and complexities of thought. Beneath the figure, beyond the narrative and the mimetic virtuosity, Norman Rockwell seeks a form of painting that is rugged, rough and arduous. Much more than the glittering surface can convey, more than the uncomplicated style and simple narrative might suggest.

4. *Artists Costume Ball*, 1921
Painting for costume ball poster
Oil on canvas, 29 x 21.5 inches
Norman Rockwell Museum Collection, Gift of Evelyn F. Hitchcock in memory of Ethan Wolcott Hitchcock, NRM.2004.1

After World War I, the New Rochelle (New York) Art Association held three annual costume balls to raise funds for a war memorial. Rockwell, then living in New Rochelle, painted this poster design in 1921 to advertise one of the balls. Since he was a member of the Association, we can guess that he volunteered his time and talents for this poster.
In her brief history of the Association, Ann Maloney Lyons said, "These galas were immensely popular and successful. Dancing lasted from 8 pm till 4 am." Artists' posters, such as this one, were auctioned off at the end of the evening, adding to the fun and raising additional funds.
From its thinly applied but broad brushstrokes, it appears that Rockwell painted this quickly, perhaps completing it within an hour and at one sitting. Though painted seven years before *Checkers*, the basic interpretation of the clown is the same. Note the white cap that hugs the clown's head, the arrow-shaped eyebrows, and the lines through the eyes and at the cleft of the chin. Each clown wears a ruffled collar, and the same circular shapes, painted in primary colors, accent the hat and the cap.
The "reverse" painting of the signature–leaving space for each letter rather than painting them–was probably done with the aid of pencil lines.

Following pages
President Abraham Lincoln Sitting at a Table, February 24, 1861

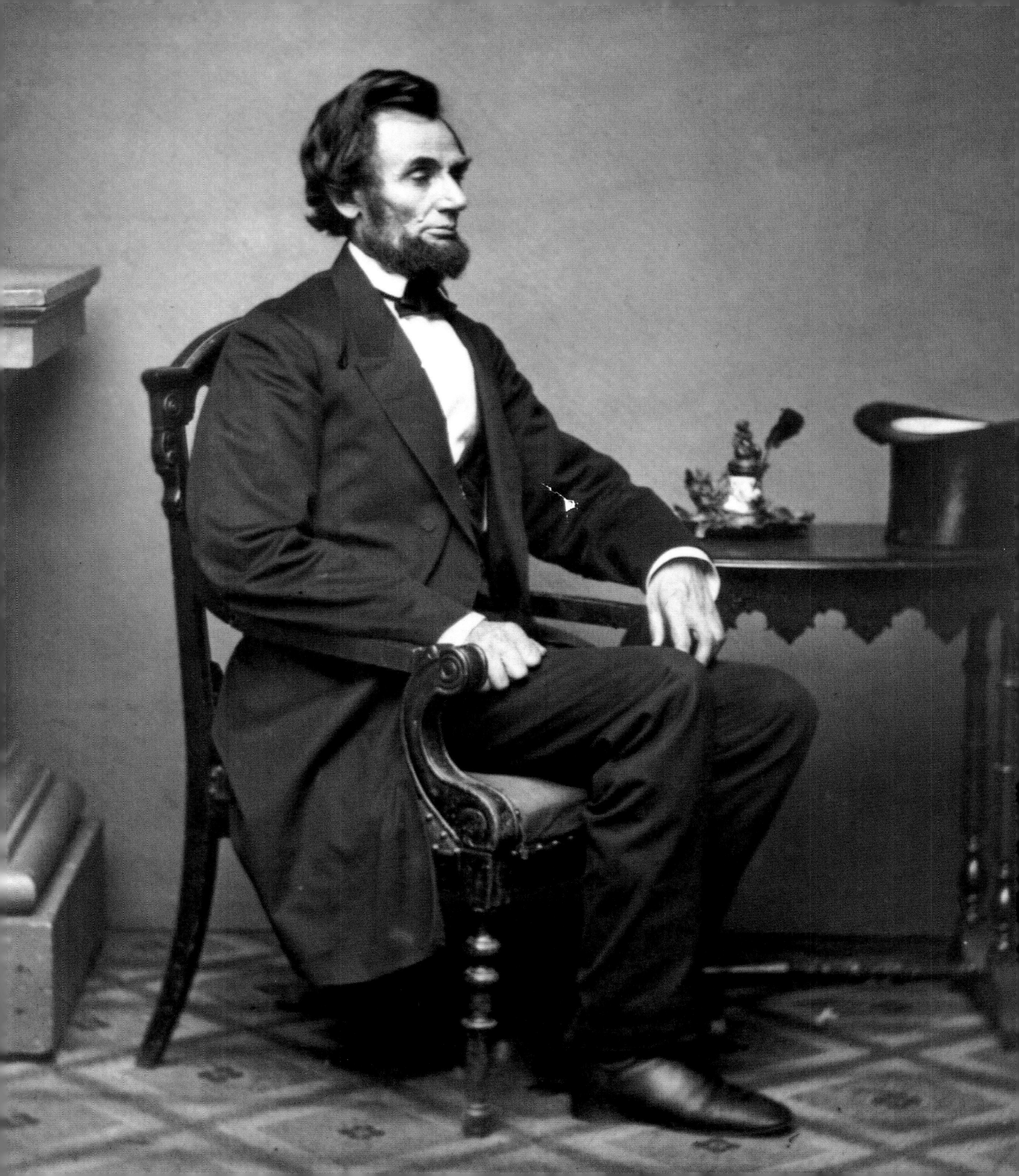

Stephanie Haboush Plunkett

American Chronicles

"I love to tell stories in pictures.
For me, the story is the first thing and the last thing."
Norman Rockwell

Stephanie Haboush Plunkett
Deputy Director / Chief Curator
Norman Rockwell Museum
Stockbridge, Massachusetts, USA

Like most creators of art for commerce, Norman Rockwell (1894–1978) worked within the realm of both aesthetics and mass communication. An astute visual storyteller and a masterful painter with a distinct, personal message to convey, he constructed fictional realities that offered a compelling picture of the life that many twentieth-century Americans aspired to. Anxiously awaited and immediately understood, his seamless narratives seemed to assure audience engagement with the publications that commissioned his work, and ultimately with product endorsements that supported the bottom line. The complexities of artistic production remained hidden to his enthusiasts, who were compelled by his vision and content to enjoy his art in the primary form for which it was intended—on the covers and pages of their favorite magazines. What came between the first spark of an idea and a published Rockwell image was anyone's guess, and far more than readers would have ever imagined.

Conceptualization was central for the artist, who drew inspiration from the world around him and called the history of European art into play, employing classical painting methodology to weave contemporary tales inspired by everyday people and places. As *American Chronicles: The Art of Norman Rockwell* reveals, his richly detailed, large-scale canvases offered far more than was necessary even by the standards of his profession, and each began with a single idea. By his own admission "hard to come by," strong picture concepts were the essential underpinnings of Rockwell's art. From the antics of children, a favored theme of his youth, to the nuanced reflections on human nature that he preferred as a mature artist, each potential scenario was first cemented with a simple drawing. What followed was a carefully orchestrated process of image development that demanded the careful integration of aesthetic concern, graphic clarity, and technical skill. We are honored to have the art of Norman Rockwell on view at the Museo Fondazione Roma, in the city that Rockwell loved for its abundance of artistic riches spanning the ages. For Rockwell, whose life was driven by unrelenting publication deadlines, travel provided refreshment, and he took every opportunity to explore the world. In the 1920s, he made three trips to Europe, and shortly after his first son Jarvis was born in 1931, the Rockwell family lived in Paris for a period of eight months. While traveling on assignment in 1956, Rockwell spent time in Rome creating lighthearted drawings of its architecture, public artworks, and fashionable citizens for a Pan American Airlines advertising campaign. In the 1960s and '70s, he became well acquainted with the city while visiting his youngest son Peter, who traveled to Rome to study the art of stone carving in 1961 and remained there ever since to raise his family and establish his career as a noted sculptor and art historian.

We are most grateful to Fondazione Roma Chair, Professor Emmanuele Francesco Maria Emanuele, for envisioning this exhibition and making it possible to share the art of Norman Rockwell with audiences in Italy. Sincere appreciation also goes to Curator Danilo Eccher and the staff of the Fondazione Roma-Arte-Musei and La Fondazione NY for their generous spirit of collaboration and all of their efforts to bring this exhibition to life.

Following pages
An unemployed man selling apples, *c.* 1929–39

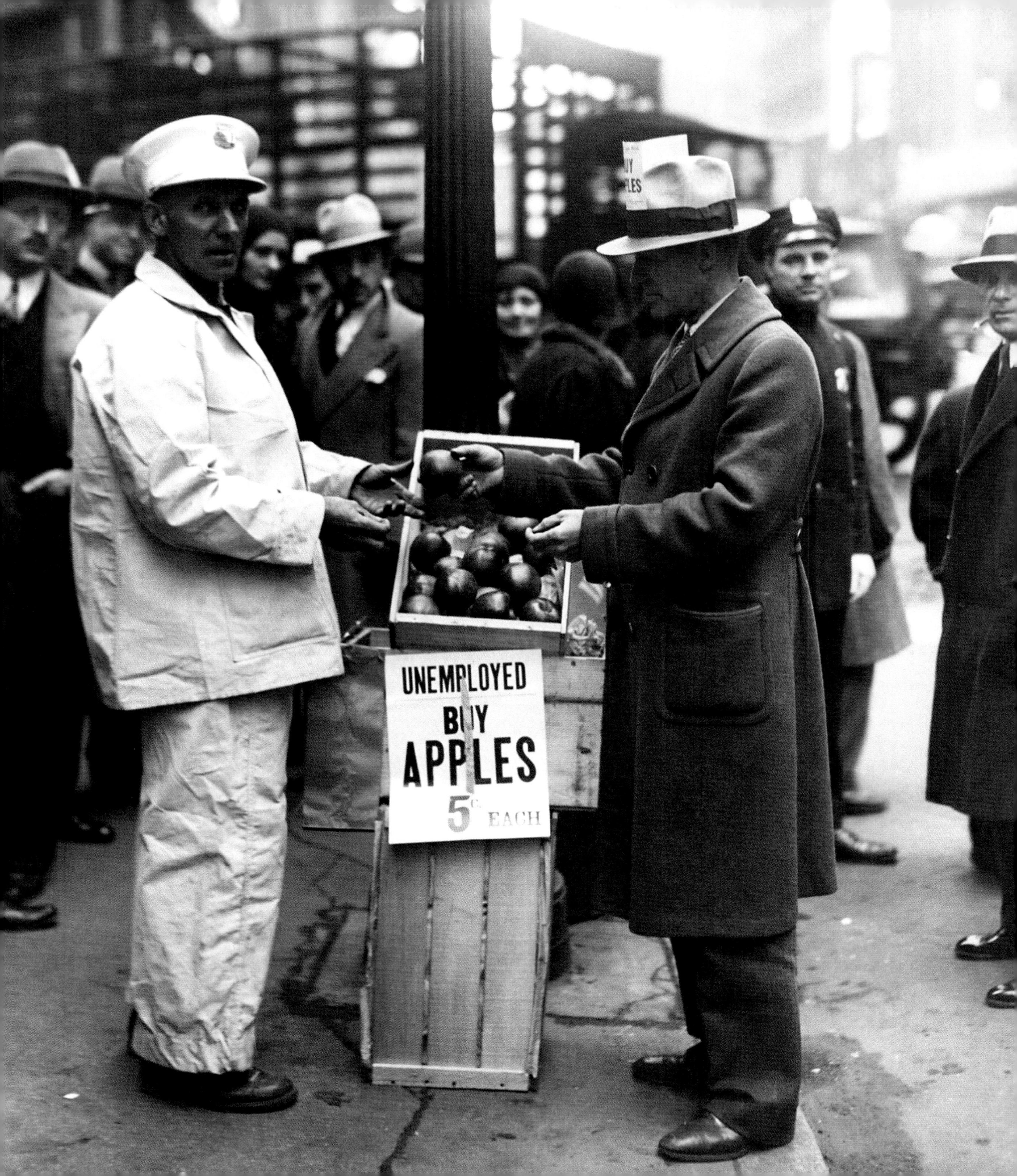
UNEMPLOYED
BUY
APPLES
5¢ EACH

Laurie Norton Moffatt

Norman Rockwell Museum: Collections in Context

Laurie Norton Moffatt
Director / CEO
Norman Rockwell Museum
Stockbridge, Massachusetts, USA

Norman Rockwell (1894–1978) was a force in twentieth-century American art. For sixty-five years, he chronicled American life on the covers and pages of the nation's most prominent journals, creating an unparalleled legacy. He is best characterized by his genius for celebrating the commonplace—for ennobling the ordinary to reveal the extraordinary. "Commonplaces never become tiresome," Rockwell wrote. "It is we who become tired when we cease to be curious and appreciative." Perhaps his greatest gift was the ability to see what was special in moments others take for granted. Throughout his career, Rockwell transformed images of everyday life into potent vignettes of humor and dignity with universal appeal, making his more than 4,000 works a window into twentieth-century life.

We are honored to have the art of Norman Rockwell on view at the Museo Fondazione Roma, an exceptional institution in the city that has inspired many of the world's great artistic masterpieces. Beautifully presented by our colleagues at the Fondazione, *American Chronicles: The Art of Norman Rockwell* is the first exhibition in Italy of Rockwell's art from the Norman Rockwell Museum, a truly momentous event. Rockwell visited Rome many times throughout his life to draw inspirations from the Italian art masters of the past, and to visit his youngest son, Peter Rockwell, who has been a long-time resident of this great city. We are most grateful to Fondazione Roma Chair, Professor Emmanuele Francesco Maria Emanuele, for envisioning and making this exhibition possible in Rome. Sincere appreciation also goes to Curator Danilo Eccher and the staff of the Fondazione Roma-Arte-Musei and La Fondazione NY for their outstanding efforts relating to every aspect of this exciting collaboration.

Few artists make such a singular impact on art and society as to merit a museum in their name. Norman Rockwell Museum in Stockbridge, Massachusetts, holds the world's largest and most significant collection of works by Norman Rockwell and includes more than 800 paintings, drawings, and studies. The artist bequeathed his Stockbridge studio to the Museum, complete with furnishings, easels, brushes, art books, reference materials, The exhibition research papers are housed in the Norman Rockwell Museum Reference Center. The Museum's mission is to study and communicate with a worldwide audience the life, art and spirit of Norman Rockwell in the field of illustration, presenting a contextual view and revealing his influence as an important artist whose iconic paintings continue to reflect American culture, society, and traditions.

Born in 1894 in New York City, Norman Rockwell entered the profession of illustration at the time of the New York Armory show of 1913, when modernism began to take hold in America. Educated at the Art Students League in the classical traditions of Western painting, Rockwell went to Europe to study the moderns and was an admirer of both Picasso and Pollock. When he launched his career, illustrators were trendsetters and were among the celebrities of their day. Rockwell hit his stride as an artist during the Cubist movement, creating what were considered to be unfashionable, narrative paintings during the age of Futurism, Abstract Expressionism, Minimalism, Dadaism, and Surrealism, ending his forty-seven-year career at the *Saturday Evening Post* during the Pop Art era of the 1960s. His career continued for another decade during which he painted documentary journalism for *Look* magazine until photography and television began to usurp the illustrator's role.

Rockwell held his first job at age eighteen as an illustrator and art editor for *Boys' Life*. He painted his first *Post* cover at twenty-two, and by the age of thirty was a nationally known figure profiled in popular magazines of the day. By the 1940s, Norman Rockwell had become a household name and his images were eagerly awaited by an admiring public. When his career ended during the 1970s, he was considered by some to be artistically outmoded, yet he had achieved the status of an elder statesman, receiving the United States Presidential Medal of Freedom in 1977—the highest civilian award in the nation. Rockwell had a finely honed sense for what made an image successful for mass-media audiences who saw themselves reflected in his art. Chronicling two world wars and the advent of radio, telephone, television, automobiles, electricity, air travel, and space exploration, his art touched a public who revered him throughout four generations. Today his work is appreciated for its narrative storytelling and sensitive understanding of human nature. His extensive body of work describes American life unlike any other collection of visual art.

5. *I'm Thinking About My Kiddie*, 1922
Raybestos brake parts advertisement
Oil on canvas *en grisaille*,
12 x 18 inches
Norman Rockwell Museum Collection, NRM.1985.6

Raybestos, a brake parts company, took a democratic approach in their 1922 advertising campaign, targeting their ads, which emphasized the importance of safety, to a wide demographic of the American public. For his seven illustrations for Raybestos print ads, Norman Rockwell portrayed a traffic policeman, a mechanic, a couple in a touring car, a bus driver, an elderly male driver, a farmer, and this image of a young urban woman and her daughter. Simple in its monochromatic rendering, the haunting gaze and Mona Lisa smile of the subject leave us wanting to know more about her and her possible relationship with Rockwell.

Ironically, as these ads stressed the improved driving safety of their products, Raybestos workers were falling ill with asbestosis, a chronic inflammatory lung disease caused by inhalation of asbestos fibers. As the company's name suggests, Raybestos brakes contained asbestos, a mineral whose microscopic strands were released into the air when woven into brake lining fabric. The American public, however, would not learn the extent of the devastating effects of asbestos for forty more years.

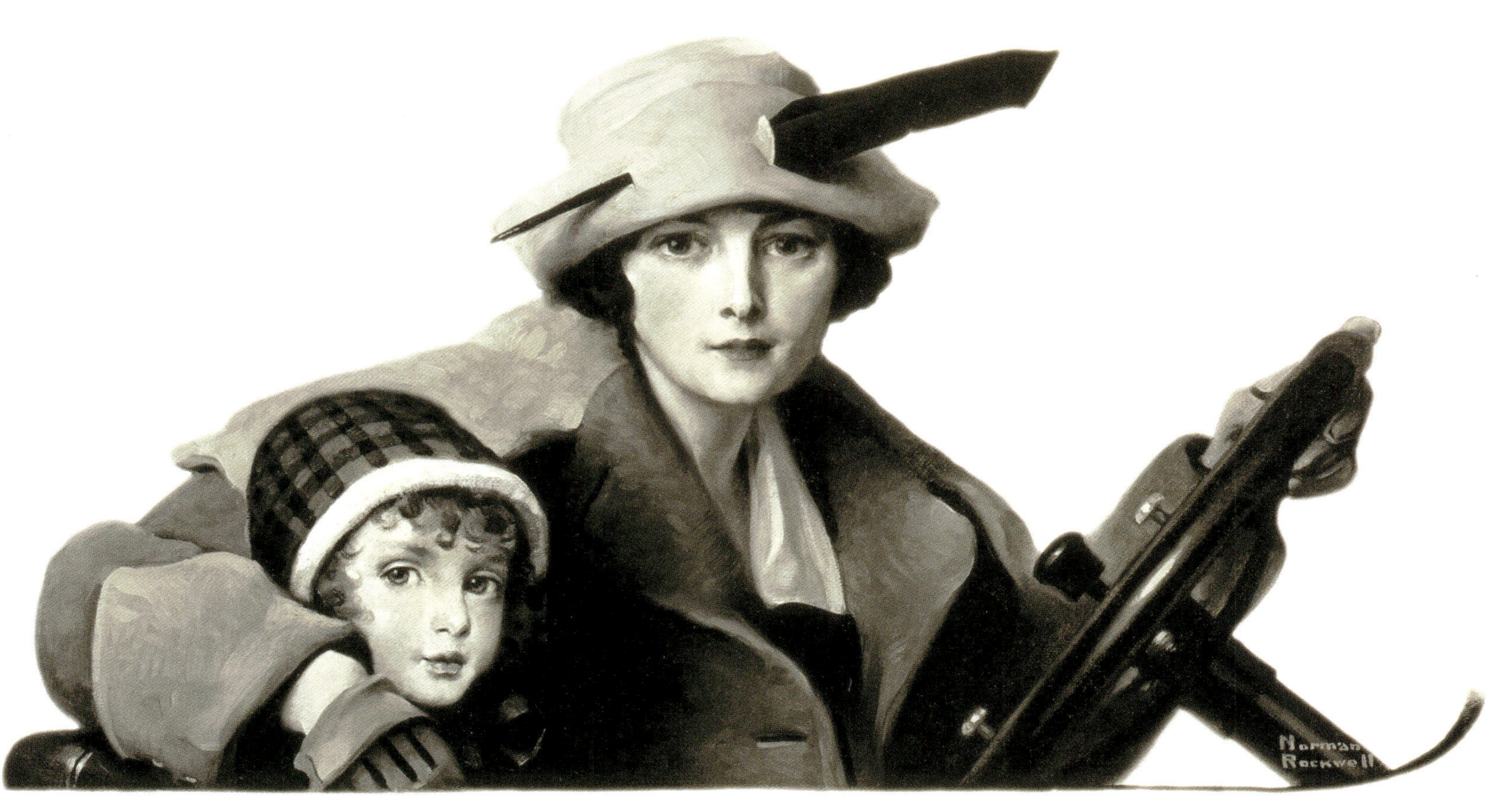

5

34

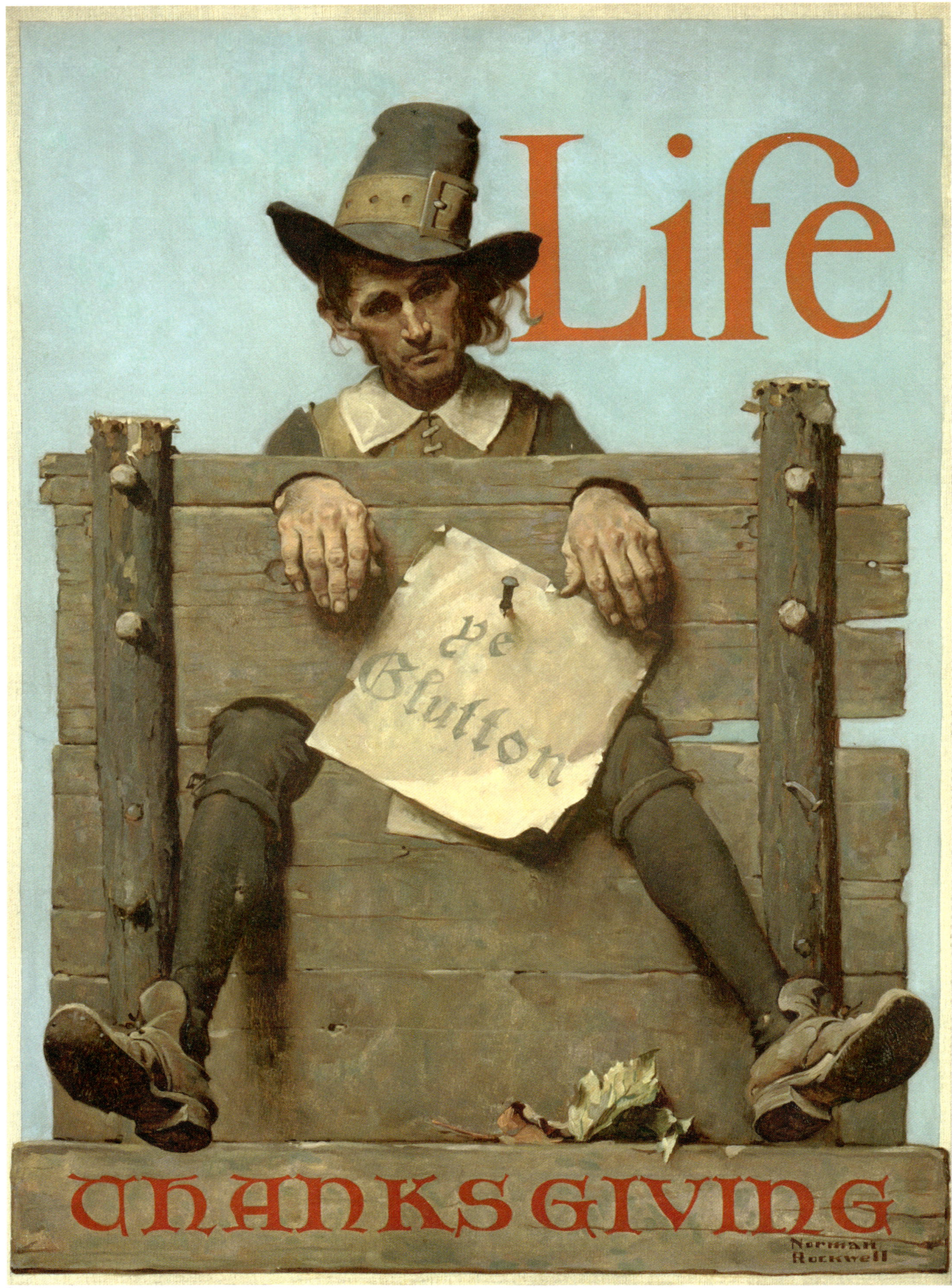

6

Rockwell's images convey our human shortcomings as well as America's ideals of freedom, democracy, equality, tolerance, and decency, but his visual reflections on populism and patriotism yearn above all for goodness to trump evil. The adjective "Rockwellian" evokes a nostalgic image of an idyllic America of a simpler era, though it is also used cynically to convey a sense of hopeless naiveté. Sharing family dinners, going to church, kindness to neighbors, love of children and pets, writing letters, talking with friends, having aspirations and dreams, desiring the idealized life; these are some of the mores and messages in Rockwell's visual language. "I can't paint evil sorts of subjects," the artist commented. His paintings portray powerful universal truths, shining a light on our highest aspirations.

Family life, attitudes toward childhood and old age, growing up, marriage, birth, and parenting are the stages of life that provided Rockwell with infinite vignettes. The ever-quickening pace of society was depicted in imagery that conveyed the evolution of communication and transportation technology. From the introduction of the telegraph, electricity, radio, magazines, telephone, trains, and the automobile during the first half of the century, to television, airplanes, computers, space travel, and the growth of the urban metropolis in the latter half of the century, America was a nation on the move, and its history was told through Rockwell's pictures. Other societal changes like increasing prosperi-

6. *The Glutton*, 1923
Painting for *Life* cover,
November 22, 1923
Oil on canvas, 31 x 22 inches
Norman Rockwell Museum Collection,
NRM.1986.3

Founded in 1883 by a group of young Harvard men as a rival publication to *Judge* magazine, *Life* targeted a sophisticated audience with its emphasis on satire and criticism. In the 1920s, *Life*'s pages featured cartoons and humorous illustrations, a format that continued until 1932 under the direction of *Life*'s longtime illustrator and new owner, Charles Dana Gibson. Presented in good fun, *Life*'s irreverent commentary on any and every subject of daily life, including prohibition, the emerging independence of women, politics, and big business, entertained weekly readers and provided a forum for the talents of the humorist-illustrators of the day.

In portraying the deadly sin of gluttony, Norman Rockwell's choice of a thin man diverged from the stereotype and presented the novel idea that anyone could be a glutton and fair game for criticism. Rockwell enjoyed the costumes and romantic settings of historical illustrations and the challenge of recording authentic details over creating imaginary ones. He often employed a professional research service in New York City, which sent him documents and tear sheets, as well as local librarians who searched out material for him.

In addition to these resources, Rockwell acquired a collection of books and prints for handy research in his studio, and rented or purchased costumes from theatrical supply firms in New York and Boston. His wife Mary searched for props in neighborhood antique shops.

Rockwell continued to do historical illustrations into the 1930s, until losing his reference collections in the 1943 fire that destroyed his Vermont studio. After that, he turned to more topical subjects.

ty, women in the workforce, access to health care, and the civil rights movement are also chronicled in his art. He addressed themes that continue to be the building blocks of our evolving culture and society to this day.

Propelled to his studio seven days a week, he produced an oeuvre of nearly 4,000 images, including 800 magazine covers, advertising campaigns for more than 150 companies, and hundreds of story illustrations. He was extraordinarily prolific and his images were ubiquitous. Seen by millions of viewers, his work helped to make the medium of illustration as potent and powerful as the Internet is today, if not infinitely more poignant and persuasive. Norman Rockwell's impact on popular culture and his influence on generations of American illustrators cannot be overstated.

Norman Rockwell Museum

Norman Rockwell Museum grew literally out of popular demand in Rockwell's hometown of Stockbridge, Massachusetts. He moved to Stockbridge in 1953 from Arlington, Vermont, to seek medical treatment for his wife Mary at the Austin Riggs Center, a private psychiatric hospital. Stockbridge is a beautiful New England village where gracious homes line the Main Street that he painted in careful detail in the great tradition of town limners. The Rockwells were soon settled and warmly embraced by the citizens of the town where he was

7. *She's My Baby,* 1927
Painting for *The Saturday Evening Post* cover, June 4, 1927
Oil on canvas, 32 x 26 inches
Norman Rockwell Museum Collection, NRM.2007.06
Gift of Mr. and Mrs. William M. Young, Jr.

On May 10, 1927, the movie "She's My Baby," about a couple whose blissful marriage turns sour but is later saved, debuted. Advance trailers for the movie may have inspired Rockwell to use the title in his June 4 *Saturday Evening Post* cover. At the time, Rockwell was reaping the popularity and financial rewards of his artistic success, and he and wife Irene were also enjoying New Rochelle, New York's high society. They gave and attended parties, and socialized at New Rochelle's yacht and country clubs. But the glamour and festivities camouflaged a failed marriage.
Like the script of "She's My Baby," the Rockwell's marriage was disintegrating; unlike the movie, it would not be saved.
Rockwell offers a mixture of textures and patterns to vary an otherwise simple composition. The sheen of the raincoat and the girl's curls contrast with the rough patina of old shoe leather and the velvety hand of felt hats. The patterned sweater and window-pane-checkered pants add more visual spice. Colors offset each other in classic complementary fashion–a bluish-green slicker against an orangey-red hat. The paint brush leads the eye to the heart symbol, the lettered "She's My Baby," and ultimately to the young girl's face.

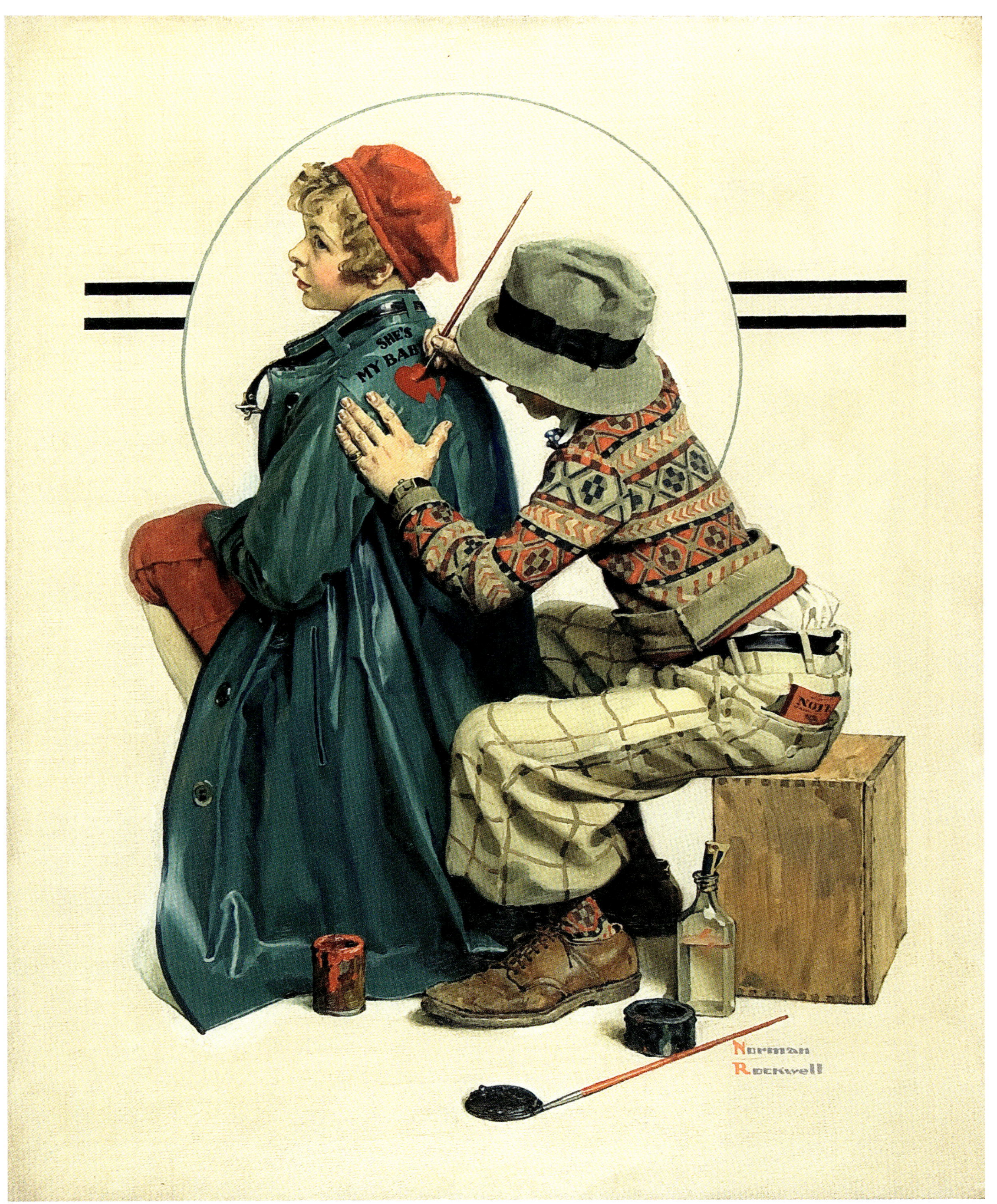
SHE'S
MY BAB
Norman
Rockwell

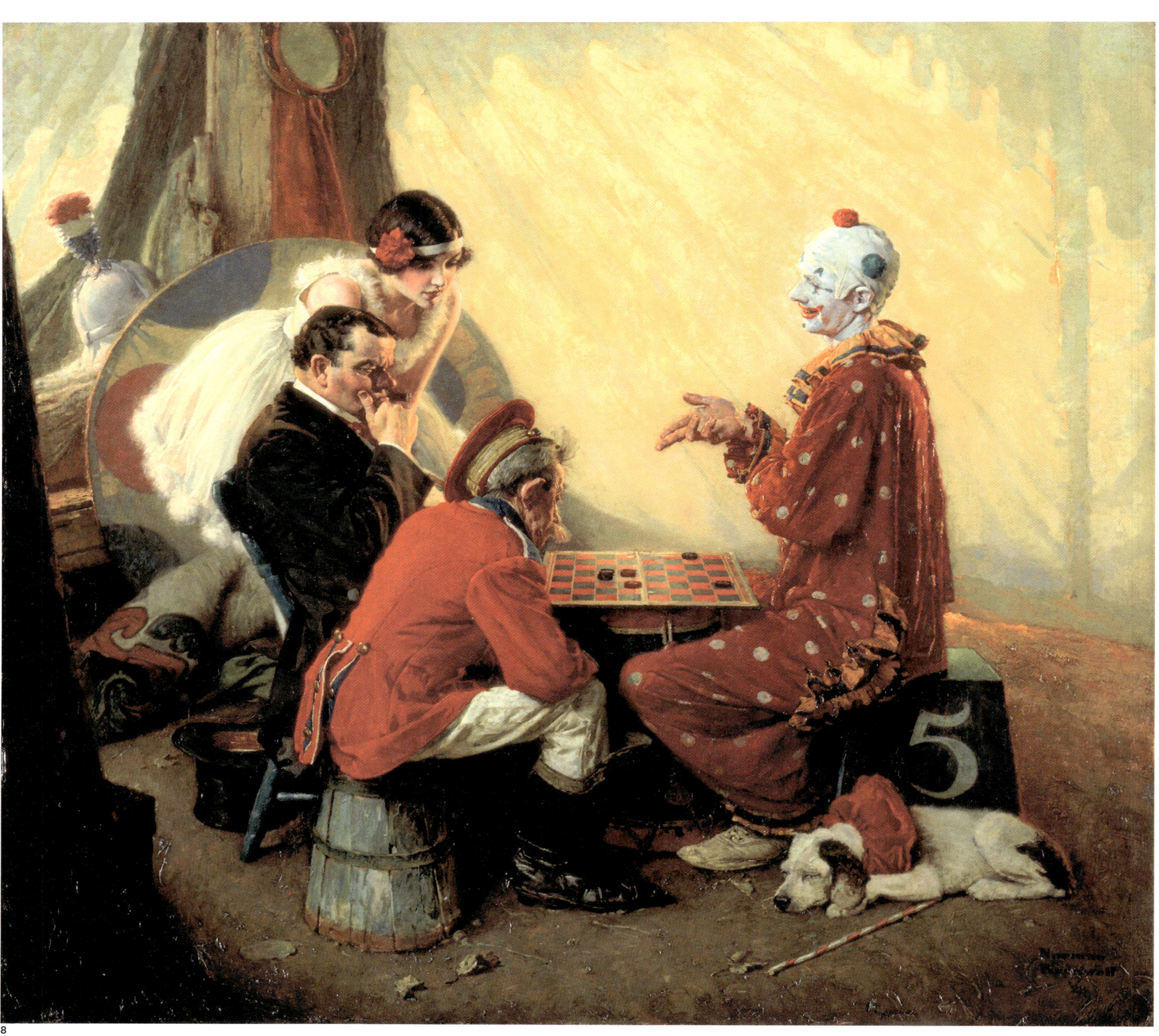

to spend his last twenty-five years. Stockbridge has a distinguished history of famous citizens, and the artist joined a community where their privacy was respected and fame understood. Townspeople were eager to pose as Rockwell's models.

The decade that followed was one of personal tumult and sadness. Mary's illness worsened and six years after moving to Stockbridge, she passed away. Rockwell was devastated. Yet it was during these years that Rockwell completed some of his most iconic scenes of childhood and domesticity, such as *Girl at Mirror* (1954), *The Runaway* (1958), and *Marriage License* (1955), as if to conjure a tranquility that was missing in his life. Paintings from this decade form the nucleus of Norman Rockwell Museum's collection.

In 1967, a group of Stockbridge citizens, among them Norman and Molly Rockwell (a retired English teacher, poet, and activist whom Rockwell married in 1961) joined in a community effort led by Norma Ogden, Patricia Deely, and Rosamund Sherwood to preserve the Old Corner House, a 200-year-old Federal period white clapboard Georgian house that was threatened with demolition on the historic Main Street. When the Old Corner House opened to the public in 1969, Rockwell agreed to lend some of his paintings to attract visitors to the restored home. For a short while, the young organization functioned as the Stockbridge Historical Society with exhibitions of the town's historical artifacts

8. *Checkers*, 1928
Painting for *Ladies' Home Journal* story illustration, July 1929
Oil on canvas, 35 x 39 inches
Norman Rockwell Museum Collection, NRM.1976.1

Checkers, published in 1929 for *Ladies' Home Journal*, illustrates a story by Courtney Ryley Cooper about a circus clown named Pokey Joe who no longer feels that he is funny.
His circus pals decide to lift his spirits and renew his confidence by letting him win a high-stakes game of checkers–the only thing he really cares about.
The subject of circus characters is fertile ground for Rockwell to create dimensional characters in exotic costumes. The drama and flair of the circus world are expressed through the richness of his colors and in a painterly style found most often in Rockwell's earlier work of the 1920s and 1930s. It is a true illustration in the sense that it describes the text of a story and adds to our enjoyment and appreciation of the tale through its visual richness.
Circus life and performers are favored themes in Rockwell's repertoire; his childhood experience of going to the circus and his experience of being around performers at the Metropolitan Opera during his art student days are fondly recalled through these images.

on loan from the neighboring library. But word quickly spread and people learned about the original Rockwell paintings on display. The Old Corner House was soon identified primarily as a center for the exhibition of original Rockwell works.

An Artist Museum

Museums dedicated to the work of an individual artist, as well as artists' homes and studios, are a growing genre in the United States. Unlike museums of generalized subject matter or encyclopedic collections, museums, homes, and studios with comprehensive collections of an artists' work and papers offer an intimate and in-depth examination of an artist's life and creative workspace. These specialized institutions provide for deeper understanding of the artist's creative process and afford research and sustained scholarship of important artistic figures. They present, study, and preserve the life and work of an influential individual, often placing the artist in the larger context of his or her genre or art movement. Cataloguing projects, scholarship, archival research, and the opportunity to view the development of an artist's style through a comprehensive collection are assets afforded by artist museums.

Norman Rockwell Museum seeks to engage a worldwide audience to inspire art appreciation through Norman Rockwell's art and to educate the public

9. *Welcome to Elmville*, 1929
Painting for *The Saturday Evening Post* cover, April 20, 1929
Oil on canvas, 33 x 27 inches
Norman Rockwell Museum Collection, NRM.1979.3

"There was one kind of idea which I didn't have to struggle over—the timely idea. I'd just keep my ear to the wind and, when I heard of a craze or fad or anything which everyone was talking about, I'd do a cover of it." *Welcome to Elmville* was one such idea. Norman Rockwell said that at the time, rather than imposing new taxes on their citizens, towns were hiring police to set up speed traps and "fine their victims heavily."
The model for this pose was not one of the many professional models engaged by Rockwell when he lived in New Rochelle. Instead, he chose Dave Campion, the owner of a local news store, for this and for other images that required a character who was tall and lean. Positioning him in a crouching position gives his body angles that create movement. The arbitrary shadow behind his body adds to this effect. The small streaks of white paint in the foreground tell us a car has just careened by.

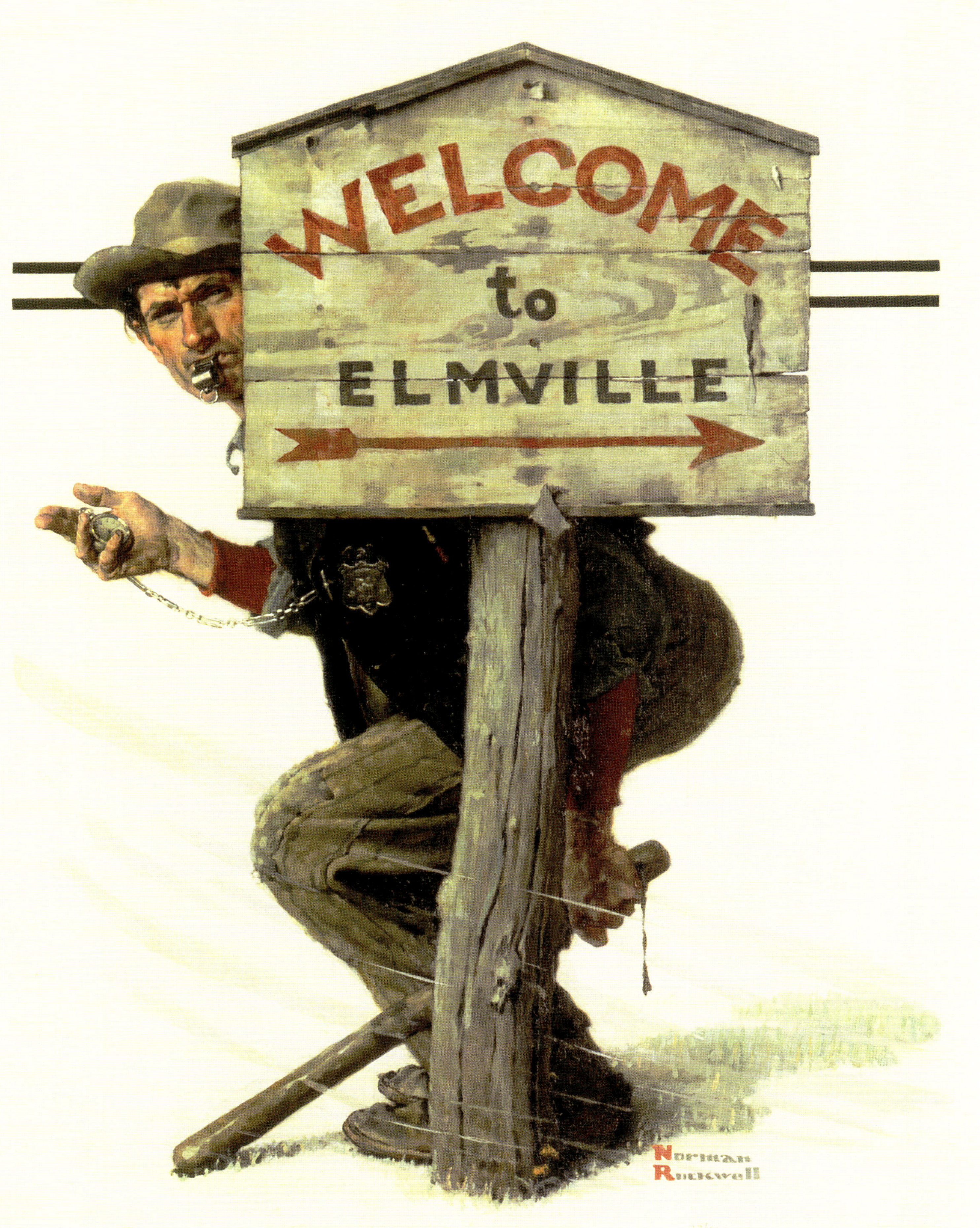
WELCOME
to
ELMVILLE
Norman
Rockwell

42

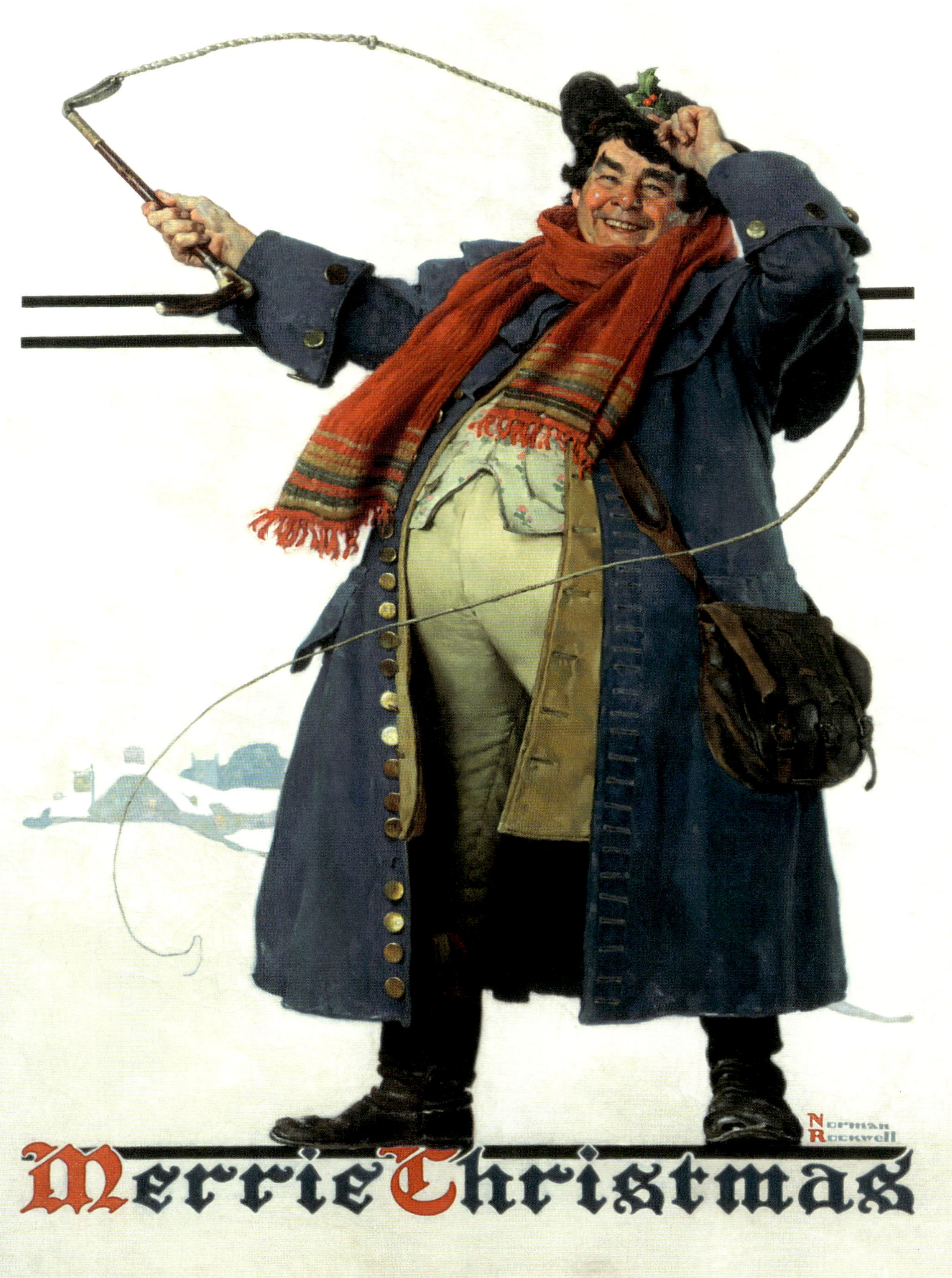

about the art of visual communication through its commitment to presenting the best illustration art and educational programs. Pressed by a lack of space for its growing collections, audience, and programs, the Museum moved in 1993 to its present home, designed by architect Robert A.M. Stern. The Museum presents Rockwell's collection in classic, naturally lit galleries and provides room for changing illustration exhibitions and an active educational program. The Museum is situated in rural Stockbridge overlooking the Housatonic River on the former Linwood Estate, which features an elegant 1859 Berkshire "cottage" built by New York attorney Charles Butler. Norman Rockwell's studio was moved to the grounds in 1986 after it was bequeathed to the Museum. Historic Linwood House contains the Museum's administrative offices. A restored Victorian carriage barn, stone potting shed, and icehouse complete the complex of buildings. An arboretum featuring ornamental specimen trees was planted here during the late 1800s.

Norman Rockwell Art Collection Trust

In 1973, Norman Rockwell established the Norman Rockwell Art Collection Trust, which forms the nucleus of the Museum's collections. The 79-year-old Rockwell created the trust as a safeguard to insure that his treasured personal collection remained intact. Designated for art education and art apprecia-

10. *Merrie Christmas*, 1929
Painting for *The Saturday Evening Post* cover, December 7, 1929
Oil on canvas, 44.125 x 33.125 inches
Norman Rockwell Museum Collection, Gift of the family of John W. Hanes, NRM.2000.3

Merrie Christmas is an embodiment of Norman Rockwell's imaginative journey with Victorian literature.
The painting awakens the sentiments of the Christmas season for all who have read Charles Dickens' works.
The portrayal of the coachman is based on Dickens' character of Tony Weller, father of Pickwick's manservant in *Pickwick Papers*. Weller is portly and robust and described as "uncommon fat." He wears top boots, a broad-brimmed hat and a tile-green shawl. "On the stage box he is king," writes Dickens. "Elsewhere he is a mere greenhorn."
In books read to him by his father, Rockwell grew up seeing the illustrations of H.K. Browne, known by his moniker, "Phiz." But Rockwell's full-color renderings bear little resemblance to Browne's linear style intended for engravings. Unlike many of Rockwell's *Saturday Evening Post* covers in which people are slightly caricatured, the flesh and blood realism of *Merrie Christmas* is so convincing that one feels Rockwell views Dickens' world as fact rather than fiction. Knowing Rockwell's empathy and predilection for the characters and imbedded messages in Dickens' works, we feel he must have yearned for a commission to illustrate his novels, but he never received one. Paintings such as this are the only tribute to the author to whom Rockwell credits his way of looking at life.
"This way of looking at things has stuck with me from those nights when my father would read Dickens to us in his even, colorless voice, the book laid flat before him to catch the full light of the lamp, the muffled noises of the city–the rumble of a cart, a shout–becoming the sounds of the London streets.... The variety, sadness, humor, happiness, treachery, the twists and turns of life; the sharp impressions of dirt, food, inns, horses, streets; and people–Micawber, Pickwick, Dombey (and son), Joe Gargery–in Dickens shocked and delighted me. 'So that,' I thought, 'is what the world is really like.' I began to look around me; I became insatiably curious."

tion, the Norman Rockwell Art Collection Trust comprises approximately 120 works that Rockwell placed in the perpetual care and custody of the young Stockbridge museum. Many of Norman Rockwell's most iconic images are in the Trust collection, including the *Triple Self-Portrait* (1960), *Going and Coming* (1947), *Girl at Mirror* (1954), the *Runaway* (1958), *Marriage License* (1955), *Main Street Stockbridge* (1967), and the *Four Freedoms* (1943).

Norman Rockwell kept the first cover that he created for *the Saturday Evening Post* throughout his life. *Boy With Baby Carriage*, from 1916, launched one of the most successful artist/publishing relationships in history. He painted 321 covers for the *Saturday Evening Post*, and during the course of his forty-seven-year-career with the magazine, his subject matter changed from the humorous, carefree scenes of adolescence of his early years to coverage of invention, history, social change, and the poignant nuances of life's transitions. His final cover for the *Post* was *Portrait of John F. Kennedy* (1960), which was published a second time upon President Kennedy's death in 1963.

Adhering to artists' centuries-old tradition of self-portraiture, Rockwell painted *Triple Self-Portrait* in 1960, revealing a self-consciousness in the act of painting a self-portrait while demonstrating his familiarity with artistic tradition. Tacked on the easel are portraits of artists Rockwell admired: Dürer, Rembrandt, Picasso, and Van Gogh. Rockwell often revealed his knowledge of art

11. *Brass Merchant*, 1934
Painting for *The Saturday Evening Post* cover, May 19, 1934
Oil on canvas, 34 x 28 inches
Norman Rockwell Museum Collection, NRM.1978.2

While other *Saturday Evening Post* artists were portraying beautiful women gazing out from the cover, Norman Rockwell was painting women engaged in activities giving them dimension and identity beyond beauty or social status. In *Brass Merchant*, Rockwell's shopper, though elegantly dressed, is driving a hard bargain for a coffee pot. Surrounding the merchant's feet are objects typical of Rockwell's studio inventory–antiques collected to decorate his studio according to the fashion of the day or for use as needed in a painting. As he sat at his drawing table sketching ideas, perhaps Rockwell's eye fell upon his own samovar, suggesting the idea for this cover. The painting's composition leaves us to guess what the outcome of the bargaining session will be. The two bodies are angled equally, giving neither an advantage, and the pot is squarely in the middle. In addition to the beauty of the symmetry, the painting is so delicately painted–almost as if the medium were watercolor and not oil–that it has a translucence yielding vibrancy and freshness. We feel the characters could walk off the page.

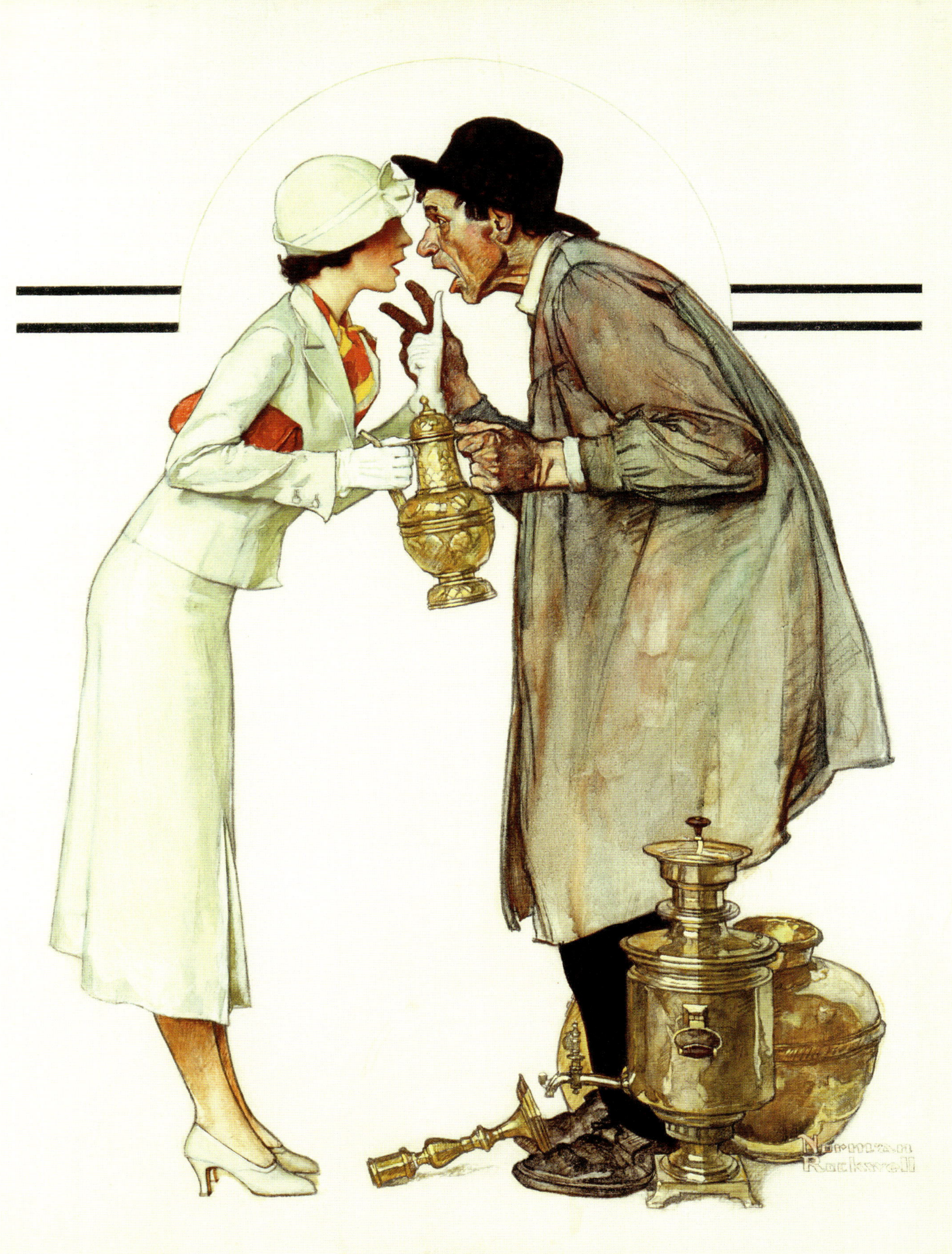
Norman
Rockwell

history in his paintings as if to say, "I may be viewed as an illustrator, but I can paint like the best of the old masters." Close examination of the painting reveals eight self-portraits: five small sketches in the corner of the easel and three major portraits. Personal mementos hint at autobiographical events: a traumatic fire in 1943 that entirely destroyed the artist's Vermont studio and an untold number of paintings; a trip to Paris where he purchased what he believed to be an "antique helmet," later discovered to be the common fireman's headgear at the time; and his love of Coca-Cola. An immaculately neat painter, he pokes fun at himself, coyly suggesting, with the brushes carelessly strewn around his easel, habits messier than the fastidious ones he actually had.

Girl at Mirror (1954) reveals an image of a young girl at the dawn of adolescence who studies herself in the mirror, another subject of art historic tradition. Not quite ready to cast aside her doll, she contemplates experimenting with brush and makeup as she compares herself with the movie star in the magazine in her lap. As so often occurs in Rockwell's paintings, we are given a voyeuristic glimpse into a private moment that is also symbolic of universal passage, in this case from girlhood to womanhood. A strong sense of connection and identification with humanity cuts across boundaries of culture and time.

The *Four Freedoms* are among Rockwell's best-known images. President Franklin Delano Roosevelt, in his 1941 State of the Union address, identified

12. *Artist Facing Blank Canvas*, 1938
Painting for *The Saturday Evening Post* cover, October 8, 1938
Oil on canvas, 38.5 x 30.5 inches
Inscribed "To my good friends Jorj and Ben Harris"
Norman Rockwell Art Collection Trust, NRACT.1973.4

An as illustrator, Norman Rockwell struggled with deadlines his entire life. He said of this painting, "Meeting deadlines and thinking up ideas are the scourges of an illustrator's life. This is not a caricature of myself; I really look like this." Commissions for advertising, story, and book illustrations came with suggestions or even imperatives for the subject of a painting, but cover art for a publication such as *The Saturday Evening Post* required Rockwell to develop his own original and, preferably, new ideas. He had never used the theme of an artist facing a deadline before, but in 1938, after returning from an extended family vacation in England, it became useful.

Though he often posed for characters in his own paintings when "extras" were needed for a scene with a lot of people, Rockwell did few formal self-portraits or paintings in which he was the sole character. *Artist Facing Blank Canvas* is one. In it Rockwell is surrounded by his references. Museum reproductions, art history books, artists' monographs, illustrators' annuals, and books and tear sheets on such subjects as birds, animals, and trees comprised his library. Photos taken for one painting were saved in files and binders, and sometimes were used a second or third time. Sketches strewn about represent rejected ideas for this *Post* cover. These elements accurately portray Rockwell.

Others don't ring true. Rockwell did have a horseshoe, but it hung on his studio wall—not from his easel, where it would have been in the way of his work. Orienting it opposite the usual upside-down placement believed to bring good luck may symbolize the bad luck he has encountered; his August due date had long passed. Rockwell rarely began a painting at the oil-on-canvas stage. By the time a canvas was primed and on his easel, he had completed a fully detailed drawing, the same size as the canvas, ready to have its basic composition traced to the final support. His palette table, which was always to the left of his easel, has been replaced by a hand-held palette on the floor to his left, perhaps as a compositional counterbalance to the sketches on the floor to his right. Rockwell's pipe, included in all his self-portraits because he thought of himself as "an inveterate pipe smoker," is in his pants pocket (which would have been uncomfortable against the chair) because he thought it would be more prominent. The kachina talisman hanging with the horseshoe reminds us of Rockwell's southwest travels during the 1930s. And, finally, Rockwell's costume is fictional, created with the idea of brightening things up.

On May 15, 1943, five years after this cover was published, Rockwell's studio burned to the ground, destroying the small collection he kept of his own paintings. Four days later, he received a letter from his friend and fellow illustrator Ben Harris expressing sorrow for Rockwell's loss. "We are sending you all of your things which we've saved—and can find—and you remember we still have that beautiful original, the back view portrait of yourself. Although it would break our hearts you may have it back any time you want it. Let us know." And so it was returned to Rockwell.

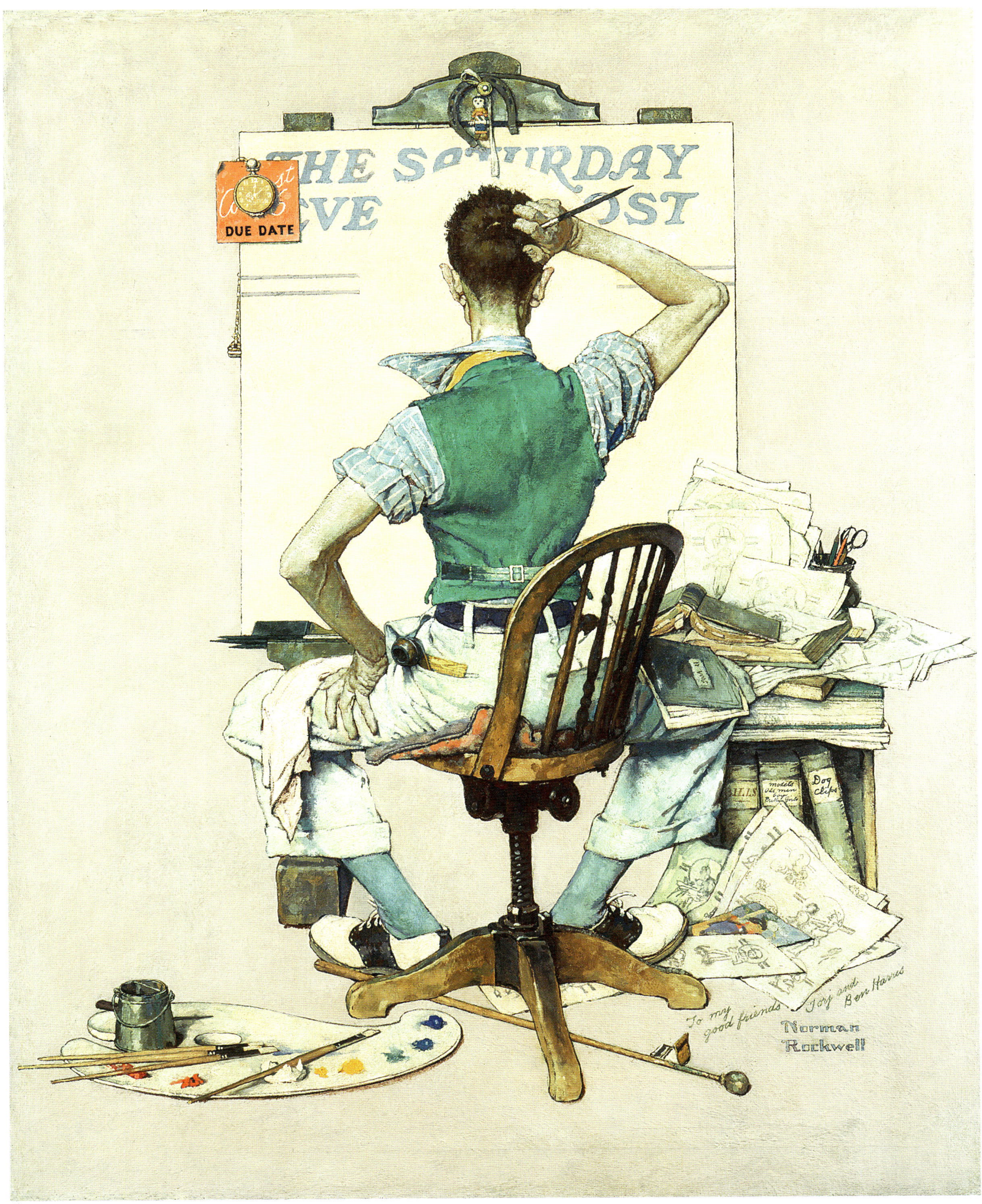
DUE DATE
Dog Clips
To my good friends Joy and Ben Harris
Norman Rockwell

47

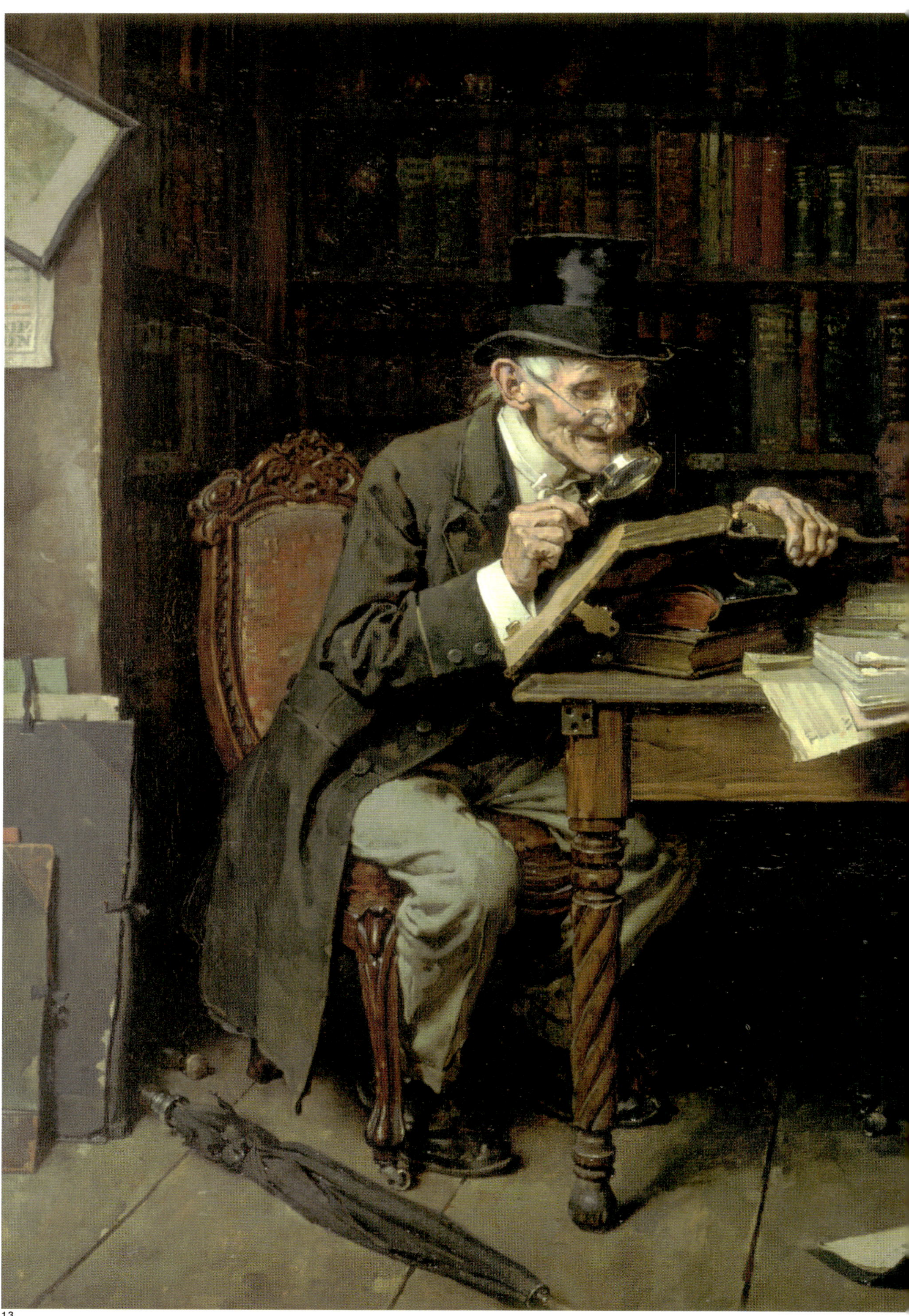

13

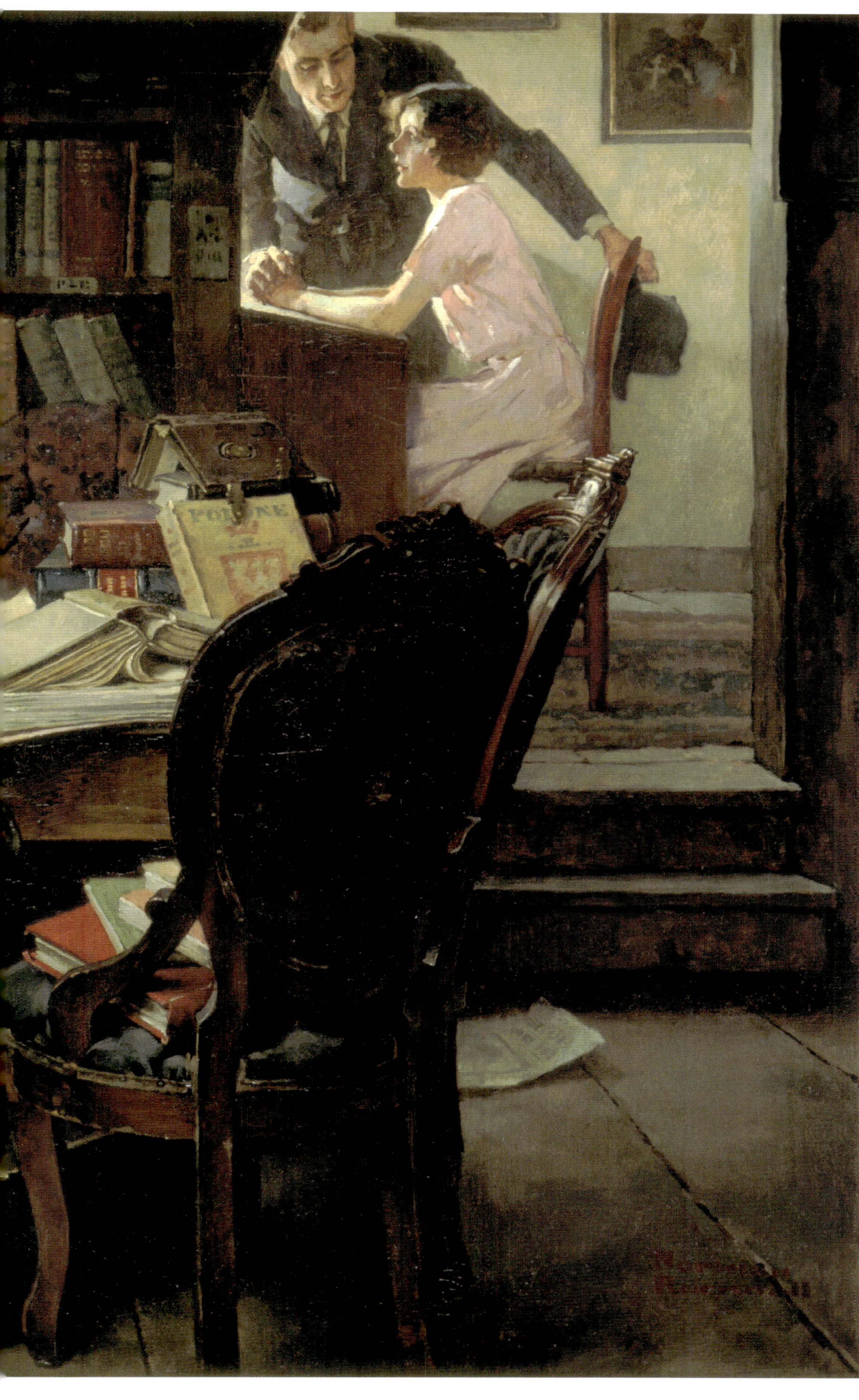

four basic human rights that should be guaranteed "everywhere in the world—freedom of speech, freedom of worship, freedom from want, and freedom from fear." Painted by Rockwell during World War II as his contribution to the war effort, these powerful works conveyed Roosevelt's ideals in terms that were understood and appreciated by a broad audience. An immediate success from their first appearance in the *Saturday Evening Post* in 1943, the *Four Freedoms* continue today to be iconic images of American democracy and freedom.

Freedom of Speech conveys the quiet dignity and strength of an ordinary American with the conviction to speak at a New England town meeting while neighbors, who may hold differing views, respectfully listen. The painting speaks powerfully to America's first-amendment rights. Rockwell inserts a self-portrait in a cameo appearance peering out of the upper left corner of the painting.

In the *Golden Rule*, painted for the cover of the *Saturday Evening Post* in 1961, Rockwell portrays a sea of faces, multicolored ethnic clothing, and religious symbols, illustrating his personal belief in tolerance and the universal oneness of mankind. Painted when he was sixty-seven, the cover was one of his last for the *Post*. In it, the artist acknowledged his dissatisfaction with a world still beset by religious and racial differences and strife decades after World War II. It was during this period in his life that he left the *Post* and began paint-

13. *Book of Romance*, 1927
Painting for *Ladies' Home Journal*, July 1927
Oil on canvas, 32 x 42 inches
Norman Rockwell Museum Collection, NRM.1985.03

In his autobiography, Rockwell wrote that, over time, many limitations were imposed on magazine illustration. An illustration "has to conform to the editors' ideas of what the reader wants." A poll conducted by *Ladies' Home Journal* found that the vast majority of women readers were interested in young love. Further, Rockwell claimed, "the one unforgivable sin in American illustration is to paint a woman who is not ravishingly beautiful."
This subject picture, which appeared unaccompanied by a story, fills the desire for beautiful young lovers, but Rockwell's focus is more directed toward the mysterious old man.

14. *Turn of the Tide (Get that Fish on My Line, Sonny)*, 1937
Painting for *American Magazine*, October 1937
Oil on canvas, 20 x 32 inches
Norman Rockwell Museum Collection, NRM.1997.18

Norman Rockwell's work for *American Magazine* was concentrated during the years 1934 to 1942. This is a strong period in the artist's career during which he excelled in the field of story illustration. Rockwell created thirty-one images inspired by narrative text for the publication. In *Turn of the Tide*, the future of both a rustic community's way of life and a pair of impoverished lovers rests on the outcome of a battle of wills between an embittered, ill millionaire and a spawning salmon swimming upstream.

ing subjects of contemporary relevance for *Look* magazine, moving away from the humor and pathos that were the hallmarks of his earlier decades.

The Norman Rockwell Art Collection Trust also holds a significant collection of drawings, striking examples of Rockwell's skill as a draftsman. Rockwell sketched every detail that would appear in his paintings to the scale of each final image. Working in charcoal, he often cut out and patched with blank paper an area or detail he desired to rework. Rockwell's skill in creating the strong "architecture" needed for his finished paintings is apparent in his drawings.

The Trust collection is also filled with experimental works created during Rockwell's late-in-life travels and from sketch classes he attended to refresh his inspiration. These efforts to rejuvenate his painting coincided with grieving the death of his wife Mary in 1959.

His 1961 marriage to his third wife, Molly Punderson, symbolized a new beginning, starting a period of travel that gave rise to increasingly political themes. Numerous works painted for *Look* magazine during the 1960s resulted from travels to the former Soviet Union, Africa, the Middle East, South America, and across the United States.

Rockwell visited Rome frequently, both on business and to visit his son Peter Rockwell, who has lived in Italy for many years. Plein air studies of the Trevi Fountain, the Colossal Statue of Emperor Constantine, and the Sistine Chapel are examples of a fresh, quick sketching style that he employed when drawing and painting from life. A loose, colorful group of sketches painted in his later years reveals a side of the artist that emerged during the rare moments he was not working for hire.

Norman Rockwell Museum Collection

Almost from the inception of the Art Collection Trust, the Norman Rockwell Museum started to collect additional Rockwell works. The collection of artworks owned outright by the Museum has been developed through purchase, gift, and bequest. The collection includes notable magazine covers, story illustrations and advertisements. To shape the most encyclopedic collection of Rockwell's work, the Museum's collecting philosophy has been to acquire fine representative works of every period and type. Early, middle, and late periods of the artist's work can be studied, as well as his artistic progression throughout his career. Numerous studies, color sketches, and working drawings reveal the artist's process.

The *Problem We All Live With*, a powerful visual narrative focusing on school desegregation in the 1960s, was the first purchase made for the Norman Rockwell Museum collection in 1975. Painted in 1964 for the occasion of the tenth anniversary of the Brown v. Board of Education Supreme Court ruling, the picture illustrates a girl being escorted to her newly integrated school by United States Marshals. The viewer's eye is drawn to the young girl walking courageously under the protection of the Marshals while epithets and objects are hurled at her. Able to address the Civil Rights movement as a respected com-

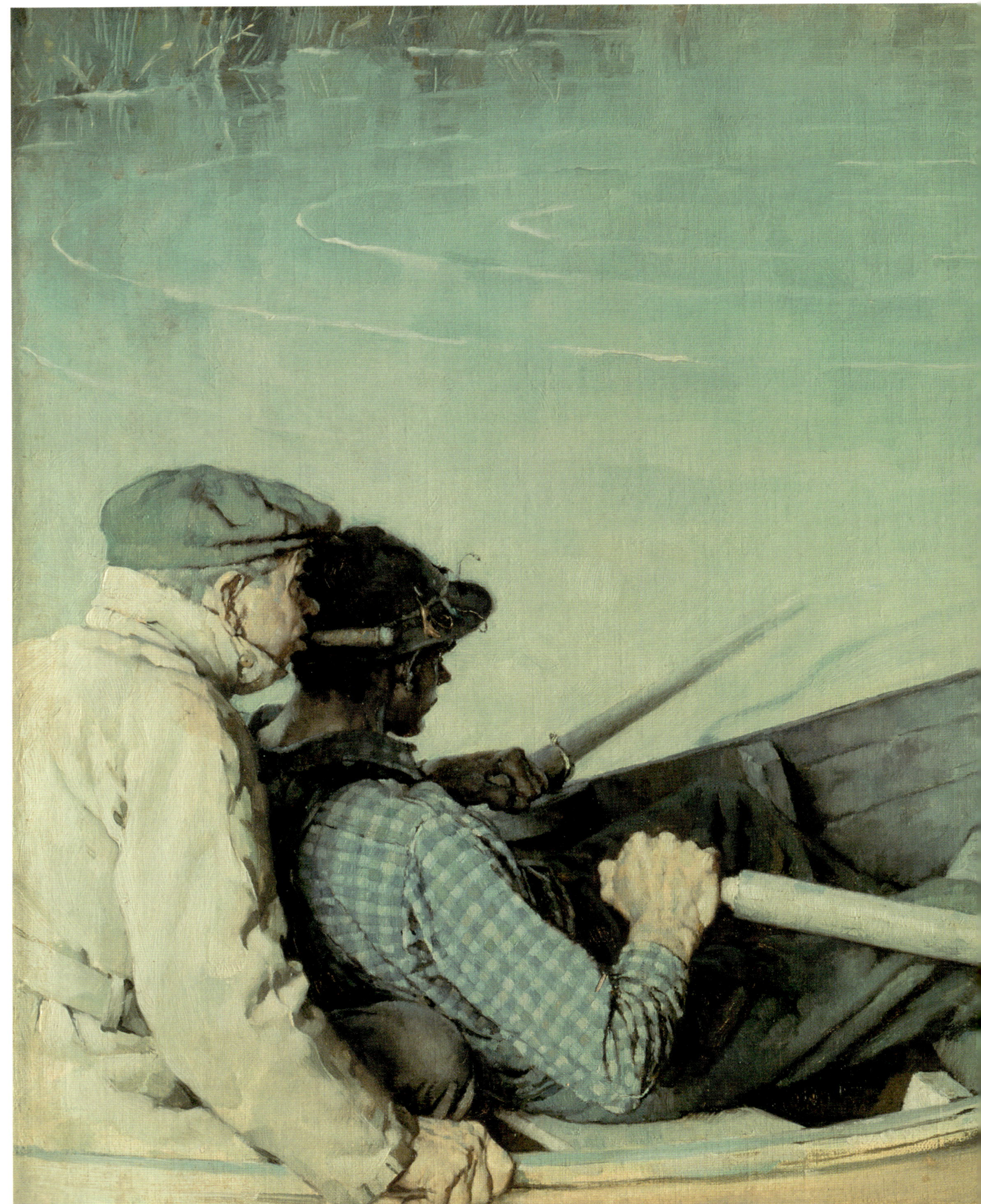

14

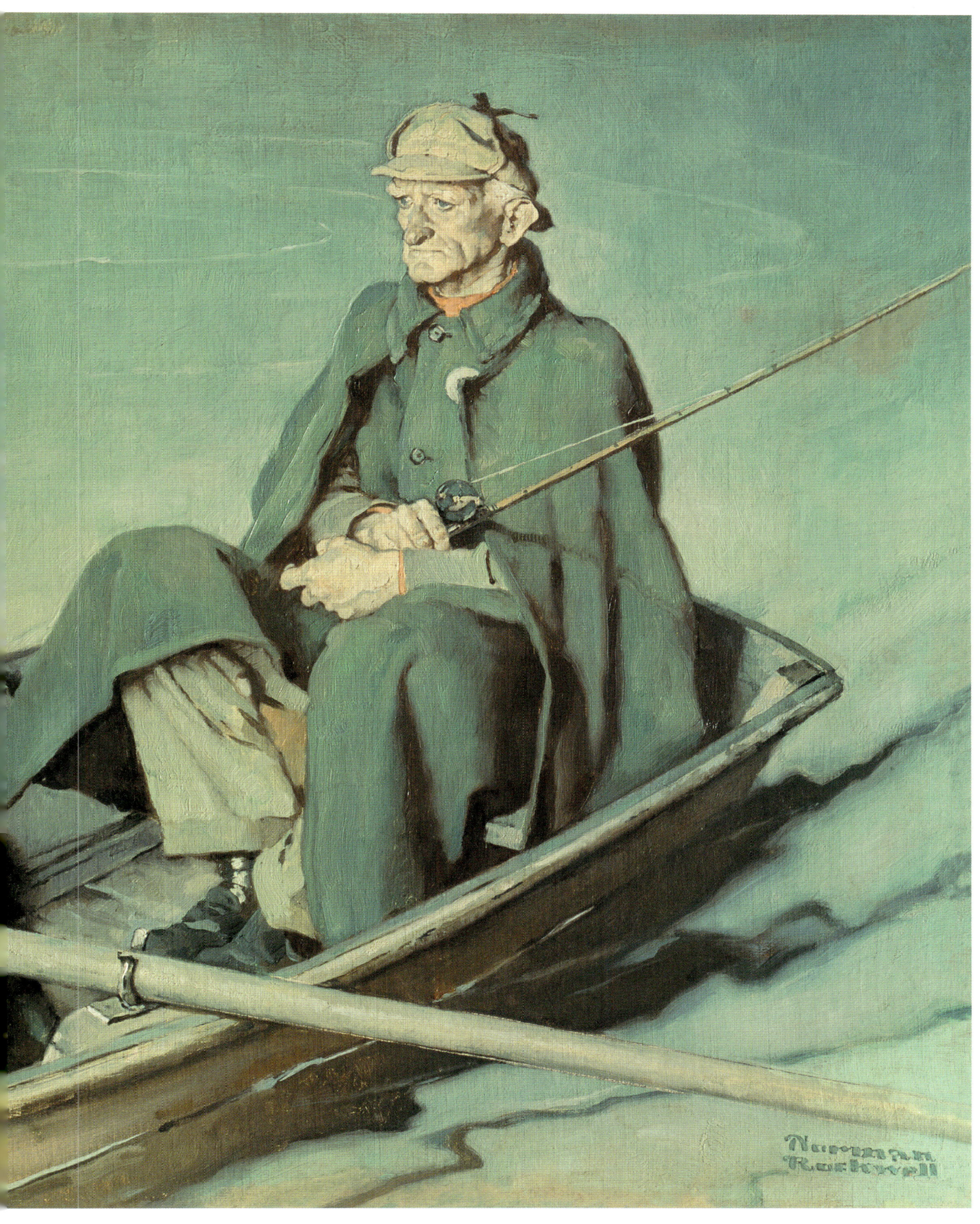
Norman
Rockwell

mentator who had earned the trust of the nation during his sixty years of painting, Rockwell painted some of the most powerful work of his career during this period. Expressing his own views on tolerance, equality, and human dignity, Norman Rockwell pleaded for brotherhood in *Murder in Mississippi* (1965) and viewed race relations through the innocent eyes of children in *New Kids in the Neighborhood* (1967).

The *Art Critic* (1955), a painting that considers the communicative powers of art, was acquired by the Museum to complement an extensive series of preparatory studies in the Trust collection. The work depicts a young art student studying a Rubenesque portrait, portrayed with the innuendo and sexual humor characteristic of the 1950s.

The art student, modeled by Rockwell's son Jarvis, who was himself a developing artist, gazes through his magnifying lens at the brooch nestled in the décolletage of the amused lady, posed for by Rockwell's wife Mary. On an adjoining wall, a group of Dutch Masters looks down in disapproval. This painting and its accompanying studies offers one of the best examinations of the artist's working process, as it is the final painting of more than eleven sketches for this subject in the Museum's collection. The thumbnail sketch for this painting is typical of the miniature idea vignettes Rockwell would sketch to pitch an illustration idea to his art editor.

15. *Ichabod Crane*, c. 1937
Unpublished illustration
Oil on canvas, 49.5 x 24.5 inches
Norman Rockwell Art Collection Trust, NRACT.1973.107

In 1936, book publisher George Macy commissioned Norman Rockwell to illustrate new editions of *Tom Sawyer* and *Huckleberry Finn*. Eager to repeat Rockwell's success with additional titles, Macy encouraged him to explore other subjects for illustrated books. Rockwell began work on a series of pictures of celebrated characters in American fiction, which would be paired with excerpts from the stories. As one of the first in the series, he chose Ichabod Crane, the schoolmaster from the 1819 Washington Irving story *The Legend of Sleepy Hollow*. Rockwell painted this first version of Ichabod and then a second, more developed version, which is now in the collection of Utah's Draper Elementary School. It is likely that Rockwell's good friend and New Rochelle model Fred Hildebrandt, who had just posed as the schoolmaster in *Tom Sawyer*, also appears in Ichabod Crane. Irving described his character as "tall, but exceedingly lank, with narrow shoulders, long arms and legs, hands that dangled a mile out of his sleeves, feet that might have served for shovels, and his whole frame most loosely hung together. His head was small, and flat at top, with huge ears, large green glassy eyes, and a long snipe nose, so that it looked like a weathercock perched upon his spindle neck to tell which way the wind blew." Rockwell's artistic interpretation departs from a version created ten years earlier by Arthur Rackham, one of his favorite illustrators. Rackham's spidery pen-and-ink rendering suits the skinny, gawky Crane, whereas Rockwell's figure is more substantial, making us feel slightly unsettled by the penetrating demeanor of his sideways glance, and fortunate that we are confronted by a painting and not the actual man.

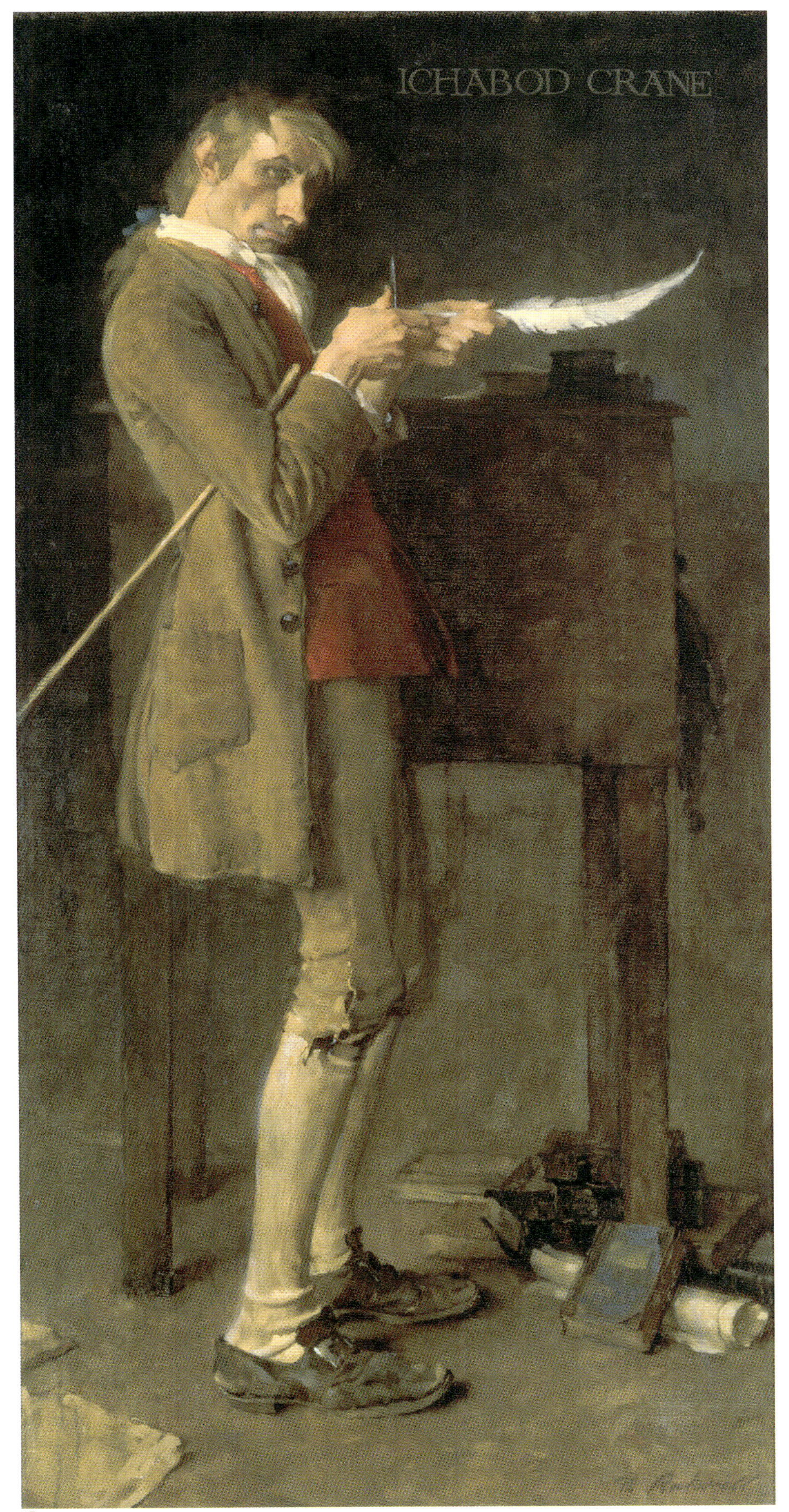

15

The Museum acquired a fine story illustration with the acquisition of *Aunt Ella Takes a Trip* (1942). Painted for *Ladies' Home Journal*, the painterly illustration demonstrates the artist's skill with light and expression. The woman drives resolutely as the girl rides joyfully at her side in their country wagon in the early morning sunlight that flits like the butterflies on the prairie. Mothers and daughters are rare as Rockwell's subjects, though one notable early 1920s work the Museum added to its collection is an advertisement, done for Raybestos brakes, depicting a mother at the wheel of her motor car with her young daughter at her side.

Of the fifty paintings done for the annual *Boys' Life* cover/calendar series, forty-four are owned by the National Scouting Museum in Irving, Texas. Norman Rockwell Museum was fortunate to add *A Scout Is Helpful* (1939), a painting of an Eagle Scout rescuing a victim of the 1938 New England flood, and *Good Friends* (1924), an early image featuring a young Cub Scout with puppies, and two recent acquisitions, *Army of Friendship* (1933) and *The Good Scout* (1935). A 1914 image of *Scouting with Daniel Boone* is a fine representation of Rockwell's work as the youthful editor of *Boys' Life* magazine.

Thirty-three sketches from Rockwell's 1956 Pan Am trip around the world, created while on assignment for the airline, are among the many works that Rockwell created for America's most prominent advertisers.

16. *If Your Wisdom Teeth Could Talk They'd Say, "Use Colgate's,"* 1924
Painting for Colgate dental cream advertisement, 1924
Oil on canvas, 26.5 x 32 inches
Collection of the Norman Rockwell Museum, NRM.1979.1

A perfect example of Norman Rockwell's early twentieth-century style of advertising illustration, this painting for Colgate toothpaste mentions but does not picture the product. Since the ads of such products in the 1920s were marketed to adults, Rockwell's subtlety would not have been missed. An assignment such as this made it easy for Rockwell to paint the kind of storytelling pictures he preferred. In keeping with his penchant for picturing children with benevolent grandfathers, Rockwell composes his scene with an elderly man and a young boy. From the body language and the props, it appears the man is telling the boy about an adventure of his own youth. The map and the Civil War memorabilia suggest that his story relates to an actual historical event. To hear firsthand of Civil War service would have been a profound learning experience for an imaginative youth. Since this image was used as a magazine print ad reduced to one-half or one-third page size, readers may have overlooked the incongruity of cavalry, infantry, officer, and drummer boy memorabilia. Later in his career, Rockwell would become extremely careful in researching information for his paintings as readers invariably wrote to him if they found errors.

In 1903, when Rockwell was nine, his paternal grandmother, Phebe Rockwell, died. So that Rockwell's grandfather would not be alone, the family moved from their New York City apartment at 103rd Street to John Rockwell's apartment at St. Nicholas Avenue and 152nd Street. They remained living together—even after moving to Mamaroneck in 1907—until 1911, when Rockwell's mother, complaining of the hardship of caring for her father-in-law, persuaded her husband to move the (nuclear) family to a boarding house in New Rochelle. During the eight years of proximity with his grandfather, it is likely Rockwell would have heard stories of his grandfather's brother, George Sigourney Rockwell, a sergeant in the Union Army, who was mortally wounded in the final days of battle at Stones River, Tennessee. Rockwell never mentioned his grandfather, nor does it appear that he used him as a model in any of his many pictures of elderly men. But just as Rockwell seems to compensate for the lack of affection and warmth in his family by painting it into his pictures, the tender grandfather-grandchild relationship is abundant in his work.

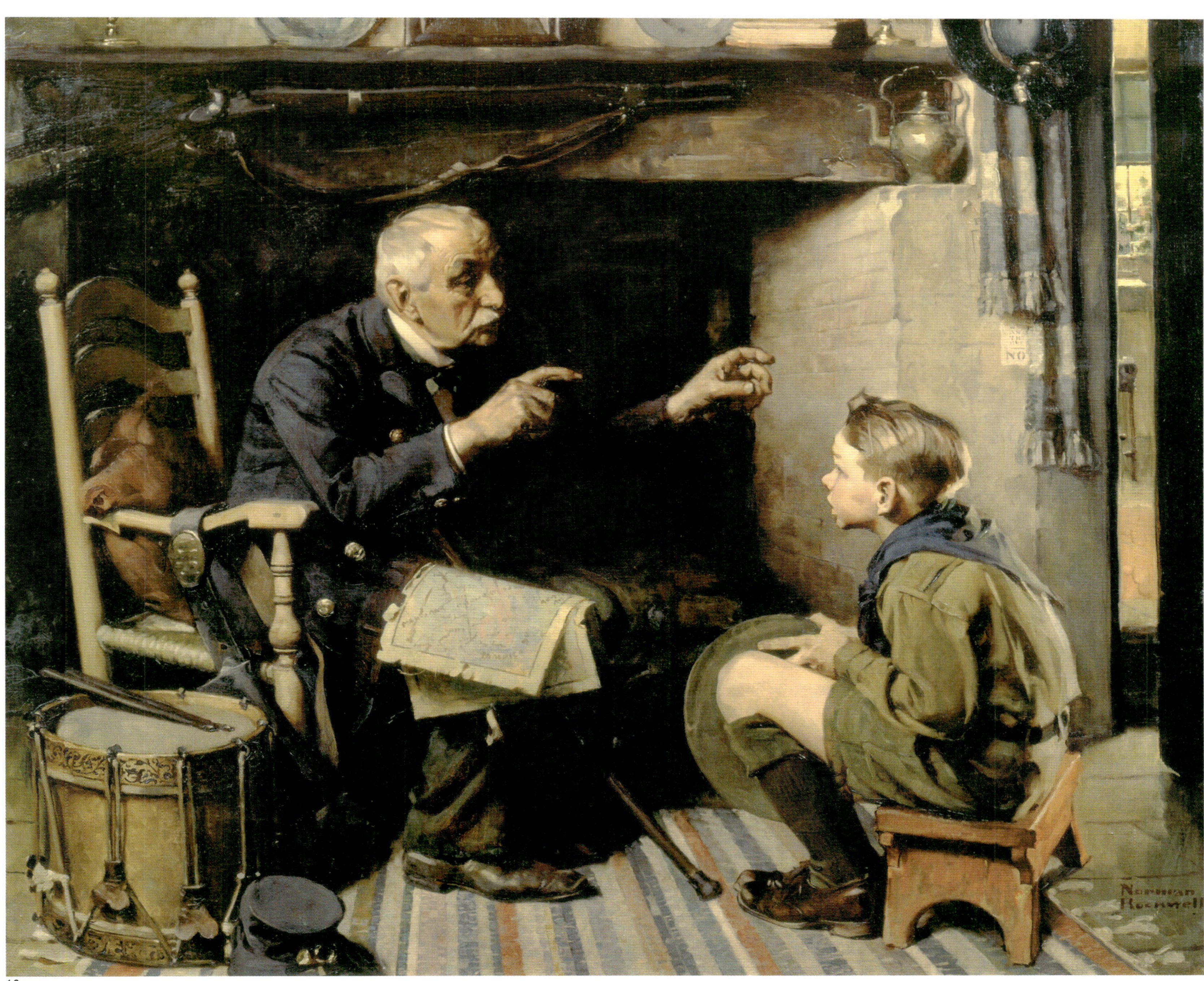

16

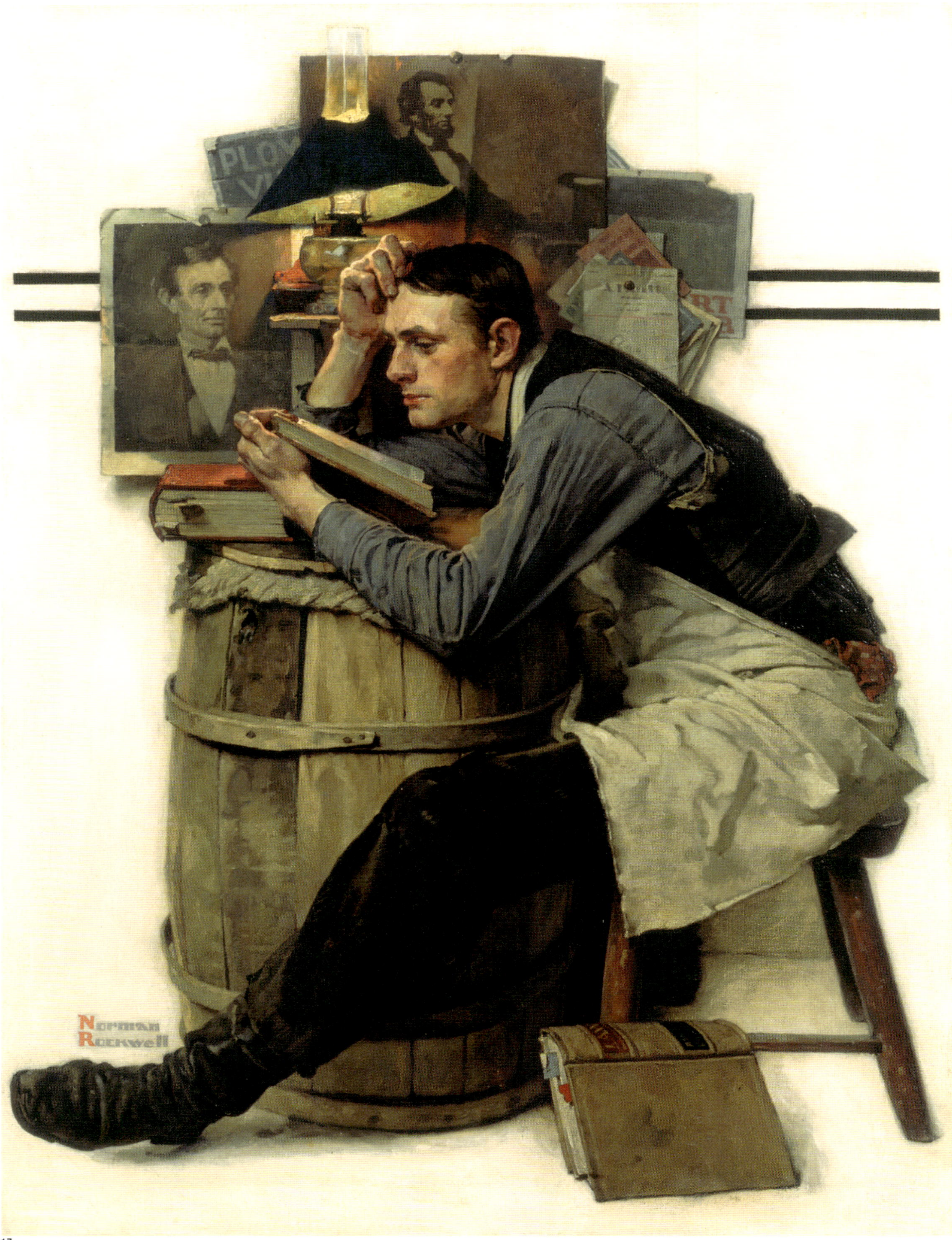

17

Norman Rockwell Studio

Norman Rockwell's Stockbridge studio, moved from the artist's home in Stockbridge, is now situated in the Museum grounds, preserved with its historic furnishings, artist materials, daily work diaries, art reference library of books and museum prints, costumes, and travel memorabilia. Open from May through October, the studio offers visitors the opportunity to become immersed in the artist's working environment. Rockwell designed the studio to his exact specifications, incorporating the best features enjoyed from his numerous previous studios. The Stockbridge studio, where he worked for his last twenty-three years, was considered his "best studio yet," a converted 1840s New England carriage barn that had been renovated by Shaker craftsman Ejner Handberg. This work space was tailored according to his preferences and years of experience, and provided for all the necessities of his workday.

The studio afforded a social place to greet and meet with guests, and consists of a spacious north-lit work space, an area for staging and posing models, a dark room and projecting room for tracing drawings, an office area for correspondence, a balcony for the storage of costumes and working studies, back storage rooms for files and supplies, and even a couch for his afternoon nap. Here he met with his secretary to go over bills to be paid, art supplies for purchase, and to review his correspondence and fan mail. Everything he needed was pre-

17. *The Law Student*, 1927
Painting for *The Saturday Evening Post* cover, February 19, 1927
Oil on canvas, 36 x 27.5 inches
Norman Rockwell Museum Collection, NRM.1979.4

To celebrate the February 12 birthday of President Abraham Lincoln, Norman Rockwell painted this picture of a store clerk reading law books. While it alludes to Lincoln's own study of law, the chronology is slightly mistaken. Though Lincoln had been a store clerk and then part-owner of a store, it wasn't until two years later, after he had begun a political career as a representative in the Illinois General Assembly, that he began to study law. The point is well taken, however, and provides a picturesque cover. Far from resembling Lincoln, the handsome Rockwell model adds to the cover's charm. Later in his career, Rockwell would paint authentic representations of Lincoln for Boy Scout calendars and historical illustrations.

Business invoices tacked to the wall identify this setting as the back room of a store. These papers, the leather-bound books, the tear sheets of Lincoln images, and the wood barrel, give Rockwell an opportunity to represent a variety of textures.

Now that *The Saturday Evening Post* was printing covers in full color (note the capitals of the signature), Rockwell could use color to enhance his composition. He added touches of vermillion strategically around the student, eventually leading the reader's eye to the rosy glow of the student's light-bathed face, framing the scene and lending it warmth.

The Law Student earns a place as one of Rockwell's symbolic portrayals of the American dream, presenting the notion that with diligence, a person of meager means can aspire to greatness. Rockwell's own diligence was leading him to financial success and illustration fame, thus securing his American dream. In 1927, he was a member of the local Yacht and Country clubs, drove a canary-yellow Apperson Jack Rabbit, and spent $23,000 (the equivalent of $253,000 in 2006 dollars) building a study next to his newly purchased $38,000 New Rochelle house. Later that summer he embarked on a four-month tour of Europe with two friends.

sent in the studio, to which he brought his storytelling ideas and models for meticulously crafting the collage of his paintings. His photographers worked closely with him in this space, capturing the poses of the models who appeared in his art. Rockwell often acted out the expression or pose he desired of his model. Family members and friends visited with him during his workday to read aloud to him from the window seat, or to offer a critique of a current work.

The studio is filled with memorabilia gathered on travels and objects used in his paintings as props. Visitors to the studio experience a sampler of the world's cultures through the unusual artifacts that Rockwell collected. A Turkish samovar, an early whaling ship model, an Ethiopian musical instrument called a masenqo, a Dutch pipe, a Navaho blanket, African spears, a southwestern kachina doll, and masks and armor are highlights of the studio collection of decorative objects. Icons of various religions gathered on travels include a mosaic shalom, a crucifix, and a God's eye. The artist's tools and equipment included a rarely used etching press, a variety of easels, a marble palette table, T-squares, canvas stretcher bars, paints, and meticulously cleaned paintbrushes. A collection of hats, sleigh bells, walking cane, powder keg, and antique muskets were among the props Rockwell used for paintings of early American scenes. A collection of authentic period costumes was destroyed in the 1943 Vermont studio fire.

18. *The Stay at Homes (Outward Bound)*, 1927
Painting for *Ladies' Home Journal* illustration, October 1927
Oil on canvas, 39.25 x 32.5 inches
Norman Rockwell Art Collection Trust, NRACT.1973.82

Over a forty-nine-year period beginning in 1924, Norman Rockwell contributed thirty-seven illustrations to *Ladies' Home Journal*. Some accompanied fictional stories, and some, like this one, told their own story, published with title only. The motif of children and the elderly was common throughout Rockwell's career. Rockwell enjoyed working with children and older adults. Because they were less self-conscious and less concerned about their dignity, he said, they were freer to act out the feelings he wanted them to express and less worried about how they might be portrayed.

When an artist depicts a person facing away from us, we are invited to place ourselves in that person's role, becoming the surrogate of the character. By offering two choices, Rockwell increases the pool of viewers who might empathize with his characters, and he offers two different—in this case opposite—perspectives. This illustration would have worked just as well in a children's publication or one for seniors, but its overall sentimentality appealed to women. Other subjects Rockwell painted for the *Journal* included a young woman dreaming of romance, a Christmas visit to a sick friend, a young actor yearning for Hollywood stardom, and a woman posing for her portrait.

The foreground of this painting indicates a New England setting. In the summer of 1912, Rockwell spent three months studying painting with Charles Hawthorne in Provincetown, Massachusetts, which was then a Portuguese fishing village. Hawthorne had studied *plein air* painting (painting out-of-doors) with William Merritt Chase. In Rockwell's painterly treatment of the roofs, waves, trees, grass, and man's trousers, we see the influence of Chase's impressionistic style.

Similar to his magazine covers, Rockwell's subject pictures often provide clues for viewers to create a story continuum. In this case, the shingle-roofed cottage in the foreground may be the home the child and grandfather have left to climb the hill for a better look at the departing ship. When the ship is out of sight, or when night approaches—the westerly setting sun has already begun to cast them in shadow—they might return to light a fire to take the chill off a damp evening or to boil water for tea and reminisce about the grandfather's sailing adventures.

Odds & Ends

The house on the right is a duplicate of Rockwell's studio, which earlier that year had been built as an attachment to his garage in New Rochelle. Where the ornamental brace is attached to the chimney, however, Rockwell had a decorative palette and brushes.

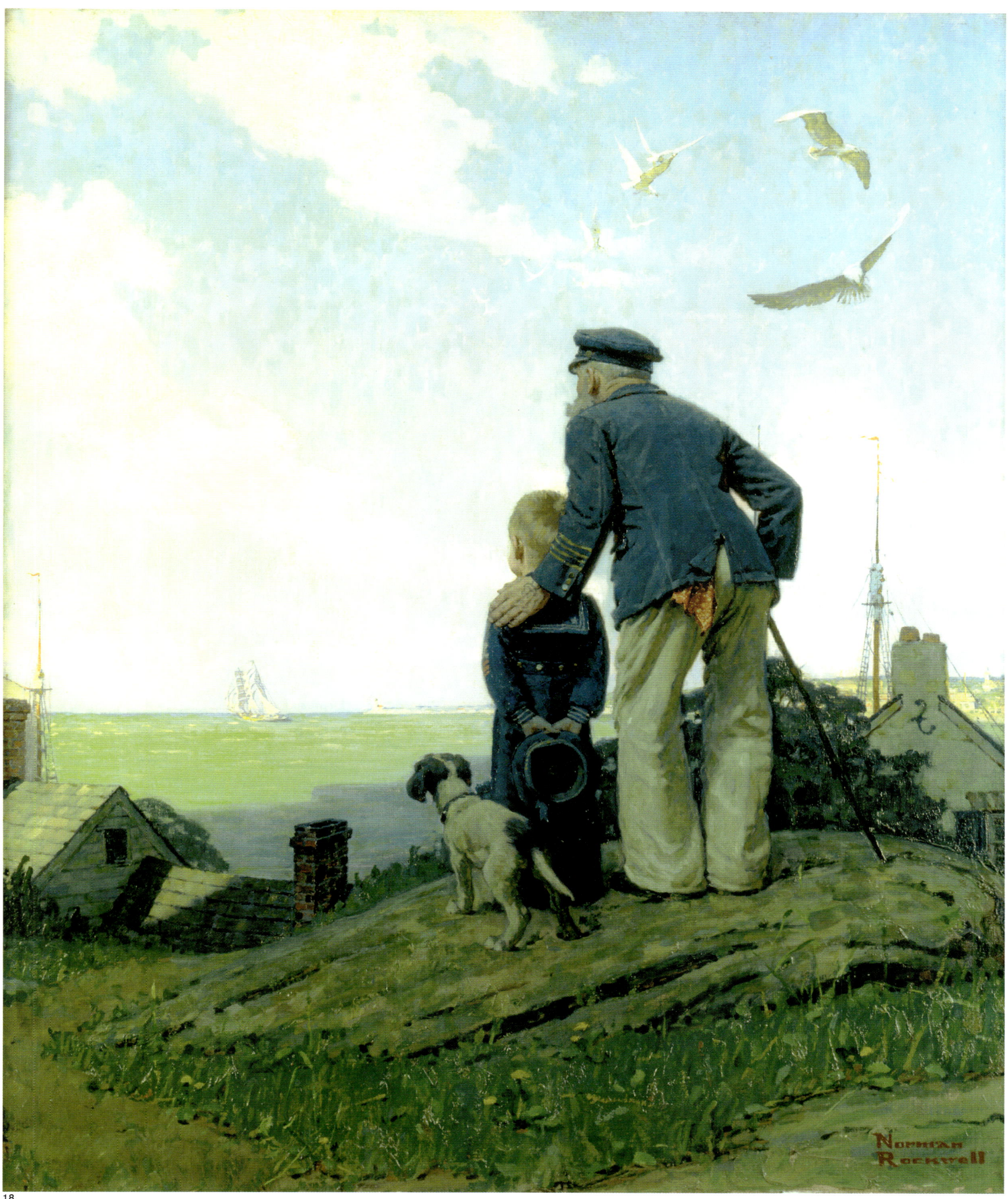
Norman
Rockwell

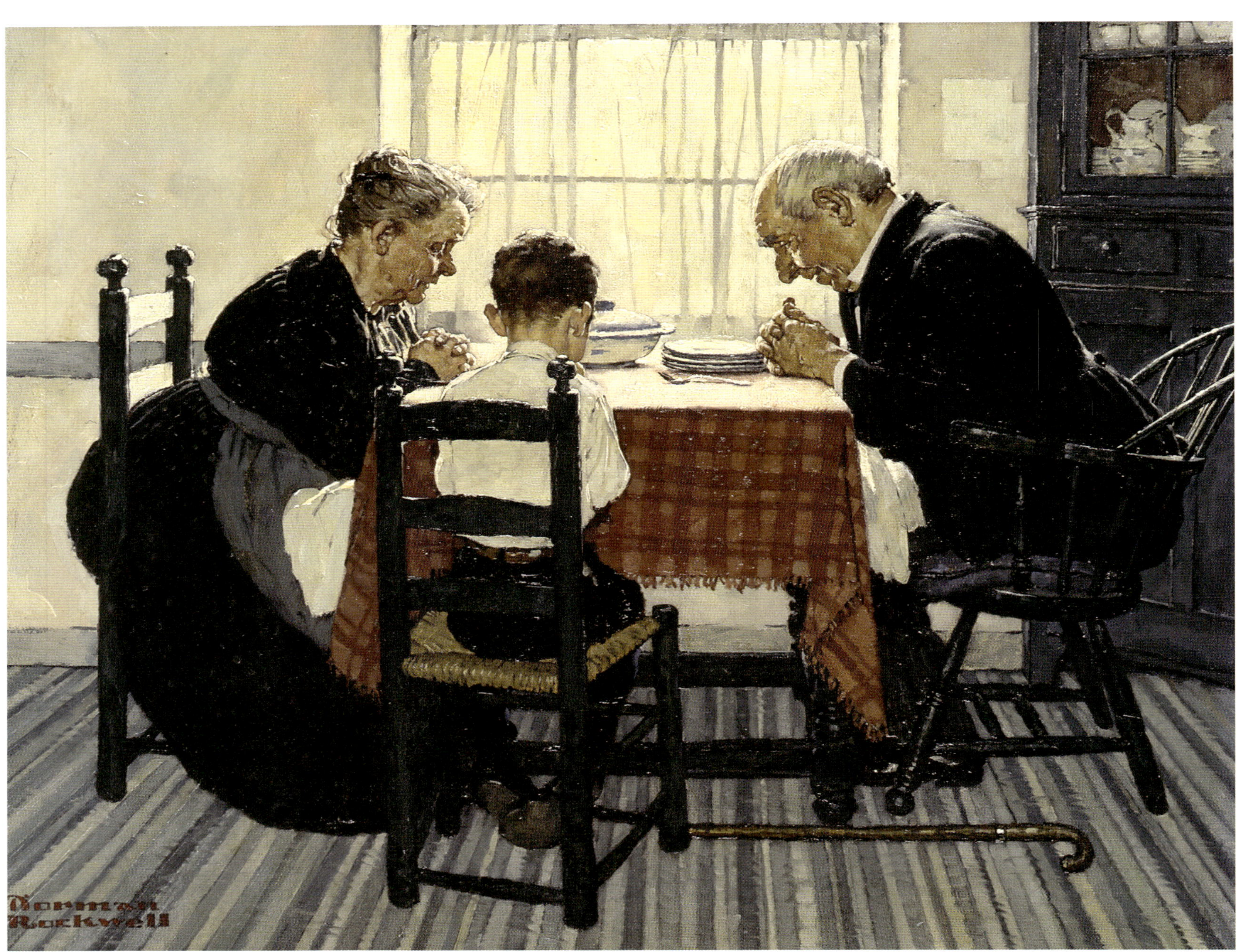

19

In his later years, Rockwell was much sought after as a portrait artist and was visited in his Stockbridge studio by such famous celebrities as John Wayne, Frank Sinatra, and Arnold Palmer. Working from photographs taken while visiting with United States presidents, Rockwell painted Dwight D. Eisenhower, John F. Kennedy, Lyndon B. Johnson, and Richard M. Nixon from his Stockbridge studio, as well as presidential candidates Adlai Stevenson, Nelson D. Rockefeller, Hubert Humphrey, and Ronald Reagan—paintings that now form the Museum's important portrait collection.

Norman Rockwell Museum Archives

The Norman Rockwell Museum Archives houses the most complete archive of the artist's papers, and many materials relating to the art of illustration. The archive contains all the published sources of Rockwell's illustrations, including thousands of original publications and several complete sets of *Saturday Evening Post* covers. Other original published source material includes full sets of Rockwell's illustrations, as well as covers and advertisements from *Boys' Life Magazine*, *St. Nicholas*, *Youth's Companion*, *Life*, *Literary Digest*, *American Magazine*, and *Look*, among others. All of his published work in early books, magazines, movie posters, and related ephemera is represented in the reference collection.

19. *Family Grace*, 1938
Lemuel remembered his mother's caution about waiting for prayer
Story illustration for "Rural Vacation" by Jake Falstaff, *Ladies' Home Journal*, August 1938
Oil on canvas, 16 x 20 inches
Norman Rockwell Museum Collection, NRM.1984.03

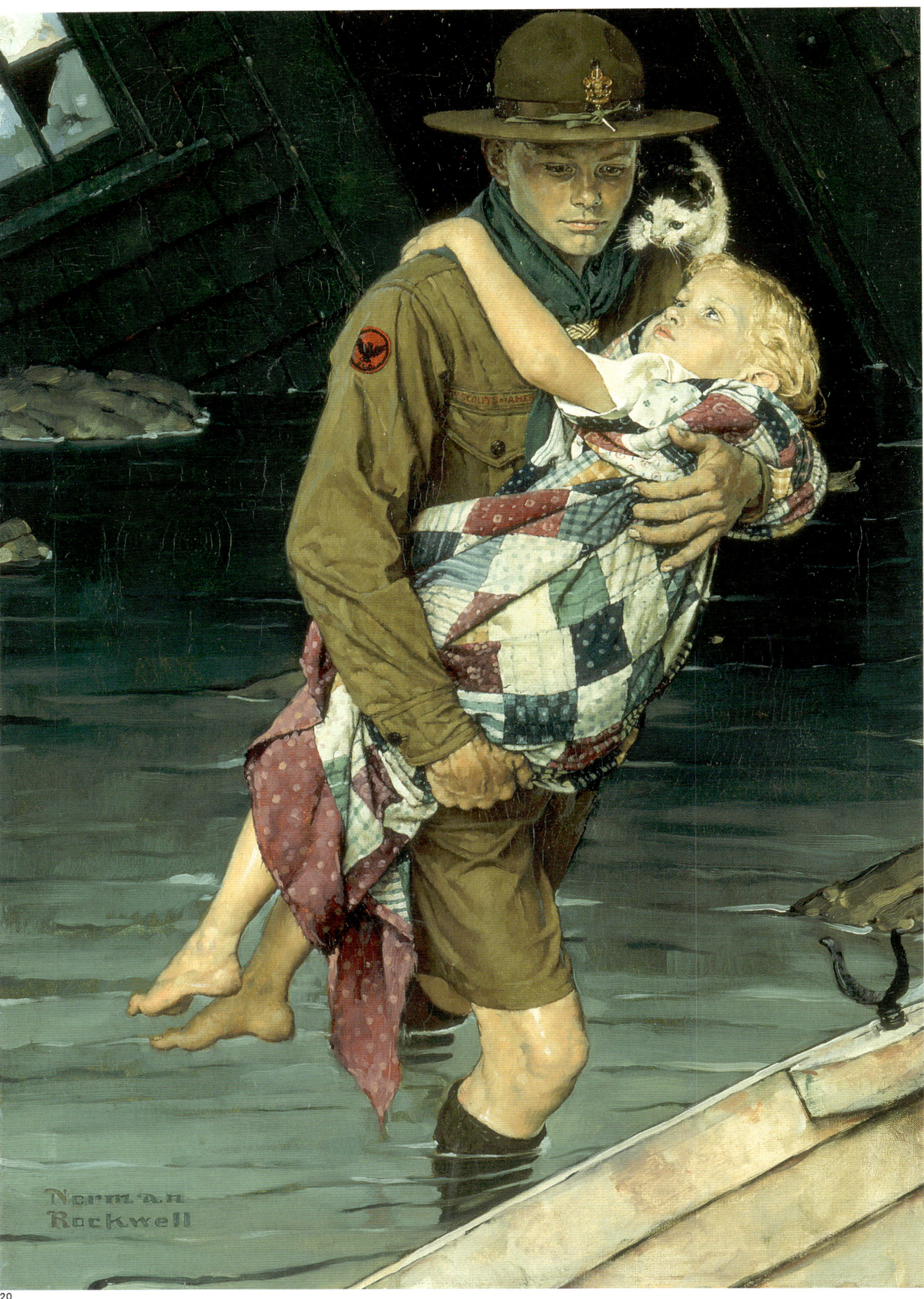

20

The artist's business correspondence with the *Saturday Evening Post* art editors and other communications offer a fascinating glimpse into Rockwell's working world. The media collection includes videotaped interviews of Rockwell models and contemporary illustrators and historians, audio and filmed recordings of Rockwell. Letters from presidents and boxes of fan mail and birthday cards attest to the enormous popularity that Rockwell enjoyed with the American public during his career. Business ledgers, cancelled checks, and personal correspondence reveal the business demands of an illustrator of celebrity status. Study sketches, numerous photography collections, and costumes offer in-depth insight into the artist's working process. Among the more notable items in the costume collection is the suede jacket used in *Freedom of Speech*, and the prom dress for *After the Prom* (1957).

The Museum published the *Catalogue Raisonné* of Norman Rockwell's work in 1986. The most complete published compilation of the artist's work to date, it contains nearly 4,000 entries of every finished painting and sketch known at that time. An addendum to the catalogue is maintained in digital format in the Museum reference center. It documents current discoveries of the artist's work, in addition to complete reference photo files on Rockwell's images. The Museum's library holdings specialize in volumes on American art and illustration art.

20. *A Scout Is Helpful*, 1939
Painting for Boy Scouts of America calendar, 1941
Oil on canvas, 34 x 24 inches
Norman Rockwell Museum Collection, NRM.1988.10

After successfully illustrating the new *Boy Scout Hikebook* in the fall of 1912, Rockwell was retained for the permanent staff of *Boys' Life*. The weekly magazine of the Boy Scouts of America had just expanded to national circulation. Six months later, Rockwell was promoted to art editor and he continued to work for *Boys' Life* until 1917. In gratitude for this early break and the valuable experience he gained, Rockwell made a lifelong commitment to the Boy Scouts of America, producing their annual calendar illustrations from 1925 to 1976. Painted in 1939, Rockwell's 1941 Boy Scout calendar illustration of a Scout rescuing a child in a swollen river was inspired by the Great New England Hurricane of 1938.* Both that storm and the Great Atlantic Hurricane of 1944 affected towns in New England as far north as Rockwell's hometown of Arlington, Vermont.

Of all Rockwell's clients, the Boy Scouts of America demanded the most in changes to his work. Rockwell often had to redraw studies or repaint portions of canvases, necessitating shipping the artwork from the publisher to Rockwell, back and forth until it was perfect. *A Scout Is Helpful* was no exception. Rockwell's first version showed the scout in long pants, which were wet from the knees down. The Boy Scouts editor asked Rockwell to put the boy in short pants, as scouts were always to be shown neat, and wet pants would not appear neat.

Odds & Ends
Neither Rockwell nor any of his three sons were Boy Scouts.

* The United States National Weather Service did not begin naming hurricanes until 1950.

Norman Rockwell Museum's comprehensive photographic collections document Norman Rockwell's working process. Photographs by Gene Pelham, Louie Lamone, and Bill Scovill captured the artist and his models at work. Famous photographic portraits of Rockwell by Yousef Karsch and others are also represented. Slides of Rockwell's travels during his later years, taken by his wife Molly, form another significant collection. A series of photographs by Los Angeles photographer Sam Calder reveals Rockwell's early use of photography in his working process. The archive has grown enormously through gifts by numerous donors and is the world's most significant biographic and artistic reference source for Norman Rockwell.

Norman Rockwell Family Art Collections

Norman Rockwell descended from and also fathered an artistic family. Ancestral works from Rockwell's maternal grandfather, artist Howard Hill, hung in Rockwell's studio. Rockwell's three sons became artists, and the Museum holds a small but distinguished collection of works by family members. Jarvis, the eldest son, is a modernist and collector of contemporary toys and action figures, and the Museum owns several of his drawings and assemblages. A significant collection of outdoor sculptures by Peter, the artist's youngest son, is well represented on the Museum's bucolic thirty-six-acre campus. Peter's site-

21. *Girl Reading the Post*, 1941
Painting for *The Saturday Evening Post* cover, March 1, 1941
Oil on board, 35.25 x 27.25 inches
Norman Rockwell Museum Collection, Gift of the Walt Disney Family, NRM.1999.3

Always aiming for the widest possible audience for his *Saturday Evening Post* covers, Rockwell pictures often have several layers of interest. To assure a successful cover, Rockwell grabs the viewer's attention with a trick–he matches the cover girl's face perfectly to the schoolgirl's body. By picturing a reader so engrossed in the *Post*, Rockwell emphasizes the interest and allure of the magazine, thus promoting its sale on newsstands. Beyond the gimmick, a story of growing up emerges in the simple scene of commuting to school. This young girl may soon leave behind her scuffed saddle shoes for polished heels, and her cozy mittens for kidskin gloves.

THE SATURDAY EVENING POST
C.B. COGGINS
Norman Rockwell
to Walt Disney
one of the really
great artists-
from an admirer
Norman
Rockwell

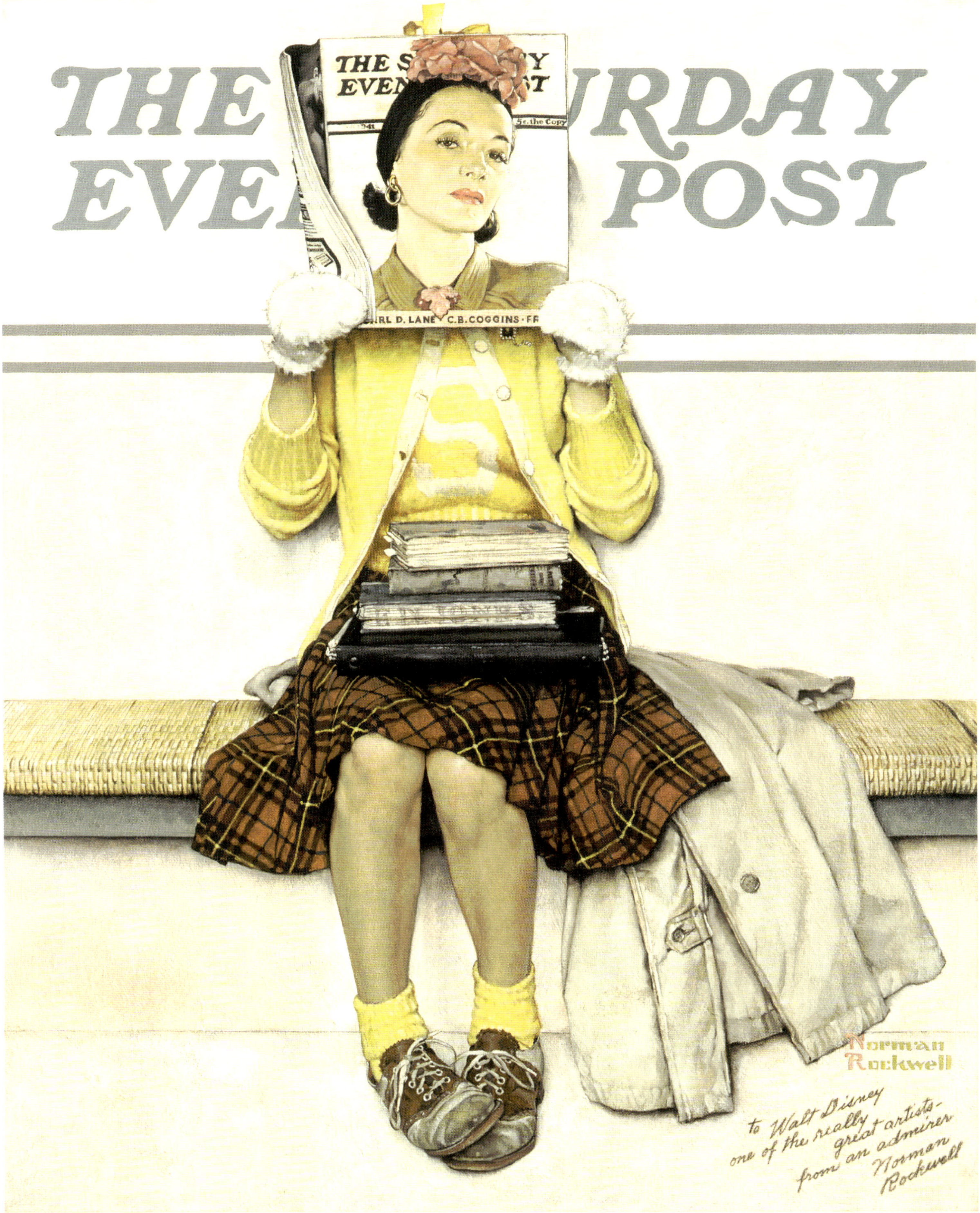

21

specific installations of life-size bronze acrobats and a carved monster plinth are designed for children to climb; a bronze fountain of acrobatic figures, and other carvings of soapstone and marble accent the grounds. A series of bronze maquettes and terracottas are also available for study. Norman Rockwell's middle son, Thomas, has authored noted books for young readers that are available in the Museum library.

Norman Rockwell Museum Illustration Collection

A gifted artist and masterful storyteller, Norman Rockwell consistently found inspiration in the work of other artists both from within the field of illustration and from the world of fine art. Norman Rockwell Museum places Rockwell's art firmly within the context of American art and European narrative tradition by preserving and collecting illustration works representative of the visual and cultural narrative of nineteenth- and twentieth-century America. By building a broader collection of original works by an expanded spectrum of illustrators, the Museum honors Norman Rockwell's commitment to his beloved profession by maintaining and presenting important works that might otherwise be lost.

Norman Rockwell Museum is in the vanguard of preserving and interpreting illustration art and highlighting its significance in our understanding of American visual culture. Norman Rockwell was a great admirer of illustrators, and over the years he acquired an important collection of illustration art, some of which has come to the Museum through the Rockwell family. Included among these historic works are drawings by Henry Matthew Brock, Edmund Dulac, Thomas Fogarty, A.B. Frost, Rico Lebrun, Maxfield Parrish, Edward Penfield, and Hugh Thompson. The Museum has established a significant collection of works by important visual communicators, both historical and contemporary, which trace the evolution of both society and the field.

America's Visual Culture

The exhibition mission of the Norman Rockwell Museum is to inspire awareness, appreciation, and understanding of the art of Norman Rockwell and its significance in the field of art and illustration. Museum exhibitions explore the impact of Rockwell's work and examine the history and evolution of his profession, placing him within the context of his colleagues. Exhibit themes speak to the meaning and presence of illustration in the world and honor the accomplishments of important visual communicators. They distinguish the Museum as an important center for study and scholarship within and beyond the field of illustration. Loans of artwork to museums around the world, an active educational program, and a popular web site expand the museum walls beyond Stockbridge.

Since its inception, the Norman Rockwell Museum has explored the impact of illustrated images and their role in shaping and reflecting our world through changing exhibitions, publications, and programs. Dedication to a deepened understanding of the art of illustration has led to the formation of the Rock-

22. *Freedom of Speech*, 1943
War bond poster
Image originally published with essay by Booth Tarkington in *The Saturday Evening Post*, February 20, 1943
Norman Rockwell Museum Collection

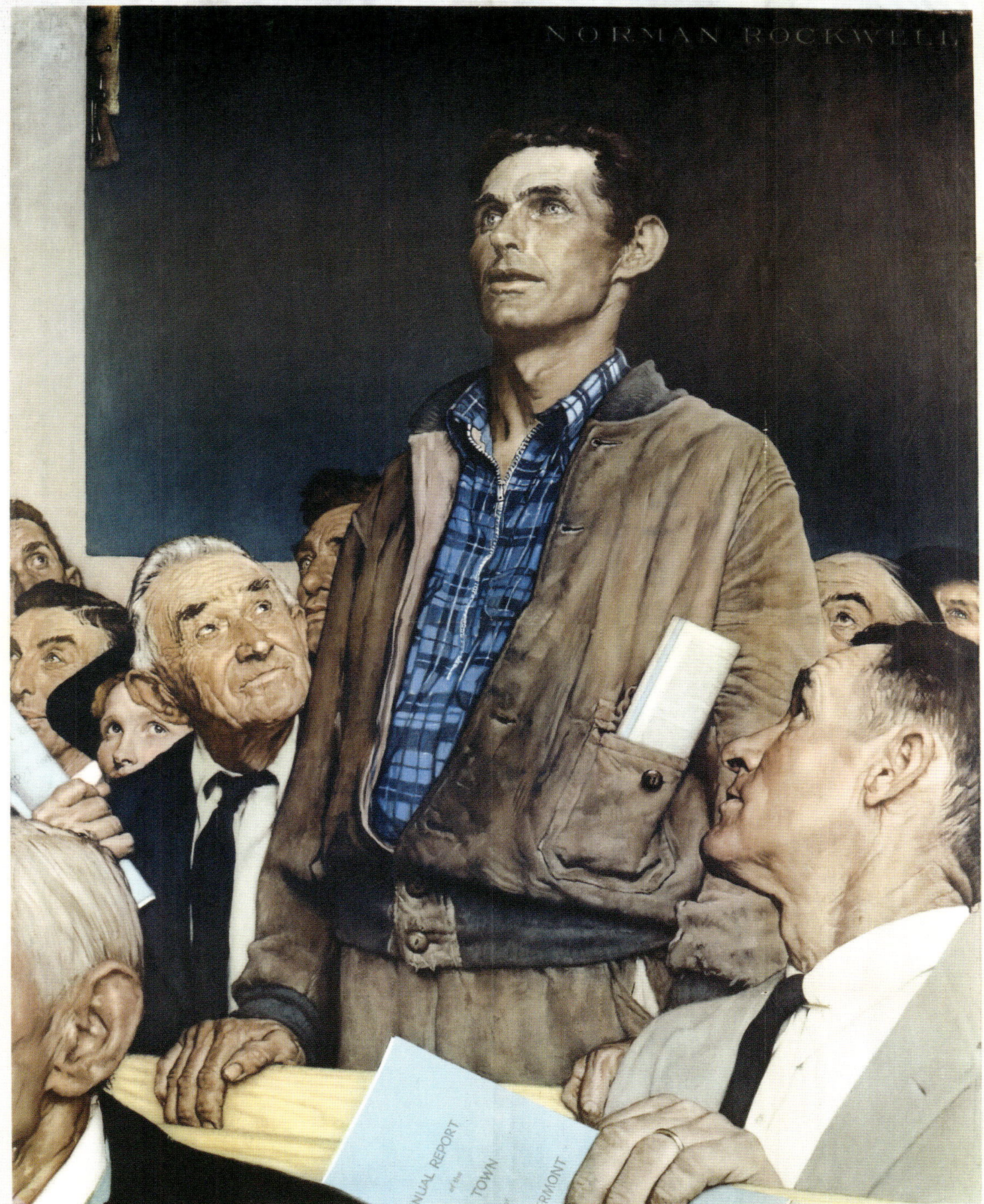

23. *Freedom of Worship*, 1943
War bond poster
Image originally published with essay by Will Durant in *The Saturday Evening Post*, February 27, 1943
Norman Rockwell Museum Collection

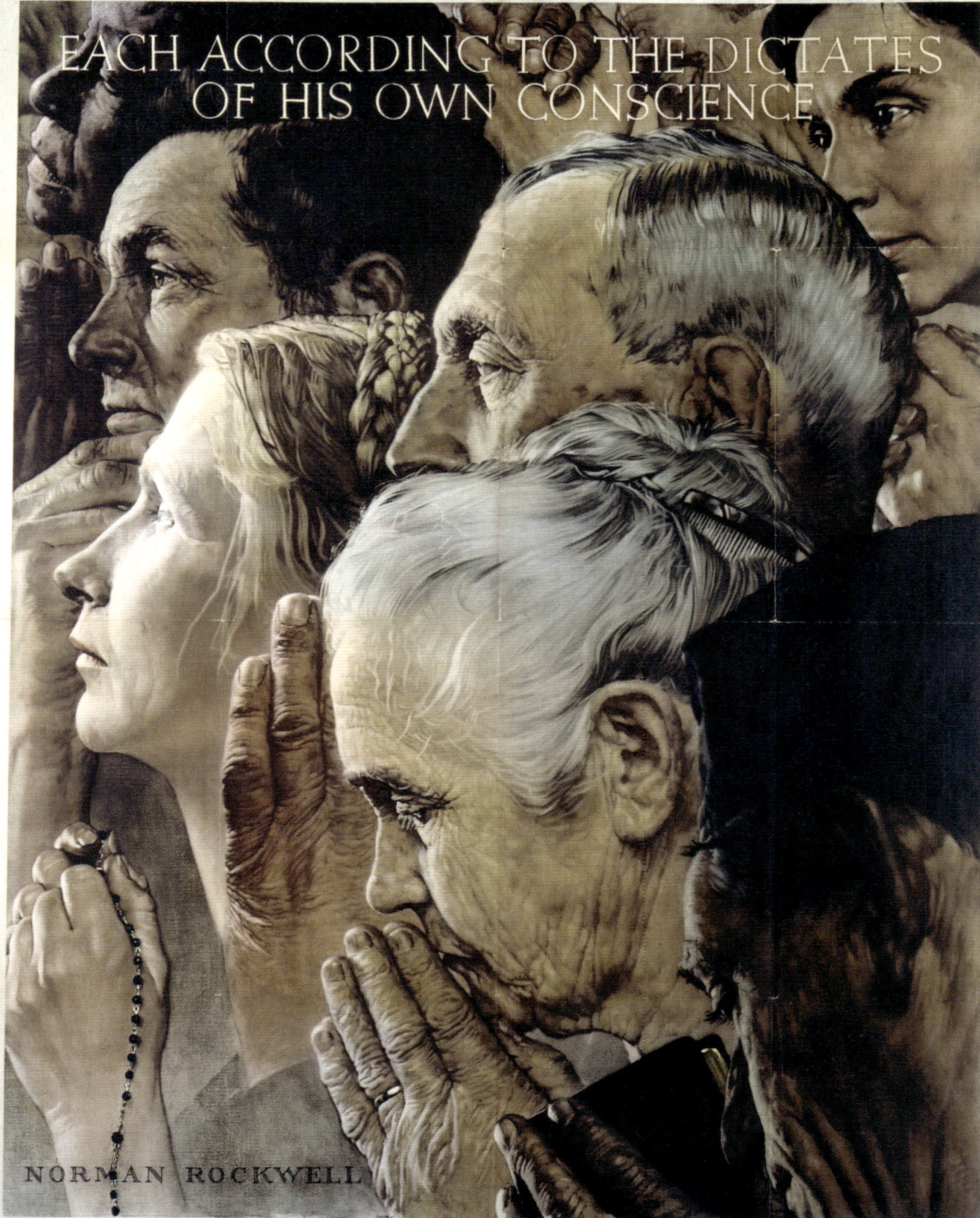

23

24. *Freedom from Want*, 1943
War bond poster
Image originally published with essay by Carlos Bulosan in *The Saturday Evening Post*, March 6, 1943
Norman Rockwell Museum Collection

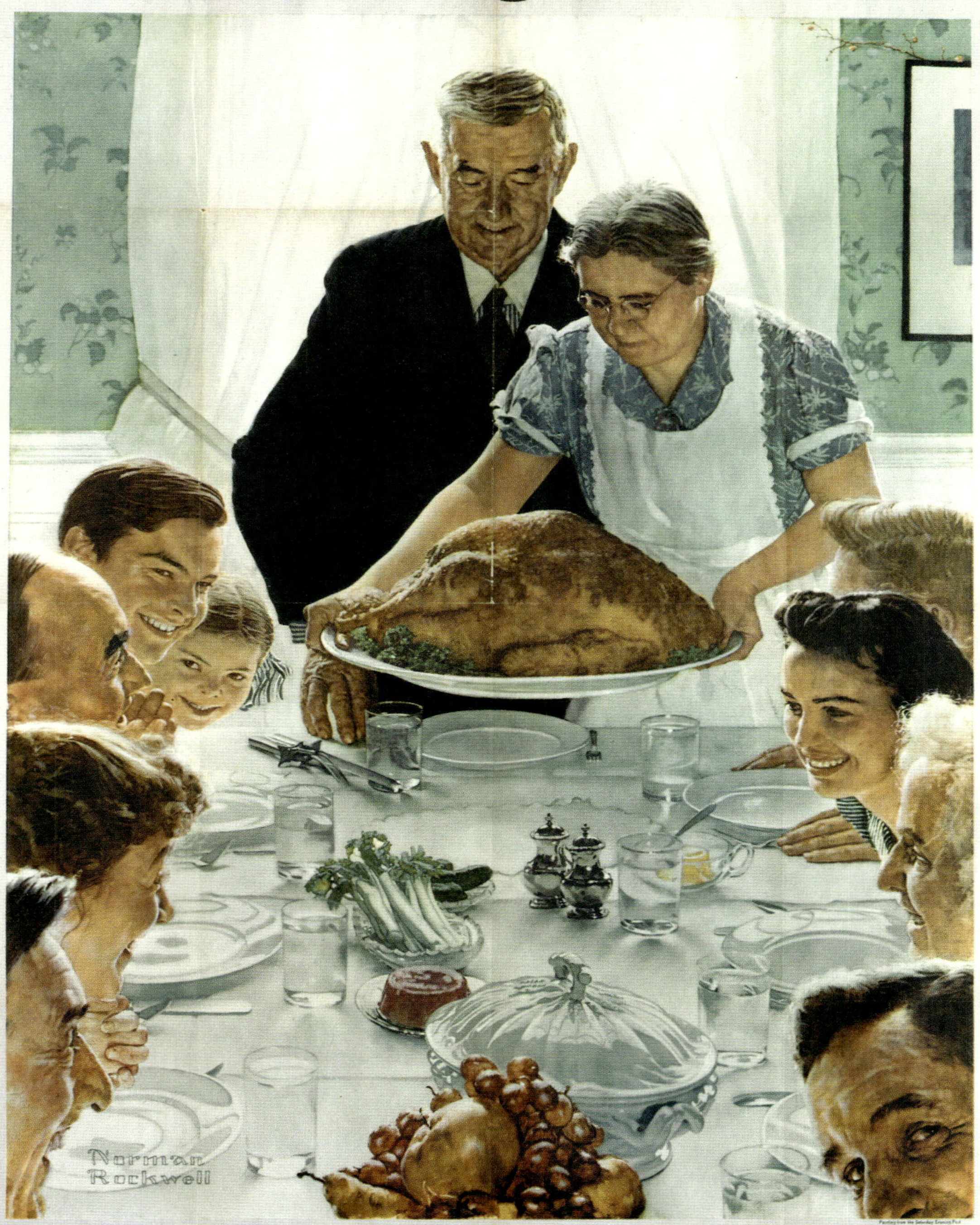

25. *Freedom from Fear*, 1943
War bond poster
Image originally published with essay by Stephen Vincent Benét in *The Saturday Evening Post*, March 13, 1943
Norman Rockwell Museum Collection

OURS... to fight for

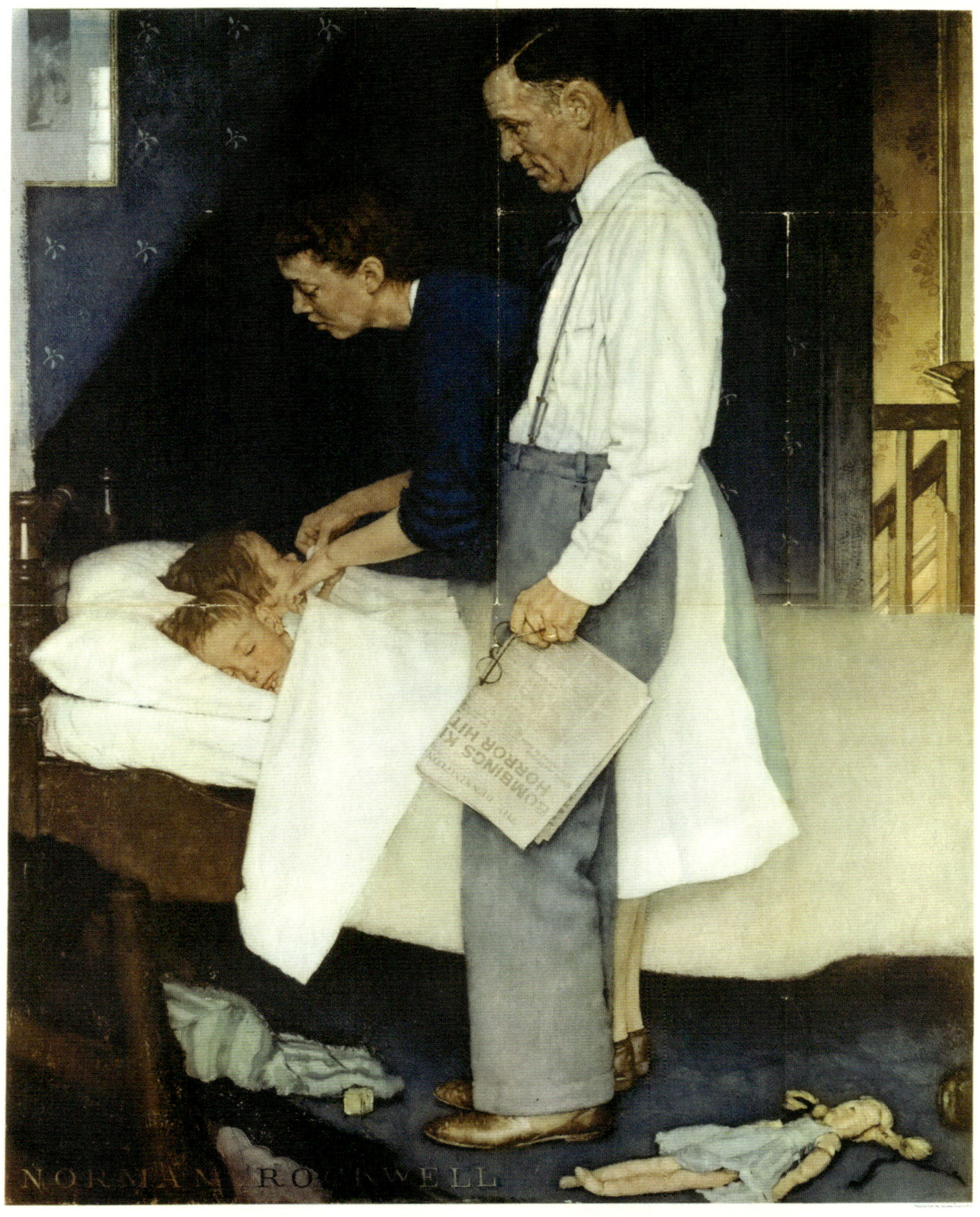

FREEDOM FROM FEAR

25

well Center for American Visual Studies. The first of its kind in the nation, this research institute supports sustained scholarship and establishes the Norman Rockwell Museum's leadership in the vanguard of preservation and interpretation relating to this important aspect of American visual culture.

Norman Rockwell Museum celebrates the work of Norman Rockwell and other outstanding visual artists who have chosen Rockwell's beloved profession to interpret, comment on, illuminate, and chronicle our world. We see and know ourselves better through their eyes.

Following pages
The Battle of Solomon Sea in Solomon Islands, Japan, November 1, 1942

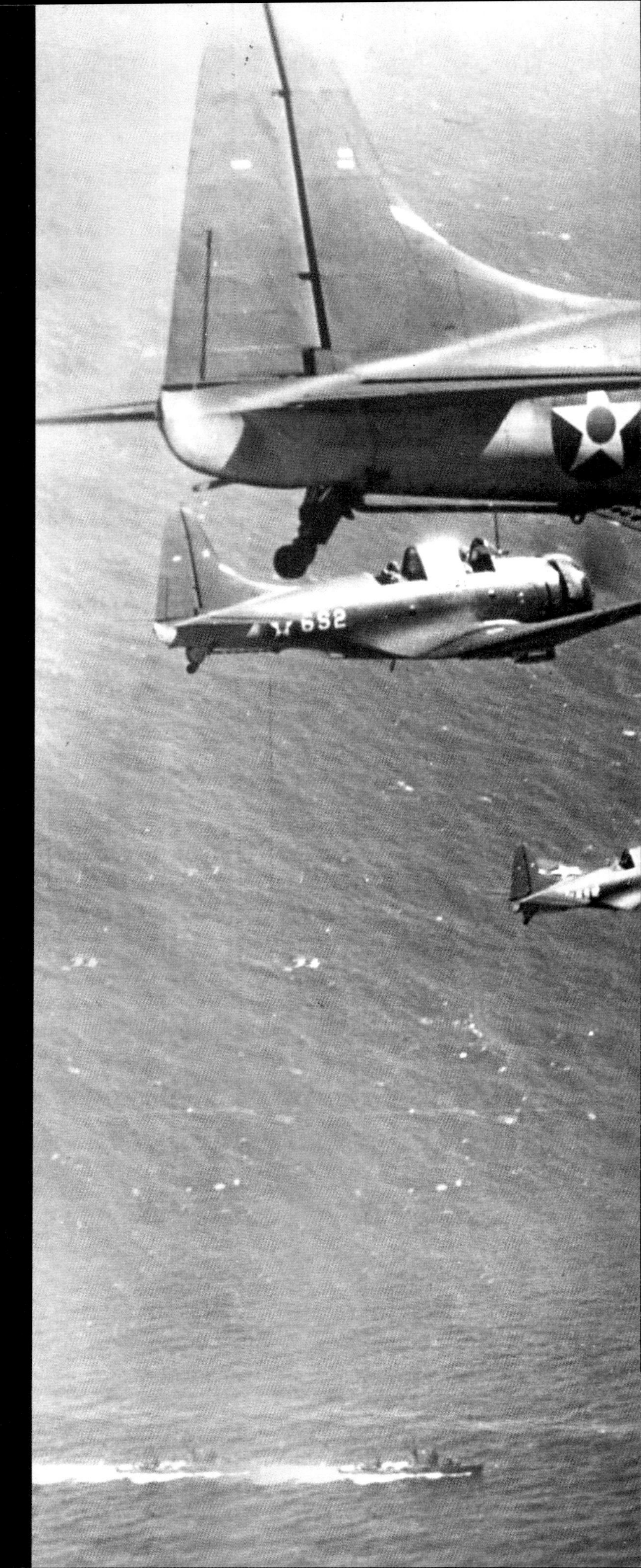
6S2

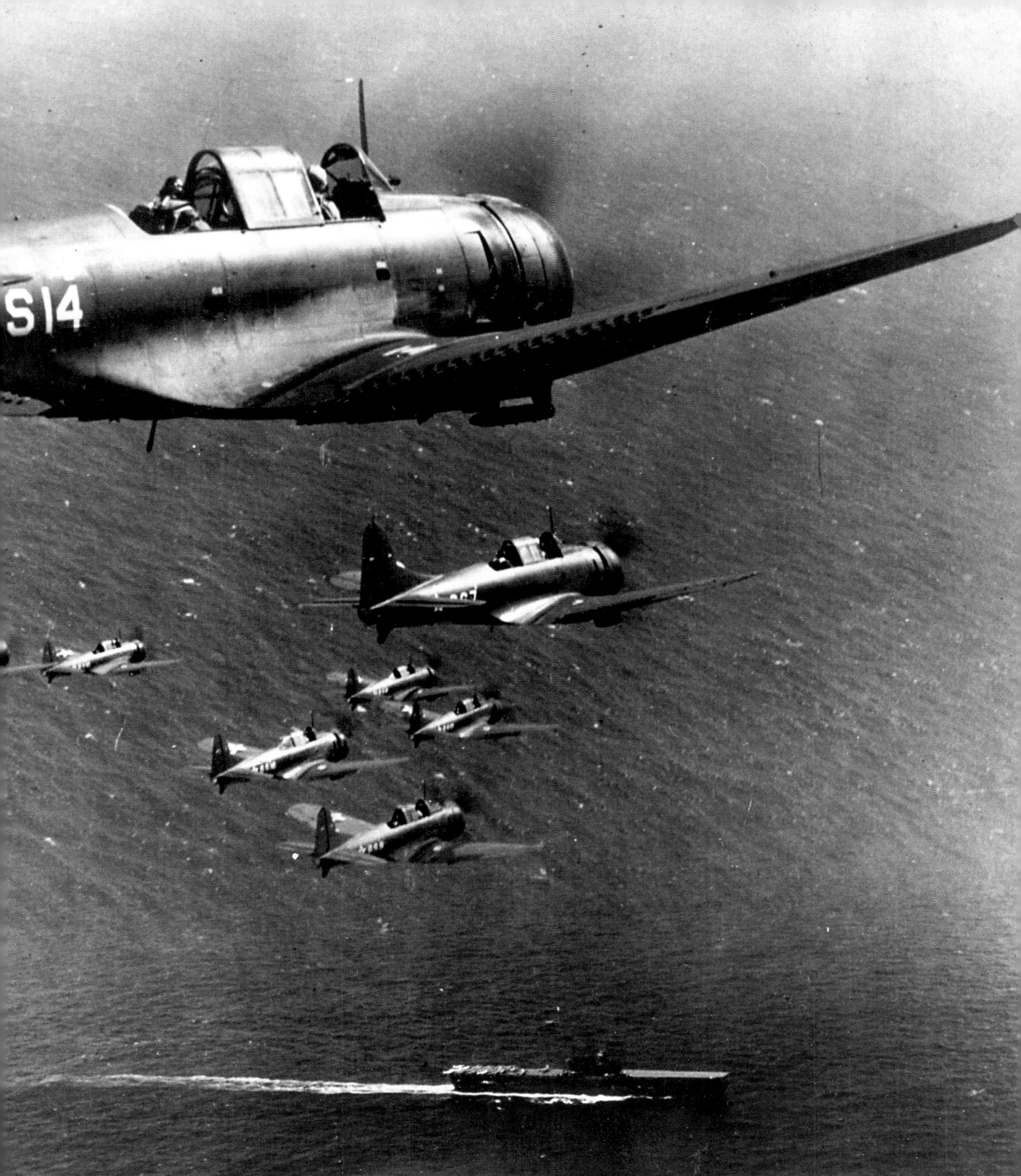
S14

Linda Szekely Pero

New York, Arlington and Stockbridge: the Life of Norman Rockwell

Norman Rockwell's consideration of art as a career was influenced on both sides of his family. His father, Jarvis Waring Rockwell, worked in the office of a textile firm, but in his spare time at home, he made copies of famous artists' drawings. Rockwell's mother's father, Howard Hill, earned his living painting meticulously detailed portraits of hunting dogs, family pets, people's homes, and wild game in lush landscapes. When commissions were absent he subordinated his skill to the manual labor of housepainting. "Norman Percevel, you have a valiant heritage. Never allow anyone to intimidate you or make you feel the least bit inferior. There has never been a common tradesman in your family. You are descended from artists and gentlemen," were words young Norman heard from his mother, Anne Mary Hill Rockwell as he was growing up on Manhattan's Upper West Side. And, Rockwell, unlike his older brother who excelled in athletics and eventually in business, would grow up to be an artist, following not his maternal grandfather's sporadically successful profession but the exciting and financially rewarding path of illustration.

Rockwell was born in New York City on February 3, 1894. The earliest evidence of his interest in art appears in his remembrance of his father copying illustrations from magazines in the evening after dinner. Rockwell said he joined him, sketching "dogs, houses and vegetables and from my imagination, pirates, whales, Indians." Later, for his older brother Jarvis and Jarvis's friend, he would draw a fleet of Spanish battleships, inspired by the 1898 Spanish-American War. After cutting them out and arranging them in battle order, the boys would use the scissors to cut up each other's ships to destroy them. "I remember it only used to take them about one second to cut down the whole fleet and it took me a whole day to draw the things."

Even more permanently etched in Rockwell's memory were images evoked by Charles Dickens. Fascinated by Dickens' stories, which were read to him and Jarvis each evening, Rockwell was inspired to draw their characters even as he listened. "I'd draw Mr. Micawber's head, smudge it, erase and start over, my tongue licking over my upper lip as I concentrated." Rockwell read Dickens throughout his life and adopted Dickens' literary view, observing the world around him and everyday life for its narratives. The powerful characterizations and rich narratives later inspired Rockwell's emotionally complex portraits. At the turn of the century, the steady influx of immigrants into New York City challenged the city's infrastructure, as well as its social structure and identity. Seeing this sometimes chaotic world around him, and viewing people as Dickens might have, Rockwell grew to be unusually perceptive of personalities, human nature, and the interactions that form the fabric of human relationships. He would become particularly interested in shared human experience.

City life, for Rockwell, was overshadowed by summer vacations the family enjoyed at upstate New York boardinghouse-farms. The annual summer idylls ingrained a store of memories and emotions in Rockwell on which he would later draw for his work. They also influenced his permanent move to the country in 1939. As Dickens' stories had confirmed to him, the city was overcrowded, polluted, and intrinsically less humanitarian. "In the city you are constantly confronted by unpleasantness. I find it sordid and unsettling."

In 1907, when Norman was thirteen years old, the Rockwell family (which now included Norman's grandfather, who had been living with them since the death of his wife in 1903), moved into Norman's deceased uncle's house in Mamaroneck, a suburban village ten miles north of the city. By this point, with the realization that his drawings impressed people, Rockwell determined that he would go to art school. He was already earning tuition money by delivering mail, by bicycle, to the outlying area of Orienta Point. One of his customers, Mrs. James Constable (of the department store Constables) commissioned him to design several Christmas cards; another hired Rockwell to tutor his two sons. This led to an offer of an inflated position as a summer-school instructor (though not of art) at the local Pennington Academy for Boys.

After his sophomore year at Mamaroneck High School, Rockwell began full-time studies at the National Academy School in New York City. After "tedious and dull" drawing from plaster casts eight hours a day for several months, he transferred to the Art Students League, where, he said, relationships between students and teachers were vital and effective—unlike the ennui he had experienced with his Academy instructors. At the League, he studied anatomy with George Bridgman and illustration with Thomas Fogarty, learning lessons that lasted throughout his career. Tackling his assignments with a dedication that earned him the nickname "the Deacon," Rockwell became one of the most promising students.

26. *Mine America's Coal*, 1944
Painting for the U.S. Office of War Information poster
Oil on canvas, 21 x 14 inches
Norman Rockwell Museum Collection, NRM.1978.12

Painted for the War Manpower Commission, this image was published as a poster, which read "Mine America's Coal. We'll make it hot for the enemy! See your United States Employment Service." World War II posters carried many varied messages. In addition to propaganda posters designed specifically to inspire fear of the enemy by showing atrocious acts committed by German or Japanese soldiers, many posters carried gentle and encouraging messages, such as appeals for increased farm production or conservation of resources like gasoline and food. Many posters encouraged workers in their war-related work, urging them not to take days off or leave their jobs. Some gave advice about how to become and stay healthy. *Mine America's Coal* showed that a middle-aged man, who was already sacrificing two children in service of the war, was willing to give even more by mining coal. Patriotism was invoked to recruit new workers for a dangerous trade.

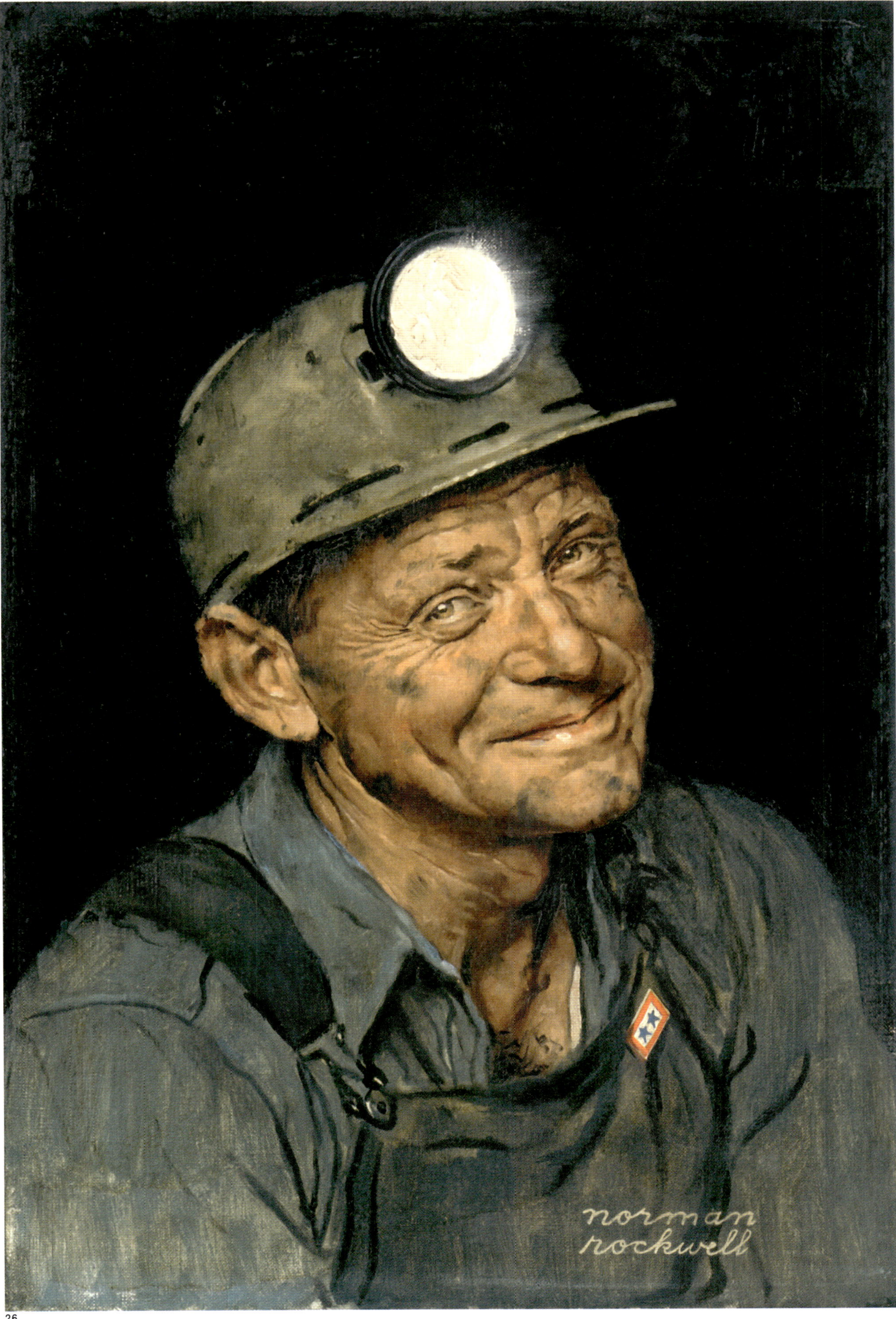

79

26

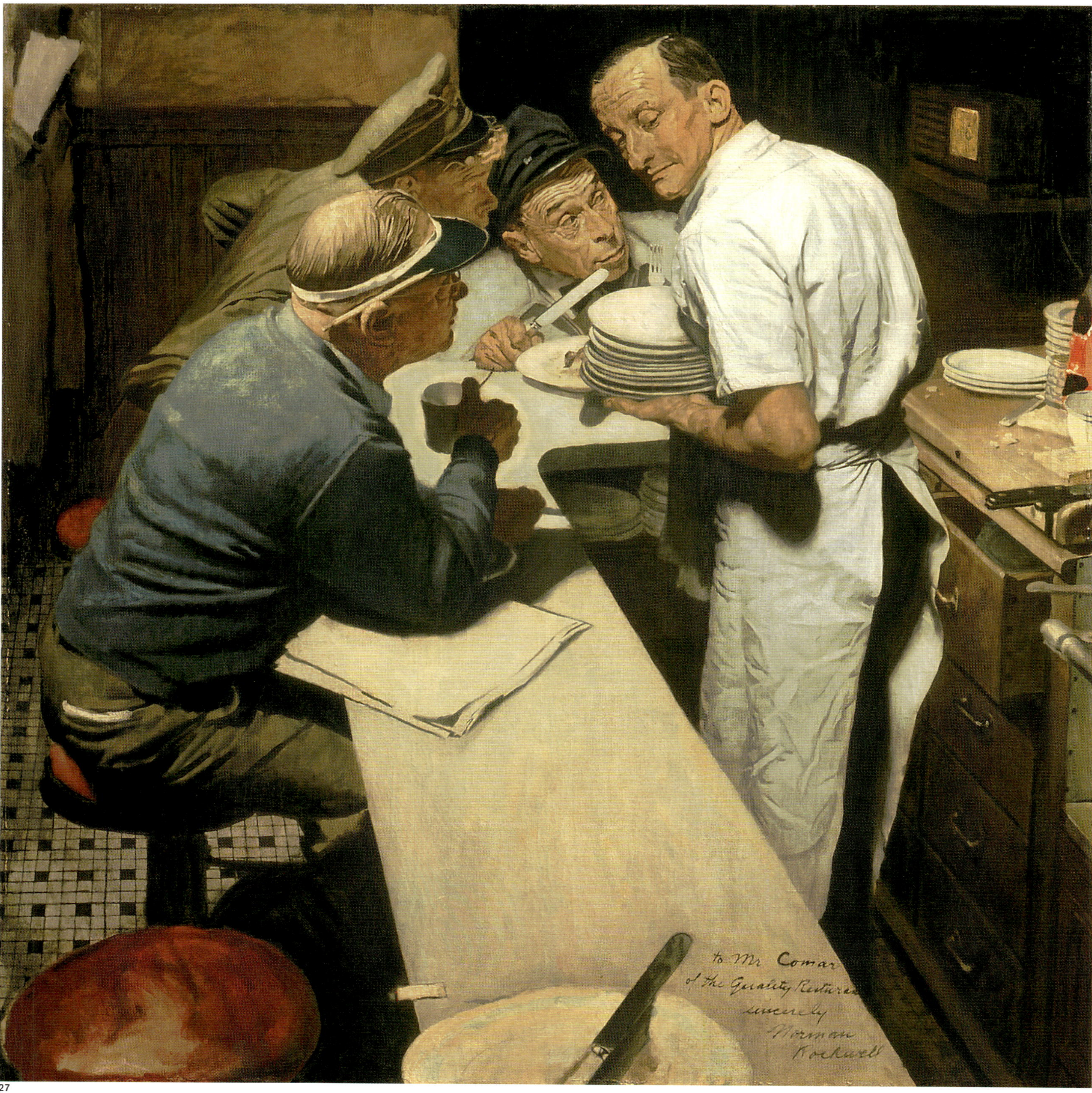
to Mr Comar
of the Quality Resturan
sincerely
Norman
Rockwell

27

With Fogarty's recommendation, Rockwell gained entry to the New York publisher McBride, Nast & Company, which hired him to do eight illustrations for an edition of C.H. Claudy's *Tell-Me-Why Stories* and four illustrations for Gabrielle E. Jackson's *The Maid of Middies' Haven*.

With the fee from his "first really professional job," as Rockwell put it, and by sharing with two other aspiring artists, he rented a studio in Manhattan's Upper West Side. Three months later, his father visited and asked the naïve studio mates if they realized their studio was in a house of prostitution. The next day the three moved to a studio in Brooklyn, next to the Brooklyn Bridge. The refuge of a studio was crucial for Rockwell during this time when he still lived with his parents. The family had recently left Mamaroneck for rented rooms in a midtown Manhattan boardinghouse, a culture of displaced persons Rockwell described as "immured in unhappiness." For an eighteen-year-old struggling for a career in a demanding and competitive field, the oppressive boardinghouse made Rockwell feel he couldn't breathe. He decided to spend the summer in Provincetown, Massachusetts, studying with the celebrated New England realist painter Charles W. Hawthorne. Inspired by Titian and Frans Hals, Hawthorne may have been a significant influence during this early stage of Rockwell's development. For example, Rockwell followed Titian in his choice of underpainting in Mars violet, a deep rose that added warmth to skin tones. His primary focus that summer was

27. *War News*, 1944
Unpublished
Oil on canvas, 41.25 x 40.5 inches
Norman Rockwell Museum Collection, NRM.1976.2

Intended as a cover for *The Saturday Evening Post* but never completed, *War News* pictures a restaurant counterman and his customers, including a Western Union boy, a clerk, and a deliveryman, gathering to listen to a radio report. Painted in January or February of 1944 about the proposed invasion of Normandy, the headline of the *Troy Times Record* of January 17, 1944, on the counter reads, "Invasion Plans At France Possible." Rockwell decided not to submit *War News* to the *Post*, perhaps because it was hard to convey what the men were hearing or to make the newspaper headline discernible. He instead went on to create a second painting of a man charting war maneuvers.

to emphasize color and depart from all the grays and muddy blacks he'd been using for children's magazines, which were reproduced in black-and-white and therefore often painted in tones of gray. Rockwell called the summer "an idyllic interlude during which I sluffed [sic] all my responsibilities, my city cares, even my ambitions, and lived the life of the most bohemian artist...." He returned refreshed and ready for new challenges.

That fall, Edward Cave, editor of the Boy Scouts' monthly magazine *Boys' Life*, asked Rockwell to illustrate a Boy Scout handbook he had just written. He also retained him for the permanent staff of *Boys' Life*, which was expanding to national circulation. Years later, Cave wrote to Rockwell: "Now I am flattered to find myself second only to the late great Condé Nast [of McBride, Nast & Company] in early recognition of your potential originality, liking for right things and regular people, and artistic skill." Rockwell's first *Boys' Life* assignment was to illustrate a story of a young scout and his Cree companion, set in the Ontario wilderness in January. The characters were all heavily clothed, providing Rockwell little opportunity to show off his Art Students League training in anatomical drawing, but Bridgman's emphasis on proportion and balance is apparent. Even in these early works, Rockwell's insistence on making each character a unique individual is clear. He did not yet have the knack of capturing nuances of expression but his choice to individualize his characters rather than to create "types," as many

28. *Boy in a Dining Car*, 1946
Painting for *The Saturday Evening Post* cover, December 7, 1946
Oil on canvas, 38 x 36 inches
Norman Rockwell Museum Collection, NRM.1988.2

Using a dining car from the New York Central's Lake Shore Limited as his setting, Rockwell captured a moment in his own son's life that he thought would touch a common chord. Inspired by H.K. Browne's illustration of a similar scene in Charles Dickens' *David Copperfield*, Rockwell's painting describes a young boy's first experience of calculating a waiter's tip. At Rockwell's request, the New York Central diverted a dining car bound for Albany to New York City where he and his ten-year-old son Peter met it for a model shoot. Once there, he decided the "20th Century Limited" was too modern, and he requested an older model. The first three dining car waiters he interviewed were unsuitable for the role. The following week, an older car and a twenty-eight-year veteran waiter were provided, all to Rockwell's satisfaction. In appreciation for the efforts of the Railroad, Rockwell included a postcard of their 20th Century Limited locomotive on the boy's table and the *Post* credited them in the cover's caption, resulting in $10,000 worth of publicity for the New York Central.

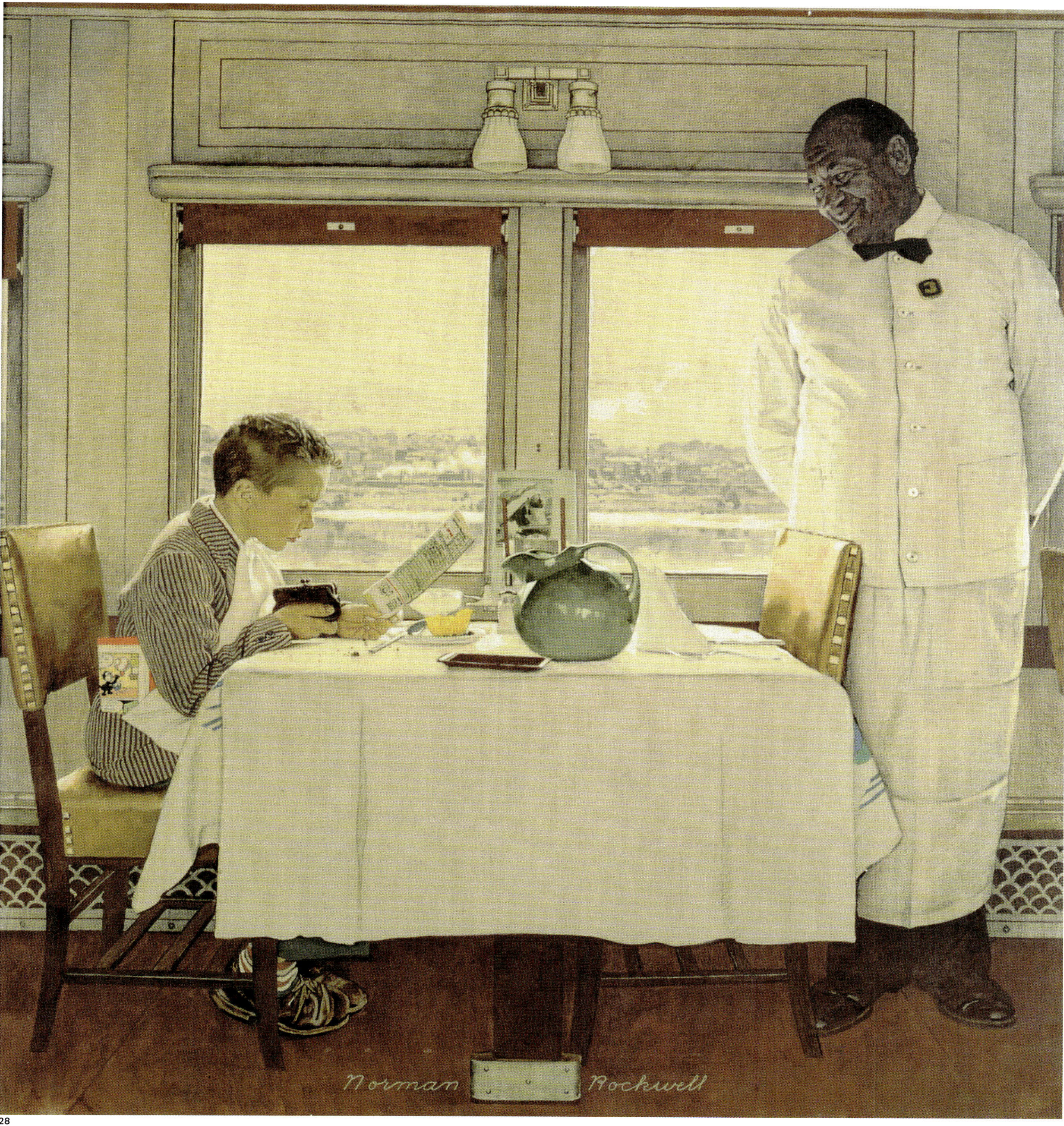
Norman Rockwell

29. Norman Rockwell posing son Peter for *Boy in a Dining Car*, 1946
Photo by Gene Pelham
Norman Rockwell Museum Collections

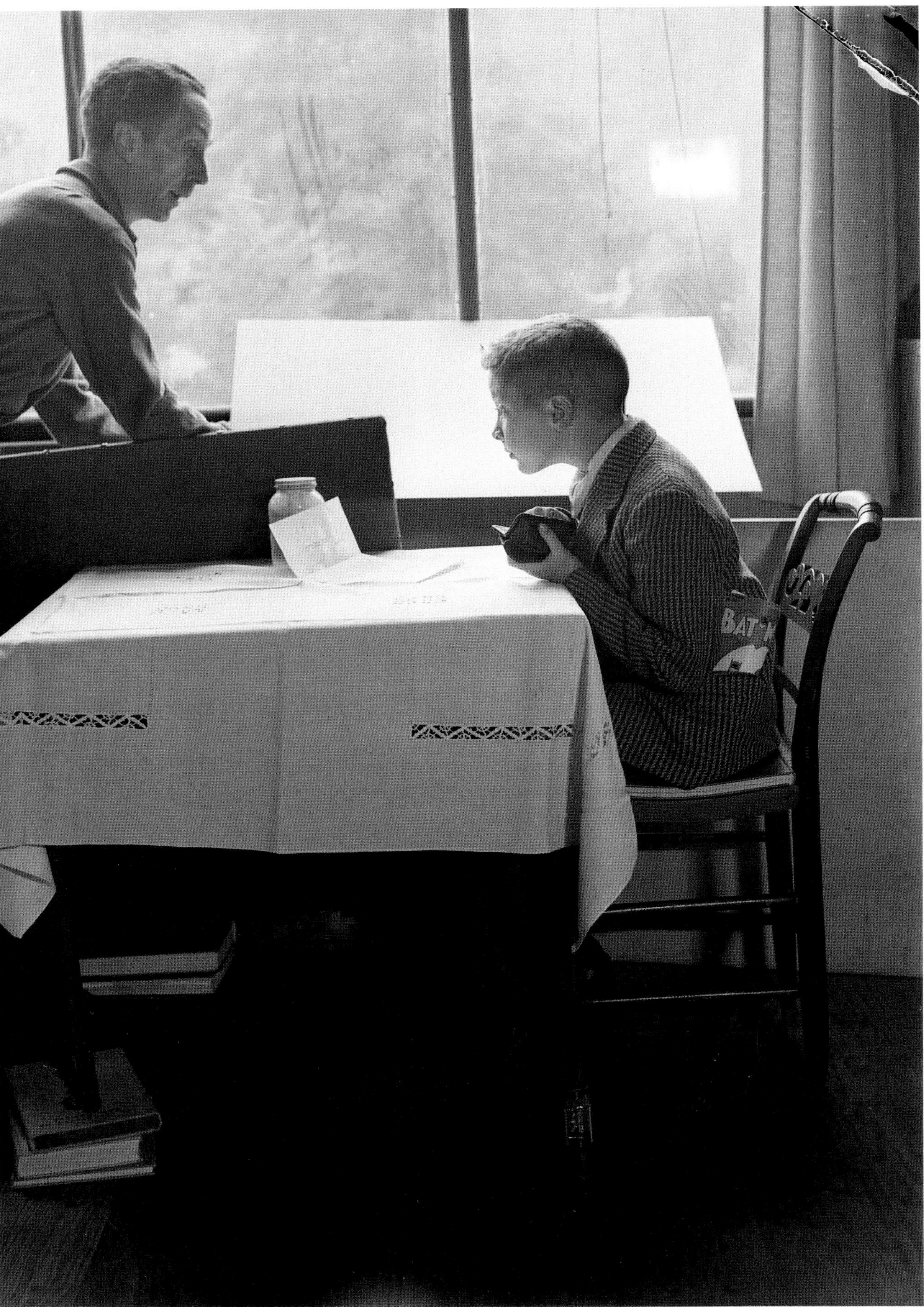

29

30. *Boy in a Dining Car*, c. 1946
Photo by Gene Pelham
Norman Rockwell Museum Collections

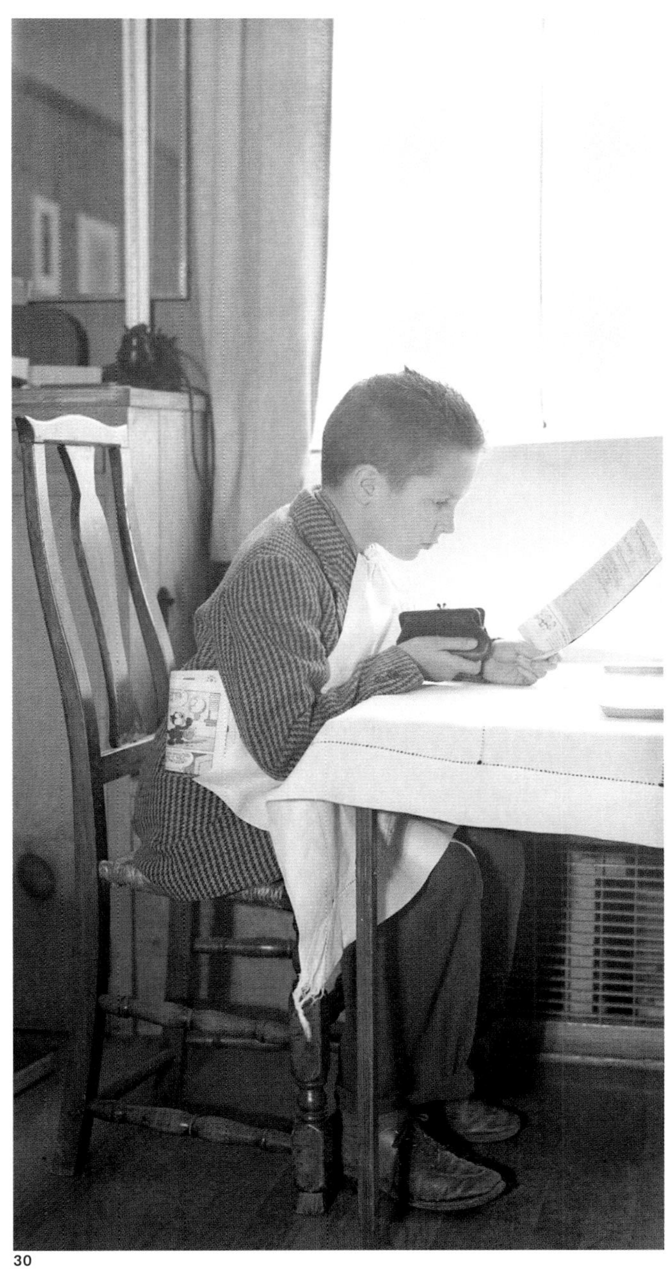

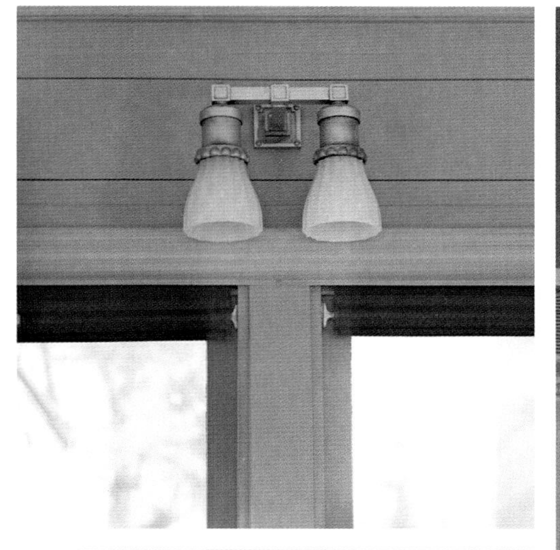

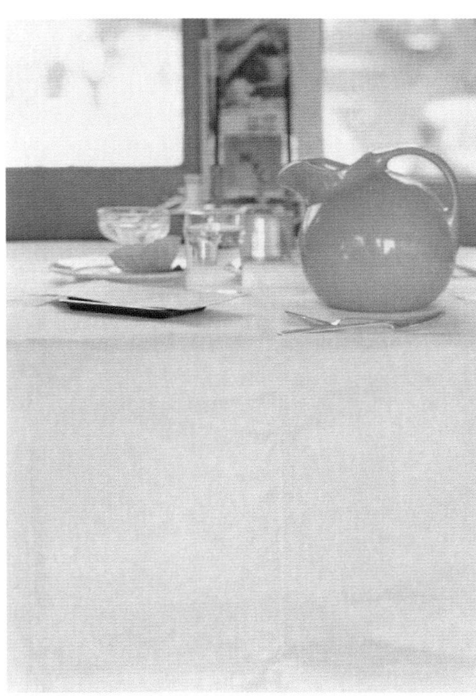

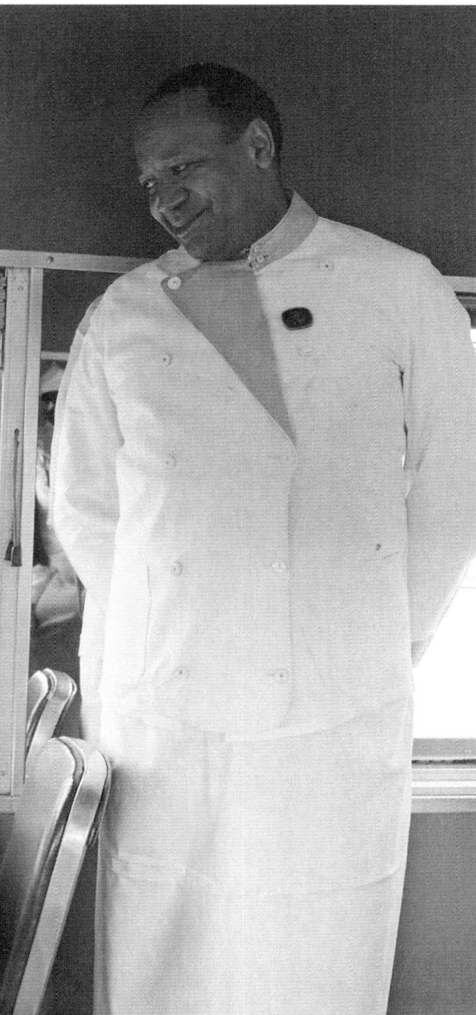

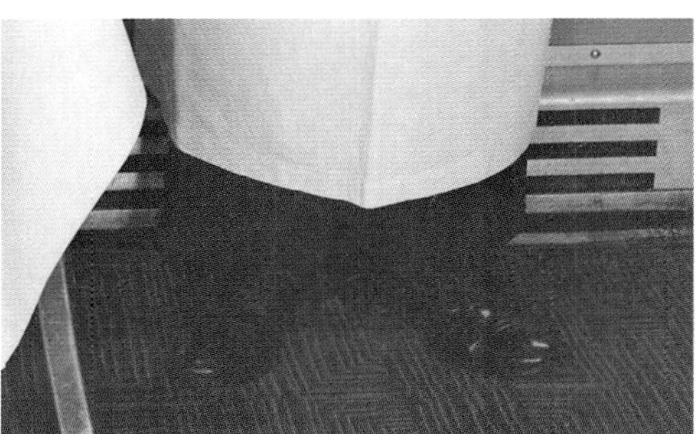

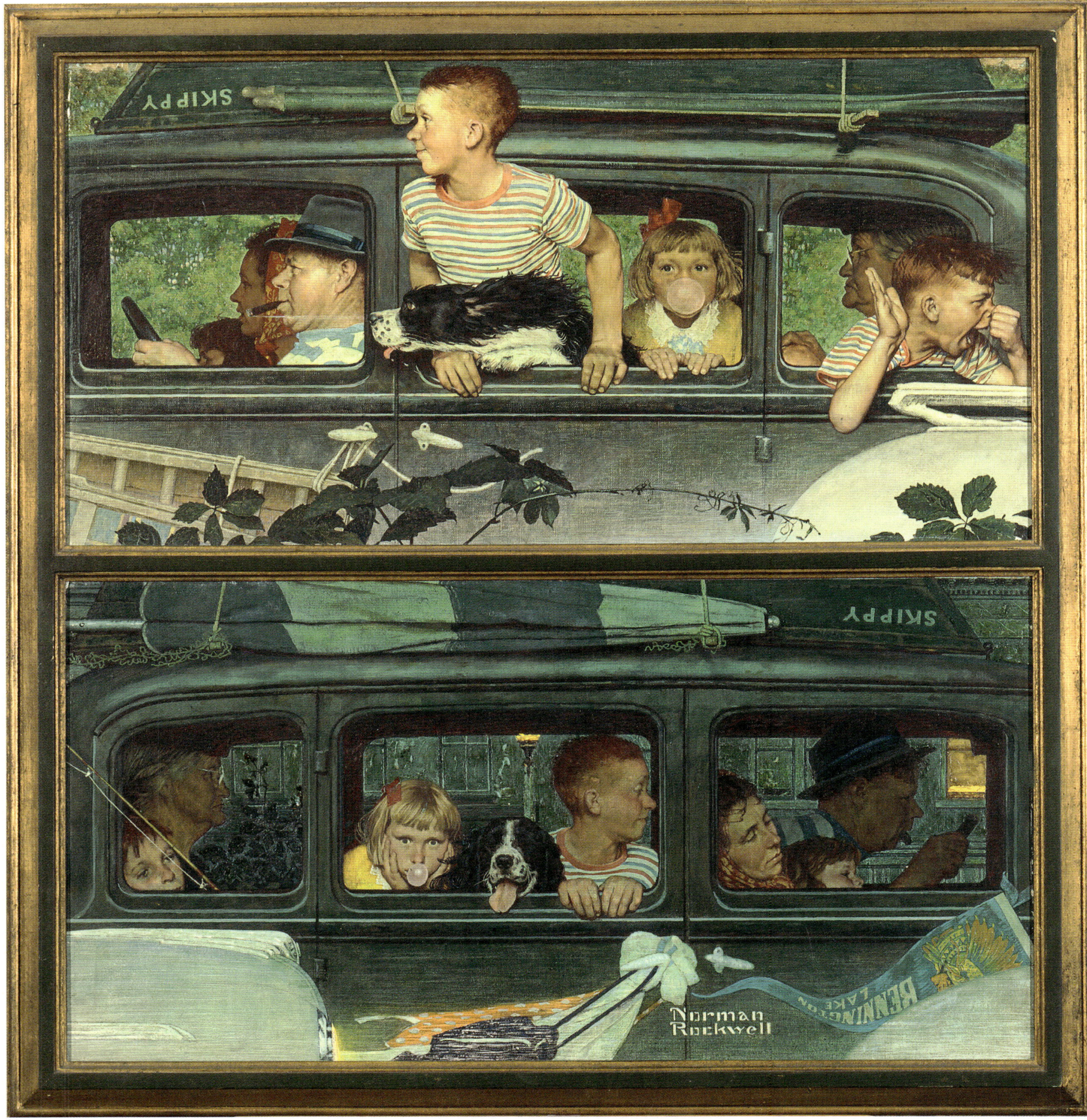

31

32. Norman Rockwell posing Butch for *Going and Coming*, 1947
Photo by Gene Pelham
Norman Rockwell Museum Collections

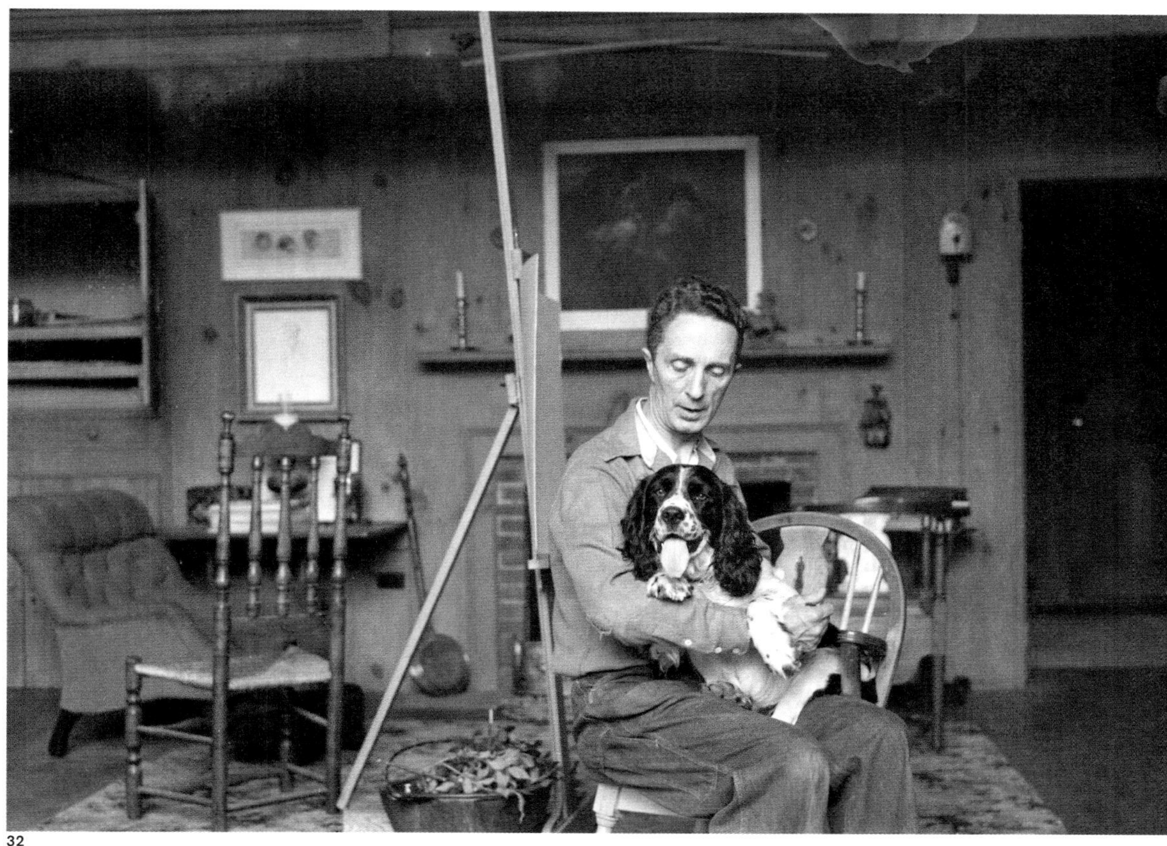
32

31. *Going and Coming*, 1947
Painting for *The Saturday Evening Post* cover, August 30, 1947
Oil on canvas:
upper canvas, 16 x 31.5 inches;
lower canvas, 16 x 31.5 inches
Norman Rockwell Art Collection Trust, NRACT.1973.9

Rockwell's *Post* covers were often of seasonal or topical subjects. This was especially true after the 1943 studio fire that destroyed his collection of historical costumes. Not only was a magazine cover intended to be a story that was easily "read" and understood, it was often intended to be relevant to the daily life of the reader.
Going and Coming, published in August 1947, is a good example of a story painting that is both seasonal and topical. The added ingredient of humor makes it even more engaging and thus contributes to its success. The use of two images within one picture allows Rockwell to be more detailed and create a continuum of time. We see the before and the after of the imagined event, a family's summer outing by the lake.

Clues abound for the reader's enjoyment in unraveling the story line. The use of a split canvas to portray a juxtaposition of an event, time, age, or place is an effective device that invites comparison of the two scenes. This technique is employed by Rockwell in only two other *Post* covers, but was commonly used by other of the magazine's illustrators. In most cases, it derives from a comic strip's use of a series of "frames" to tell a story. In this case, however, artist Don Spaulding, who studied with Rockwell in 1950 and spent several months living in the schoolhouse on the West Arlington Green, cites George Hand Wright's painting of *Going to and Returning from the Seashore* as the inspiration for *Going and Coming*.

illustrators would do, was one of the elements of his work that would set him apart from many of his peers. In a 1972 interview, Rockwell's son Peter recalled his father saying, "Do you know why Brueghel was able to paint such beautiful trees? Because Brueghel painted each tree as an individual." The opportunity for Rockwell to work on his fine sculptural drawing of the human form, through the sheer volume of work he would have, would come very soon. Following its expansion to national circulation, *Boys' Life* promoted Rockwell to art editor just six months later. Rockwell's responsibilities included illustrating the cover and one set of story illustrations per issue, interviewing illustrators, assigning stories, and approving finished artwork. "The extraordinary part of it," he later said, "was that I had to okay my own work."

In 1913, Rockwell relocated to the artist-rich community of New Rochelle, New York. From 1913 to 1916, his commissions came from children's magazines, *Boys' Life*, *Everyland*, *St. Nicholas*, and *Youth's Companion*, and two book publishers, Harper & Brothers and D. Appleton & Company, for which he illustrated nine books. Almost all were illustrations that described authors' texts. But soon Rockwell would take on the challenge of developing his own narratives and moving beyond the realm of children's interests. In 1916, at the suggestion of his studio mate, artist and cartoonist Victor Clyde Forsythe, Rockwell submitted his work to the premier showcase for America's top illustrators, *The Saturday Evening*

33. *Christmas Homecoming*, 1948
Painting for *The Saturday Evening Post* cover, December 25, 1948
Oil on canvas, 35.5 x 33.5 inches
Norman Rockwell Museum Collection, NRM.1978.10

The desire to focus his artistic energy on painting the human condition was so strong that to please his art editor, who urged him to fill his canvases, Rockwell packed his picture with figures until the only remaining background was a foot or so of floor area. With the barest reference to Christmas, Rockwell conveys a festive holiday scene purely through the smiles on all of the faces and a few touches of bright red paint. The entire Rockwell family is in this cast. Son Peter (with eyeglasses) appears in the left corner; son Tom is in the plaid shirt; wife Mary is hugging son Jarvis who has just arrived from school, and Norman looks on from their right. In the upper left corner, good friend and fellow *Post* illustrator Mead Schaeffer looks on, as does painter Grandma Moses. Behind Peter is Mead Schaeffer's daughter Patty and between Jarvis and Norman, his other daughter Lee. Mary Atherton, daughter of illustrator Jack Atherton (another close friend and neighbor of Rockwell), waves from behind Mary Rockwell.

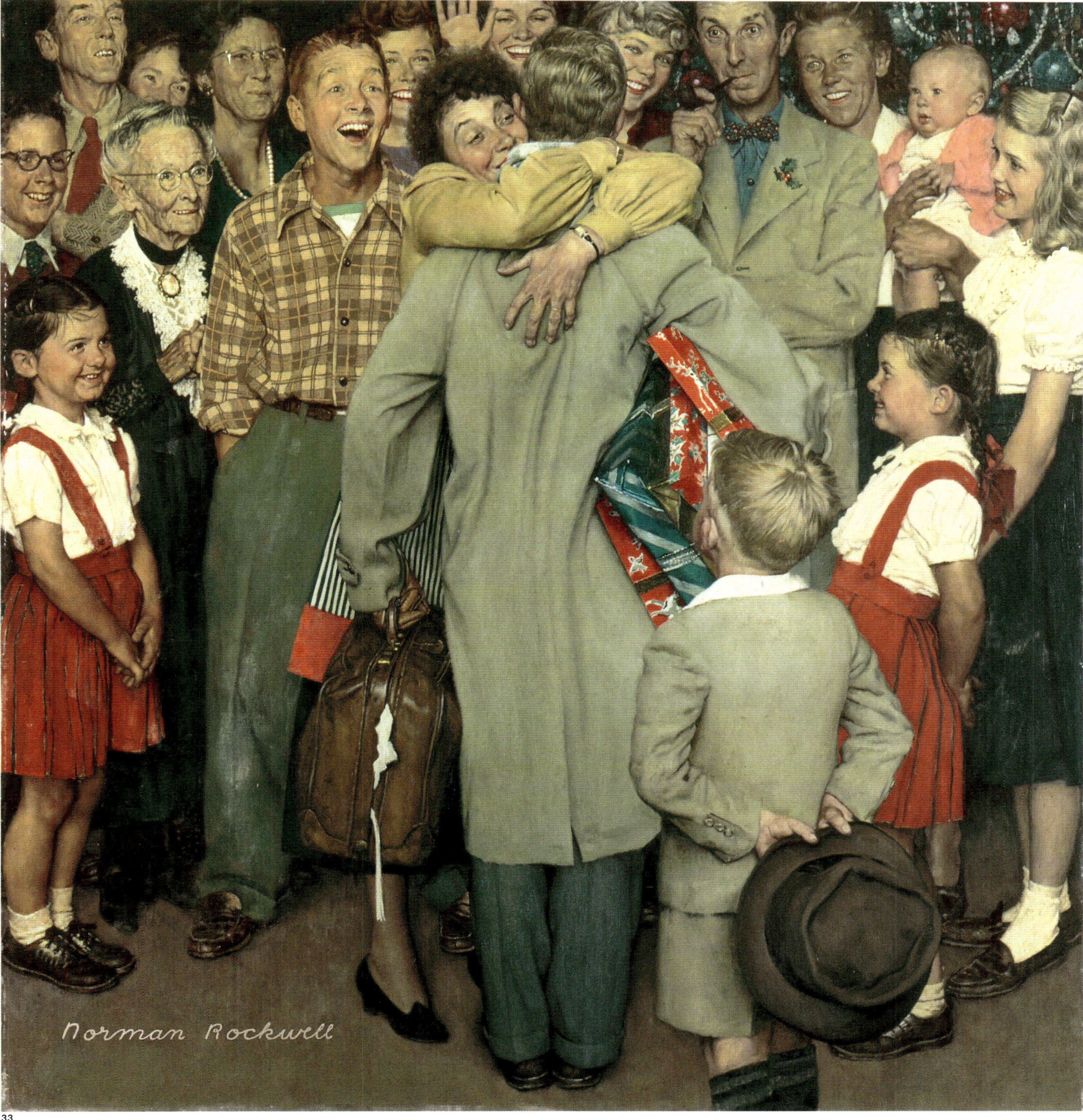

33

34. Norman Rockwell and Jarvis Rockwell posing for *Christmas Homecoming*, 1948
Photo by Gene Pelham
Norman Rockwell Museum Collections

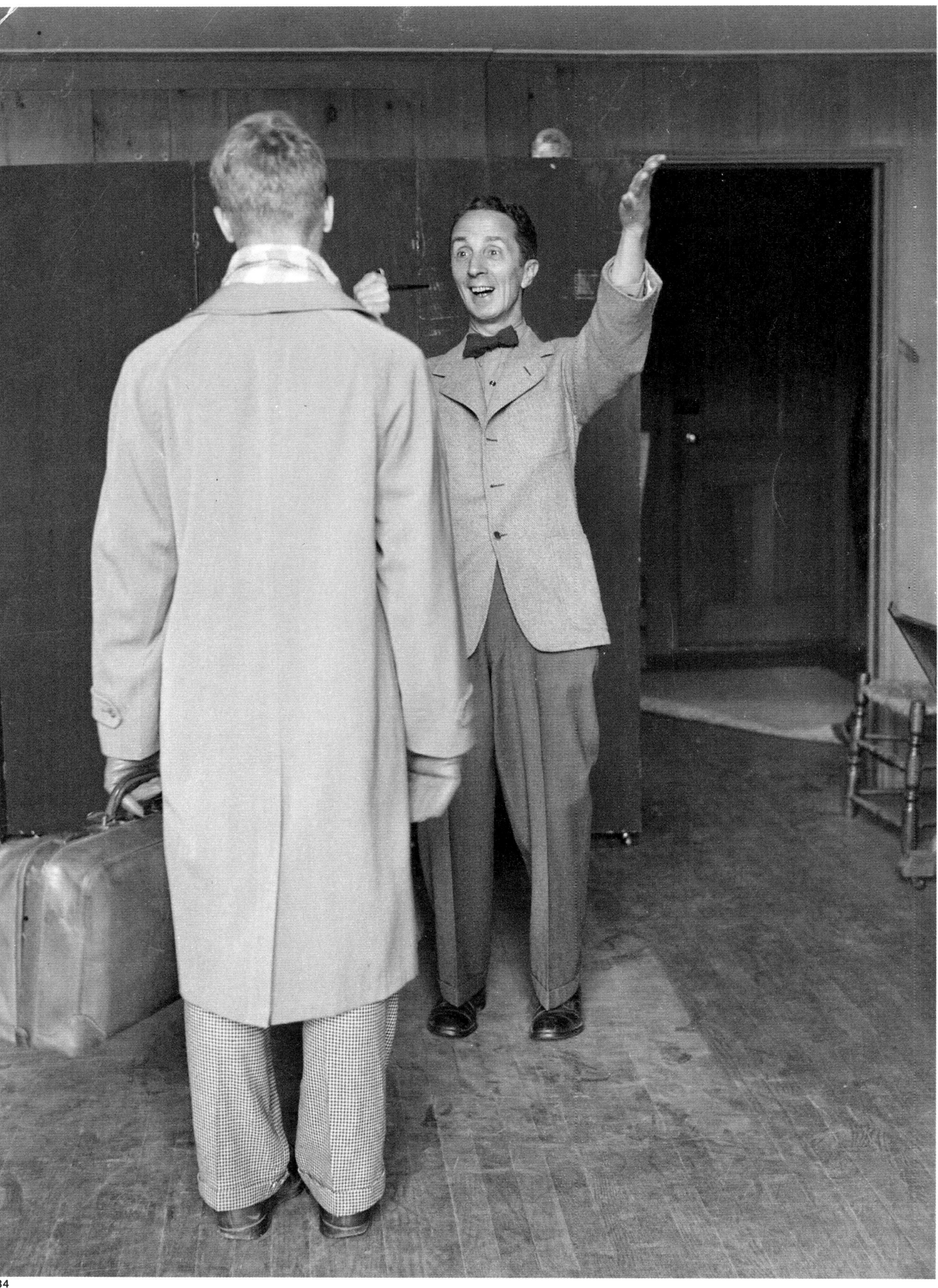

34

Post. Though years of diligence at *Boys' Life* had honed Rockwell's skills, he wasn't an instant success. His second *Post* cover, of a boy pitching a baseball to an elderly gentleman, had to be repainted five times before it was accepted for publication. Gradually his covers began to include adults, first with children, and later with adult activities and pursuits. Children, however, never completely left his repertoire.

Bolstered by his expectation of financial stability, now that he was added to the roster of *Post* cover artists, Rockwell asked a young lady living in the same boardinghouse as his family, Irene O'Connor, to marry him. She accepted and the two moved to their own apartment in New Rochelle. From all accounts, the two lived somewhat separate lives. Though trained as a teacher at Potsdam's Normal College, Irene seemed interested only in pursuing an active and increasingly affluent social life. For a while, when not at his easel, Rockwell joined her in doing some things together—hosting and attending parties, or visiting Irene's family in Potsdam. But Rockwell's recollections of this period paint a picture of emotional distance and incompatibility. Meanwhile, Rockwell was becoming prominent in a community known for its superstar illustrators. In the 1920s, New Rochelle was the state's most affluent city, and had more artists per capita than almost any city in the country. It was home to such illustration titans as Edward Penfield, art editor of *Harper's* magazine; J.C. Leyendecker, the *Post*'s top cover artist and

35. *Day in the Life of a Little Girl*, 1952
Painting for *The Saturday Evening Post* cover, August 30, 1952
Oil on canvas, 45 x 42 inches
Norman Rockwell Museum Collection, NRM.1980.2

This is a companion painting to *Day in the Life of a Little Boy*, Rockwell's prior cover painting for the *Post* published three months earlier. It would seem that painting thirty-seven heads is far more work than one or two, but to Rockwell, whose forte was portraiture, telling a complete story using this method was far less challenging than a cover with a detailed background. The events of the girl's day were so typical to the American child that this cover could be appreciated by large numbers of viewers. In other countries, Rockwell's *Post* covers were popular because their images were easily interpreted as the essence of American culture.

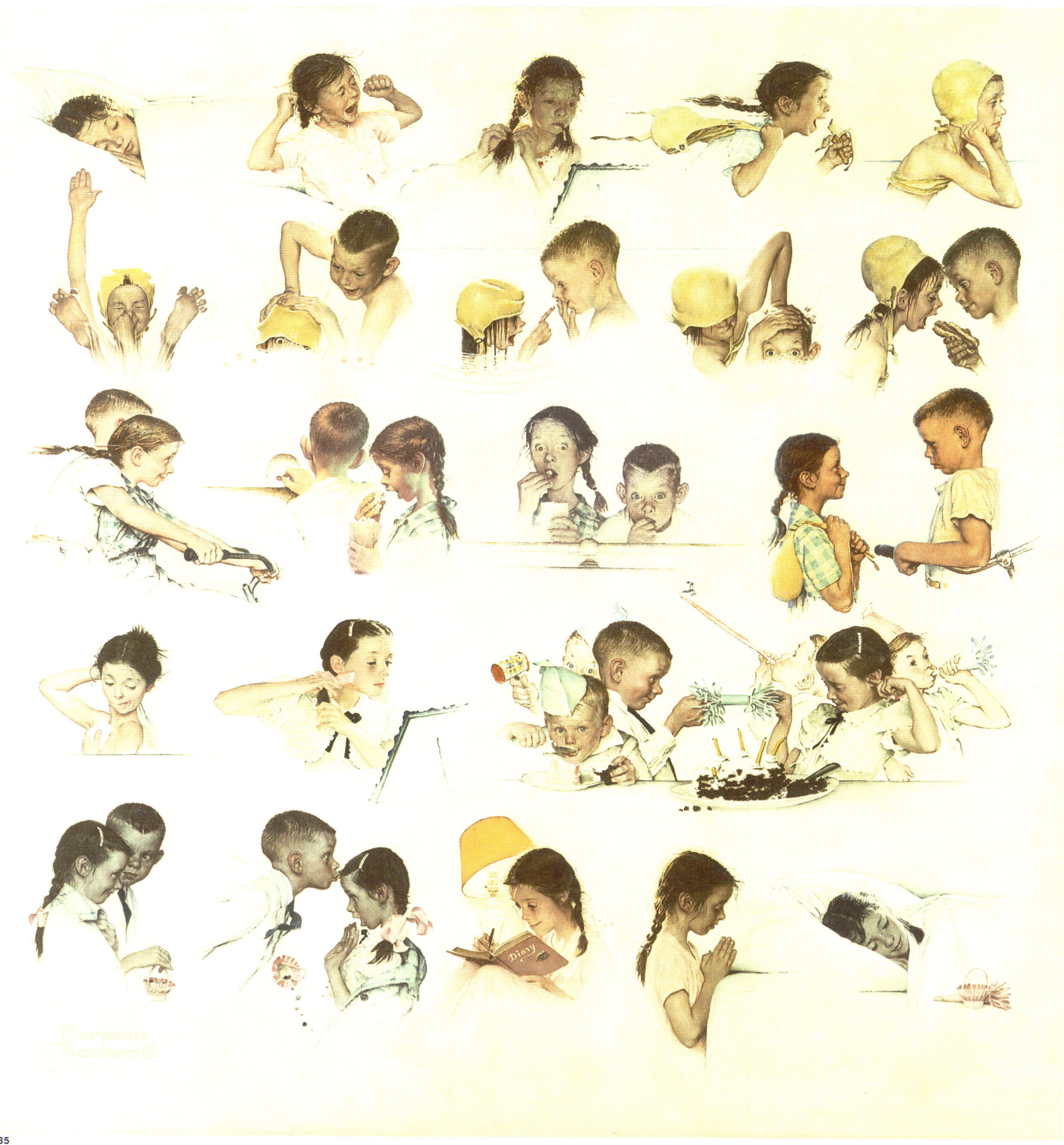
Diary

36. *Day in the Life of a Little Girl*,
c. 1952
Photo by Gene Pelham
Norman Rockwell Museum Collections

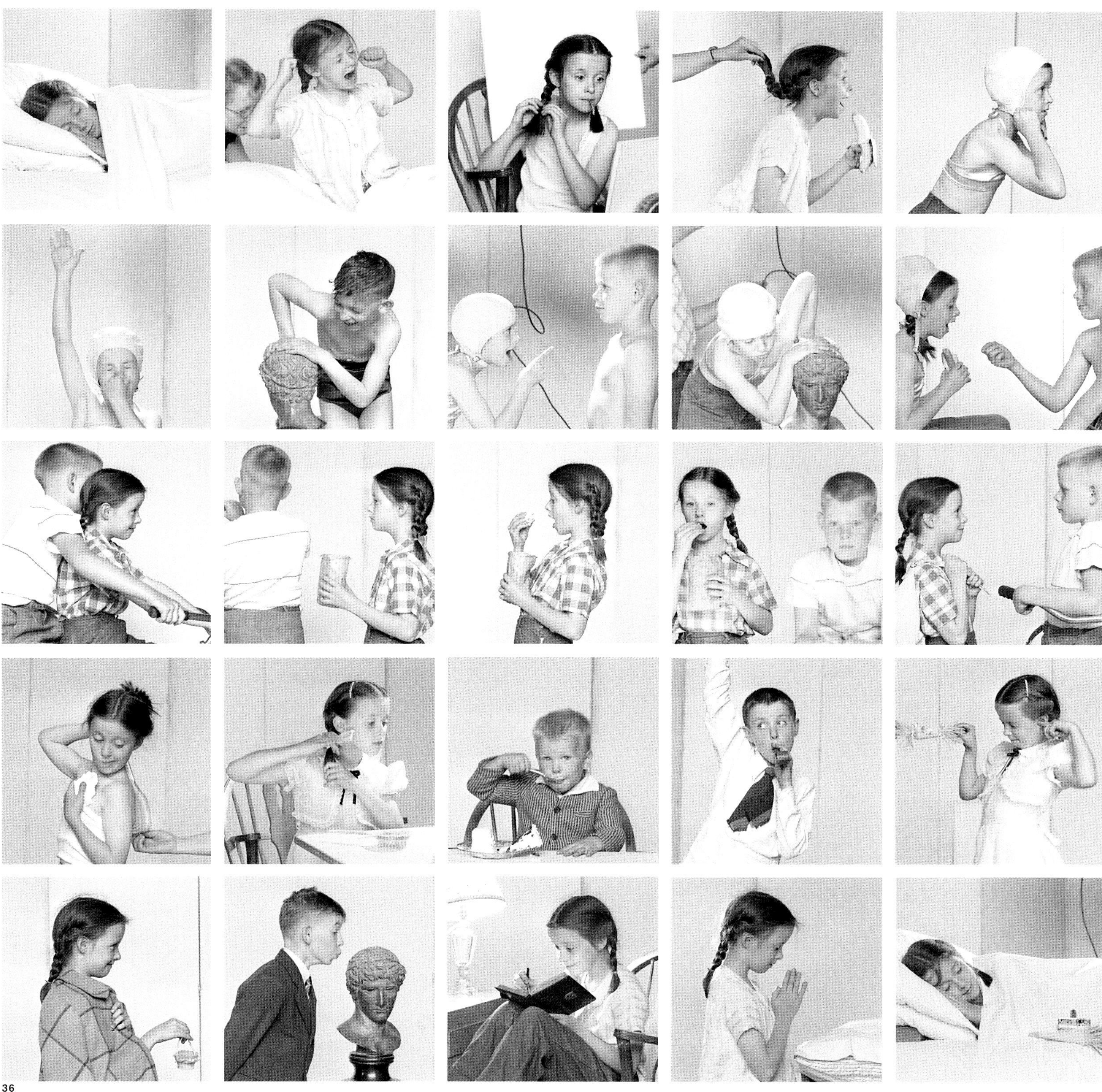

37. *Day in the Life of a Little Girl*,
c. 1952
Photo by Gene Pelham
Norman Rockwell Museum Collections

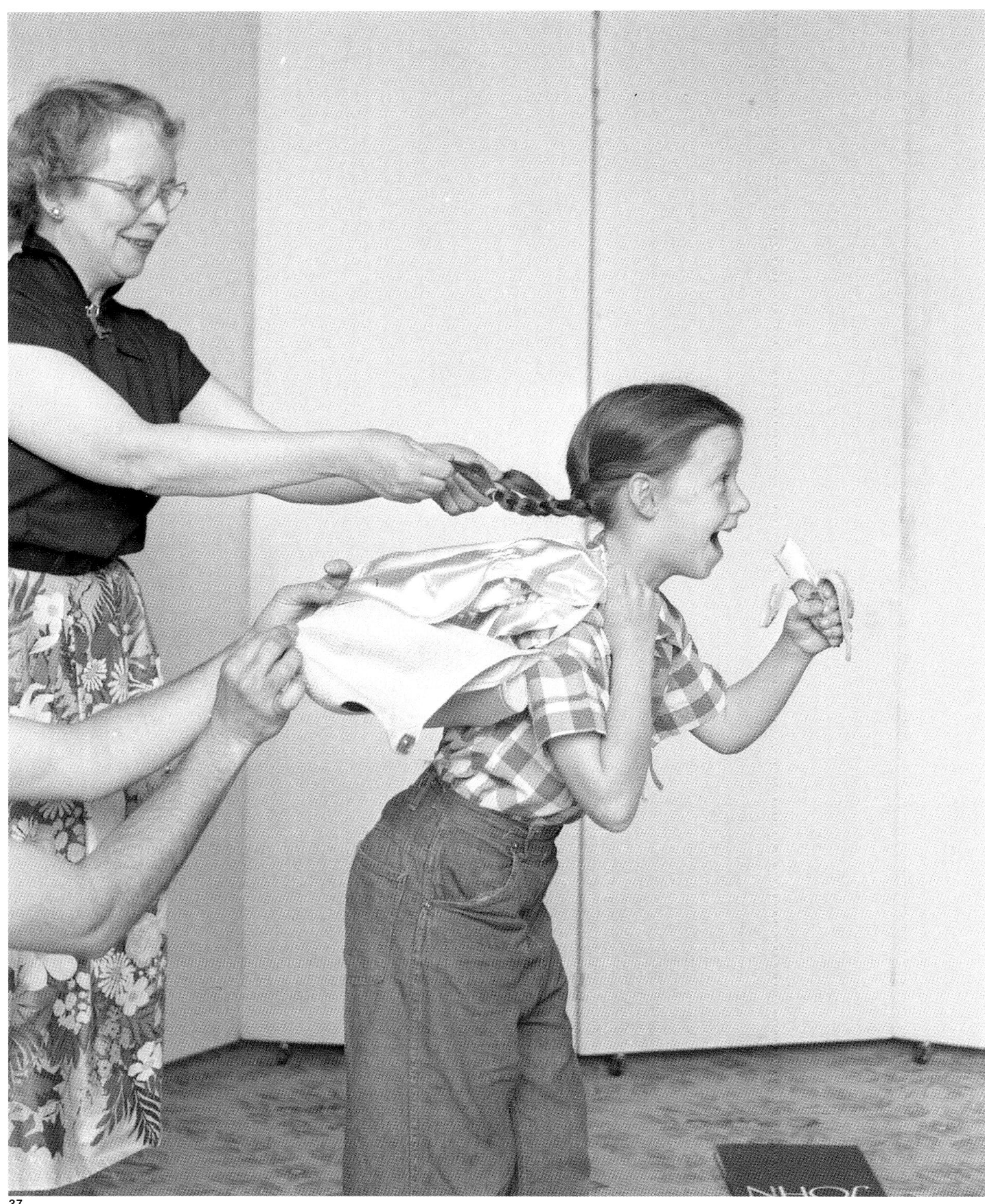

37

38. *Day in the Life of a Little Girl*,
c. 1952
Photo by Gene Pelham
Norman Rockwell Museum Collections

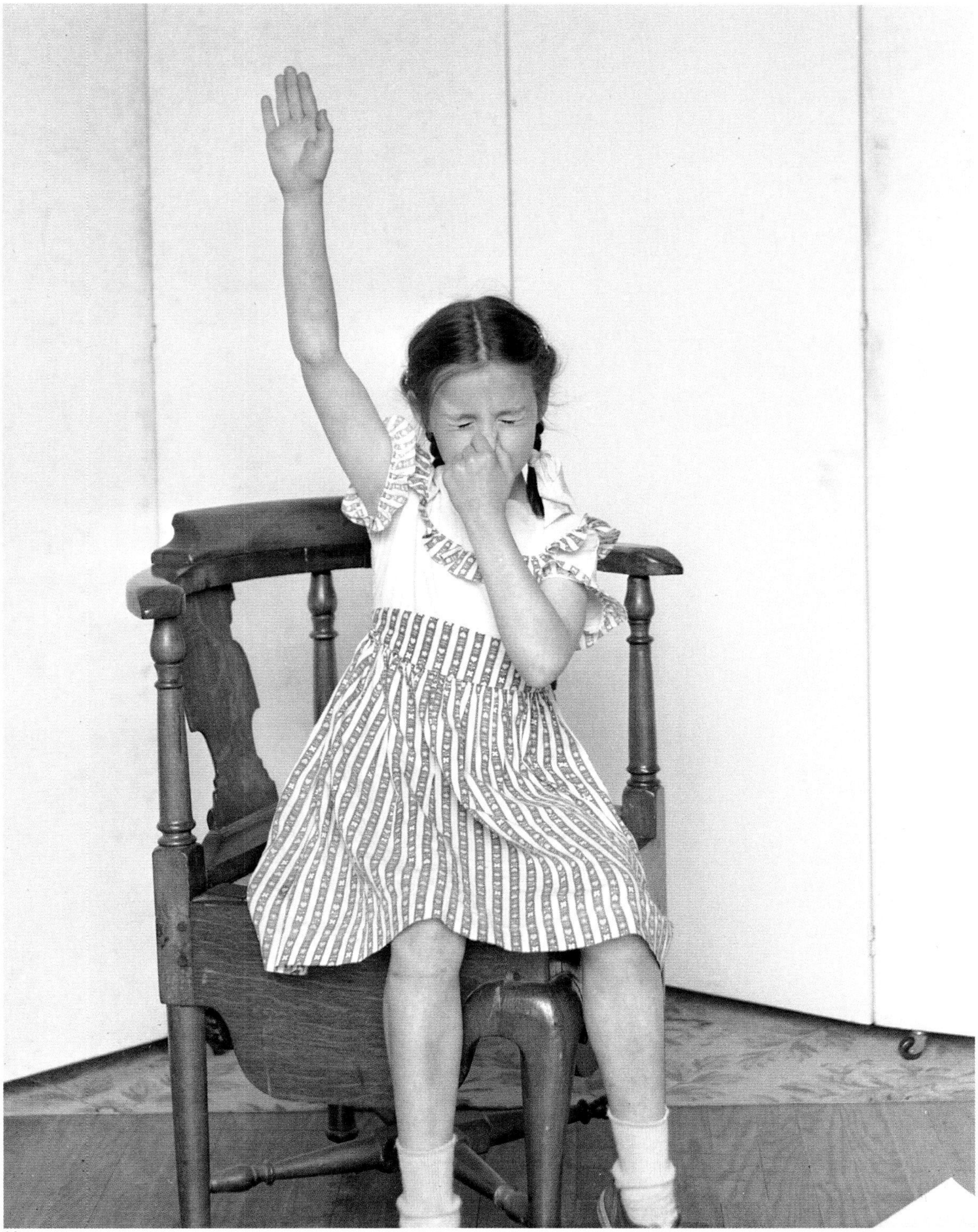

38

39. *Day in the Life of a Little Girl*, c. 1952
Photo by Gene Pelham
Norman Rockwell Museum Collections

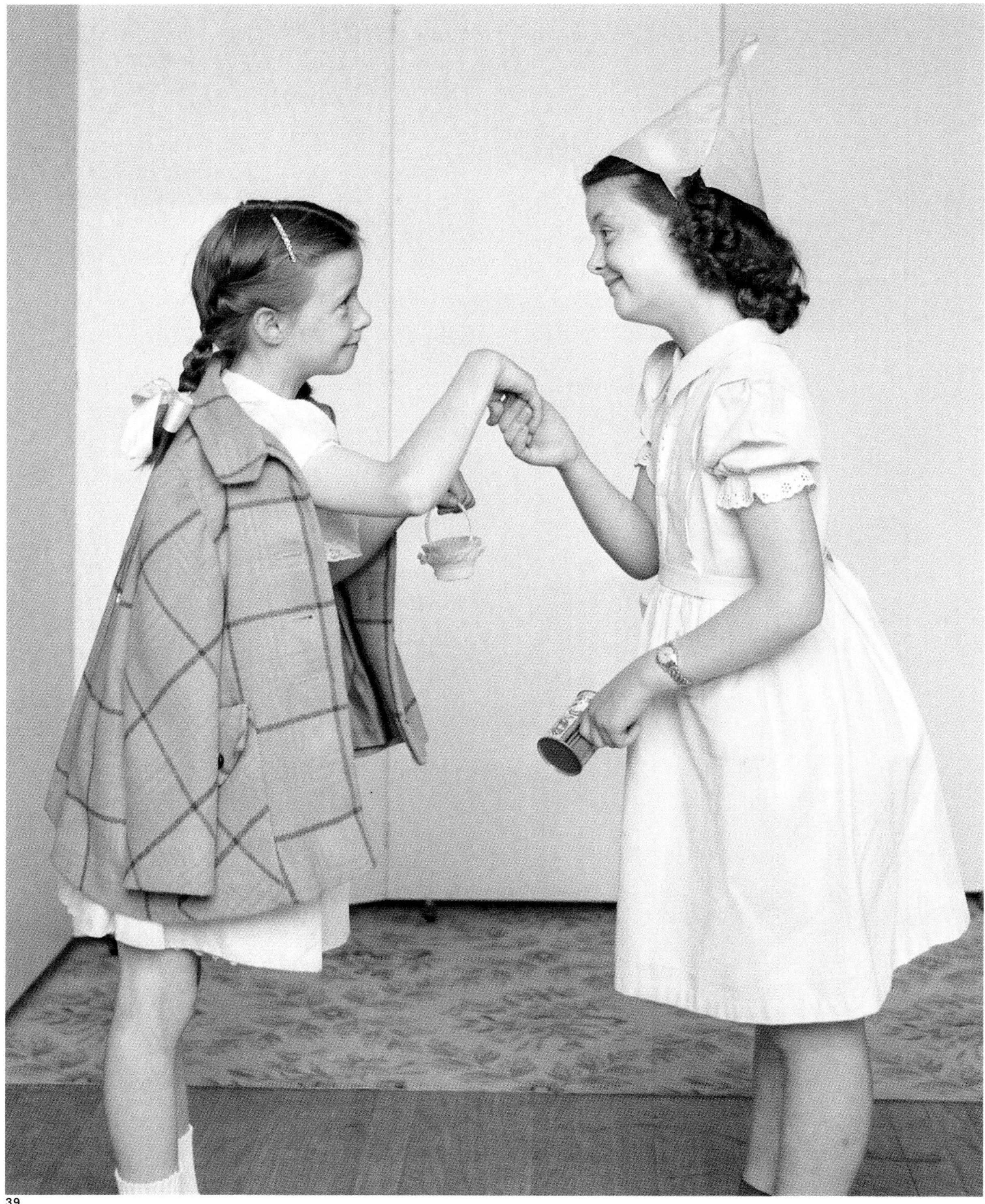

39

40. *Day in the Life of a Little Girl*,
c. 1952
Photo by Gene Pelham
Norman Rockwell Museum Collections

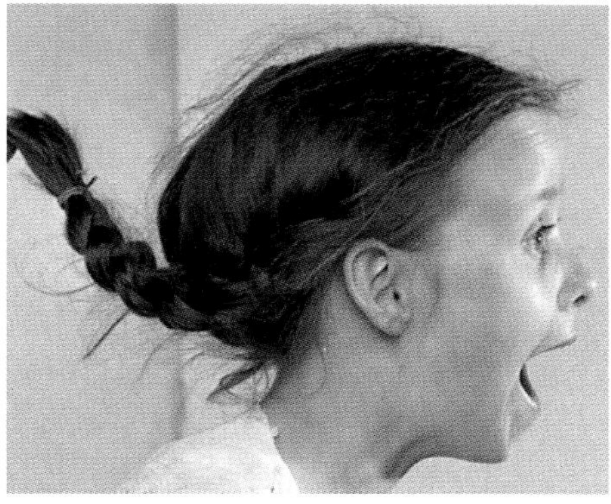

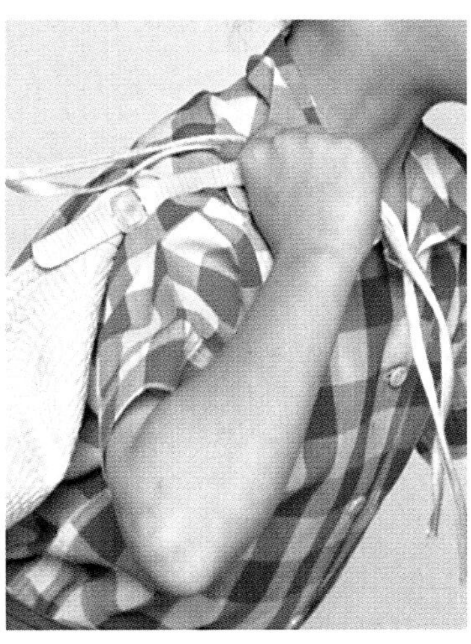

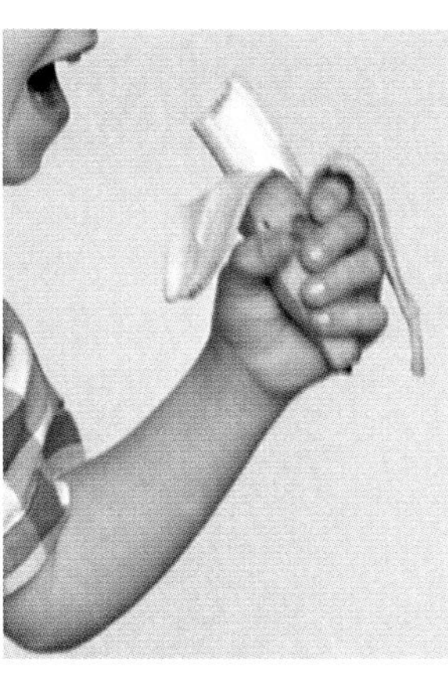

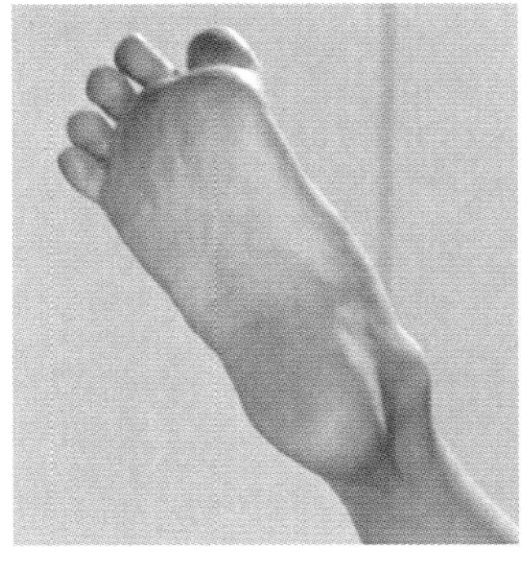

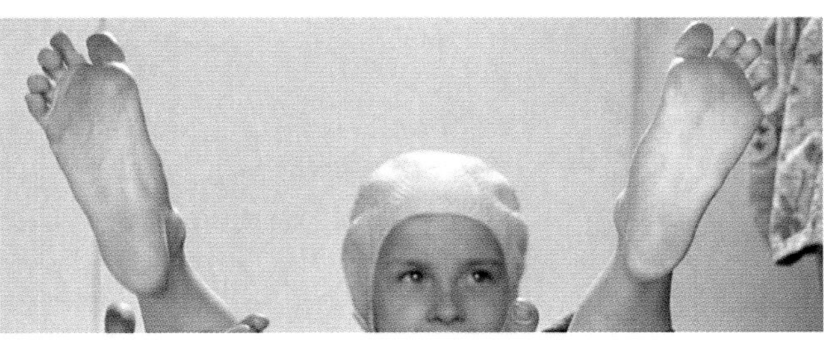

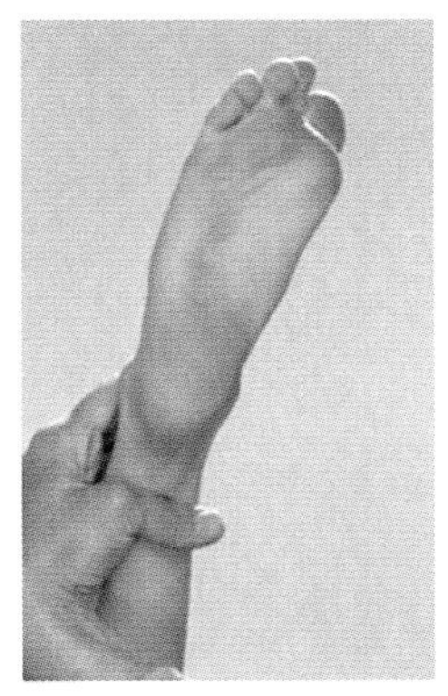

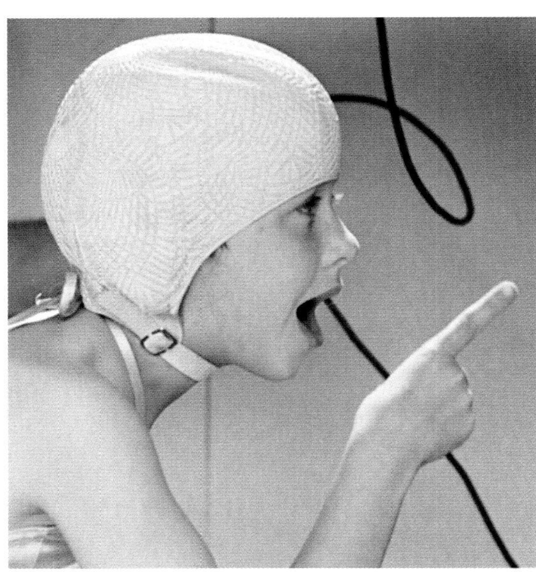

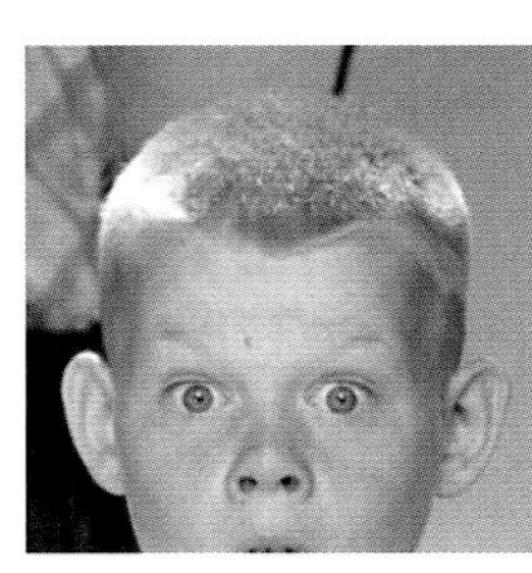

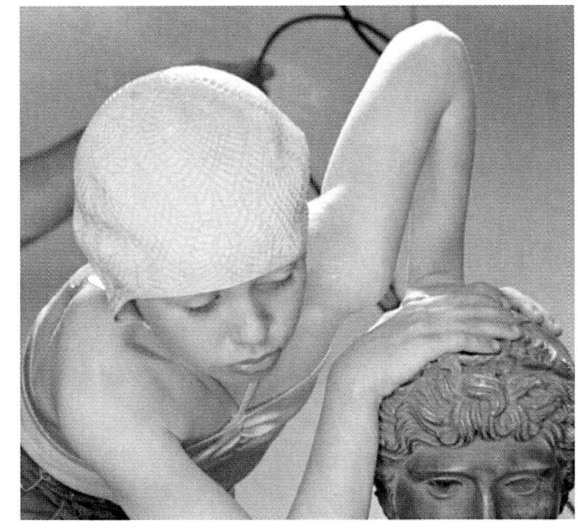

40

illustrator of Arrow collar ads; Coles Phillips, famous for the fade-away girl; and Mead Schaeffer, illustrator of fictional classics for Dodd Mead & Co. Many of the artists met socially, shared models, and critiqued each other's work.

In addition to The New Rochelle Art Association, New York's Society of Illustrators and Salmagundi Club offered the illustrators additional networking opportunities, and in 1920, the Art Directors Club of New York was formed to promote advertising art. The Club's first exhibition, held at the National Arts Club in Gramercy Park in 1921, included works by N.C. Wyeth, F.R. Gruger, Maxfield Parrish, J.C. Leyendecker, Edward Penfield, Dean Cornwell, and Norman Rockwell. In this pre-television era when people eagerly awaited the weekly arrival of *The Saturday Evening Post* for its humor, stories, and current events, illustrators became celebrities. As celebrities, they were chosen to judge Atlantic City's annual Miss America Beauty Contest. Rockwell was a judge at the second, third, and fifth contests, in 1922, 1923, and 1925, sharing the dais in 1922 with Coles Phillips, Willy Pogany, and Howard Chandler Christy, and 1923 with Dean Cornwell.

Taking notice of his *Post* covers, art directors of *Life*, *Judge*, and *Leslie's* offered Rockwell work. In 1924, at age thirty, he typically spent twelve to fourteen hours a day in his studio. As Rockwell's popularity soared, Curtis Publishing pulled in its reins and became the sole publisher of Rockwell illustrations in its three magazines, the *Post*, *Ladies' Home Journal*, and *Country Gentleman*. In

41. *Sis*, 1954
42. *Beanie*, 1954
43. *Freckles*, 1954
44. *Girl with String*, 1955
Paintings for Kellogg Company corn flakes advertisements
Oil on canvas, 14.75 x 14.75 inches each
Collection of the Norman Rockwell Museum, NRM.1993.1, NRM.1993.3, NRM.1993.4, NRM.1993.6,
Gift of Kellogg Company

In the early 1950s, with a stroke of creative acumen, Chicago advertising director Leo Burnett paired popular icons Superman, Howdy Doody, and Norman Rockwell with Battle Creek's star cereal maker Kellogg.
With an innovative color palette and contemporary design, the ad campaign changed the look of cereal boxes and inspired shoppers to eagerly reach for them on their grocery store shelves. Central to the success of corn flakes were Rockwell's signature fresh-faced kids, who beamed out at us from store displays and magazine print ads with enthusiasm, happiness, and most of all, good health.
American companies such as Kellogg found in Rockwell qualities they wanted associated with their products: honesty, artistry, competence, and status. Using words such as "distinguished" and "noted" and phrases such as "American Legacy," "elegant taste and discrimination," "unexcelled craftsmanship," and "accustomed to the finest," advertisements described their products or their customers while alluding to Rockwell.

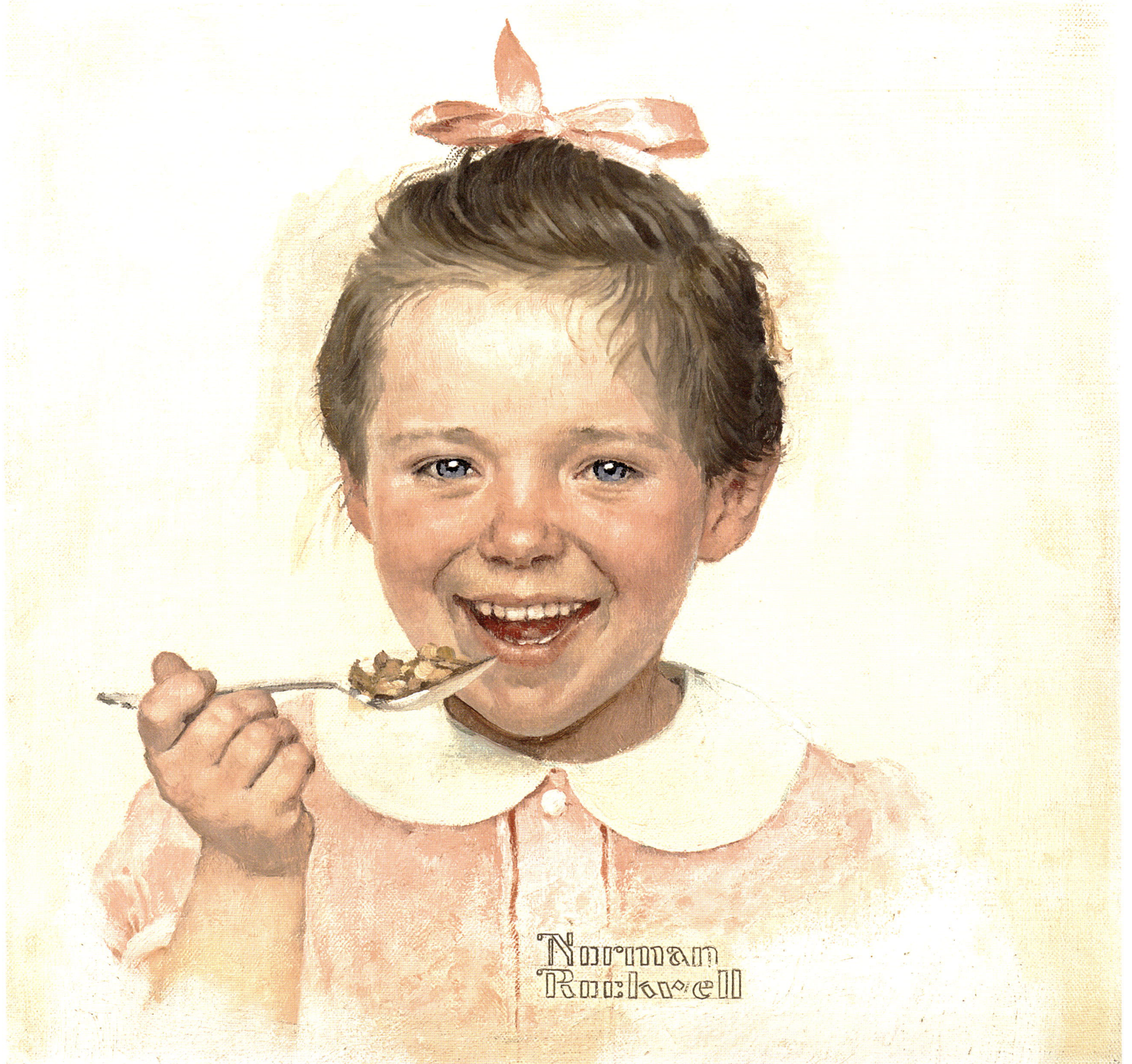

41

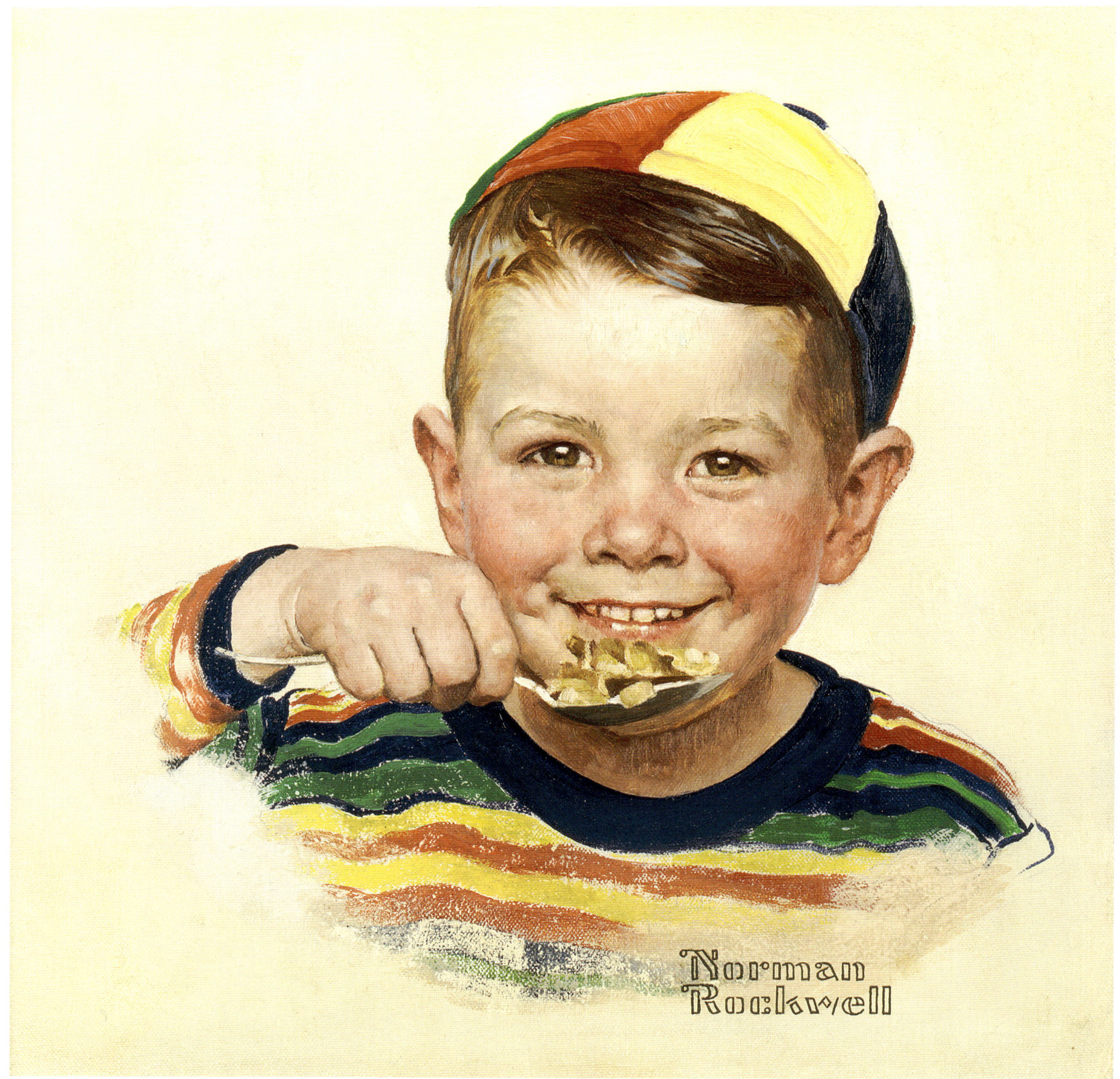
Norman
Rockwell

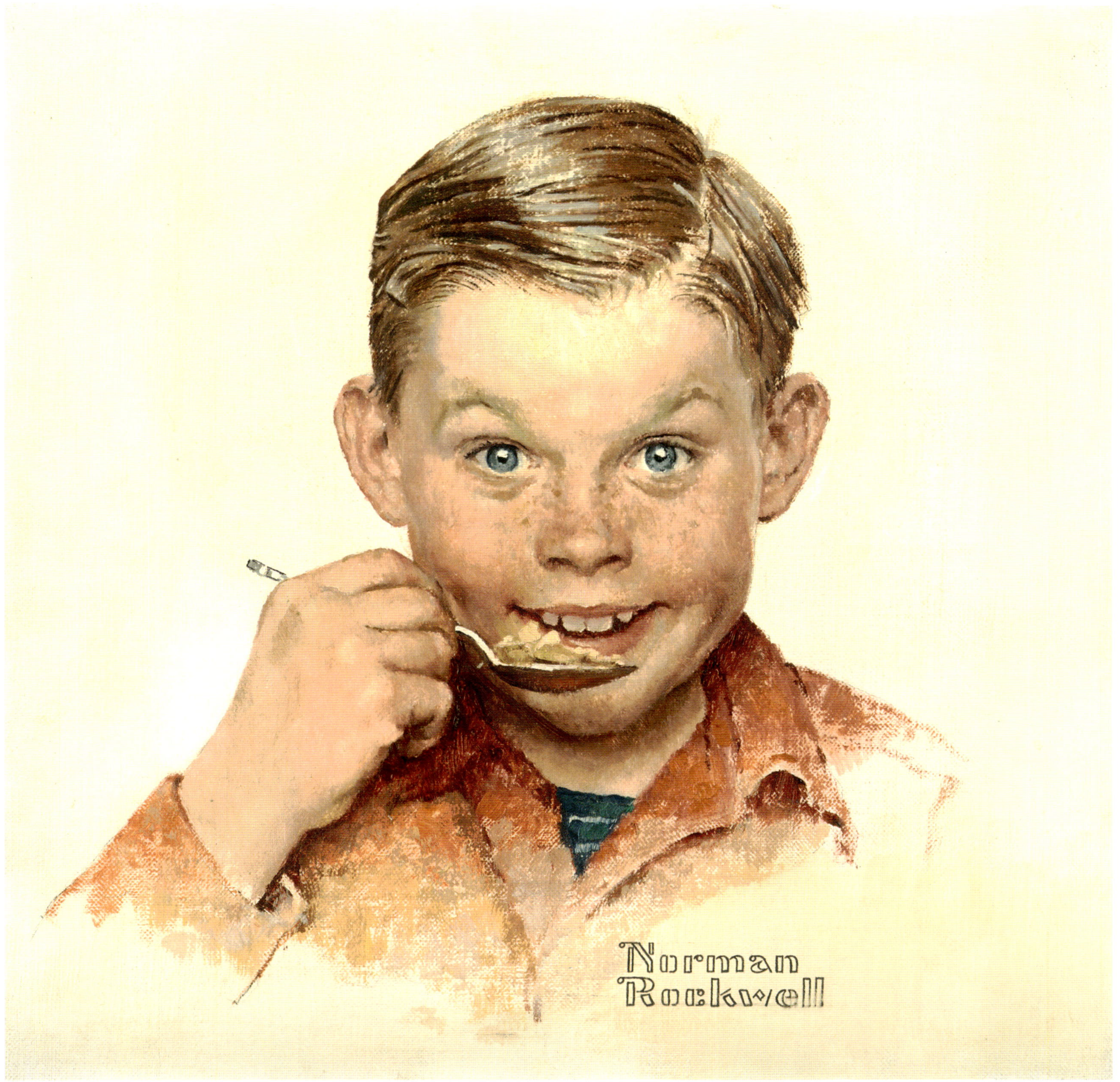

43

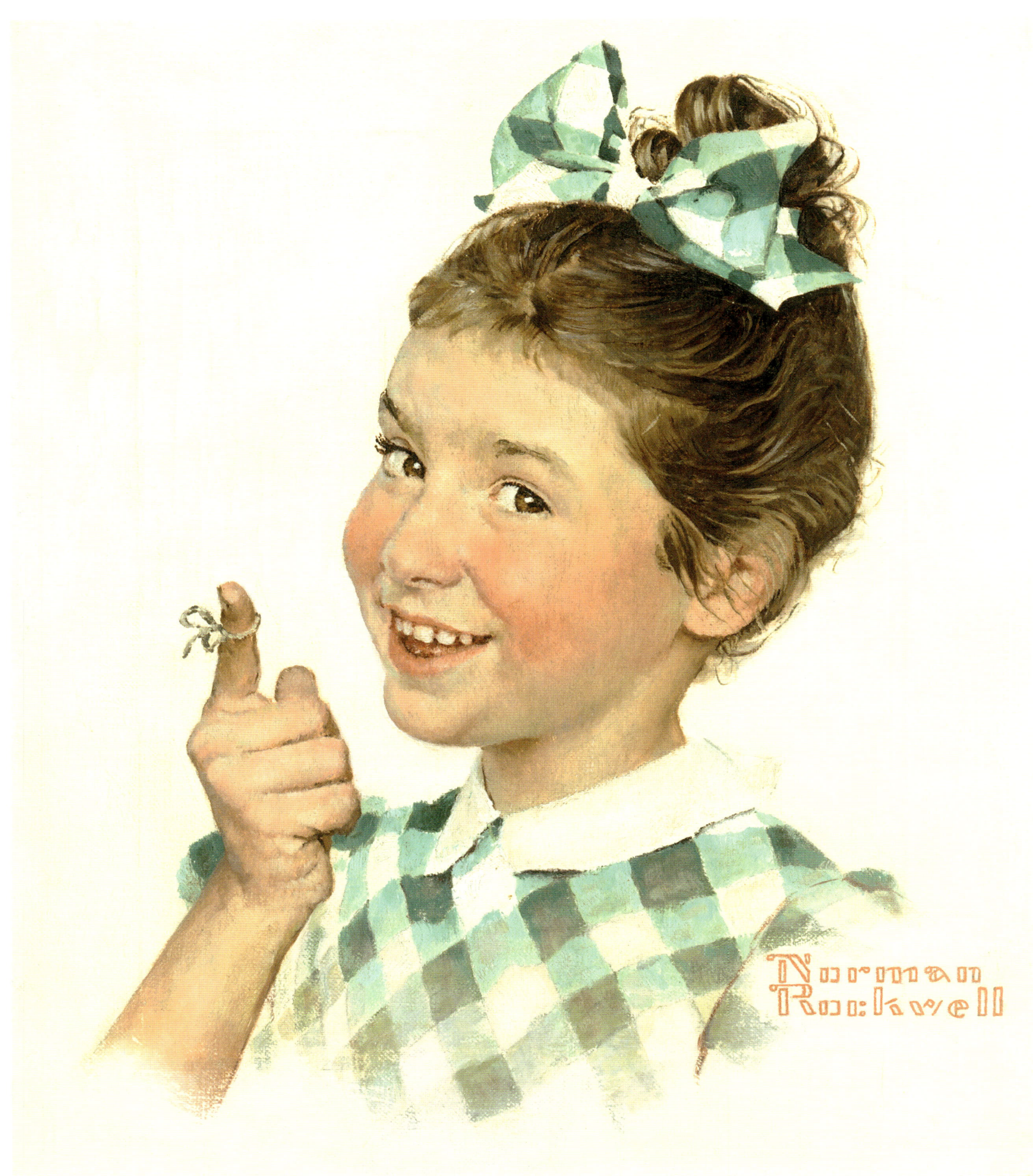
Norman
Rockwell

1934, assignments began to appear in *American Magazine*—but no other serial publication. Though it was understood that Rockwell could do work for her sister publications, the *Post* still expected Rockwell to give them priority. In 1939, Rockwell received a letter from art editor Pete Martin expressing his distress upon hearing his next assignment would be late because he was redoing a picture for *Ladies' Home Journal*. "The fact that the other magazine is another Curtis publication has no possible bearing on the case," admonished Martin. The embargo on non-*Post* work was still intimated in 1950 when Rockwell received a letter from editor Ben Hibbs expressing shock at seeing one of Rockwell's Boy Scout calendar images reproduced in the rival publication *Look*. "To find a picture of yours in another magazine—and especially in *Look*—was ... quite a shock. I just hope this doesn't mean that your work is to be used by others of our competitors." So proprietary was *Post* management about Rockwell's work that later that year, when publicists wanted to run an article in *Country Gentleman* about Rockwell's Hallmark Christmas cards, Hibbs said he was against it even though the *Post* had "no legal right to prevent [it]." Fortunately, other types of illustration such as advertising and book illustration were excluded from this "understanding," enabling Rockwell to take lucrative assignments from major American corporations—possibly one reason for his prodigious output of advertising illustration (he did illustrations for more than 160 companies).

After a separation from Irene O'Connor in 1929, Rockwell, now living alone in the Hotel des Artistes, was invited to spend a vacation in California by his former studio mate Clyde Forsythe, who had returned to his native southern California to pursue his career as a painter of western subjects. Forsythe introduced him to twenty-two-year-old Mary Barstow, recently graduated from Stanford University, who was teaching primary school mathematics. Instantly they hit it off, and in three months they were married. They returned to Rockwell's apartment at the hotel, where they lived for several months until the relocation of the tenants of Rockwell's New Rochelle house (Irene had asked for nothing in the divorce settlement). On August 6, 1931, Rockwell's father died of stomach cancer at the age of 63. His father, he later recalled, was the "gentlest and kindest man that ever lived," attributes any son would have cherished in a role model. (Indeed, in a 1988 interview, Norman Rockwell's doctor's summation of him was that "he was a gentle, kind man.")

One month after the death of Rockwell's father, Rockwell and Mary's first son, Jarvis, was born. (Their second son, Thomas, was born in 1933, and third son, Peter, arrived in 1936.) Despite his family bliss of the early 1930s, Rockwell encountered a major impasse in his work. A break from his surroundings, he felt, would do him good and the stimulation of the arts scene in Paris might give him inspiration and unblock his creative flow. In February 1932, with six-month-old Jarvis and pet German Shepherd Raleigh in tow, the family boarded the *Mauretania* for Paris. Rockwell had vacationed in Europe a number of times before, but this trip was intended to kick-start a new direction, or at least to inspire new work. From Mary's letters to her family in California, it appears that Rockwell wanted to shorten the time it took to paint covers and ship them back to the *Post* in

Following pages
Two boys playing baseball arguing,
September 28, 1965

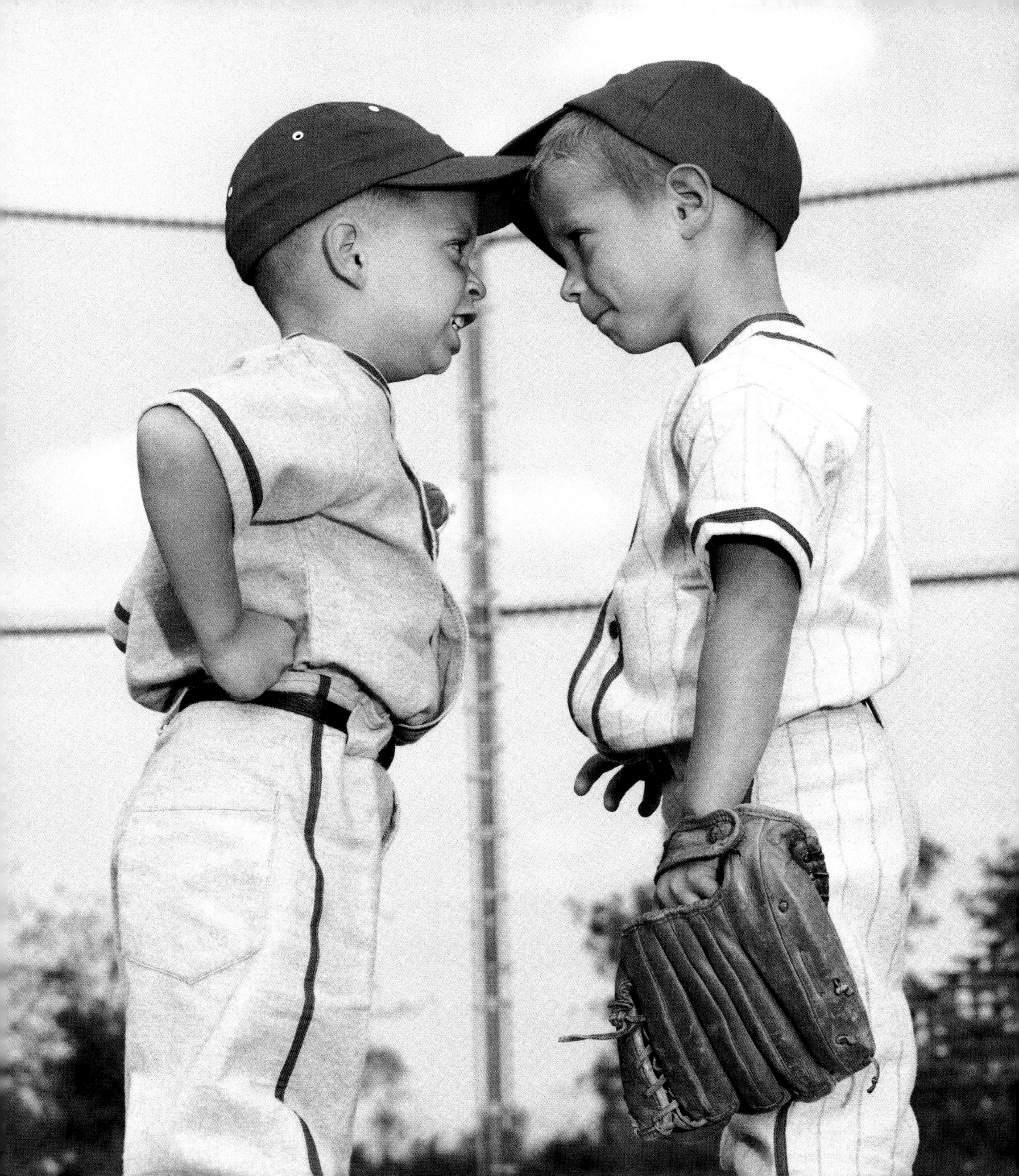

order to spend most of his time on non-illustration painting. The success of the plan hinged on whether or not editor George Horace Lorimer would accept Rockwell's new work, which had undergone some modernization. When no word came from the *Post*, there was nothing to do but return. In October, after almost deciding to relocate permanently to Paris, the family returned to New Rochelle.

The next major influence on his work came not from an artistic movement or style or a new way of handling light or color, but from using photography. One of the time-saving methods Rockwell had used in Paris had been to photograph models' poses. "The wear and tear and strain that working with living models placed on me was awful. I would sit for eight hours yelling, 'Lift eye brows!', 'Raise that arm a little!', and 'Make that smile bigger!' I would carry out all these gestures and facial expressions myself, and by the end of the day I was so tired and nervous that I was ready to drop." Rockwell said he never got over the feeling it was cheating, and in a letter to Mary's sister wrote that when J.C. Leyendecker visited his studio, which had photos "plastered" over the floor, "neither one of us appeared to notice them but it was just as though a fresh corpse I had just murdered lay there." Four years passed before Rockwell publicly admitted using photographs—for his 1936 *Tom Sawyer* book illustrations.

In 1937, Lorimer retired as editor of the *Post* and Wesley Winans Stout succeeded him. Aside from his aloof tone with Rockwell, Stout's letters were signed

45. *Girl at Mirror*, 1954
Painting for *The Saturday Evening Post* cover, March 6, 1954
Oil on canvas, 31.5 x 29.5 inches
Norman Rockwell Art Collection Trust, NRACT.1973.8

Girl at Mirror follows a long tradition of fine artists who have pictured a woman contemplating her reflection. George Hughes, fellow *Post* cover artist, said that a painting by Edouard Manet inspired this painting. Two paintings by other artists stand out as strong candidates, however. Included in Rockwell's reference files are examples of Picasso's *Girl at Mirror* and Elisabeth Vigée Le Brun's *The Artist's Daughter*, each of which could have directly influenced this work.

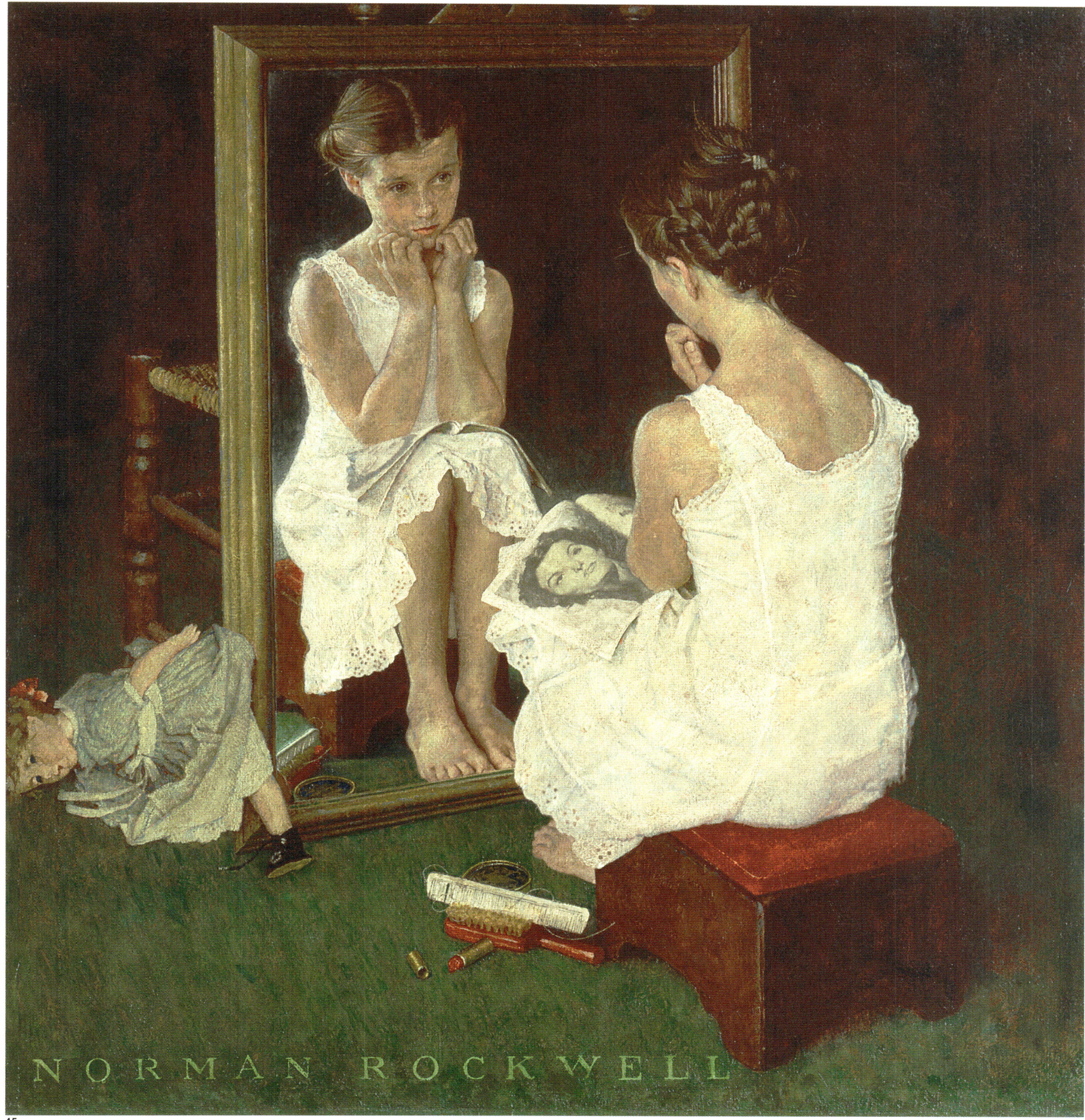

45

with the noncommittal and ambiguous single word "Truly." Truly what? Rockwell may have wondered, for he remembered this period as one of increased insecurity. Stout was always asking for changes.

His "constant nagging," Rockwell said, "sapped my inspiration." Ironically, as Rockwell was feeling the sting of Stout's edits, he was garnering the praise of the wider publishing community. In 1938, less than midway in his career, *Judge* magazine honored Rockwell with its High Hat Award. Their list of Rockwell's accomplishments prophesied the success he would achieve in the next thirty-eight years of his career: "[For] having become, while still a young man, a tradition in art; for having kept alive the affectionate interest of America by his re-creation of figures of the late eighteenth and early nineteenth centuries; for having faithfully portrayed persons and scenes familiar to the common man; for having painted one of the finest murals in the Nassau Tavern at Princeton; for having developed his camera eye for fine detail, which has proven that careless modernization is not part of good craftsmanship; for having been the inspiration for a school of drawing; for his faithful and grateful attachment to the Saturday Evening Post and its traditions; for his encouragement given to aspiring young artists; for his story-telling ability; for his youthful enthusiasm for, and curiosity about, all things; for his tireless energy; for his splendid sense of humor; and for his fine private life."

46. *The Discovery*, 1956
Painting for *The Saturday Evening Post* cover, December 29, 1956
Oil on canvas, 35.25 x 32.5 inches
Norman Rockwell Art Collection Trust, NRACT.1973.5

Intending it to be used as a September or October cover, Rockwell sent this painting of a small boy discovering a Santa suit in the bottom drawer of his father's dresser to *The Saturday Evening Post* in July. But the *Post* ran the image as the December 29 cover. Though the obvious interpretation of the painting is the boy's discovery that Santa does not exist, the *Post* in its contents section provided an alternate explanation (one that ignored the presence of mothballs): Santa had left his clothes to be sent to the cleaners. In *The Discovery*, Rockwell makes use of *doorkijkje*, a device favored by seventeenth-century Dutch artists, which literally means a "look through." An open door through which a distant view can be seen creates another picture plane, which adds depth. This is one of very few images set in a room in Rockwell's own home. The bureau and pipe were Rockwell's as well, but the Santa suit was not.

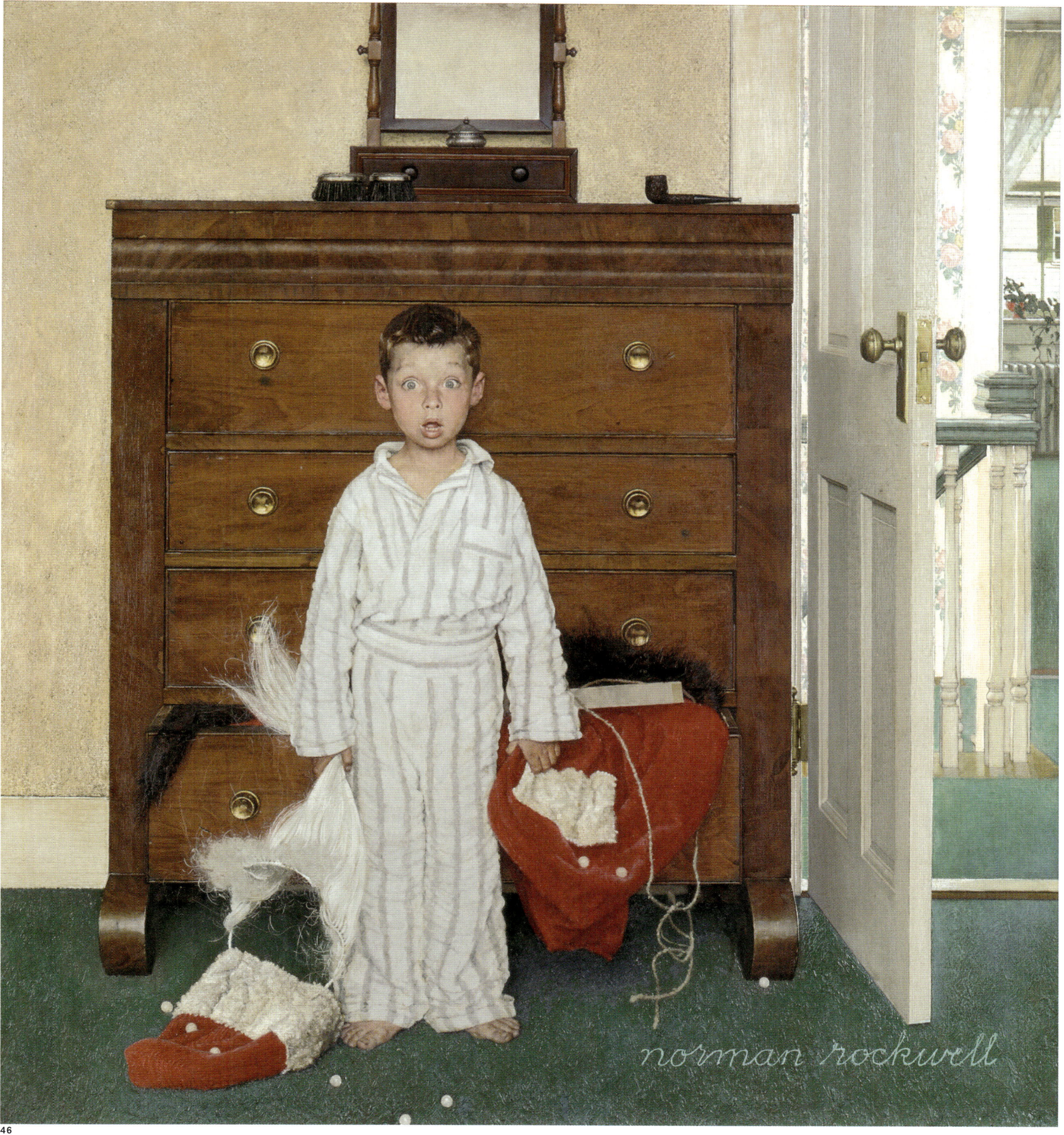
norman rockwell

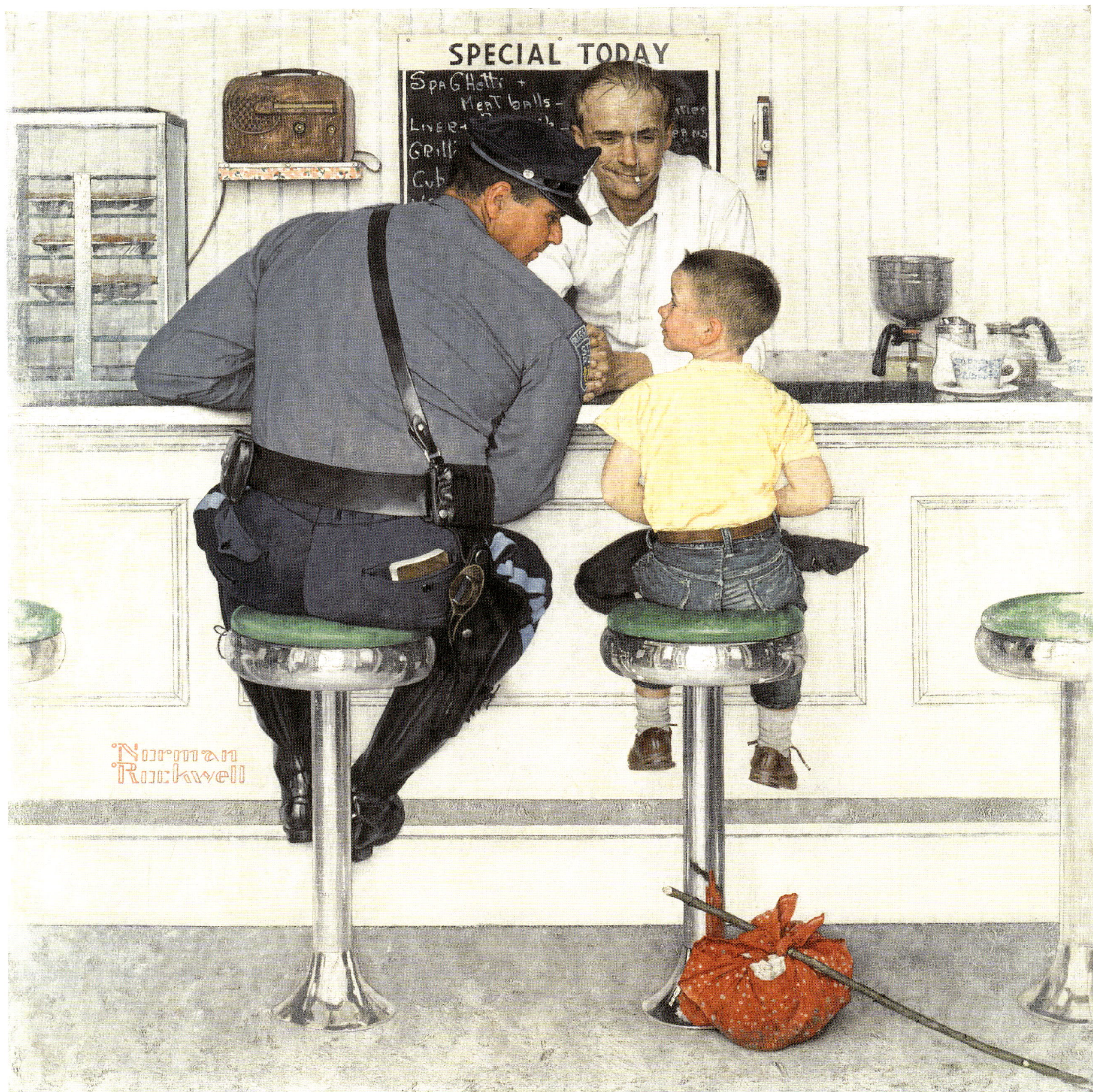
SPECIAL TODAY
SpaGHetti +
MeaT balls -
Norman
Rockwell

48. *The Runaway*, c. 1958
Photographer unknown
Norman Rockwell Museum Collections

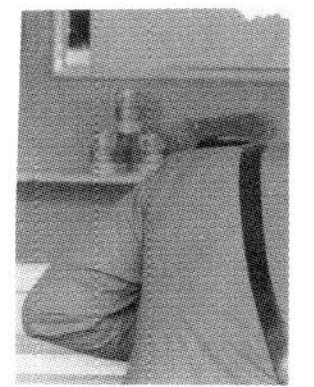
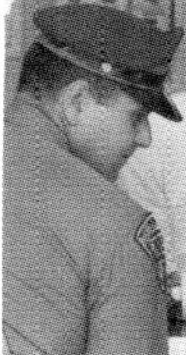
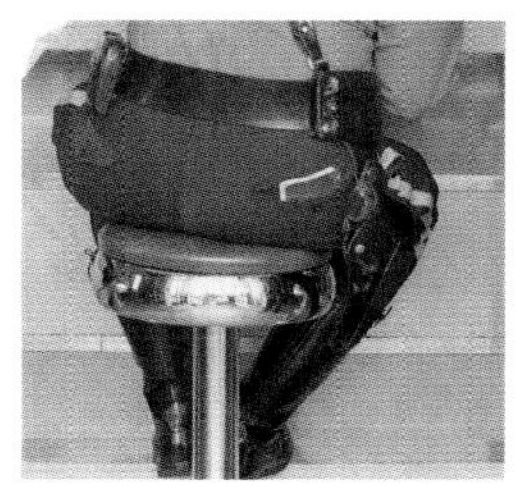
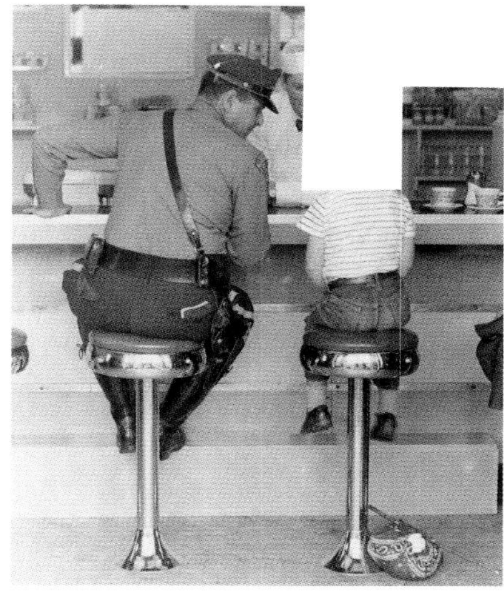
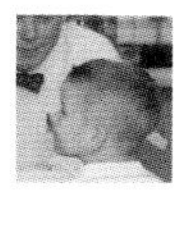
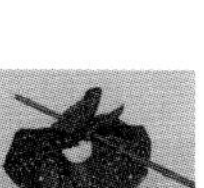
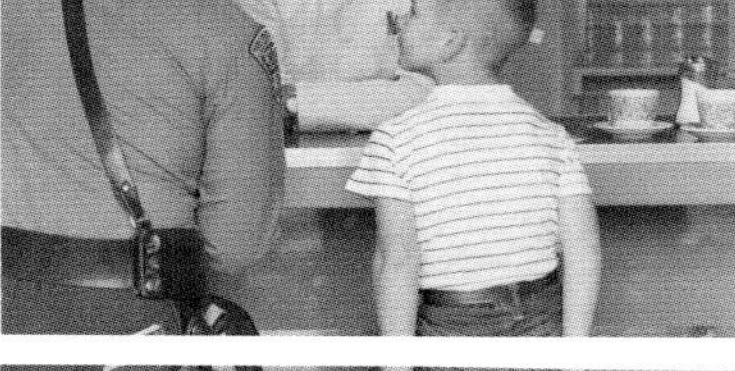
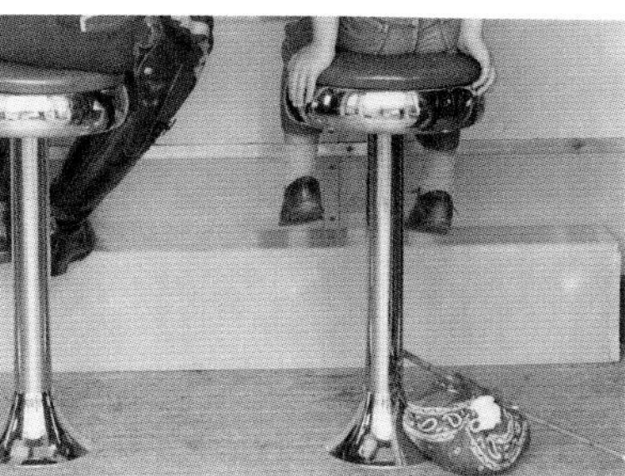
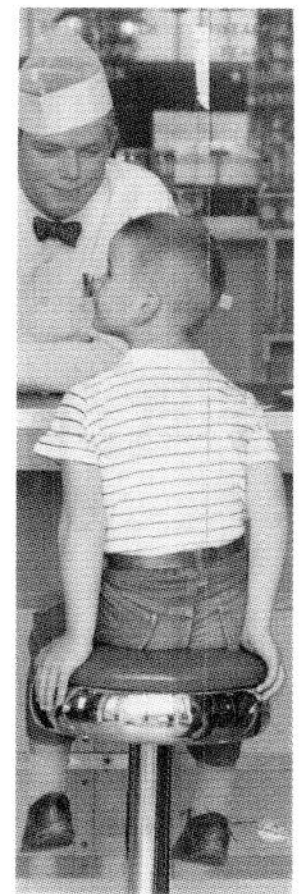
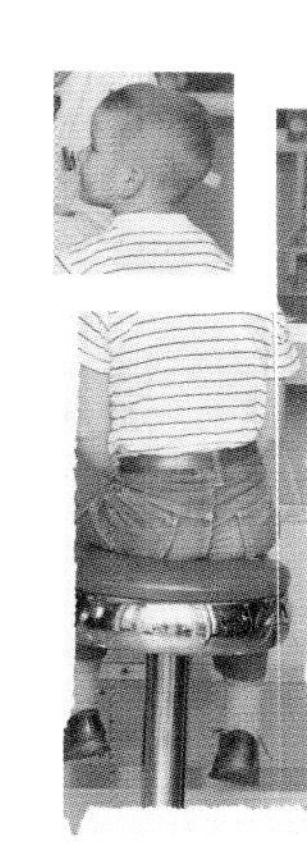

48

47. *The Runaway*, 1958
Painting for *The Saturday Evening Post* cover, September 20, 1958
Oil on canvas, 35.75 x 33.5 inches
Norman Rockwell Museum Collection, NRM.1973.18

Norman Rockwell's boyhood experience growing up just north of New York City provided inspiration for this popular painting. "I ran away from home when I was a kid in Mamaroneck and mooned around the shore, kicking stones and watching the whitecaps on Long Island Sound," he said. "Pretty soon it began to get dark and a cold wind sprang up and moaned in the trees. So I went home." Many years later, Rockwell brought eight year-old Ed Locke and Massachusetts state trooper Dick Clemens to a restaurant in Pittsfield, Massachusetts, where they were photographed as models for *The Runaway*. After completing a first canvas capturing the restaurant's modern décor, Rockwell rejected it and produced a second version with a sparer setting. Asked by Clemens why he made the change, the artist explained that he wanted a rural background "to give the impression that the little boy had gotten further out of town." This subtle revision heightened the significance of a moment shared by the would-be runaway and a compassionate trooper who, ensured that "no harm [will] come to that kid."

49. *The Runaway*, c. 1958
Photographer unknown
Norman Rockwell Museum Collections

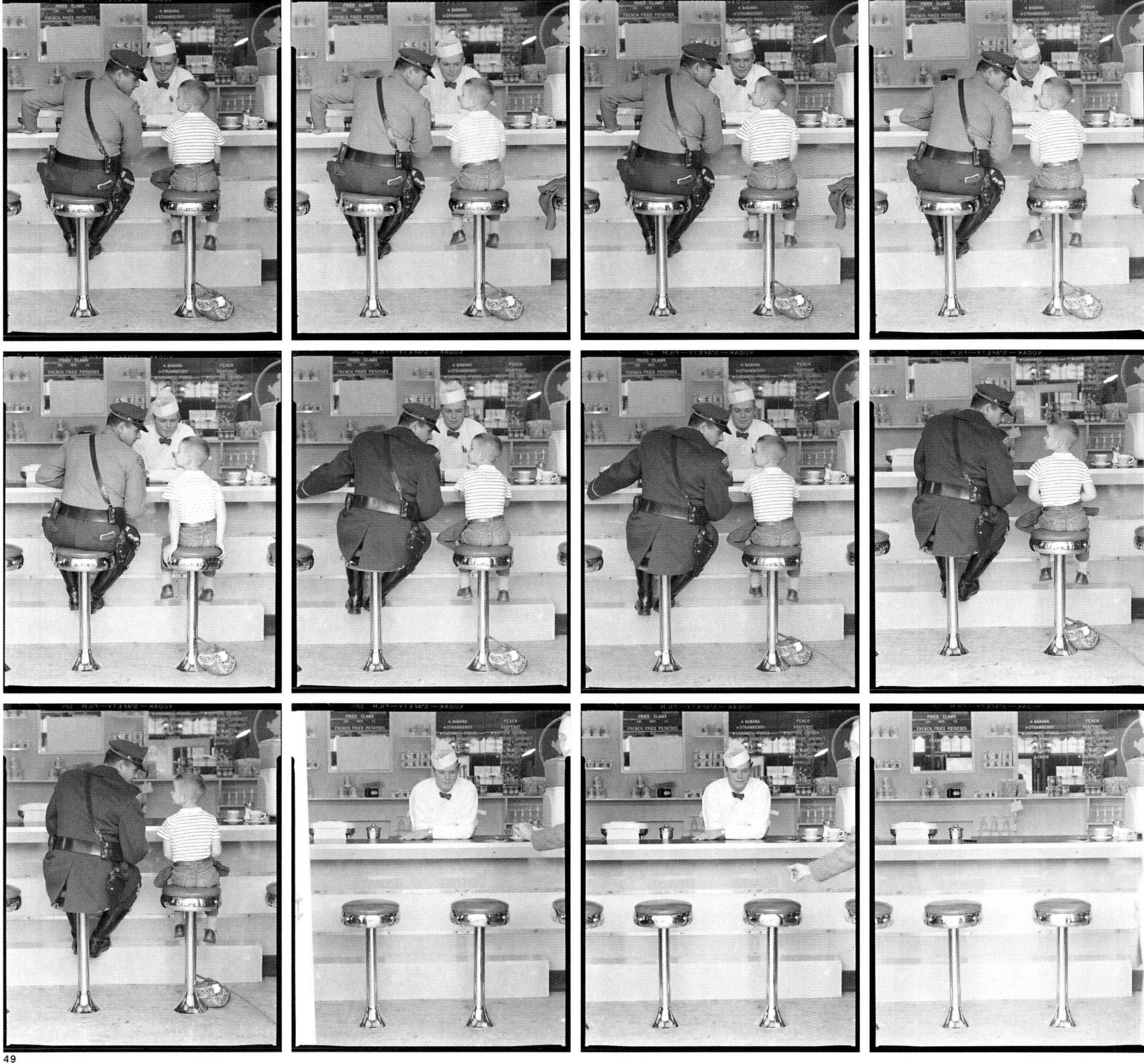

49

A three-week trip to England in 1938, during which the artist visited prominent illustrators Arthur Rackham, Edmund Dulac, and George Belcher, put the Rockwell family, now including three young sons, on a new course. Exploring by bicycle the countryside near Oxford, Rockwell recollected his youthful summer idylls in upstate New York, and on their return home, Norman and Mary began a search for a summer home in the country. In the valley that lies below Red Mountain, Minister Mountain and Swearing Mountain in Arlington, Vermont, there sat an eighty-year-old farmhouse with two cow barns. Rockwell purchased this sixty-acre property on the Batten Kill River, and arranged for renovations of the house and the smaller barn, which became his new studio. There, the Rockwell family spent an extended summer in 1938, returning the next summer to make the small community of 1,200 their year-round residence. Describing the charms of country life—picking blueberries, taking long walks in the mountains, climbing through old apple orchards, and enjoying the honesty and integrity of his new neighbors—Rockwell said he'd "fallen into utopia." The move to Vermont brought a whole new retinue of models, and after a 1943 fire destroyed his studio complete with costume, reference, and prop collections, he reevaluated his choice of subjects as well. Rockwell had always wanted to be topical and record the current scene, and now his artistic path was fixed.

Soon after Rockwell's move to Vermont, he was joined there by fellow *Saturday Evening Post* cover artist Mead Schaeffer and by artist John Atherton. Avid fishermen, Schaeffer and Atherton divided their time between painting and fly-fishing for trout in the Batten Kill and Green Rivers. In 1946 they were joined in Vermont by illustrator George Hughes. Living in close proximity, the four artists inspired, cajoled, criticized, and supported one another. And though they all drew on the same pool of models from the town and all contributed to the *Post*, they worked very differently in style and subject. Like a patchwork quilt in one of Rockwell's paintings, pieces of their personal and professional lives began fitting together in a pattern of relationships between the four illustrators. Just as Rockwell had been inspired by the narrative humor of A.B. Frost, Carl Spitzweg, and H.K. Browne, George Hughes, to some extent, incorporated some of Rockwell's anecdotal motifs into his own work. Atherton's vision and style were so unique that his work seemed to remain untouched by what the others had on their easels. Rockwell and Atherton had enormous admiration and respect for each other. Their disparate styles didn't distance or keep them from long discussions about painting. Sharing ideas nourished and sustained these geographically sequestered painters in a way similar to that in which creativity is fostered in an artists' colony, and for Rockwell the fellowship turned Arlington into Camelot.

This balanced blend of peaceful surroundings, family, close friends, good neighbors, and the stimulation of artists and illustrators fostered an artistic period in which Rockwell created paintings that were instantly regarded as his finest work. Although he'd had several public showings at the New Rochelle Art Association in the 1910s, now his participation in gallery and museum exhibitions snowballed. The 1943 sixteen-city tour of his *Four Freedoms* paintings catalyzed his burgeoning celebrity, and in 1945, Rockwell shared billing with American

Following pages
The Guggenheim Museum,
August 8, 1959

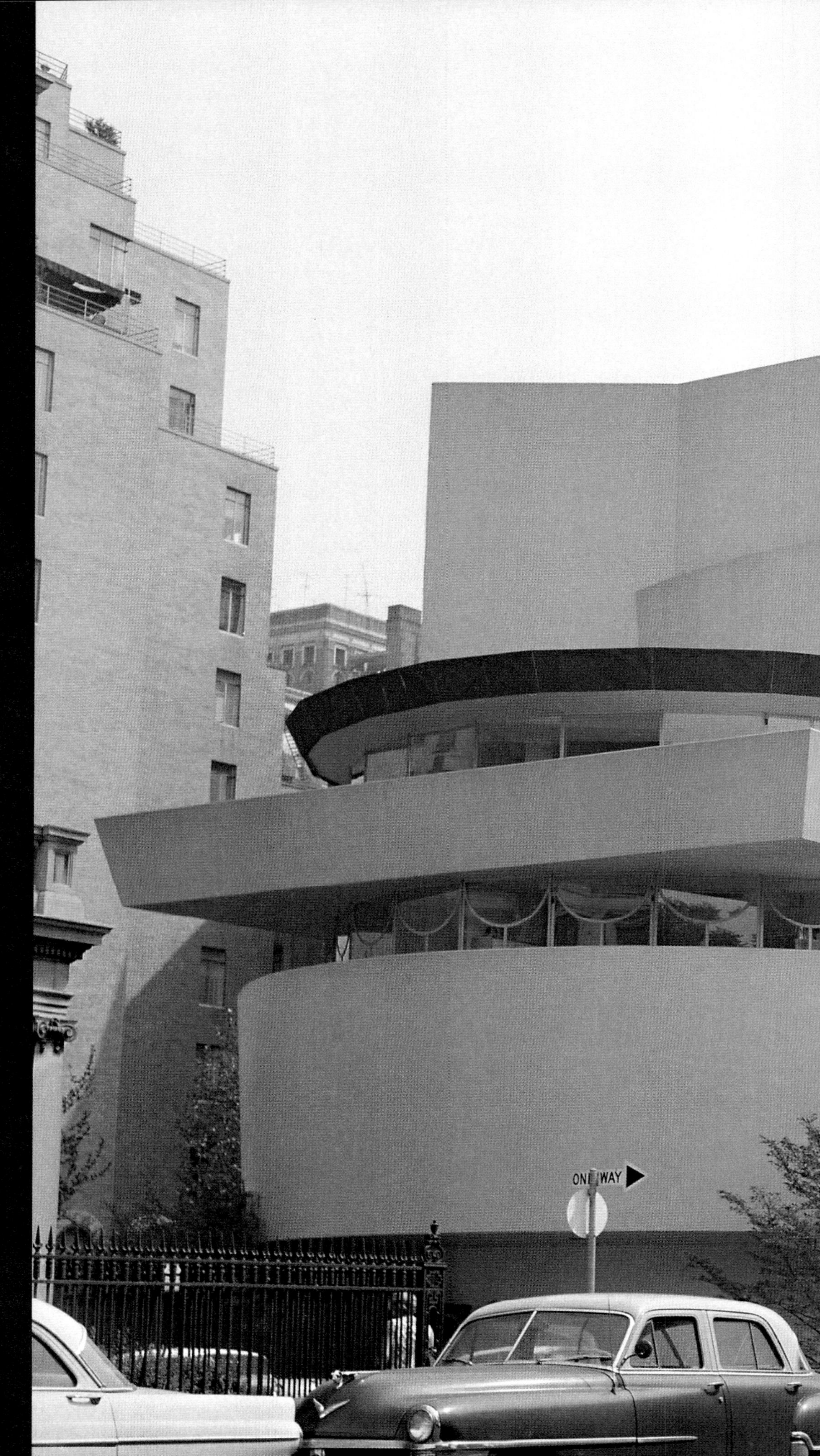
ONE WAY

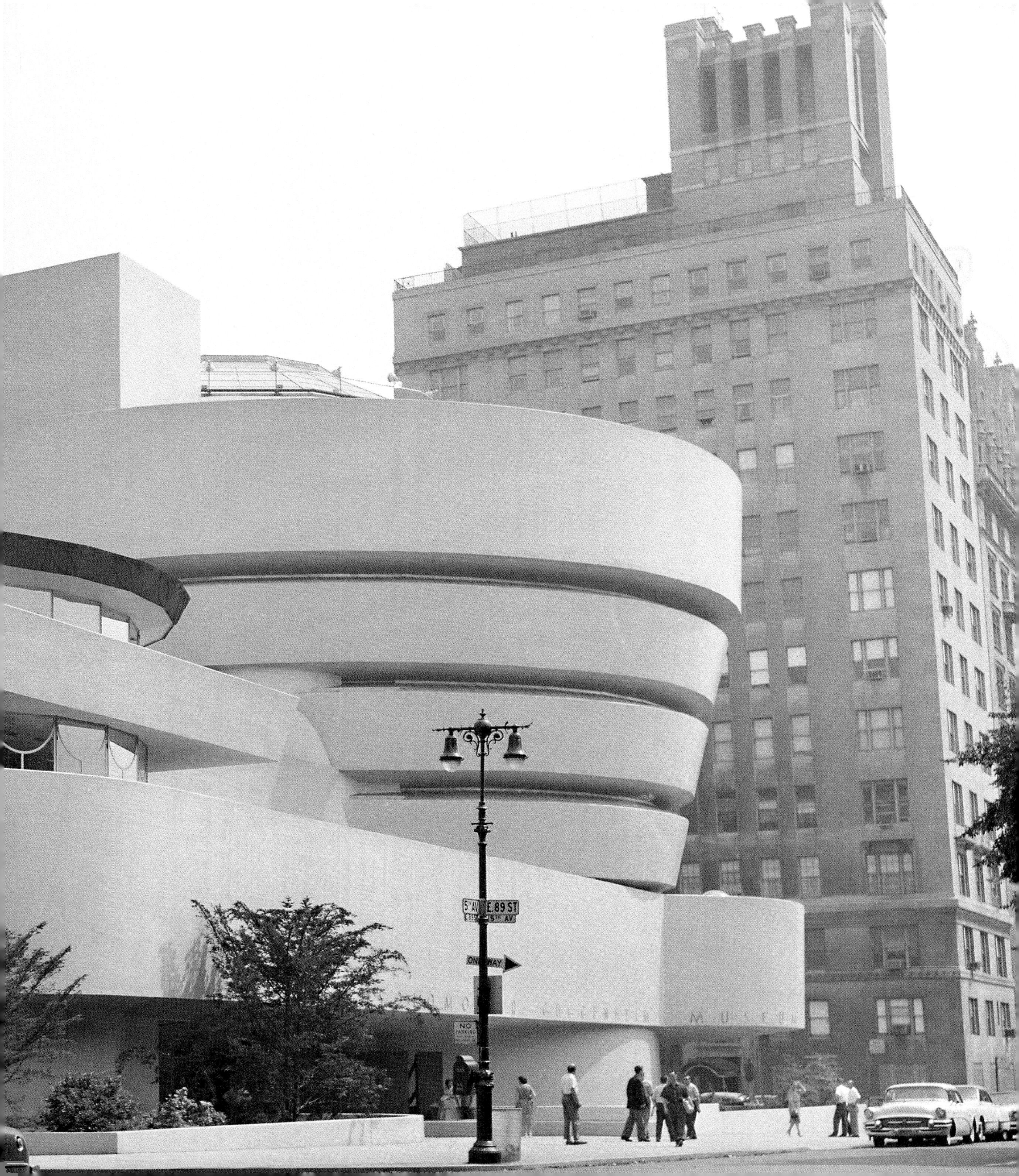
5TH AV E. 89 ST

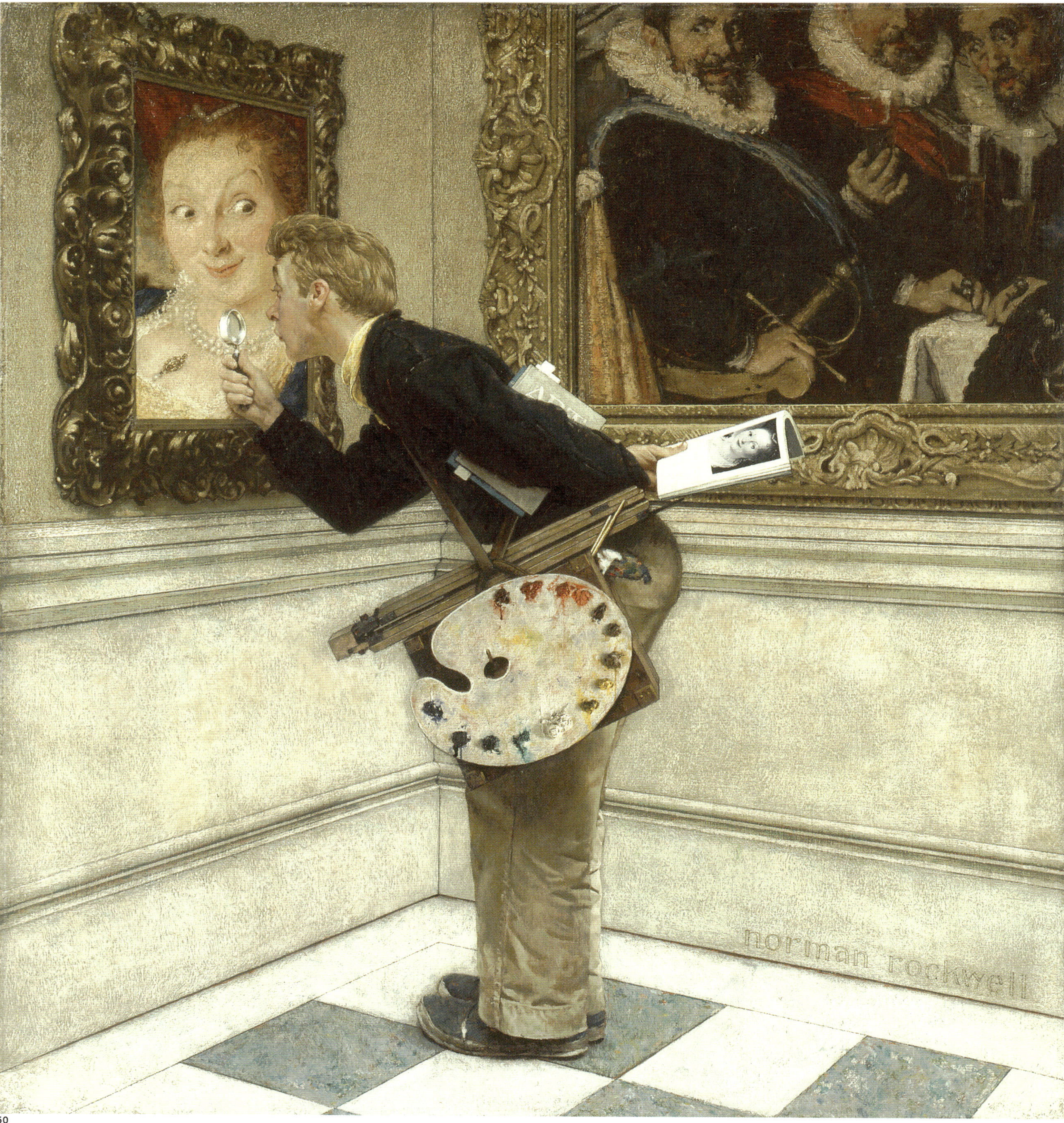
norman rockwell

painters Charles Burchfield, Thomas Hart Benton, John Stuart Curry, John Sloan, and Charles Sheeler at San Francisco's Palace of the Legion of Honor. Two years later, the Metropolitan Museum of Art included Rockwell's paintings for the movies *The Song of Bernadette* and *The Razor's Edge* in an exhibition of Motion Picture Art, and in 1951 his *Post* cover *Soldier's Return* was included in a show of works by Art Students League artists. When the Metropolitan Museum purchased a Rockwell painting for its permanent collection in 1952, the *Saturday Evening Post* announced that Rockwell had "arrived."

From 1946 to 1949, eight illustrators were responsible for all but fifteen *Saturday Evening Post* covers. Since four of these eight all lived in the same remote hamlet, *Post* art editor Ken Stuart often traveled to Vermont for consultations with the artists. The camaraderie of the group lessened the pressure of these visits, and upon Stuart's departure they could gather and talk shop. Stuart, an illustrator before his 1943 hire as art editor, had strong opinions about the magazine's artistic direction. One of his first policies was to have the artists paint what they did best—even if it wasn't traditional *Post* cover fare. Stuart didn't want the artists copying a cliché or a predetermined style just because it had once worked. This gave Jack Atherton the freedom to paint mostly fishing and hunting subjects. For Hughes, it meant that his characters could take on a greater measure of sophistication and urbanity honed during his years as a fashion illustrator. For

50. *Art Critic*, 1955
Painting for *The Saturday Evening Post* cover, April 16, 1955
Oil on canvas, 39.5 x 36.25 inches
Norman Rockwell Museum Collection, NRM.1998.4

Norman Rockwell once said he envied students who swooned when viewing the *Mona Lisa* because he never felt such passion. Rockwell may have seen himself as a more analytical artist, such as the one examining a seventeenth-century Dutch painting in his 1955 *Art Critic*. His original draft depicts a student examining painter Frans Hals' technique in a portrait of a Dutch housewife. In that study, a Dutch landscape on an adjacent wall places the student in a gallery of Dutch artwork. But a recurring Rockwell theme of fantasy and reality exchanging places seems to have taken over, and the painting changed course.
With typical humor, Rockwell replaced the homely woman with one more alluring–based on a Peter Paul Rubens portrait of his wife. The Dutch landscape became a group of Dutch cavaliers, brought to life with animated facial expressions. They are wary and concerned. Is the student getting too close to the painting? Is he being too personal with their gallery colleague? The scene's movement from reality to fantasy refutes the view that Rockwell's work is only photographic.

Odds & Ends
On the student's palette, three-dimensional dollops of paint remind us that we too are standing in a gallery looking at a painting.

51. *Art Critic*, c. 1955
Photo by Bill Scovill
Norman Rockwell Museum Collections

52. *Art Critic*, c. 1955
Photo by Gene Pelham
Norman Rockwell Museum Collections

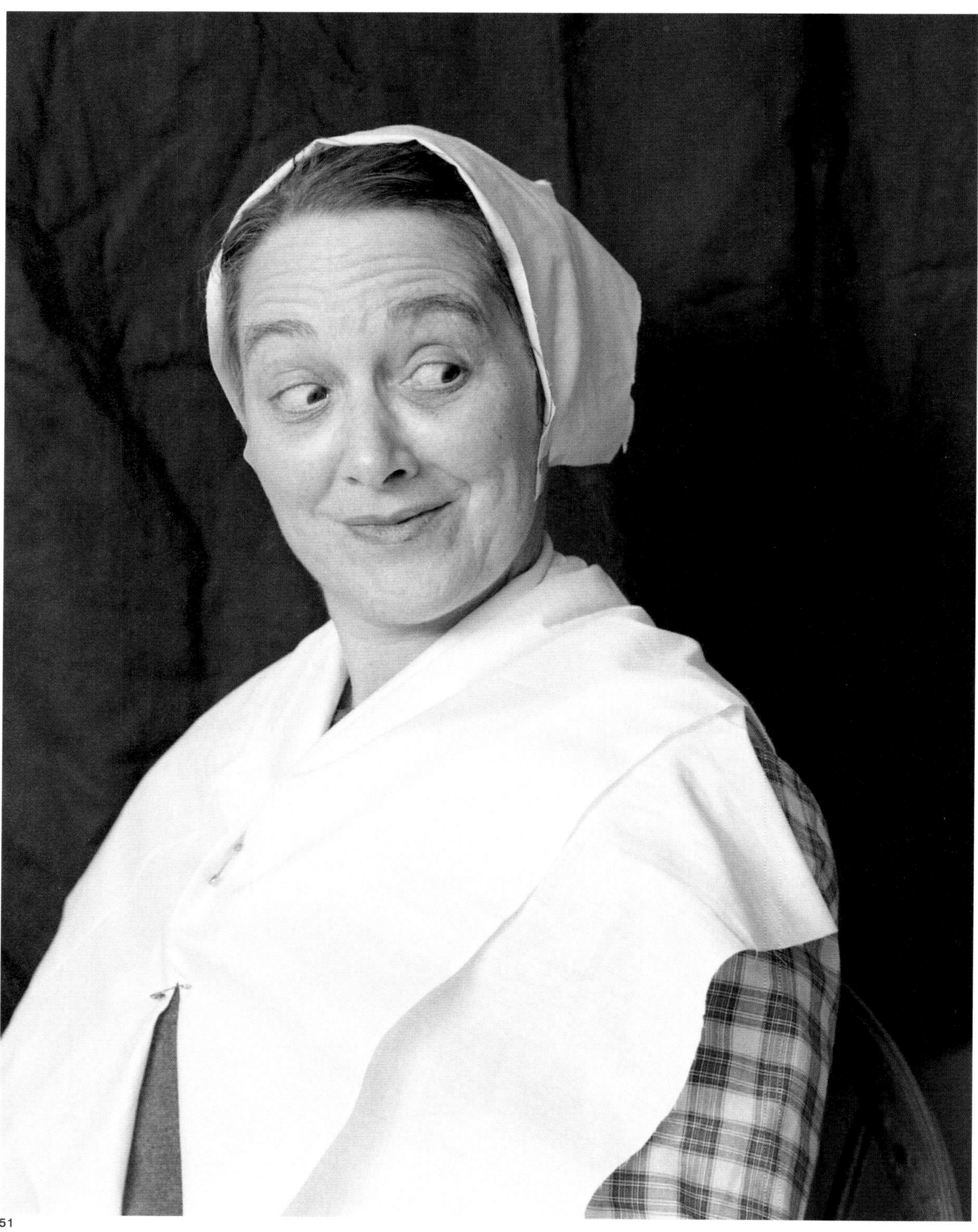

51

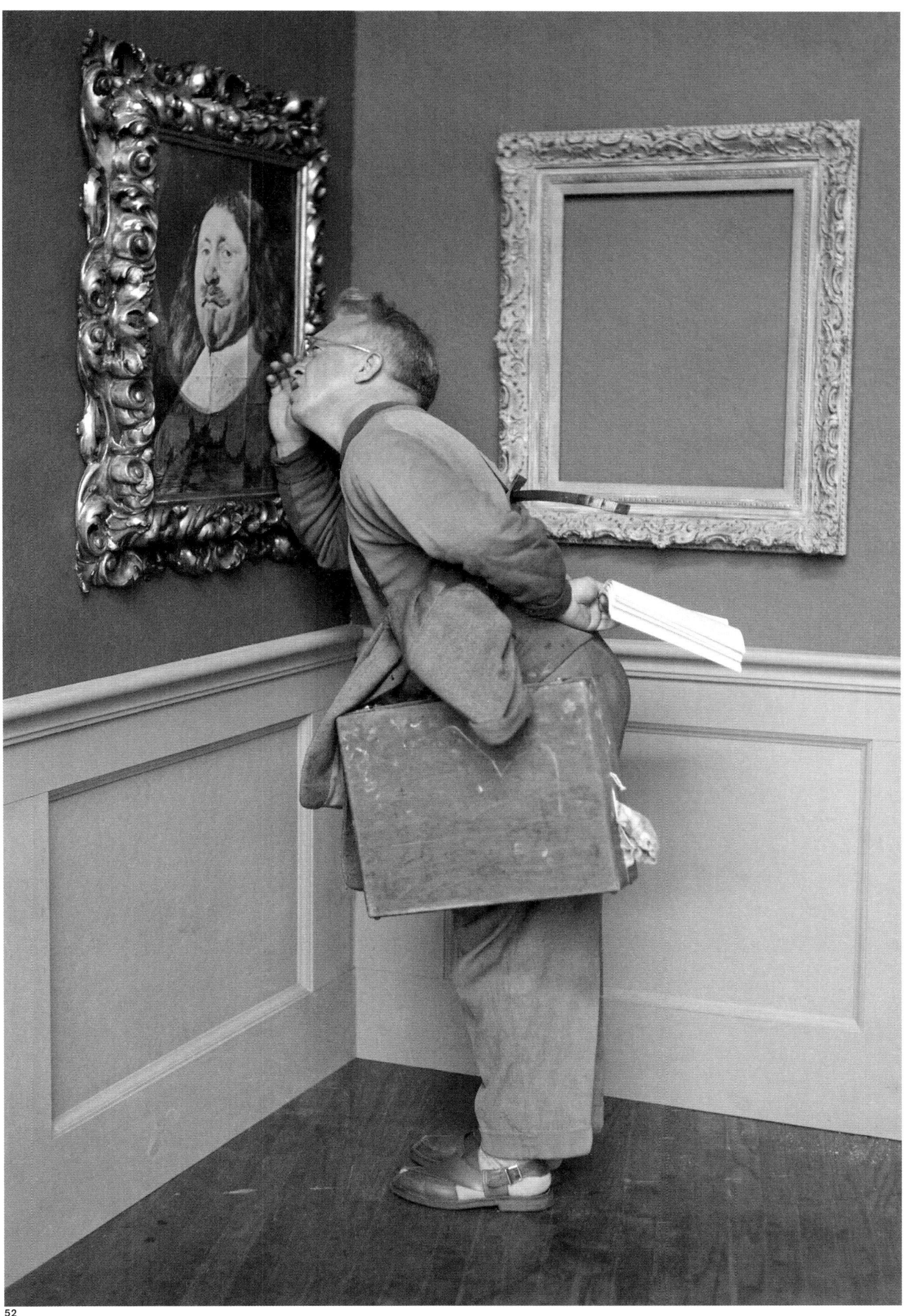

52

53. Study for *Art Critic*, *c.* 1955
Print
Norman Rockwell Museum Collections

54. Study for *Art Critic*, *c.* 1955
Print
Norman Rockwell Museum Collections

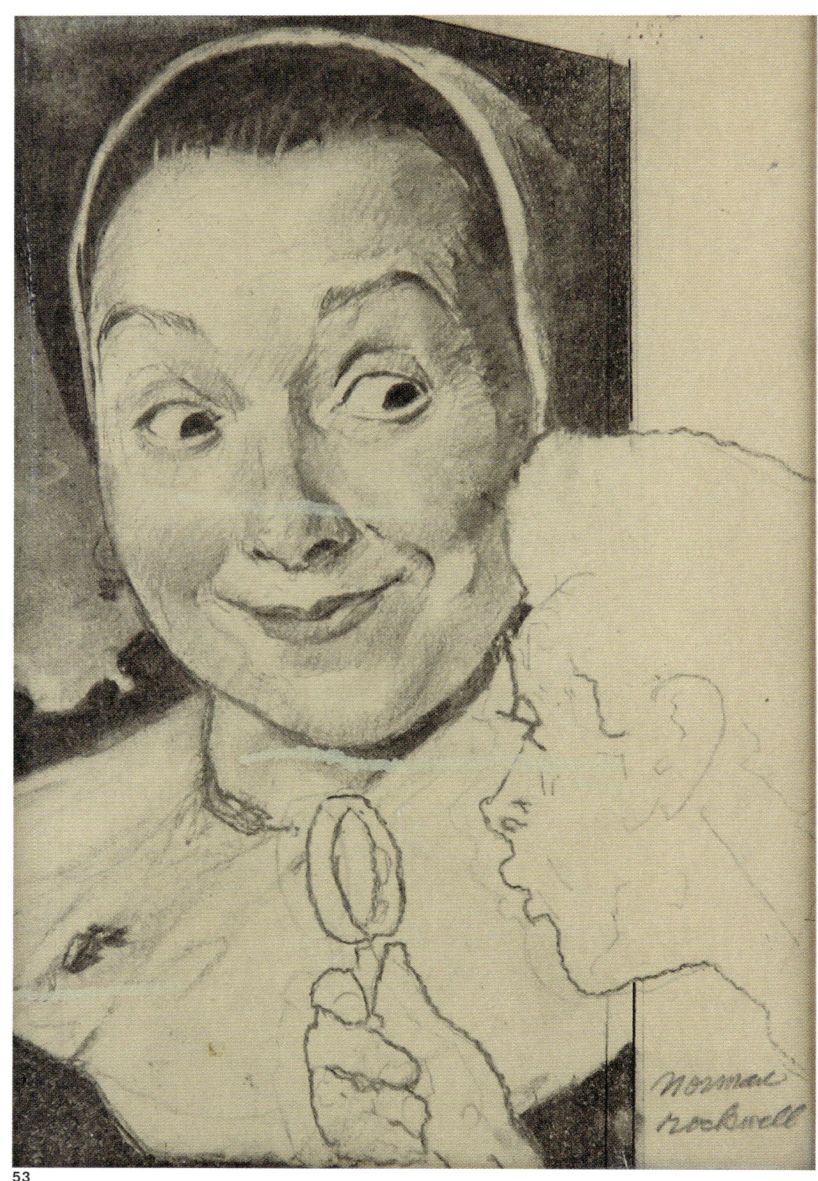

53

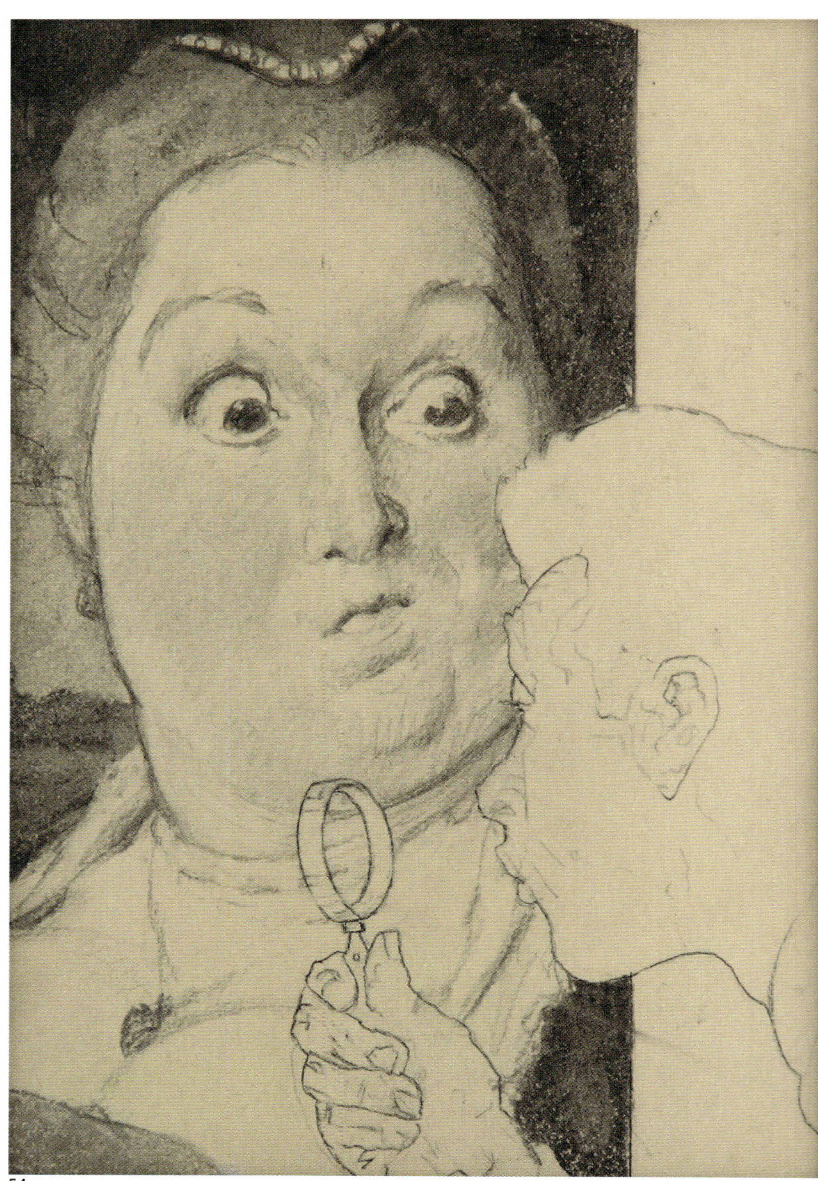

54

55. Study for *Art Critic*, *c.* 1955
Print
Norman Rockwell Museum Collections

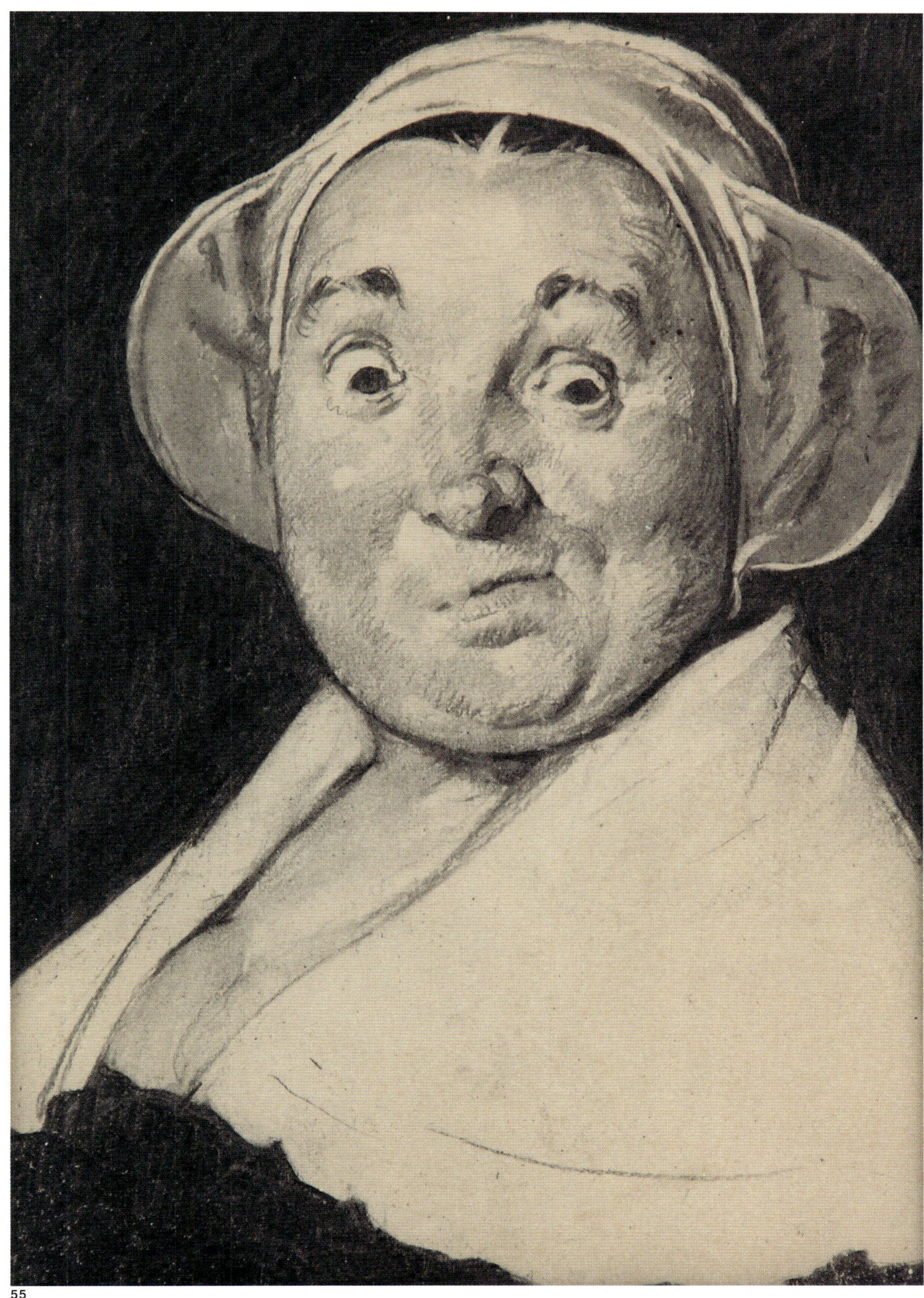
55

56. Study for *Art Critic*, *c.* 1955
Print
Norman Rockwell Museum Collections

57. Study for *Art Critic*, *c.* 1955
Print
Norman Rockwell Museum Collections

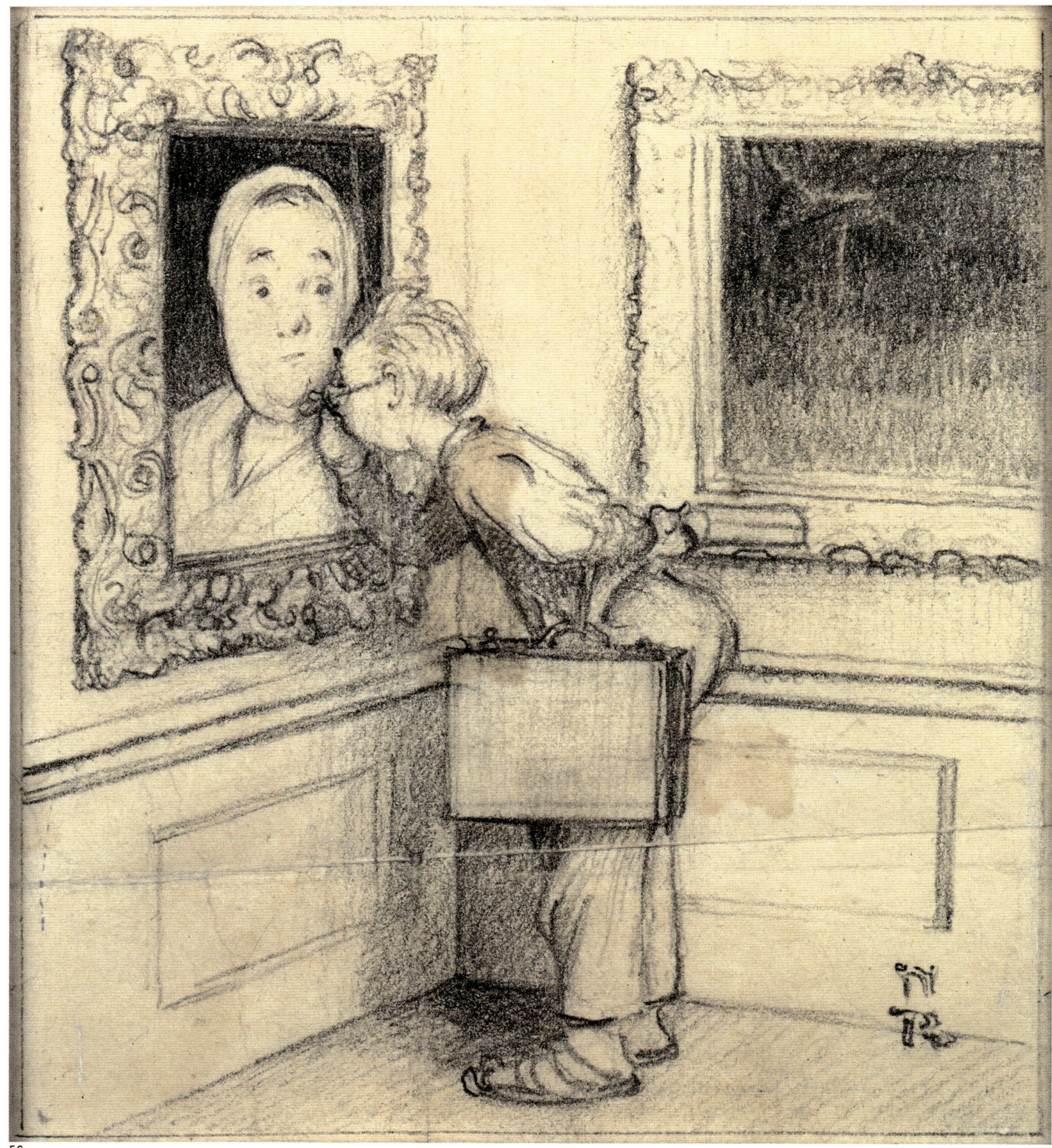

56

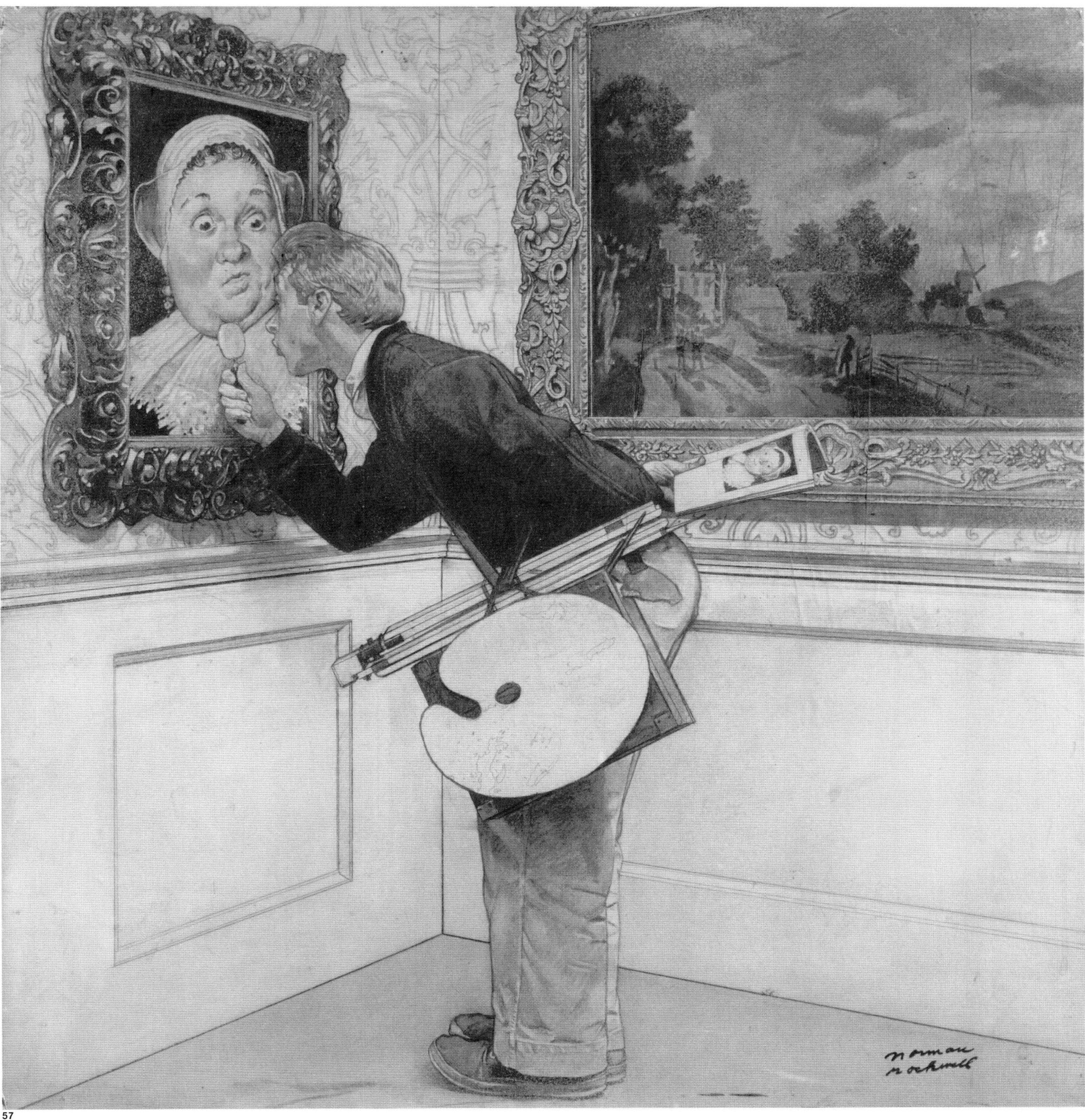

57

124

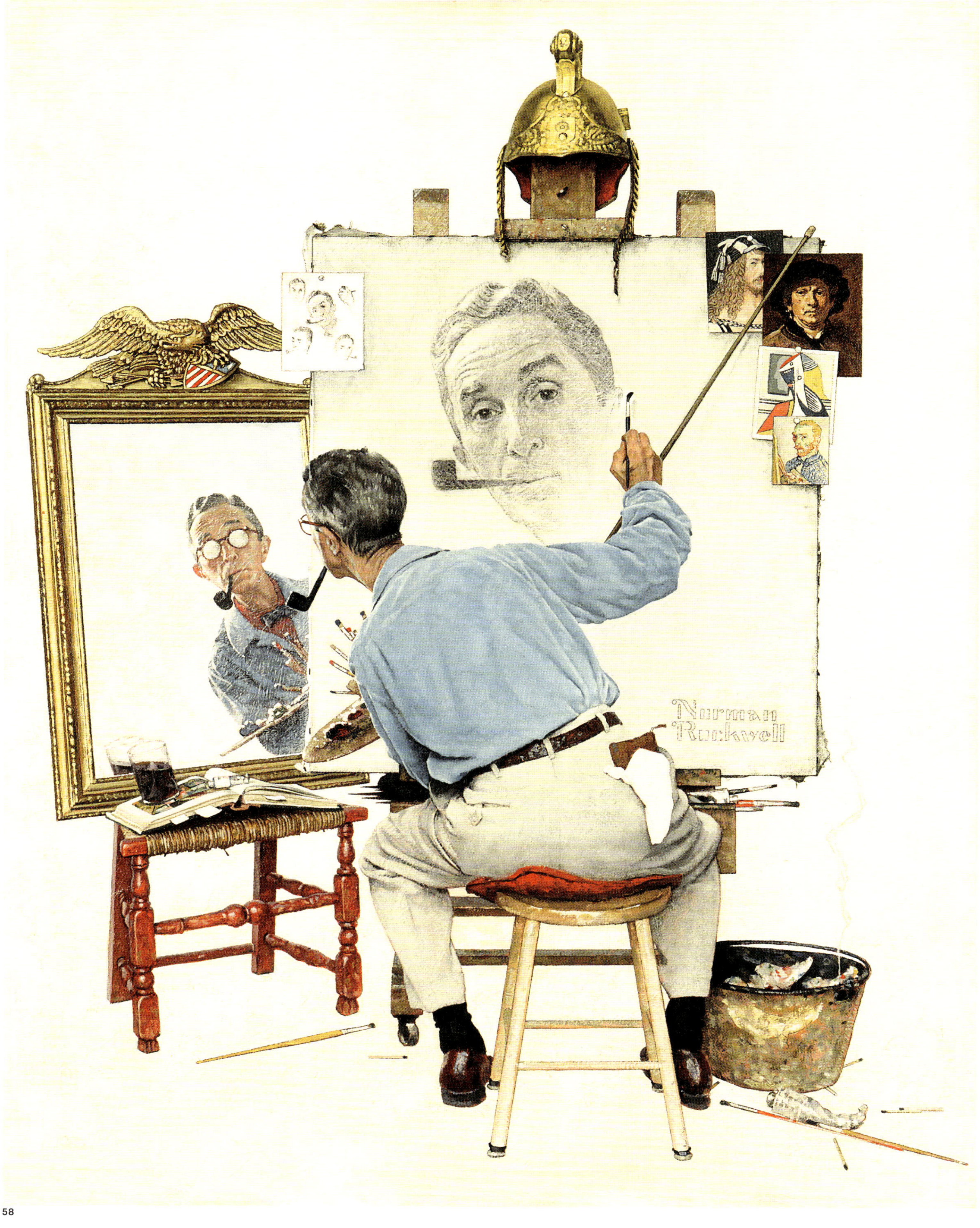

Rockwell it was an affirmation. Attuned to each new movement in contemporary art, he regularly held his work in comparison and questioned its relevance. Stuart's sanction endorsed his penchant for everyday scenes of neighbors and friends doing typical things, depicting their wisdom and follies, their sufferings and joys. But Stuart also encouraged Rockwell to move from his usual close-up composition to a longer view with a more detailed background. Editorial changes of this kind sent the illustrators into lively discussions during their 5 p.m. cocktails. Rockwell called these playful interludes by the forty-year-olds "the children's hour."

Despite his seclusion in the Vermont hills, Rockwell found ways to refresh his ideas and spirits, away from the long, cold winters. When cabin fever became too much, the Rockwell family took trips to southern California where friends' studios were always available and Mary's relatives were nearby. Rockwell often traveled to New York to lunch or to give lectures for gatherings of the Society of Illustrators or to see new exhibitions—sometimes of his own work. Distant from the activities of the war raging in Europe, Rockwell was challenged to record his interpretation of the effects of World War II on the servicemen and Americans at home. For Rockwell, an unassuming private whose name, Willie Gillis, was coined by Mary from the 1938 Munro Leaf story *Wee Gillis*, told the story of one man's army in a series of fourteen *Post* covers, on which he was depicted doing everything from peeling potatoes to reading his hometown newspaper to proud-

58. *Triple Self-Portrait*, 1960
Painting for *The Saturday Evening Post* cover, February 13, 1960
Oil on canvas, 44.5 x 34.75 inches
Norman Rockwell Art Collection Trust, NRACT.1973.19

Humor and humility were essential aspects of Norman Rockwell's character, so when asked to do a self-portrait that would announce the first of eight excerpts of his autobiography, the result was lighthearted and somewhat self-deprecating.
The painting provides the essential elements not of his life as an illustrator, but of the specific commission. Rockwell's life is far too eventful and complex to begin to approach summation in a single work, so he limits the composition to himself, his artists' materials, his references, a canvas on an easel, and a mirror.
There are more inconsistencies in this painting that are cause for wonder. Rockwell was a stickler for neatness, but here he has scattered matchsticks, paint tubes, and brushes over the studio floor. The glass of Coca-Cola, Rockwell's usual afternoon pick-me-up, looks as if it will tip over at any moment. Other discrepancies can be explained away. He has traded his usual Windsor chair for a stool (easier to see more of him?) and his milk glass palette table for a hand-held wooden palette (an economy of picture space?). In real life, Rockwell's mirror was not topped with an eagle holding arrows, cannon balls, and a shield. The eagle, taken from the outside of Rockwell's studio for use as a prop, may have been added to send a message. Most of the features ring true: He did tack or tape studies to his drawings or canvases and he did immerse himself in favorite artwork before beginning a project.
That Rockwell's eyes cannot be seen bothers some who try to find a psychological significance. But the reference photos of Rockwell posing show he could not have seen his own eyes; his mirror was directly opposite his studio's massive north window, causing the reflected glare on his lenses.
As Rockwell's assistant, Louie Lamone, recalled, paint rags and pipe ashes sometimes conspired to ignite small fires in Rockwell's brass bucket, so the wisp of smoke in the painting rings true. Rockwell's brass helmet, usually placed on an unused easel, crowns this one. Just as the smoke is a reminder that once Rockwell's studio caught fire as a result of his carelessness with pipe ashes, the helmet reminds us of a favorite Rockwell story. While in Paris in 1923, Rockwell acquired it from an antiques dealer who sold it as a military relic rather than as the contemporary French fireman's helmet Rockwell later found it to be. Alluding to its real provenance, *Post* editors noted for their readers when the painting was published that the helmet "could come in handy when the fire in that receptacle gets going."
The four self-portraits on his canvas—Albrecht Dürer, Rembrandt van Rijn, Pablo Picasso, and Vincent Van Gogh—are his references. They invite us to compare (as he did) how other artists tackled the problem of a self-portrait. Influenced during his student years by Durer's superb draftsmanship, Rockwell puts him at the top of his canvas. Next in line is Rembrandt, whose painting style Rockwell admired above all others. Below it is Picasso, whom Rockwell admired greatly but whose work, he admitted, was opposite his own.
Last is Van Gogh, a painter with whom Rockwell never identified, and whose style his own work never resembled. Unlike Rockwell, all four artists produced numerous formal self-portraits. Rockwell produced only two other full-color self-portraits: *Norman Rockwell Painting the Soda Jerk*, showing the artist from the waist up at work on his 1953 *Post* cover, and *The Deadline*, a 1938 *Post* cover composed much the same as this one—the rear view of the artist at work at his easel. Both are unselfconscious portraits, confirming that in 1953 and 1960 Rockwell's view of himself continued unchanged.

The Saturday Evening POST

June 1, 1961

15c

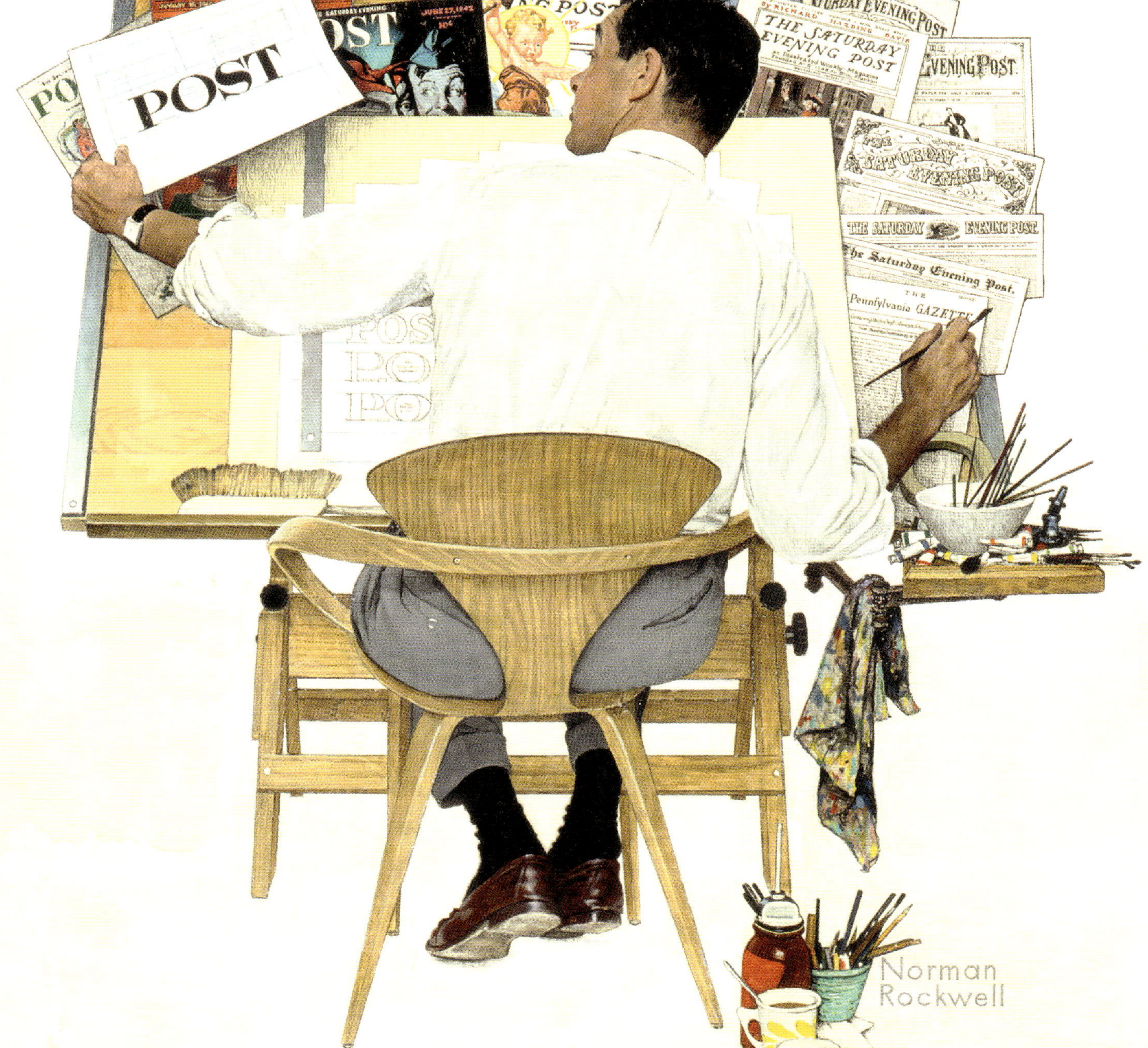

59

ly receiving a care package from home. Rockwell's only image of a soldier in battle—designed to stimulate ammunition production at munitions factories—featured a powerful machine-gunner for the poster *Let's Give Him Enough and on Time.* Rockwell later wrote that he "didn't like to do pictures that glorified killing, even in a good cause." By 1942, Rockwell had finished seven Willie Gillis covers and was at work on the motivational poster for the U.S. Army, but he wanted to do more for the war effort. He decided to illustrate President Franklin D. Roosevelt's concept of the four basic human freedoms, a job he later said "should have been tackled by Michelangelo."

On May 21, Rockwell and Mead Schaeffer visited the Ordnance Department in Washington with a progress report on Rockwell's machine!gunner painting. At home in Vermont, they had discussed how they could make a significant contribution to the war effort. With their official business completed, they pitched their proposals. Rockwell would interpret Roosevelt's Four Freedoms ideals and Schaeffer would paint a series of portraits of U.S. servicemen. According to published accounts, the War Department didn't have the time to publish their posters nor could they pay Rockwell or Schaeffer their customary fees. Rockwell later said he offered his work free of charge. On their way home, Schaeffer and Rockwell stopped at Curtis Publishing in Philadelphia and showed their sketches to Ben Hibbs, who had recently succeeded Wesley Stout as editor at the *Post.* Hibbs ea-

59. *Lubalin Redesigning the Post*, 1961
Painting for *The Saturday Evening Post* cover, September 16, 1961
Oil on canvas, 34 x 26.5 inches
Norman Rockwell Art Collection Trust, NRACT.1973.13

Hoping to lure back advertisers, who had switched their attention to television, *Saturday Evening Post* designer Herbert Lubalin was assigned to create a new, more contemporary, logotype. To help readers accept the change, Rockwell was hired to create the first *Post* cover with the new logotype. In the1961 cover, also known as *Modernizing the Post*, Lubalin is shown creating the logotype. Strewn over his drawing table, as he prepares the new design, are logos dating back to the beginning of the century. Instead of its position in the upper left corner, the new "Post" spread across the width of the page. Reporting on the Savoy Hilton presentation of the cover to more than 200 advertisers, the *Wall Street Journal* announced, "*Saturday Evening Post's* New Format Appears to Impress Advertisers." Just six months later, the magazine returned to its old format.

Odds & Ends
Rockwell's choice of Plycraft's bent-plywood chair makes a contemporary statement, as does his simplified signature. Unlike most artists, Rockwell changed his signature to suit the style of each of his paintings.

60. Norman Rockwell with
The Golden Rule, 1961
Photo by Louie Lamone
Norman Rockwell Museum Collections

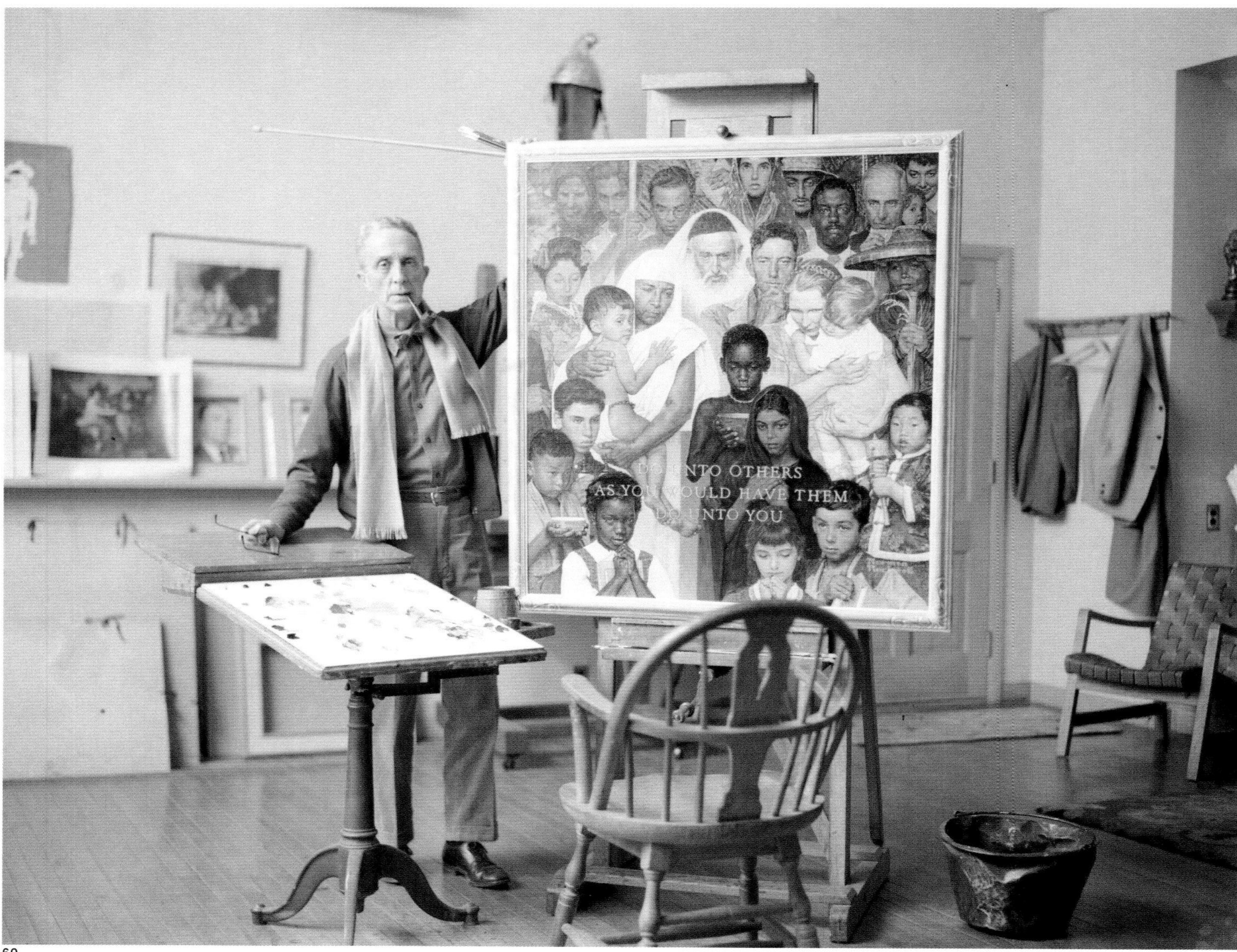

60

61. Norman Rockwell with
The Connoisseur, 1961
Photo by Louie Lamone
Norman Rockwell Museum Collections

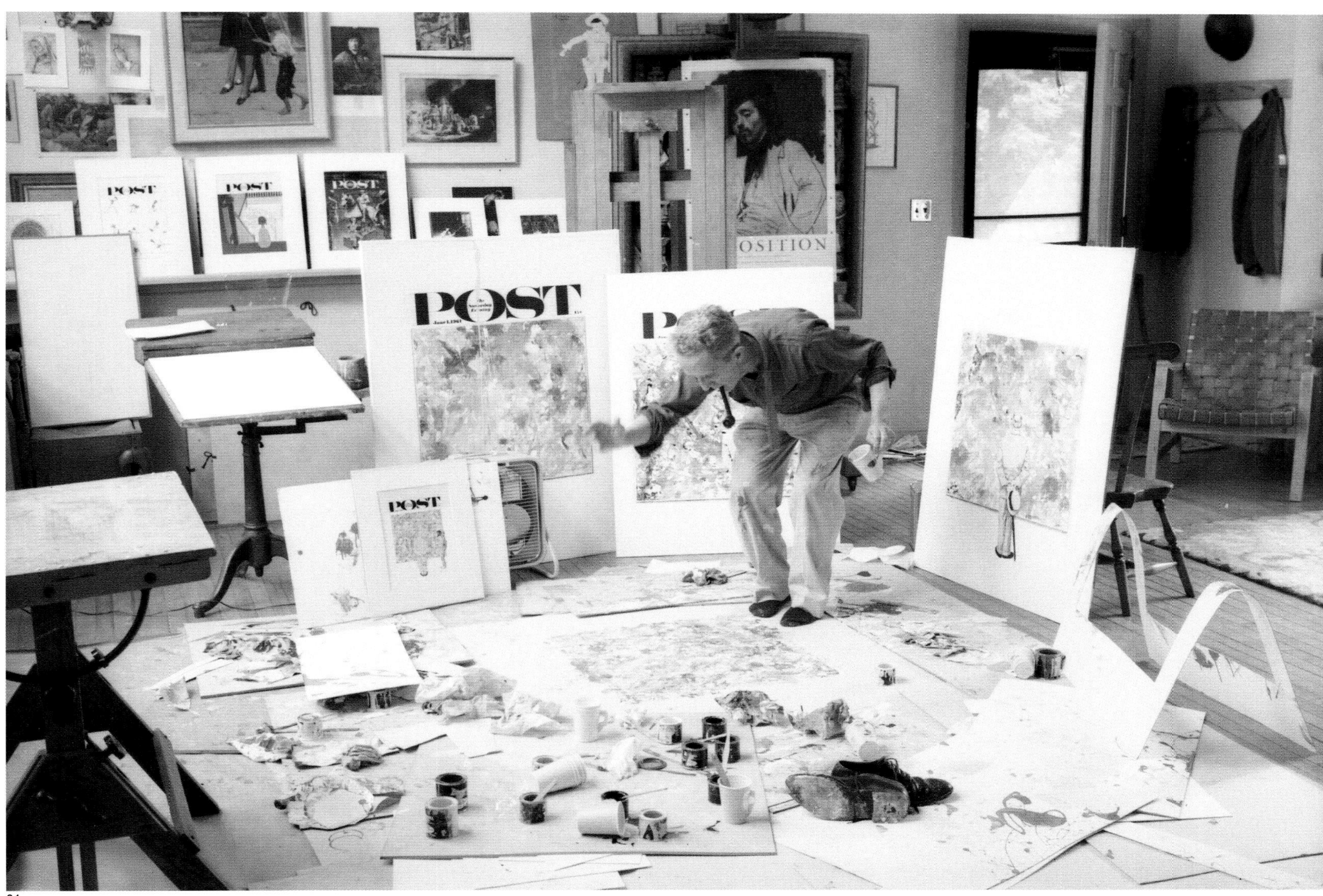

61

gerly embraced their ideas and made plans to include them in the magazine. Rockwell was given permission to halt all other *Post* work while concentrating on the *Freedoms*, but when he returned to Vermont he resumed and finished painting two Willie Gillis covers already in development.

Work on the *Four Freedoms* began in earnest in July when Rockwell posed eight models for *Freedom of Speech*. He revised his picture concept and canvas four times until it evolved into the painting we know. In addition to working on the problems with *Freedom of Speech*, Rockwell spent two months on *Freedom to Worship*, changing the subject from a barbershop scene to the less narrative treatment of a composite of profiles. Numerous requests for illustration work streamed in while Rockwell was at work on the *Four Freedoms*. To protect his time, Rockwell refused most of the requests, using the excuse that only subjects that carried a war message would be considered. By the beginning of 1943, Rockwell completed all four of his *Freedoms* paintings. They took six months instead of the three he had expected, but they were appreciatively received. In his autobiography, Rockwell quoted Hibbs' generous praise of his work. "The result astonished us all. Those four pictures quickly became the best known and most appreciated paintings of that era. They appeared right at a time when the war was going against us on the battle fronts, and the American people needed the inspirational message which they conveyed so forcefully and so beautifully."

62. *Portrait of Ann-Margret*, 1965
Painting for *Stagecoach* Movie Poster
Oil on canvas, 20 x 16 inches
Norman Rockwell Museum Collection, NRM.1973.024

63. *Portrait of Stefanie Powers*, 1965
Painting for *Stagecoach* Movie Poster
Oil on canvas, 20 x 16 inches
Norman Rockwell Museum Collection, NRM.1973.032

64. *Portrait of Bing Crosby*, 1965
Painting for *Stagecoach* Movie Poster
Oil on canvas, 20 x 16 inches
Norman Rockwell Museum Collection, NRM.1973.028

65. *Portrait of Red Buttons*, 1965
Painting for *Stagecoach* Movie Poster
Oil on canvas, 20 x 16 inches
Norman Rockwell Museum Collection, NRM.1973.025

66. *Portrait of Mike Connors*, 1965
Painting for *Stagecoach* Movie Poster
Oil on canvas, 20 x 16 inches
Norman Rockwell Museum Collection, NRM.1973.026

67. *Portrait of Slim Pickens,* 1965
Painting for *Stagecoach* Movie Poster
Oil on canvas, 20 x 16 inches
Norman Rockwell Museum Collection, NRM.1973.031

Norman Rockwell and his wife Molly went to Hollywood, where Rockwell posed and painted oil sketches of three cast members: Slim Pickens, Mike Connors, and Alex Cord. In July, the Rockwells traveled to Denver, and then to Boulder, Colorado, where Rockwell painted the remaining cast: Van Heflin, Ann-Margret, Keenan Wynn, Red Buttons, Bing Crosby, Bob Cummings, and Stefanie Powers. In an area 17 miles southwest of Boulder–the movie's second shooting location–Rockwell directed photos for his stagecoach scene, to be used later in his studio as reference.
Norman Rockwell tried to convince *Stagecoach* producer, Martin Rackin, to use his spontaneous oil sketches of the actors, created on location, for the movie poster. "I just feel they are a lot more exciting than the type of portrait I do from photographs," he said, "After all, *Stagecoach* is an exciting, dramatic thing and I think the more exciting and dramatic type of sketches would be a little more appropriate." But Rackin preferred the slicker, more detailed portraits made from photos, as seen here, and replied to Rockwell that "the many years of *Saturday Evening Post* training that you have given the American public has become your own trap." Rockwell's portraits also appeared with the actors' credits at the end of the movie along with a symbol representing the essence of the character played.

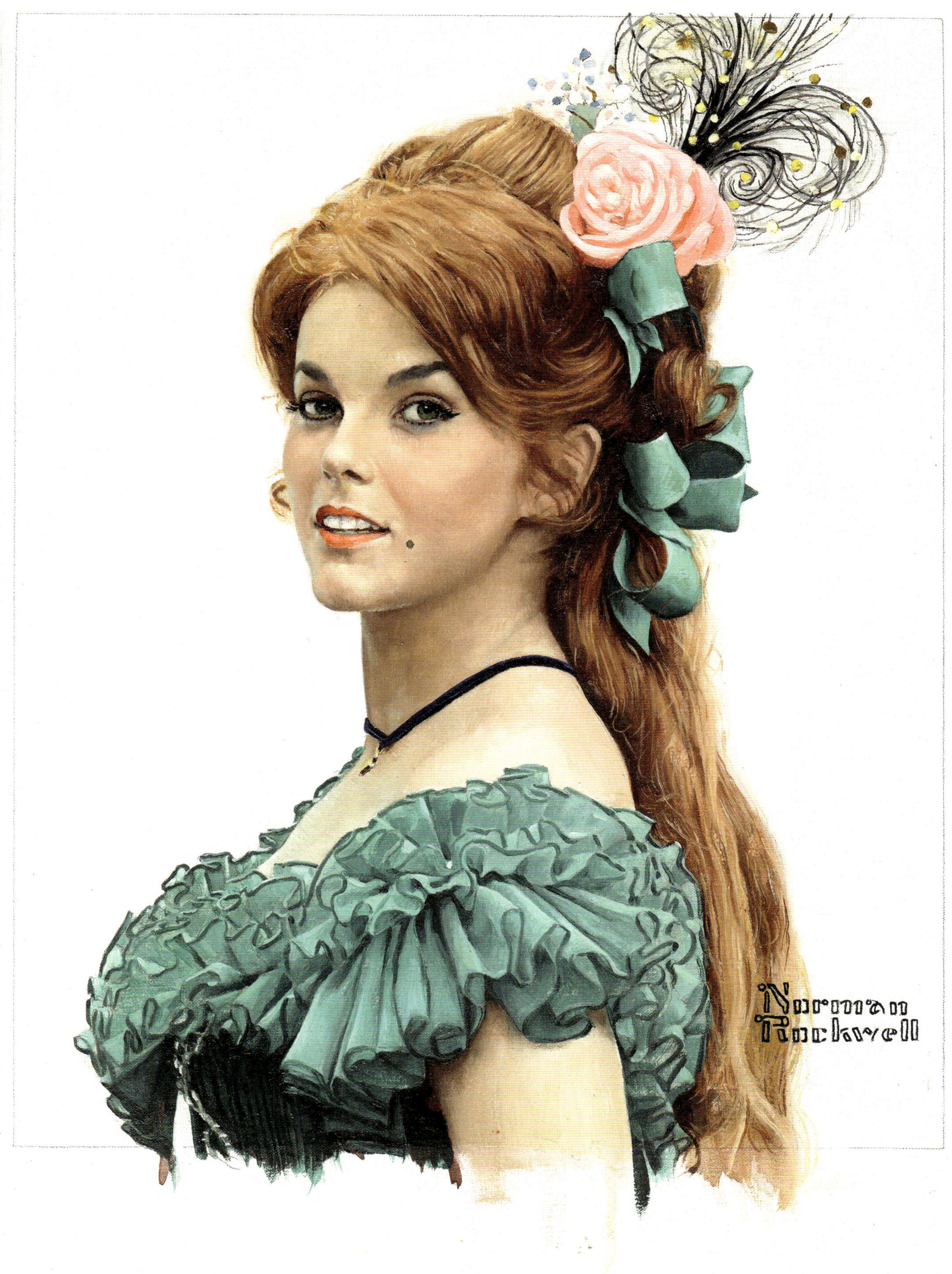

131

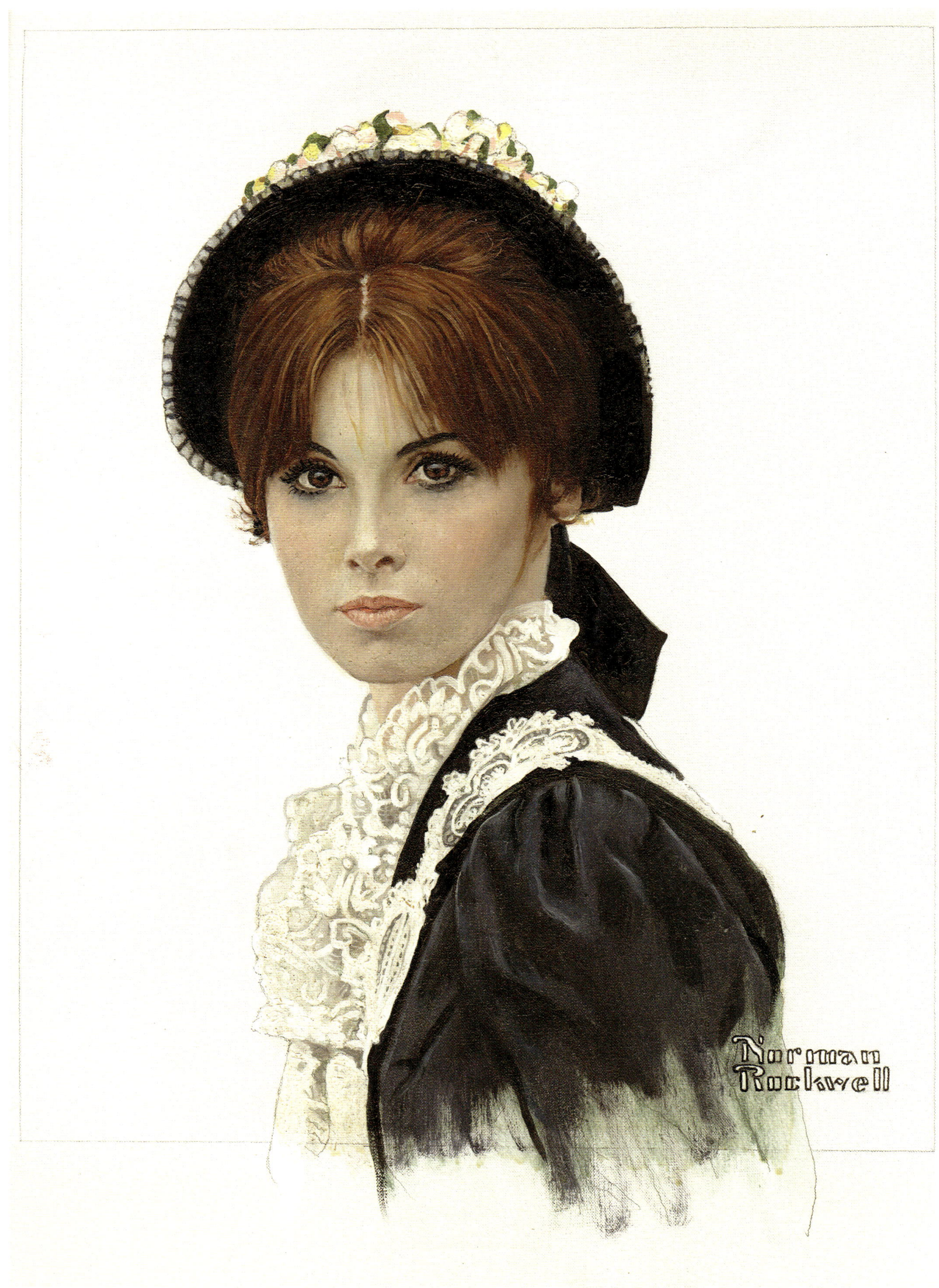

63

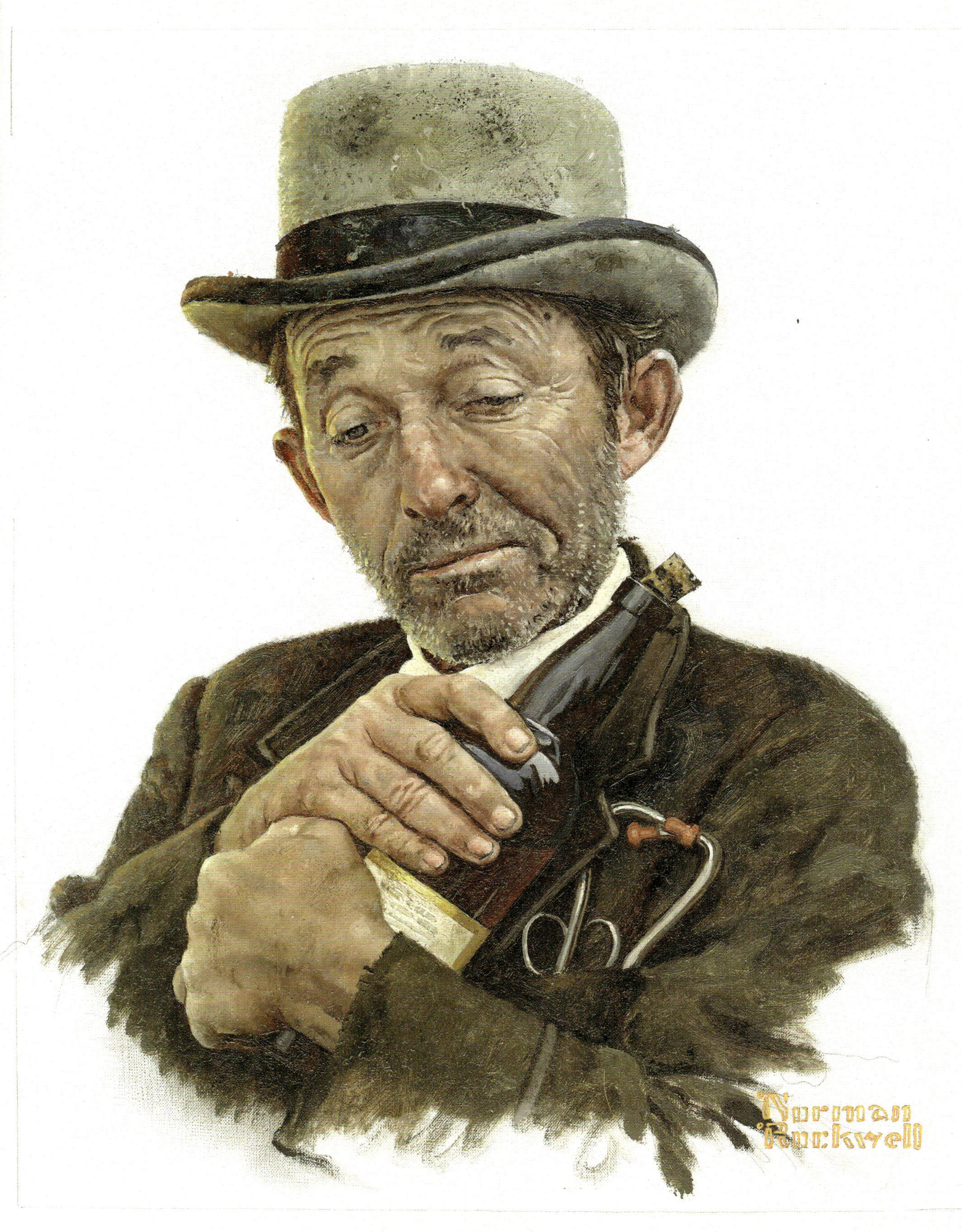

133

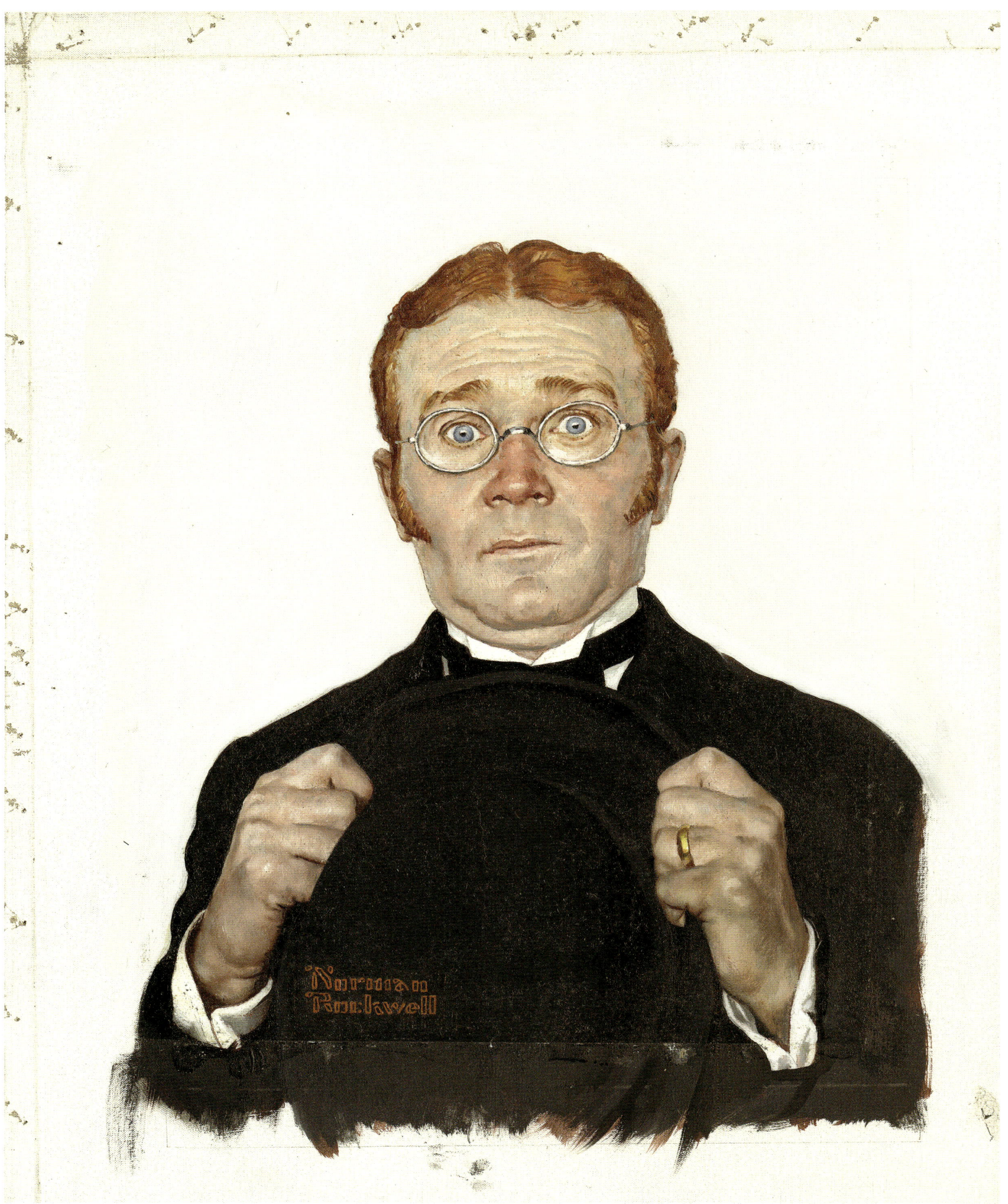
Norman
Rockwell

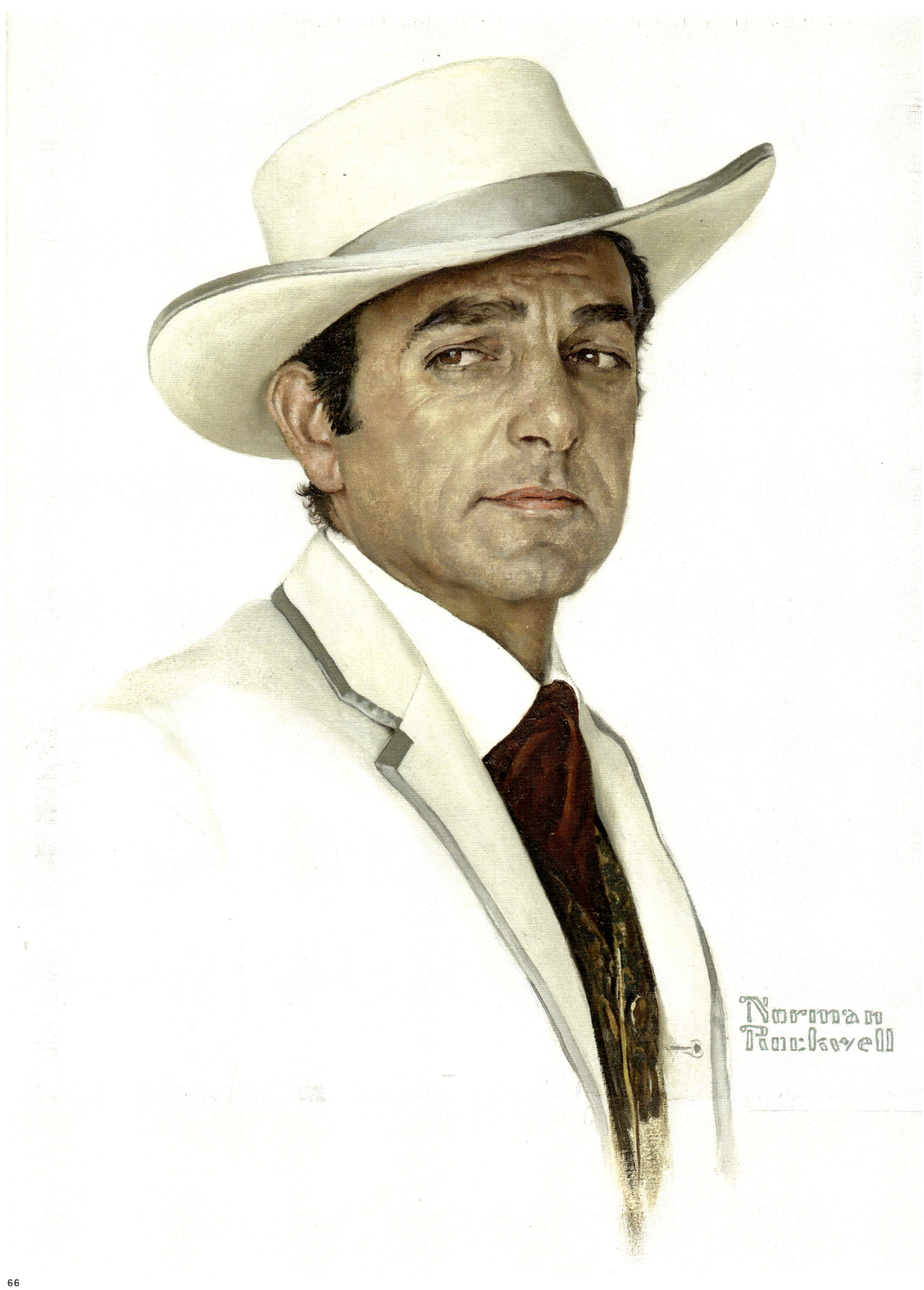

135

136

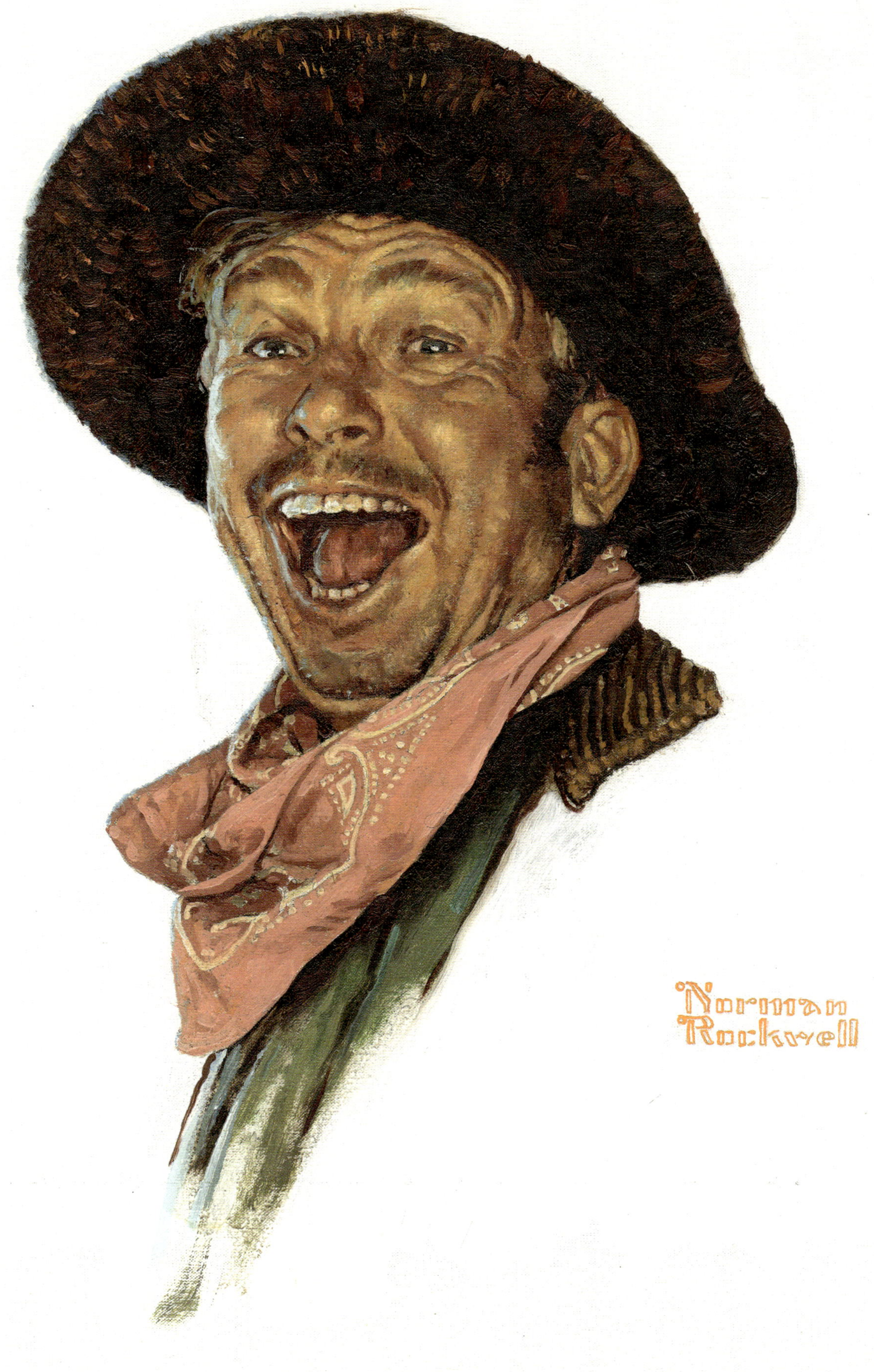

68. *Stagecoach*, 1966
Filmed by 20th Century Fox
Movie Poster Illustrated
by Norman Rockwell, 41 x 27 inches
Norman Rockwell Museum Archival
Collection, RC.2005.4.2

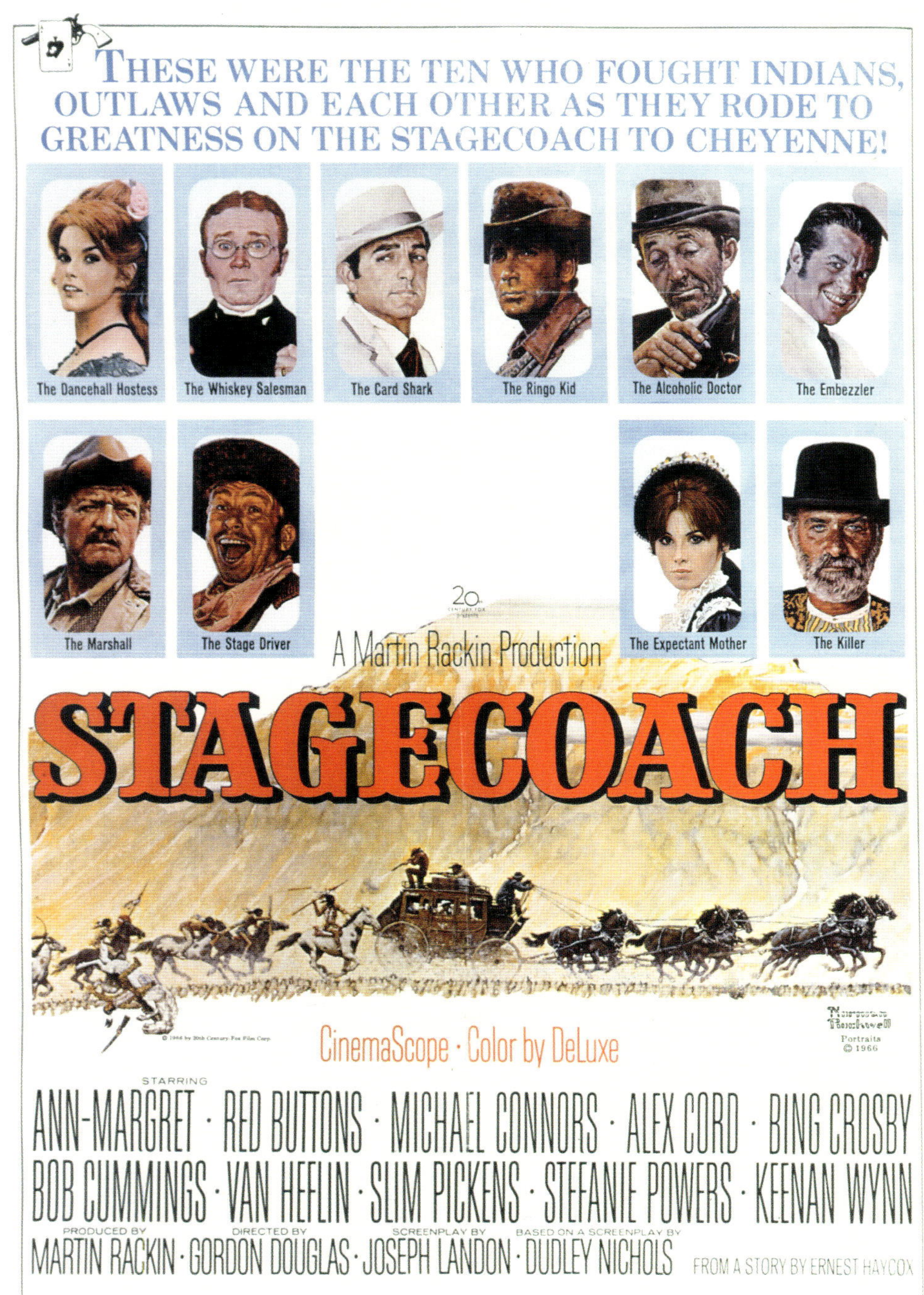

68

69. Location shot on the set of *Stagecoach*, Hollywood, California, 1966
Actors Stefanie Powers (left) and Mike Connors (right) are seated in the stagecoach
Photo by Pete Todd
Norman Rockwell Museum Collections

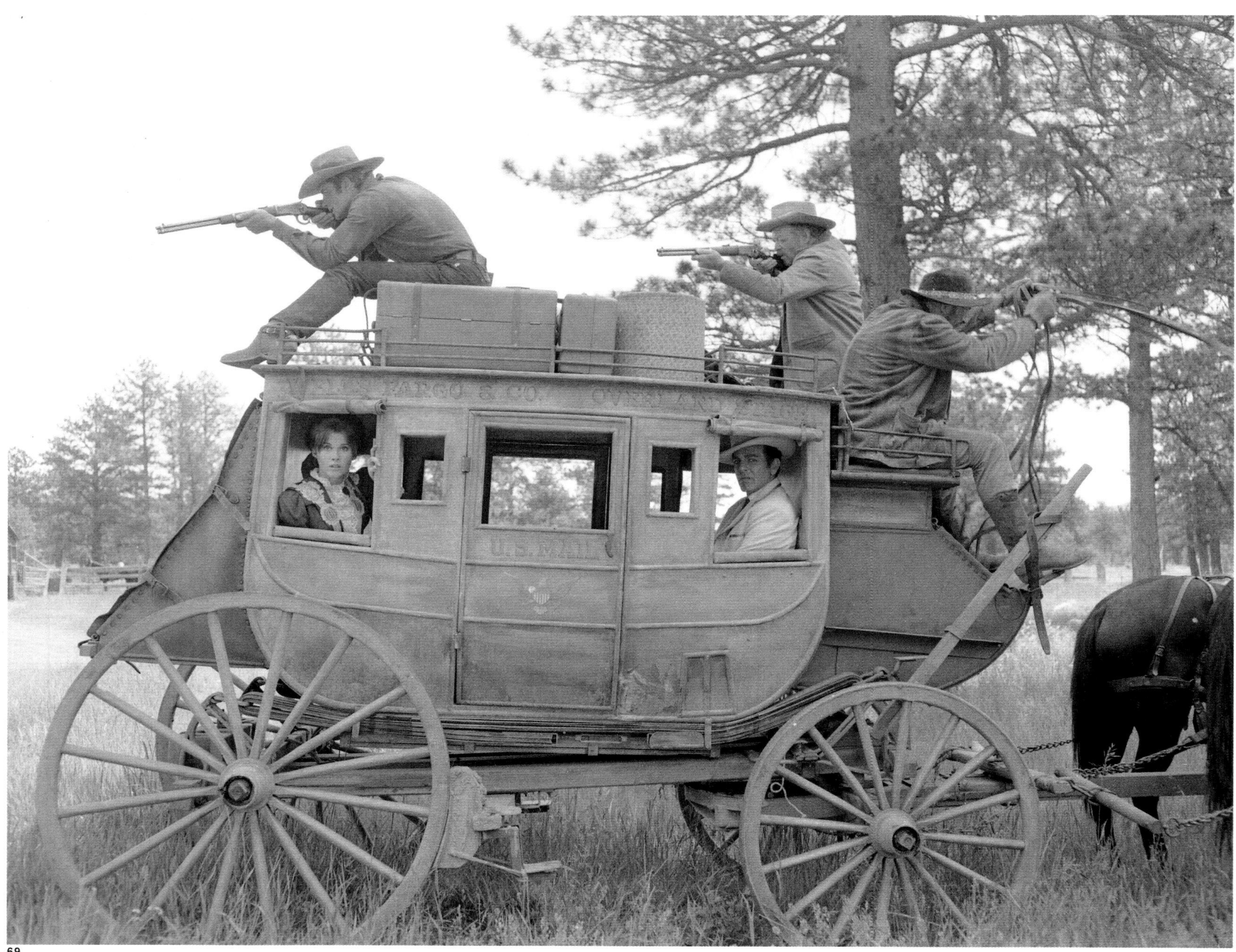

69

70. Actress Ann-Margret with Norman Rockwell on the set of *Stagecoach*, Hollywood, California, 1966
Norman Rockwell is dressed in costume as a gambler named Busted Flush, who appeared briefly in the film
Photographer unknown
Norman Rockwell Museum Collections

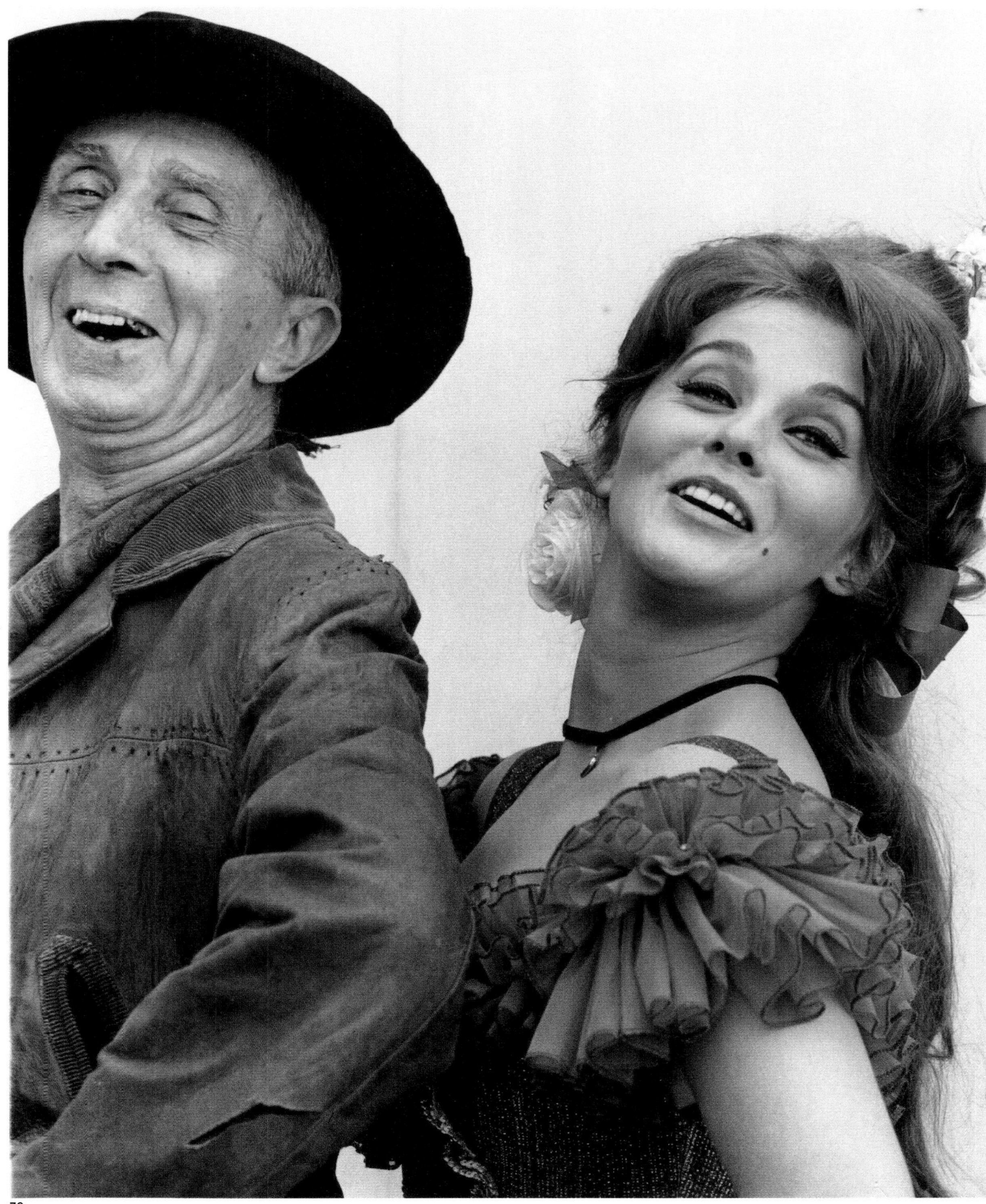
70

71. Norman Rockwell paints actor
Bing Crosby for *Stagecoach* poster,
1966
The artist's wife, Molly Rockwell,
is seen on the terrace of their
Hollywood, California hotel room
Photographer unknown
Norman Rockwell Museum Collections

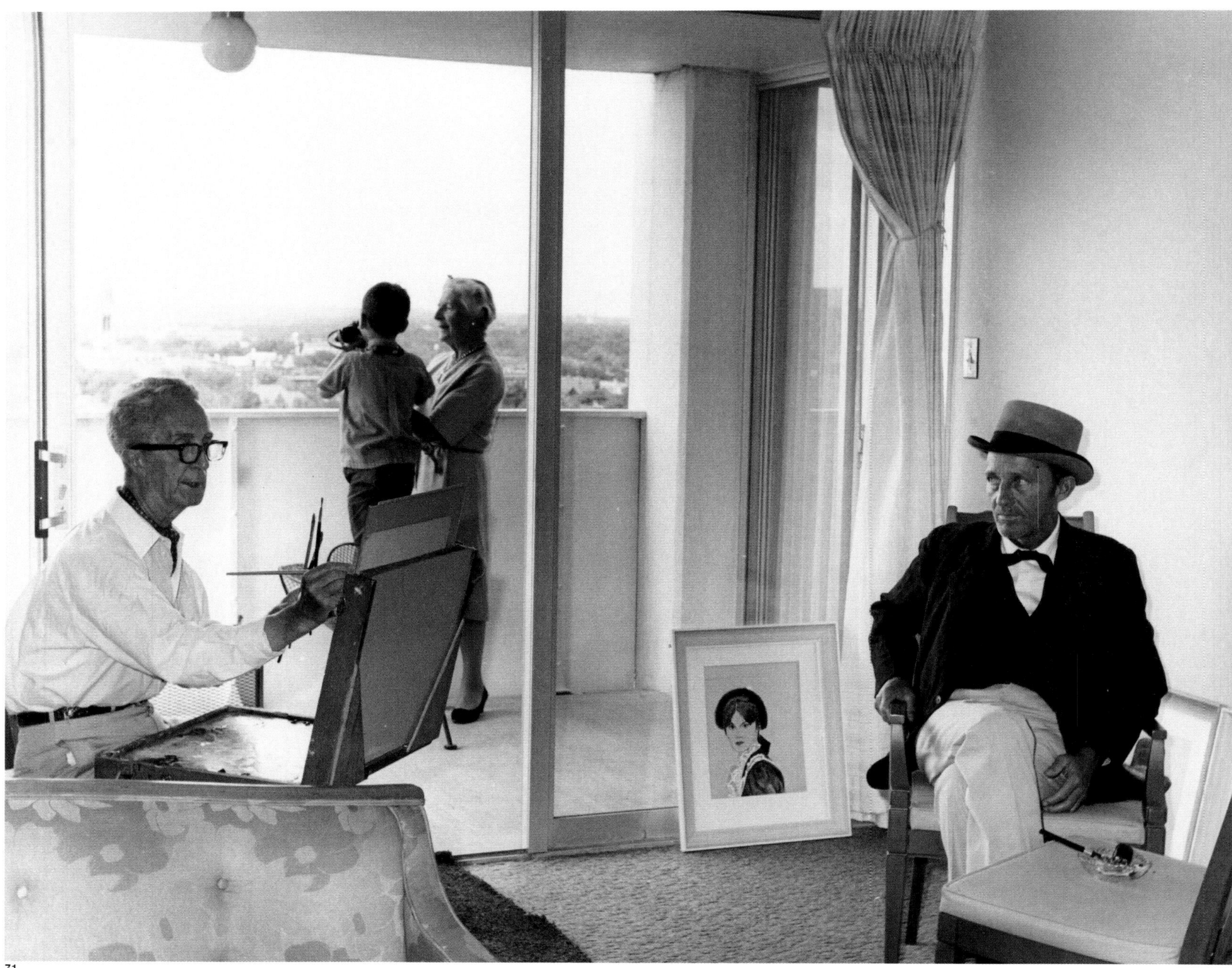

71

72. Movie still featuring Norman Rockwell as down-and-out gambler Busted Flush, engaged in a game of poker with actor Mike Connors, 1966
Photographer unknown
Norman Rockwell Museum Collections

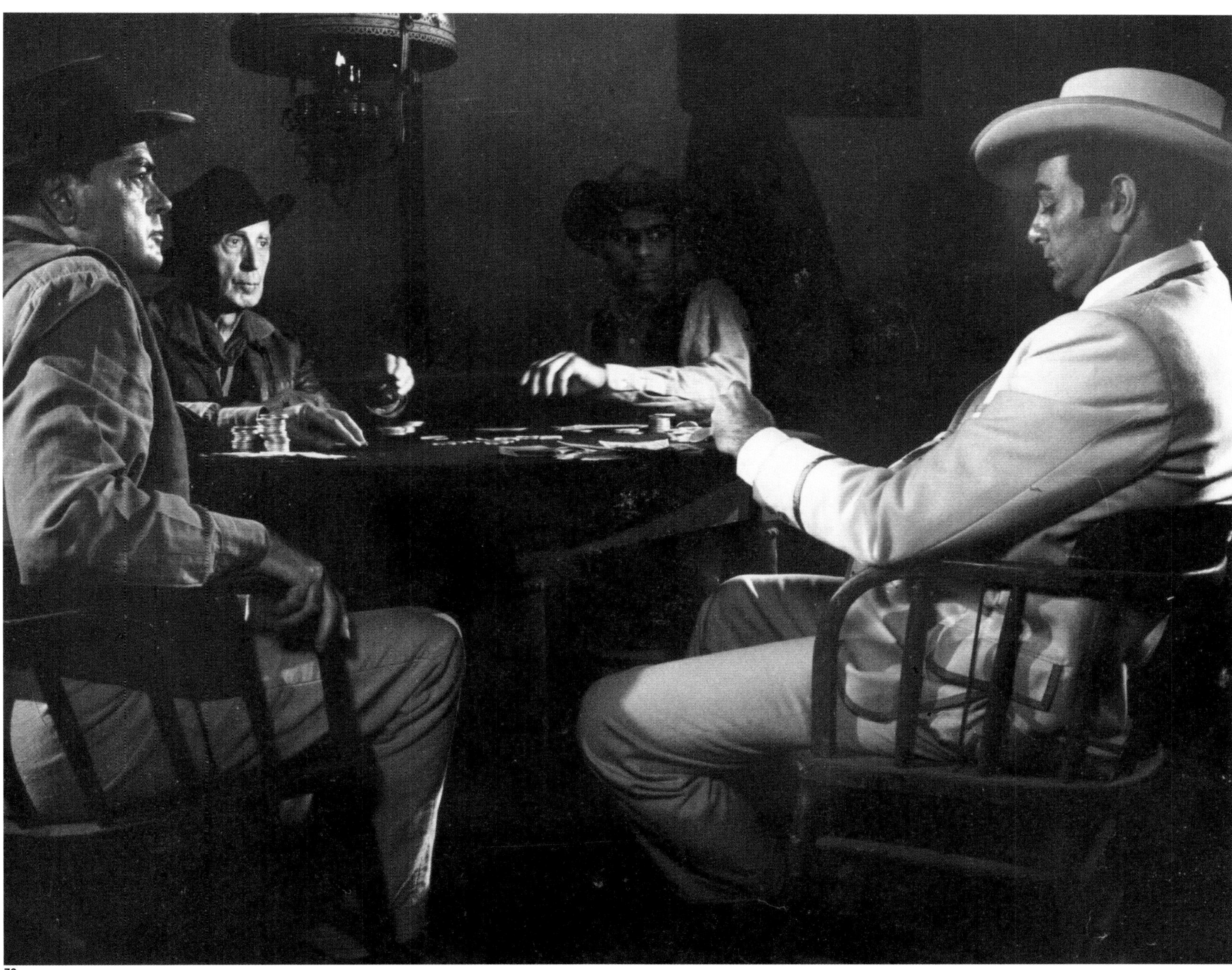

72

73. Movie still featuring actor
Slim Pickens in action as Buck,
the stagecoach driver in *Stagecoach*,
1966
Photographer unknown
Norman Rockwell Museum Collections

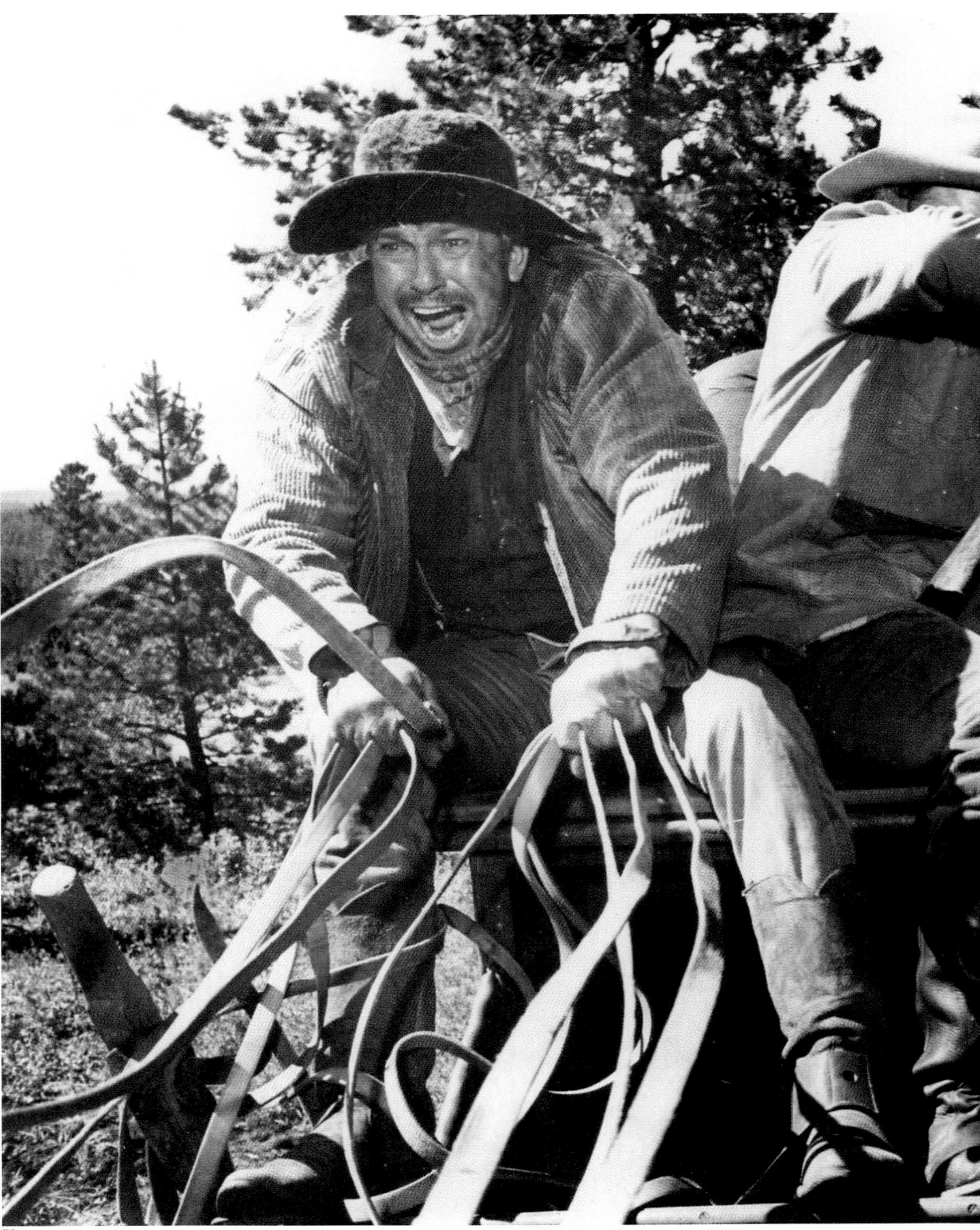

73

74. Norman Rockwell paints *Stagecoach* landscape in his Stockbridge, Massachusetts studio, 1966. Portraits of Ann-Margret and Mike Connors appear on the artist's print ledge
Photo by Louie Lamone
Norman Rockwell Museum Collections

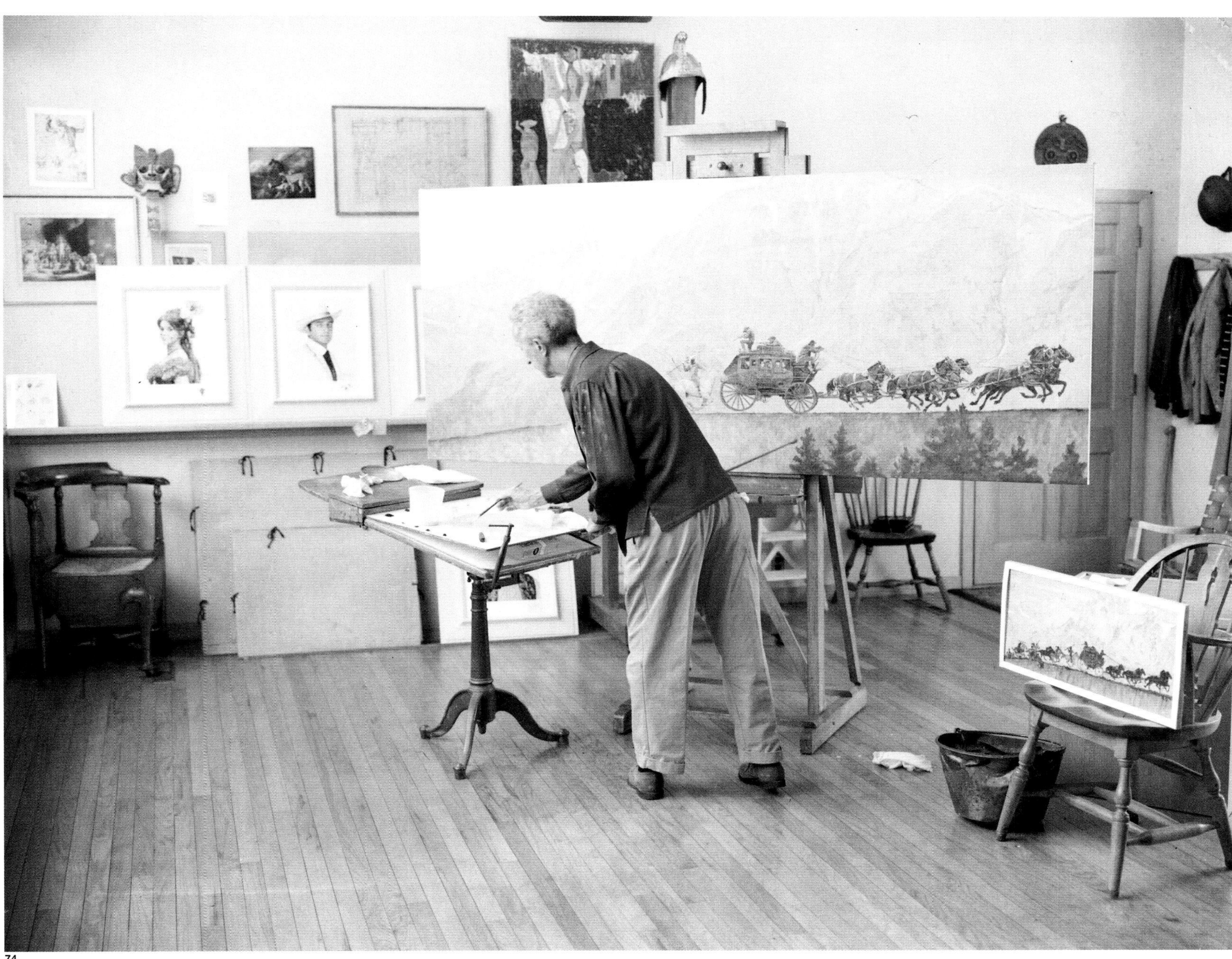

74

In the middle of the night on May 15, 1943, Rockwell's son Thomas awoke to see the studio in flames. He banged on his father's bedroom door yelling, "Pop, the studio's on fire." Because the phone was wired through the studio, the line was already dead, and Rockwell couldn't call for help. Sending his hired man to the nearest neighbor to summon the fire department, Rockwell dashed to the studio to see what he could save. Suddenly, rifle cartridges and shotgun shells, kept in a drawer in the studio, began exploding. Rockwell and his family could only stand and watch while flames consumed the studio and most of the adjacent barn. Lost were a dozen of Rockwell's favorite paintings, a collection of costumes, props, artist materials, reference files, prints, books, antique guns, and his favorite pipes. Rather than rebuild, Rockwell bought a house closer to town and hired a carpenter to build a new studio. That summer, while his new studio was under construction, Rockwell shared Mead Schaeffer's studio. Schaeffer later said Rockwell so convincingly rationalized how the setback had been beneficial by forcing him to reexamine his work that he was nearly convinced to burn down his own studio.

The paintings of his Vermont years, more than any others, comprised the indelible images that forged Rockwell's identity as an American artist; *The Four Freedoms*, *Rosie the Riveter*, *Shuffleton's Barbershop*, *Saying Grace*, and *Breaking Home Ties* created the Rockwell brand. Though Rockwell's *Post* readers had al-

75. *Family Tree*, 1959
Painting for *The Saturday Evening Post* cover, October 24, 1959
Oil on canvas, 46 x 42 inches
Norman Rockwell Art Collection Trust, NRACT.1973.7

In 1959, Rockwell began telling his life story to his son Tom Rockwell, who was ghostwriting his autobiography, *Norman Rockwell, My Adventures as an Illustrator*. Recording his family history may have inspired Rockwell to trace the lineage of an American family in a painting, as the final chapter is devoted to a day-by-day account of how *Family Tree* was created. The basic structure for the painting, a tree, is taken from a twelfth-century Dutch family tree, a photo of which was found for Rockwell by the reference librarian at the Berkshire Athenaeum. To simulate the appearance of aged parchment, Rockwell stained the background of his painting with brown paint and sketched in trompe l'oeil cracks. For even greater authenticity he rubbed dirt, gravel, and twigs into it, shook it off, then rubbed in more. He then sandpapered the surface, which he said gave it a "beautiful texture." The consistency of family features through the generations is assured by Rockwell's use of the same model for either the man or the woman in each couple on the tree. The lineage begins with a pirate and a Spanish princess taken by the pirate from a sinking Spanish galleon. The galleon is based on a painting by Rockwell's favorite illustrator of historical subjects, Howard Pyle, whose initials are on the treasure chest. Rockwell loved the idea of having the "all-American" boy descend from a pirate and his stolen Spanish princess, though it troubled his friend and therapist Erik Erikson. "Do you think you ought to start off the family with him, a cutthroat, a barbarian?" Erikson asked. Rockwell experimented with changing the pirate to a Puritan, then a buccaneer, but finally returned to the original. "Everybody," he said, "had a horse thief or two in his family."

Odds & Ends
Initial work for the painting began on April 27, 1959. It was completed four months later on August 18. Seven days later, Rockwell's wife Mary died.

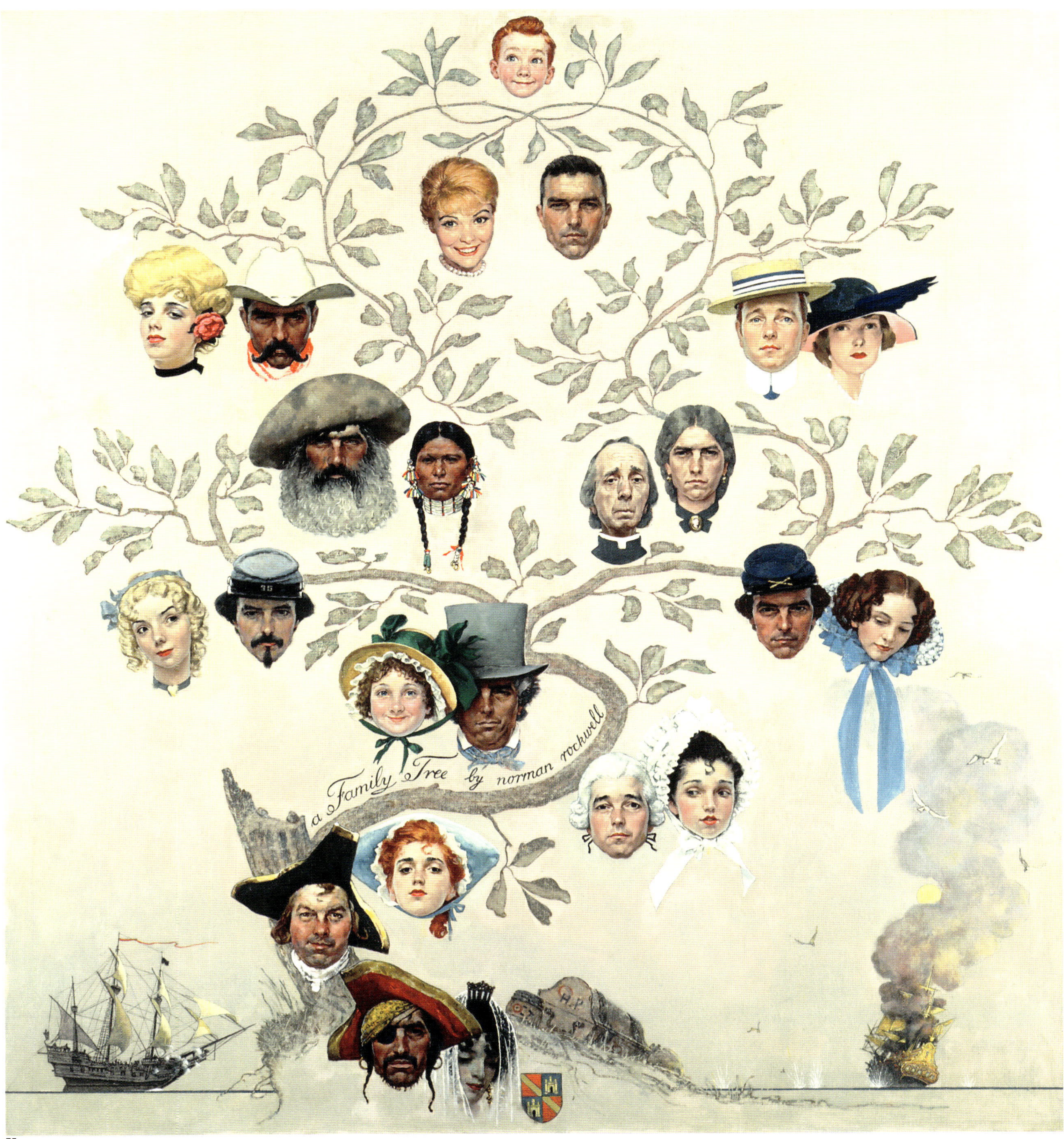
a Family Tree by norman rockwell

ways enjoyed the antics and exploits of his child models, they now were asked to look at Rockwell's work in a new way. Childhood in America and Rockwell's reflection of it were altering. On the edge of a changing world, his post-war children were about to meet new challenges. Developments after World War II—including the population swell of the baby boom, the new role and self-image of women forged by their recently acquired skills and opportunities, and, most important, the proliferation of nuclear weapons—forced us to see our world, and ourselves, in a different light. Despite an overt sense of prosperity, there was a new unease; we had exchanged our parents' struggles during the Great Depression and in a real war with the pervasive fear and threat of nuclear war. As a perennial idealist, Rockwell didn't include the worries of the new generation in his work, but he did look more seriously at the subject of youth, depicting adolescents as more complex, dimensional people. Children were seen less at play and more at learning how to grow up, ultimately to face the problems of a modern world and deal with issues that were previously, in Rockwell's words, "swept under the rug."

Rockwell's association with the *Post* lasted forty-seven years, and though painting covers was what he most liked to do, working for the *Post* had its downside. Ironically, his success was usually the cause of friction with the *Post*, as they often put pressure on him for additional work. In January 1939, the *Post* told Rockwell they were increasing his per-cover price in exchange for being able to

76. *Lincoln for the Defense*, 1961
Painting for *The Saturday Evening Post* story "Lincoln for the Defense" by Elisa Bialk, February 10, 1962
Oil on canvas, 49.75 x 17.5 inches
Norman Rockwell Art Collection Trust, NRACT.1973.77

No other statesman appears more in Rockwell's work than Abraham Lincoln, who is included in eight of Rockwell's paintings between 1927 and 1964. Rockwell enjoyed painting Lincoln, not only as an affirmation of his private views but also because of the complexity of painting Lincoln's face. In later years, Rockwell publicly stated that he thought Lincoln was the greatest American.
In 1959, discussing the use of photography in preparing an illustration, he told students of the Famous Artists Schools, "If you want to exalt a subject, you shoot up at him. To humiliate him, shoot down."
Two years later, Rockwell welcomed the opportunity to paint Lincoln for Elisa Bialk's story, *Lincoln for the Defense*, about the trial of accused murderer William "Duff" Armstrong. The prosecution's case was based on a witness testifying he saw Armstrong commit the murder between ten and eleven at night. When Lincoln asked the witness how he could see him so clearly at that hour, the witness said it was a bright moonlit night. Lincoln won the case using an almanac to prove there was no moonlight on the night of the murder.
The groundwork for the painting—posing and photographing models and props—was done in Hollywood shortly after Rockwell's marriage to Molly Punderson on October 10, 1961. After a brief stay at New York's Plaza Hotel, the honeymooners traveled to Hollywood, where Rockwell's addiction to work compelled him to begin his assignment.
Taking advantage of Hollywood's abundance of actors, he hired four men to pose as Lincoln, two for Armstrong, and a middle-aged couple as onlookers (later omitted from the painting). Returning to his studio, he referenced thirty different magazine photos of Lincoln for the head and for period clothing. Then he proceeded with his painting.

Odds & Ends
The impressionistic brushwork and combining of different colors to achieve the nuances of shading in the whites of Lincoln's clothing remind us that this painting would be reduced to a much smaller size for a reproduction, in which the separate colors and chunky brushstrokes would blend.

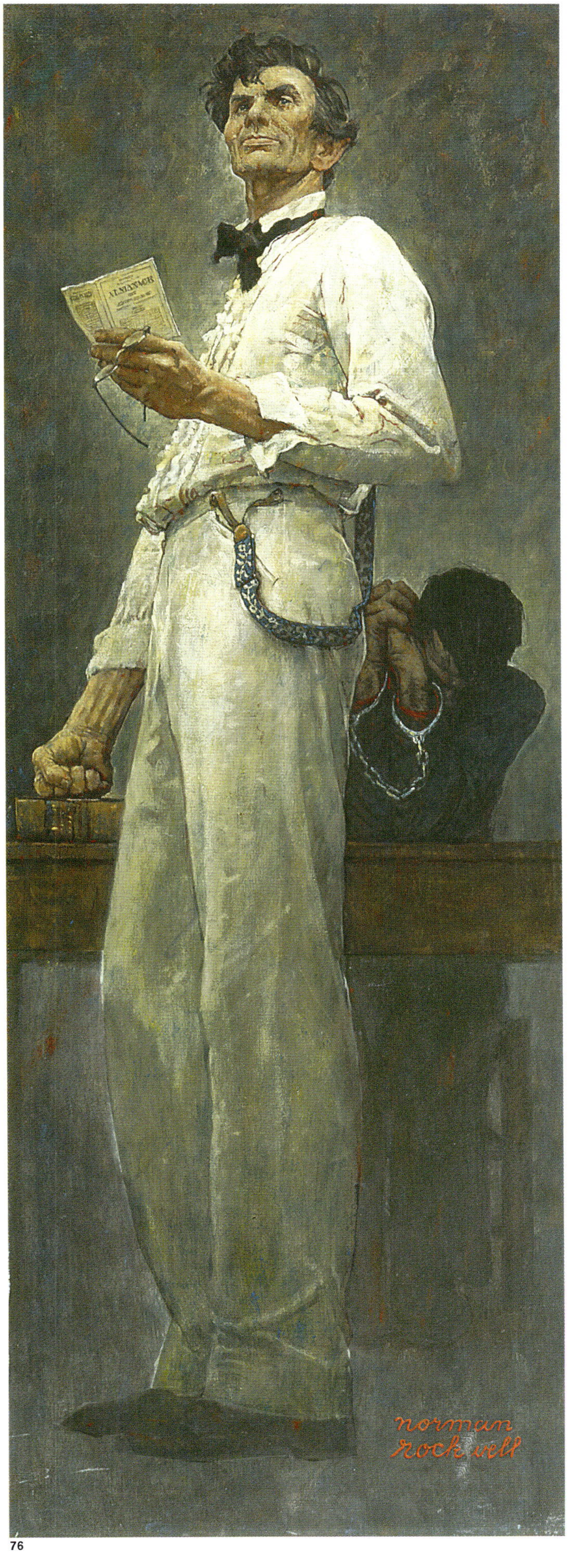

76

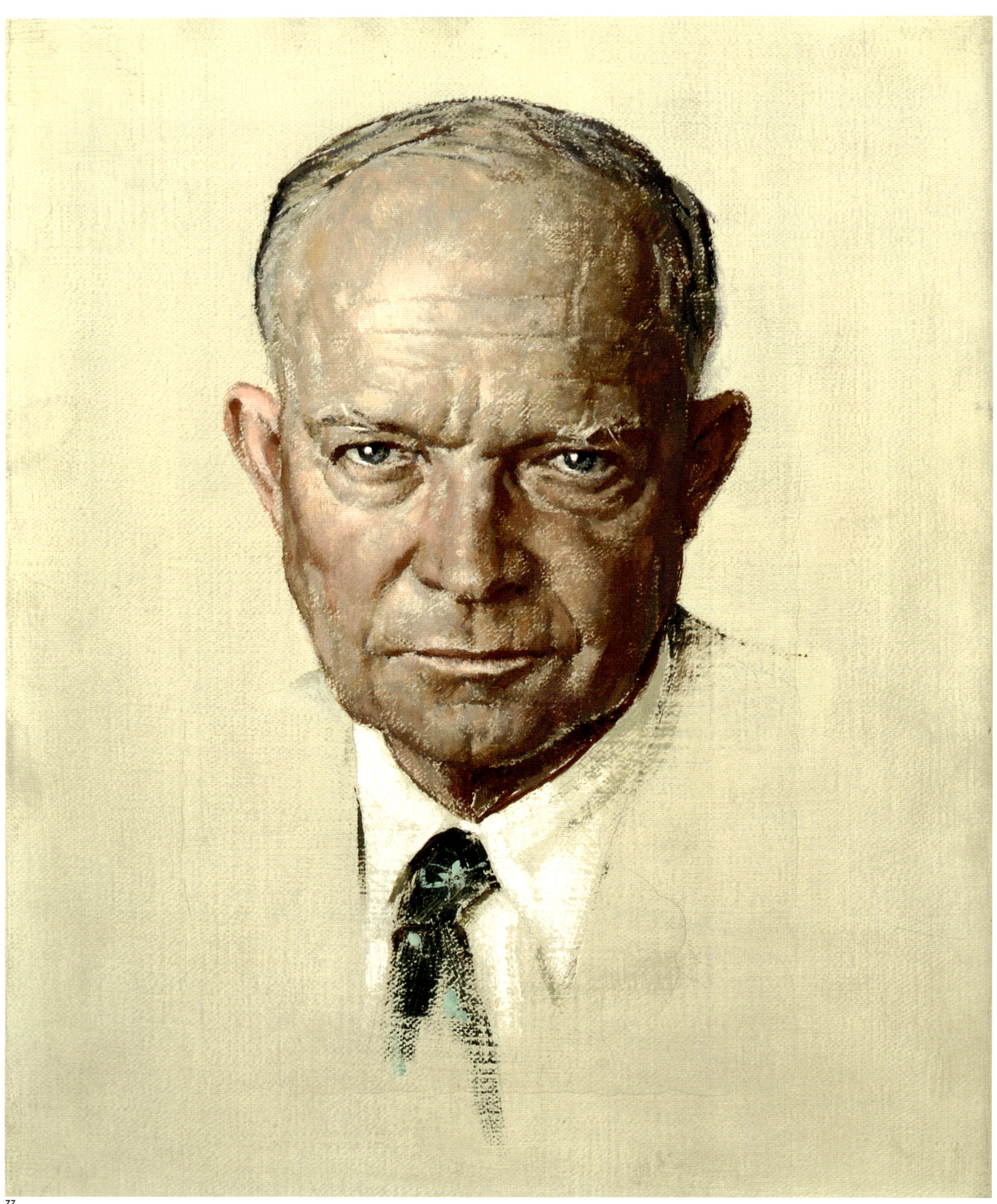

make more demands on his time. Wanting it to appear they had his interest at heart more than theirs, they told Rockwell the arrangement was intended to give him more time for his *Post* cover work (implying he wouldn't need work from others). But the greatest source of anguish to Rockwell was the altering of his paintings by the editorial staff. He accepted the occasional addition of a staff-artist signature, made because his was too close to the bottom of his canvas where it might impinge on the cover's text. But in 1937, a colored background was painted into one of his covers. And in the summer of 1949 while Rockwell was in California, three consecutive *Post* covers were altered.

In the cover *Umpires*, of April 23, 1949, the color of the visiting team's uniforms was changed, a portion each of sky and grass was added, part of a sign was relettered, and scoreboard letters were redefined. In *Roadblock*, his next cover, a replica signature was in-painted to replace Rockwell's when several inches of painting were (photographically) cropped off the bottom. And finally, his cover of September 24, 1949, *Before the Date*, was partly repainted at the direction of art editor Ken Stuart, who said readers would not be able to tell that the man and woman were getting ready for their date in separate rooms. In reply to a letter in which Stuart rationalized his alterations, Rockwell wrote, "Whether or not these things are necessary is not the question with me. It's the feeling I suffered under when Mr. Stout was there—that try as I might it was not good enough. If this is so

77. *Portrait of Dwight D. Eisenhower*, 1952
Painting for *The Saturday Evening Post* story illustration, October 11, 1952
Oil on canvas, 11 x 8 inches
Collection of the Norman Rockwell Museum, NRM.1986.2

The first use of a Norman Rockwell portrait on the cover of *The Saturday Evening Post* came in 1952 when Rockwell painted General Dwight D. Eisenhower as the Republican candidate for the presidency. Not a new phenomenon for the *Post*, which often published portraits on its covers, it was new for Rockwell, who thought of himself not as a portraitist but as a storyteller. In addition to the cover portrait, the *Post* published Rockwell's account of his session with Eisenhower, titled *The Day I Painted Ike*, complete with five additional portraits of Eisenhower (including the one seen here) and a portrait of his wife, Mamie. The *Post* revealed its Republican bias by running an Eisenhower cover but not one of Adlai Stevenson, the Democratic candidate. (In 1956, however, they ran a Rockwell portrait of Stevenson on the October 6 cover and a Rockwell portrait of Eisenhower on the October 13 cover.) Publishing the Rockwell-authored essay in the 1952 issue would also influence public opinion and garner support for the Republican Party's candidate.
When Rockwell arrived in Denver for the modeling session, he said Eisenhower's "eyes were far away." He thought the General might be thinking about the fishing trip he was scheduled to make after the session. In an attempt to get a smiling Eisenhower, Rockwell threw out a few remarks. The one that most changed Eisenhower's expression was "How are those grandchildren, General–pretty nice, eh?" It was the smile after this remark that Rockwell captured for the cover. The two men continued talking, first about painting–Eisenhower dabbled in oils–then about the imminent fishing trip. The conversation turned to the presidential campaign. According to Rockwell, Eisenhower remarked that even though a leader might need advisors, there was no need for a leader to give up his freedom of speech, and then said, "I'd rather be defeated than not say in my campaign exactly what I believe." The *Post* published the portrait seen here with the caption: "The campaign? Instantly, he was deeply serious. No punch-pulling for him! He'd rather lose the election than not tell the people just what he thinks." Later, Rockwell received a letter from *Post* reader John Maass of Philadelphia pointing out that the quotation was virtually the same as one from Stevenson's July 26 nomination acceptance speech: "Better we lose the election than mislead the people, and better we lose than misgovern the people." Maass continued, "You are famous for your warmth and sincere liking for people, but this election is a terribly serious matter and you should not let yourself be taken in by a nice smile. Even as an Eisenhower worshiper [Rockwell had ended his essay by saying "I'm an Eisenhower worshiper"] you ought to know that the General campaigns entirely by reading off ghostwritten speeches." The *Post* published four letters from readers about the Eisenhower cover, but not the one from Maass.

I had better bow out. I have plenty and more than enough to do. If I could just feel that you people believe in me, and within the necessary limits give me a free hand, I could paint some real pictures. But the worry and doubt and the thought of what will happen to my picture before it is reproduced kills my drive."

Early in 1951, Rockwell's wife Mary began treatment for depression at the Austen Riggs Center in Stockbridge, Massachusetts. As a regular patient, Mary made the tiring commute from Vermont frequently. A car accident on Halloween night, 1952, in Pownal, Vermont, must have shaken her confidence about the long drive; her car was badly damaged and a child in the car she hit was cut and bruised. In early 1953, Mary began living at the Homestead boardinghouse on Sergeant Street around the corner from the Riggs Center. In the summer of 1953, Rockwell's mother, who was cared for in a convalescent home in Warwick, Rhode Island, died at the age of 87. A few months later, after almost a year of living apart, Rockwell joined Mary at the boardinghouse in Stockbridge and rented studio space in town. Rockwell had intended to stay in Vermont—he had purchased burial spaces in the Arlington cemetery—but Mary's illness necessitated a permanent move to Stockbridge, where she could continue to receive treatment. Rockwell's closest friends had already left Vermont—Mead Schaeffer had moved to New York in 1950 and Jack Atherton had died suddenly of a heart attack in 1952.

78. *Portrait of John F. Kennedy*, 1960
Painting for *The Saturday Evening Post* cover, October 29, 1960
Oil on canvas, 16 x 12 inches
Norman Rockwell Museum Collection, NRM.1978.01

In 1960, Norman Rockwell was commissioned by *The Saturday Evening Post* to paint portraits of Presidential candidates Senator John F. Kennedy and Vice President Richard M. Nixon. Kennedy appeared on the October 29 cover and Nixon on the November 5 cover. To prepare for the painting of Kennedy, Rockwell arranged to pose and photograph Kennedy at his home in Hyannis Port, Massachusetts. When Rockwell arrived, Kennedy, in his pajamas, leaned out of an upstairs window and told Rockwell to go right in, and that he'd be down in a minute. While Kennedy ate his breakfast, Rockwell chose a room for the session. Rockwell suggested it would be best to use a dignified pose that didn't emphasize Kennedy's youth (he was just forty-three); Kennedy agreed. After photos were taken, the two men walked to the breakwater to see Kennedy's sailboat. Now more relaxed, and feeling he had been a little stiff during the photo session, Kennedy suggested they return to the house for a second shoot. Rockwell was pleased with the result: "His expression was just what I wanted–serious with a certain dignity, but relaxed and pleasant, not hard." Rockwell's modeling session with Nixon was even briefer, squeezing the photo shoot into a forty-five-minute Senate recess.

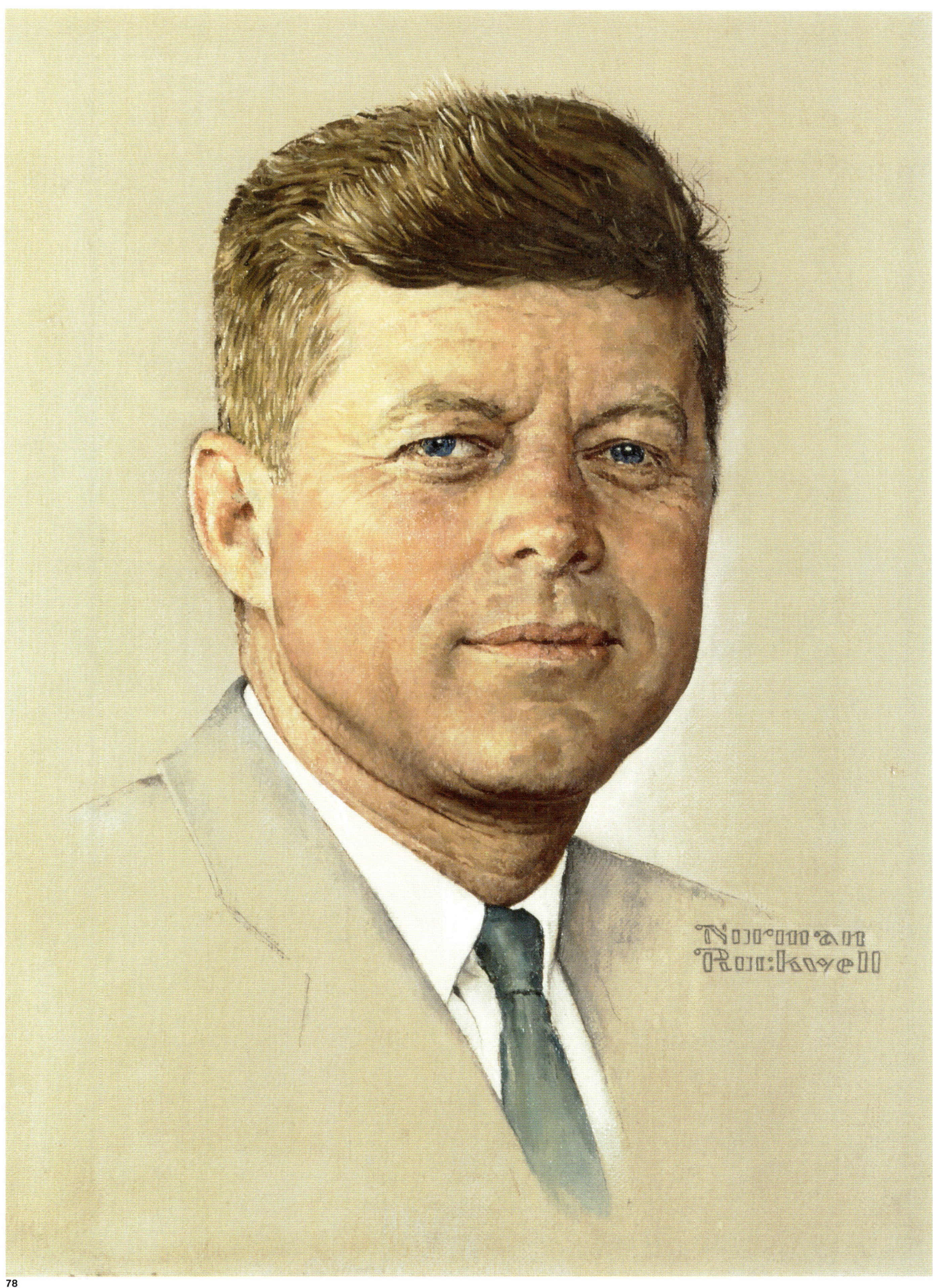

151

79. The Rockwell's South Street home
in Stockbridge, 1960
Photograph by Bill Scovill
Norman Rockwell Museum Collections

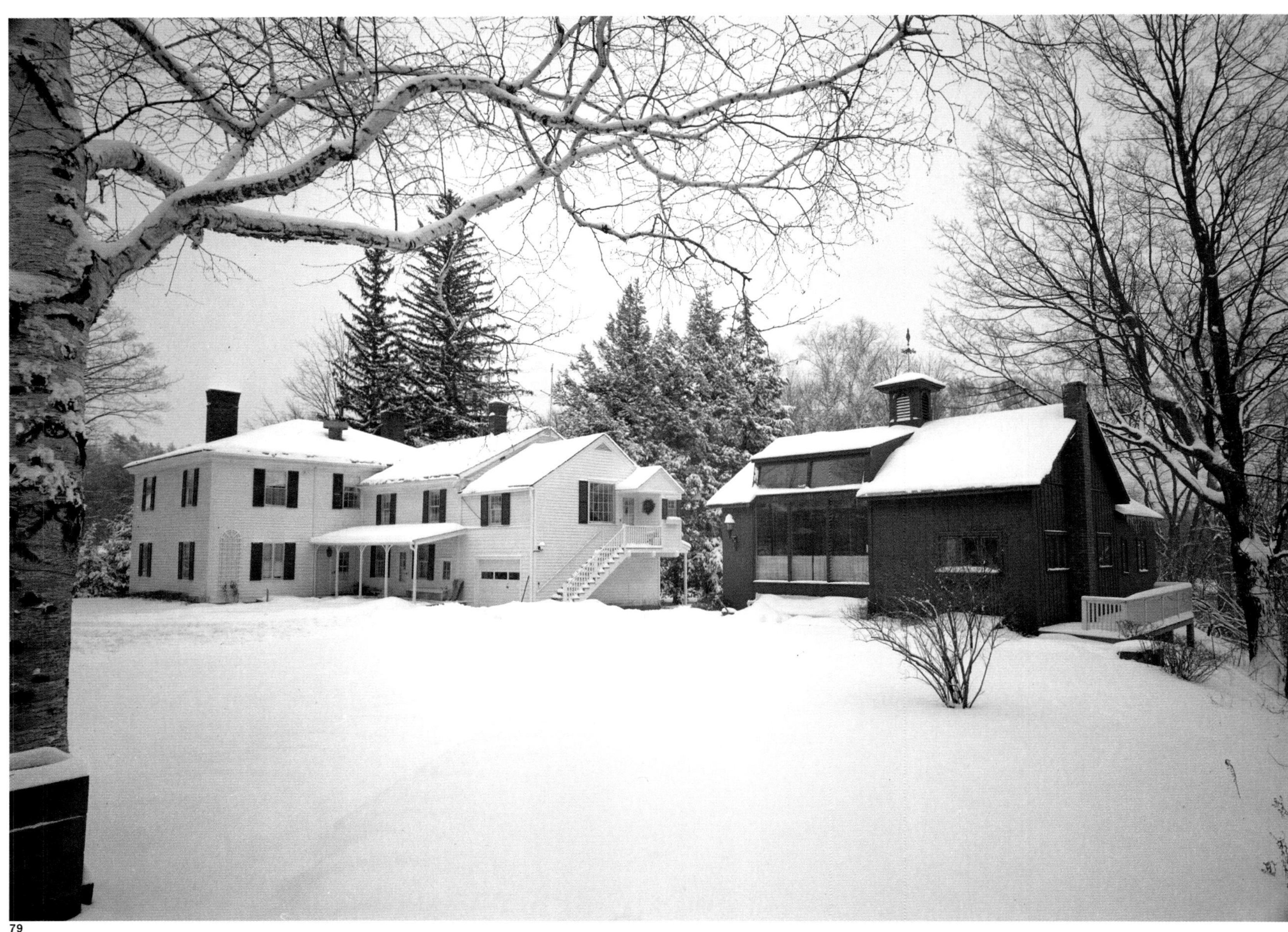

79

In 1953, Norman Rockwell and wife Mary relocated from Arlington, Vermont, to Stockbridge, Massachusetts. The small town of 2,100 people provided new faces and new inspirations for such pictures as *Family Tree*, which traced the lineage of the "all-American boy" from a sixteenth-century pirate and his Spanish princess captured on the Caribbean Sea. In progress were several of his most memorable paintings—*Girl at the Mirror*, *Breaking Home Ties*, and *Choir Boy*—and, as always, deadlines loomed. He continued to hire neighbors to pose for everyday scenes, choosing a professional model only when he needed a woman to pose naked for his 1955 *Mermaid* cover.

In January 1954, Rockwell finished painting his *Post* cover of a choirboy. Appropriate for the Easter season, it was also an echo of his many years as a choirboy in New York City and Mamaroneck. Although Rockwell no longer attended church ("If I don't go to church now I still have a pretty good average," he once said), it was still a part of his visual iconography. Rockwell had summoned *Choir Boy* from his past, but his next cover painting was influenced by more timely events. In 1952, all three Rockwell sons were away from home. Jarvis was in the Air Force stationed in Korea, Thomas had started Bard College, and Peter was attending prep school in Putney, Vermont. The loss of their companionship and possibly Mary's, who was suffering from depression, inspired one of Rockwell's most poignant paintings. Continuing an artistic tradition of communicating the rite of passage that is a child leaving home, Rockwell created *Breaking Home Ties*. Annual commitments of artwork for Hallmark, Brown & Bigelow, and Boy Scouts of America were a concern for the busy artist. Four images for Hallmark, due in the fall of 1953, went undone. Rockwell pleaded for an extension saying he had "gotten into an unbelievable jam." Worried that his relationship with Hallmark might be in jeopardy, he asked his secretary to write a second letter admitting that Rockwell was having "personal problems" and asking for confirmation that Rockwell was still in their good graces. It was March 1954 before Rockwell shipped off his four watercolor paintings for Hallmark's next Christmas series, and they were among his best. Each featured a Santa Claus, always the favorite of card buyers.

Finding the need for more space in his Main Street studio, Rockwell rented the room next door, and with permission, removed the dividing wall between the two and enlarged its north window. To announce Rockwell's Stockbridge move to their readers, the *Saturday Evening Post* published photos of Rockwell looking out from the window of his new studio. In March, Norman and Mary purchased a house adjacent to a cemetery on West Main Street. In addition to *Breaking Home Ties*, Rockwell spent his spring and summer on a Rock of Ages painting, a new series of *Four Seasons* sketches for the Brown & Bigelow calendar company, a painting of a doctor and boy for Upjohn Pharmaceuticals, and a Massachusetts Mutual Life Insurance picture of a family at a circus. Then, according to Rockwell biographer Laura Claridge, Rockwell was admitted to Pittsfield's St. Luke's Hospital in October for "a rest." Only one more *Post* cover was produced that year in the Main Street studio: another autobiographical work, called *Art Critic* (1955), it was inspired by Rockwell's experiences as an art student and the experiences of his son, Jarvis, then enrolled at the School of the Museum of

154

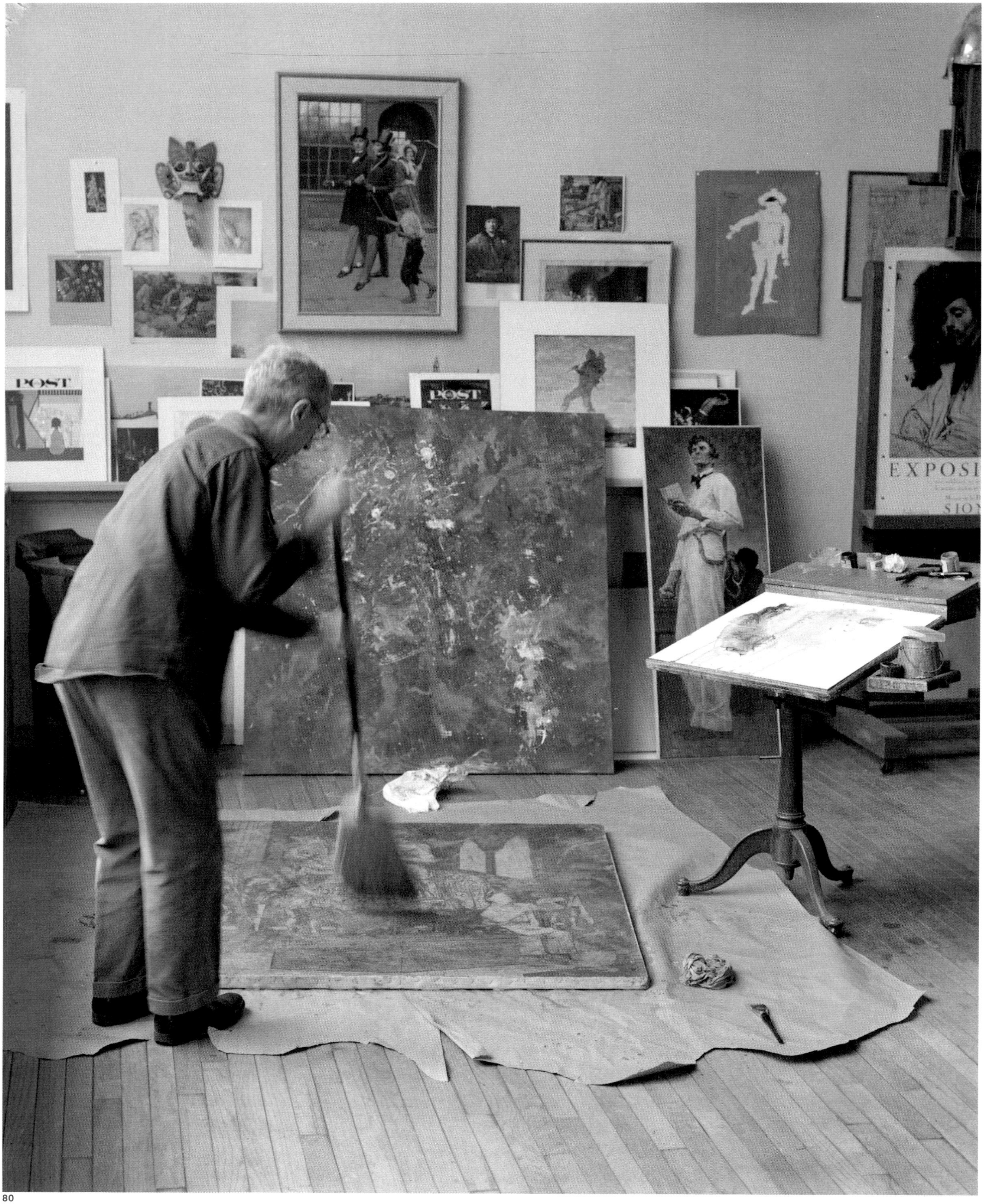

80. Norman Rockwell "sweeping"
Lunch Break with a Knight, 1962
Photo by Bill Scovill
Norman Rockwell Museum Collections

81. Norman Rockwell in his
Stockbridge studio, 1964
Photo by Louie Lamone
Norman Rockwell Museum Collections

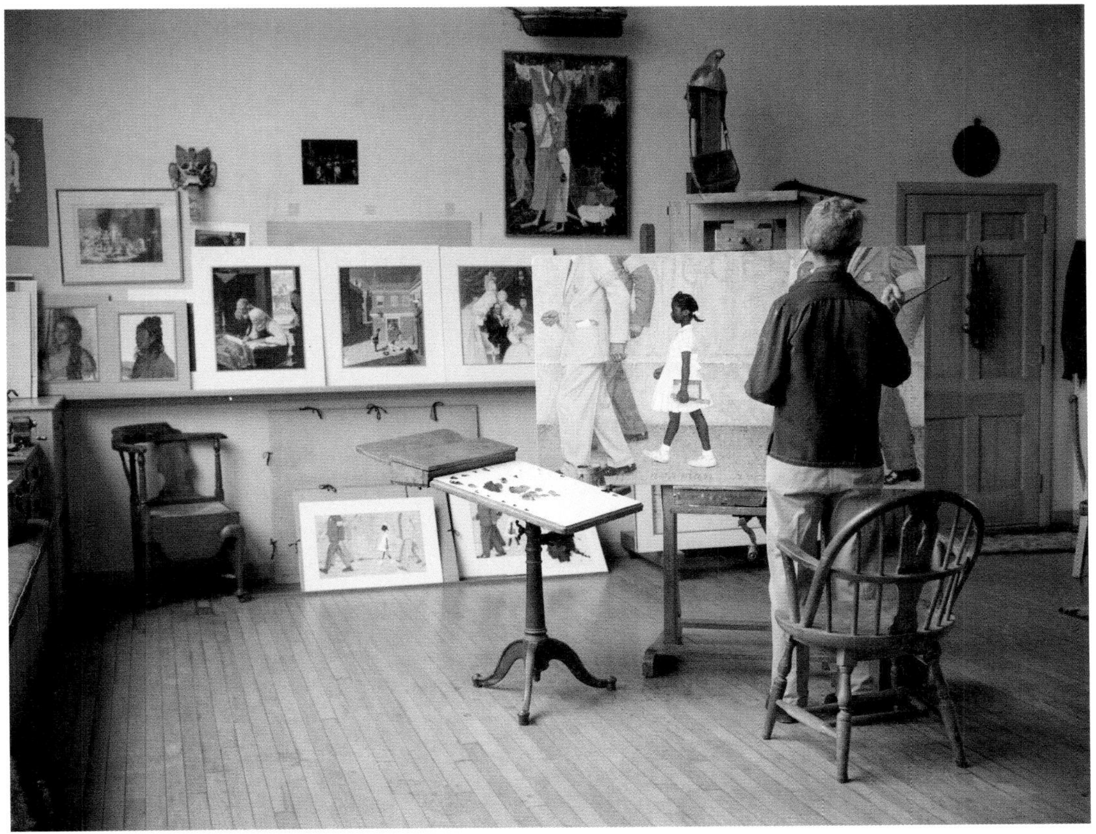

81

82. *The Problem We All Live With*, 1964
Painting for *Look* illustration,
January 14, 1964
Oil on canvas, 36 x 58 inches
Norman Rockwell Museum Collection,
NRM.1975.1

Rockwell's first assignment for *Look* magazine was an illustration of a six-year-old African-American schoolgirl being escorted by four U.S. marshals to her first day at an all-white school in New Orleans. Ordered to proceed with school desegregation after the 1954 Brown v. Board of Education ruling, Louisiana lagged behind until pressure from Federal Judge Skelly Wright forced the school board to begin desegregation on November 14, 1960.

Letters to the editor were a mix of praise and criticism. One Florida reader wrote, "Rockwell's picture is worth a thousand words.... I am saving this issue for my children with the hope that by the time they become old enough to comprehend its meaning, the subject matter will have become history." Other readers objected to Rockwell's image. A man from Texas wrote, "Just where does Norman Rockwell live? Just where does your editor live? Probably both of these men live in all-white, highly expensive, highly exclusive neighborhoods. Oh, what hypocrites all of you are!"

The most shocking letter came from a man in New Orleans who called Rockwell's work "just some more vicious, lying propaganda being used for the crime of racial integration by such black journals as *Look*, *Life*, etc."

But irate opinions did not stop Rockwell from pursuing his course. In 1965, he illustrated the murder of civil rights workers in Philadelphia, Mississippi, and in 1967, he chose children, once again, to illustrate desegregation, this time in our suburbs.

In an interview later in his life, Rockwell recalled that he once had to paint out an African-American person in a group picture since *The Saturday Evening Post* policy dictated showing African-Americans in service industry jobs only. Freed from such restraints, Rockwell seemed to look for opportunities to correct the editorial prejudices reflected in his previous work. The *Problem We All Live With* and *Murder in Mississippi* ushered in that new era for Rockwell.

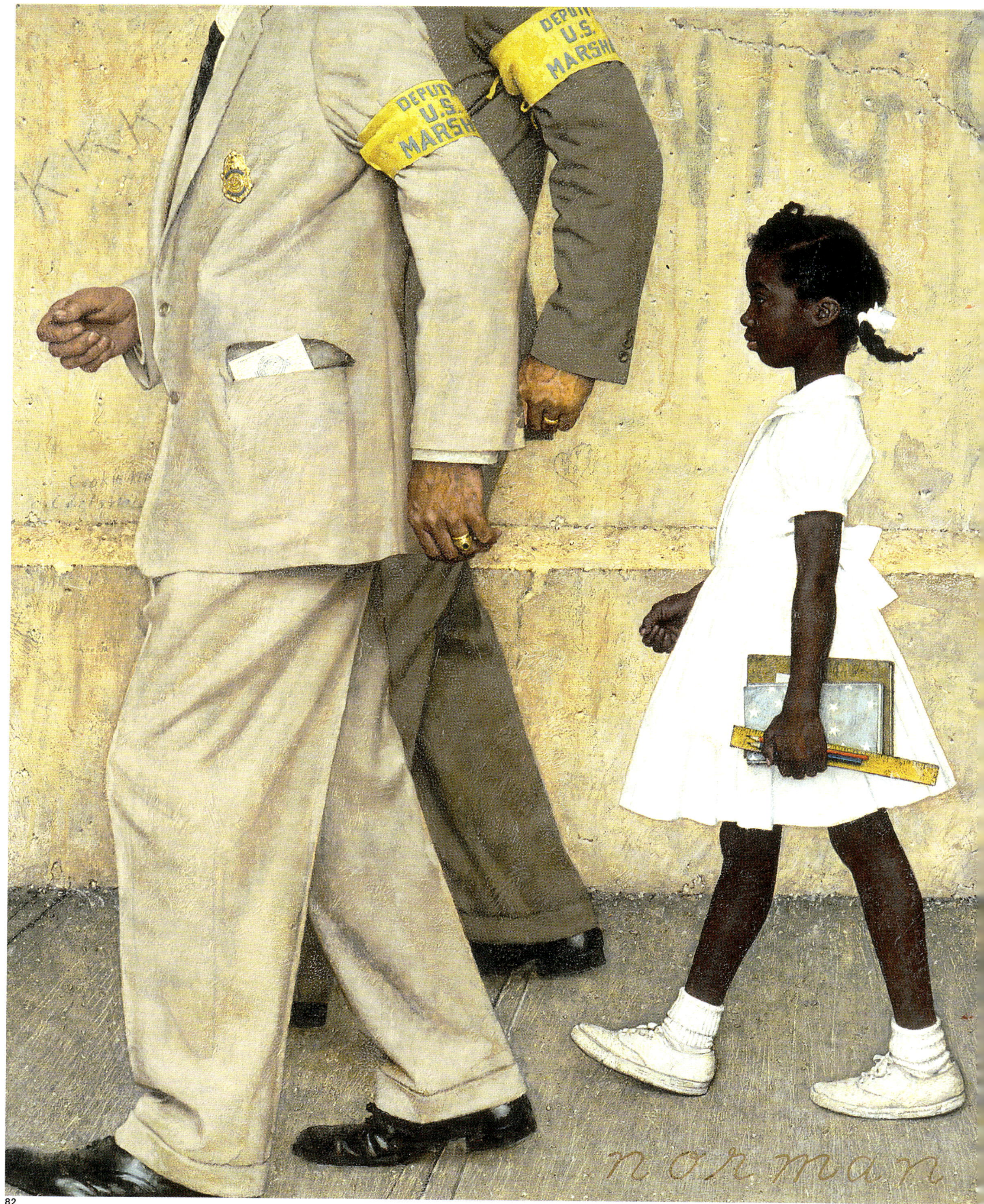

82

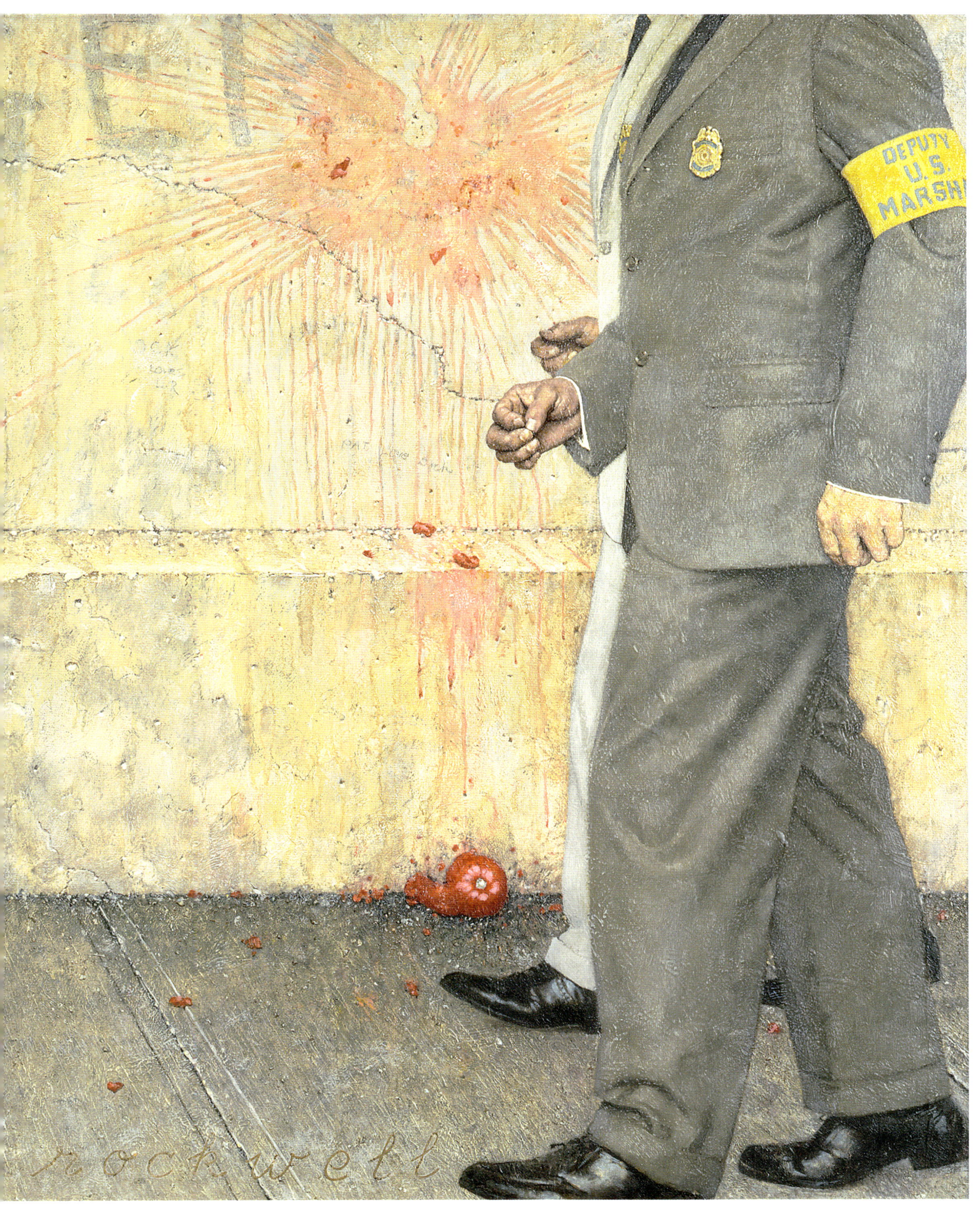
DEPUTY
U.S.
MARSH
rockwell

Fine Arts in Boston. Rockwell labored over *Art Critic* to the exclusion of other work, producing more than a dozen preliminaries for the portrait within the painting and three versions of the Dutch scene in the painting's background. Photographer Bill Scovill said Rockwell had more trouble with *Art Critic* than with any other painting. The result was worth the angst; to this day, *Art Critic* delights museum visitors—and art critics.

The following year, Rockwell was asked to travel around the world for a Pan American Airways advertising campaign. Accompanied by a representative from Pan Am's ad agency, J. Walter Thompson, and a Pan Am photographer, Rockwell would travel to seventeen cities in thirteen countries, recording impressions in his sketchbook. These would be the basis for full-color paintings for ads in the *Post*, *Life*, and *Holiday*. But shortly before the September departure date, Rockwell grew concerned about leaving Mary alone. In addition to her Riggs therapy, she was now receiving treatment at the Institute for Living in Hartford, Connecticut, and Rockwell, with the consultation of Mary's Riggs doctor, decided it would be best to place her in their care for the duration of his trip. Rockwell accompanied her to Hartford to spend a week with her before leaving for London. When the local press discovered him there, he used the pretense that he was sketching Bushnell Park's historic monuments and sculptures as warm-up for his Pan Am trip.

83. *Murder in Mississippi*,
March 5, 1965
Study for *Southern Justice* by Charles Morgan, Jr., *Look*, June 29, 1965
Digital print from archival negative of oil on board, 15 x 24.5 inches
Norman Rockwell Museum Collection

At the beginning of 1965, Rockwell began work on an illustration for *Look* about the murders of three young civil rights workers that took place in Philadelphia, Mississippi, on June 21, 1964. Michael Schwerner and his chief aide, James Chaney, were in Philadelphia to assist with training summer volunteers, one of whom was Andrew Goodman. Schwerner had been targeted by the Klan for his organization of a black boycott of white-owned businesses and for his attempts to register blacks in Meriden. Hearing of a Klan attack against blacks and of arson at Mount Zion Church, the three men drove to the site.
On their return to the Meriden office of Congress of Racial Equality (CORE), they were taken into custody by Deputy Sheriff Price, by some accounts for speeding and by others for supposedly setting the fire. After releasing them later that night, Price tailed them. Once outside of town, Klansmen intercepted them and hustled them into Price's car.
They were driven to a remote location and shot point blank. Their bodies were then taken to the farm of one of the Klansmen, dumped into a dam site, and covered by tons of dirt pushed over them by tractor.
Rockwell conceived *Murder in Mississippi* as a horizontal composition to run across two pages. The young men would be pictured on the left page and Philadelphia Deputy Price and the posse of Klansmen wielding sticks (we later learned all were armed with rifles and shotguns) on the right. His next idea was to do two separate vertical pictures—the first showing the civil rights workers and the second showing the Mount Zion Church. Rockwell hired local architect Tom Arienti to draft a church steeple, but later decided against including the church.

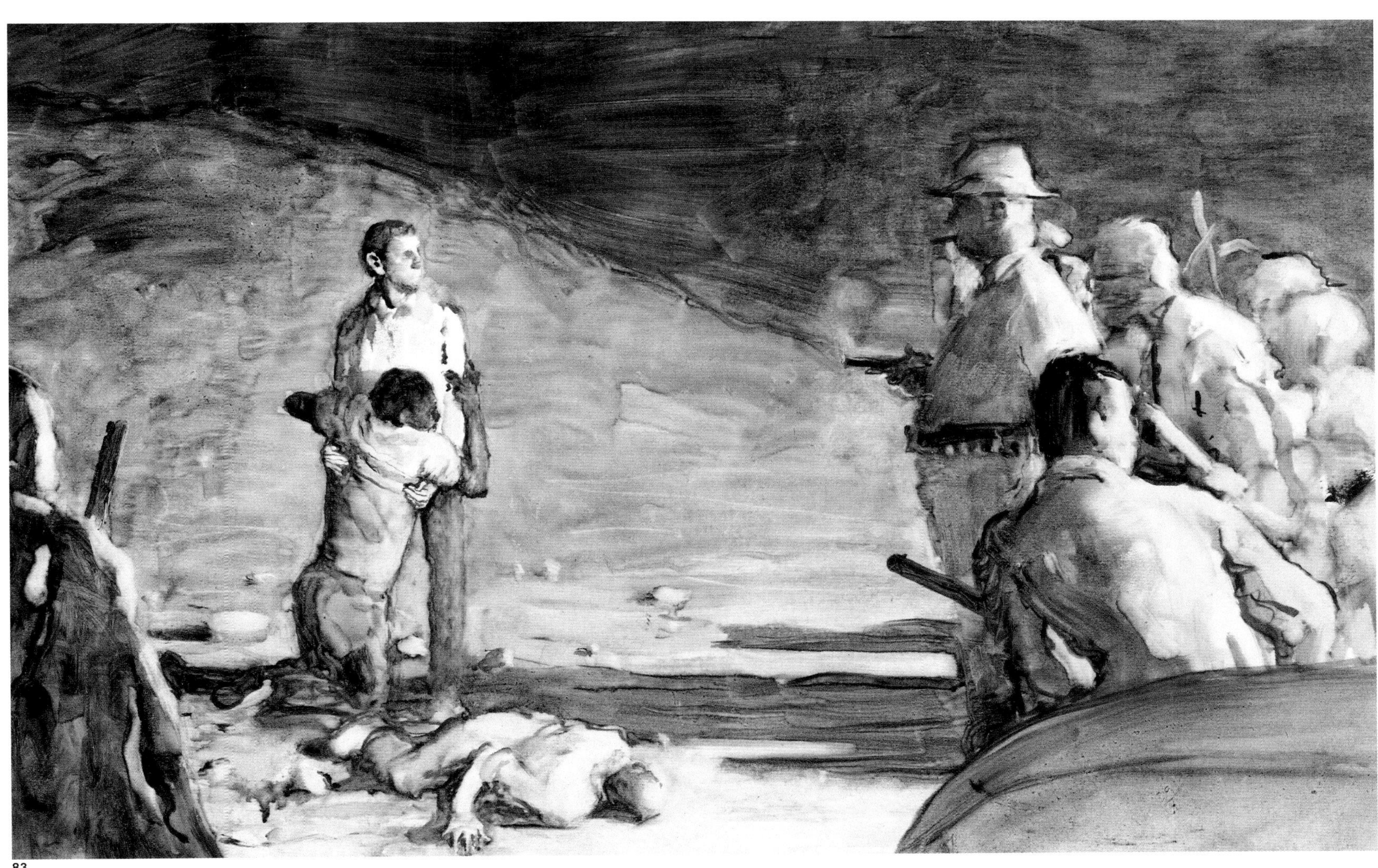

83

84. Hector Rondon
Aid from the Padre, June 2, 1962
Tear sheet of photograph,
13.875 x 9.625 inches
Norman Rockwell Museum Collection

85. *A 2nd Body is Found in the Mississippi*, 1964
The New York Times, July 14, 1964
Tear sheet, 22 x 14.75 inches
Norman Rockwell Art Collection Trust,
Studio Collection

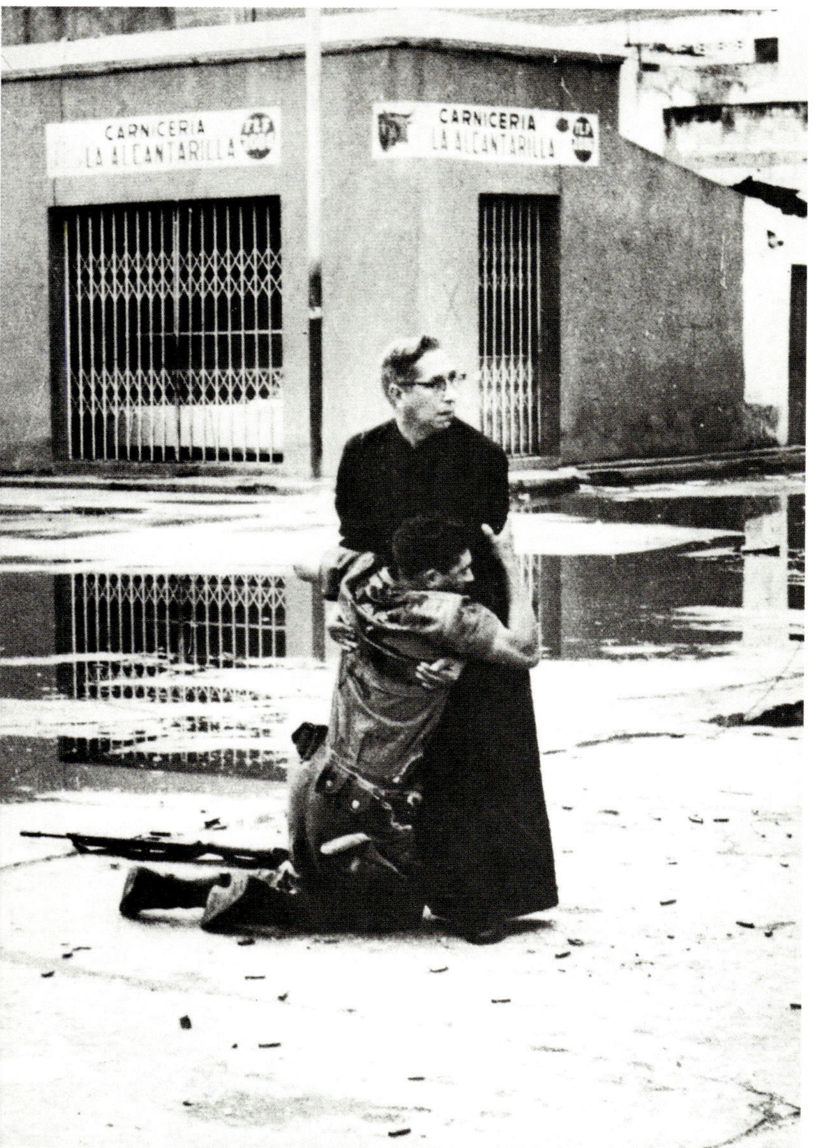

84

16 C THE NEW YORK TIMES, TUESDAY, JULY 14, 1964.

A 2D BODY IS FOUND IN THE MISSISSIPPI

No Link Seen to 3 Missing Civil Rights Workers

By JOHN HERBERS
Special to The New York Times

JACKSON, Miss., July 13 — The Mississippi River yielded a second body today. The discovery indicated a previously undisclosed racial killing in southwest Mississippi, the center of terrorist activity in recent months.

Both bodies were tentatively identified as those of Negro males from Meadville, a small town in the Homochito National Forest 25 miles east of Natchez.

Authorities said their deaths apparently had no connection with the civil rights workers who have been missing since June 21 and are presumed dead.

A Tenatative Identification

The body discovered today was believed to be that of Henry Dee, of whom little was known. It was found five miles downstream from the point where the partial remains of a youth believed to be Charles E. Moore, a 20-year-old college student, were found yesterday.

At the same time, Adams County atuhorties announced that two more Negro churches were burned by arsonists early Sunday morning near Natchez, and that night riders attempted to set fire to the home of a Negro contractor in Natchez.

The body believed to be Dee was discovered at midday on the Louisiana side of the river near Vicksburg by one of the local authorities participating in the search. It was Decapitate and badly deteriorated, but fully clothed.

The Federal Bureau of Investigation was to bring it to Jackson to make a positive identification.

The lower hald of the first body, also badly deteriorated, was found by fishermen. Authorities at Alcorn A. and M. College said they were sure it was the body of Mr. Moore, a freshman who was expelled for participating in a campus demonstration.

Alcorn is a state-supported Negro institution in rural Claiborne County 25 miles north of Natchez and 30 miles northwest of Meadville. It is in this area that white terrorist groups have been active. Negroes say that members of their race have been killed and others flogged or run out of town in the past months.

'Left School' in April

Dr. J. D. Boyd, a Negro who is the president of Alcorn, said Mr. Moore "left school" in late April. Dr. Boyd said he had been told that the young man's mother, Mrs. Maisey Moore of Meadville, had said her son went to Louisiana to visit relatives and she had not heard from him since.

Mr. Moore's roommate, Robert Haynes, had a different story. He said in a telephone interview that Moore was "sent home by the president" after a campus riot on April 20.

Little was known about the disturbances on the campus April 20. Students, as they had done in the past, staged demonstrations in protest of what they called lack of social activities on the campus, which is 10 miles from the nearest small town.

The State Highway Patrol was sent to restore order and the next day the school dismissed a number of students who had participated.

The body was identified as Moore by a key in the pocket of the jeans. It bore the number of the key assigned to Moore by the college. A buckle with the initial "M" found on the body also was identical to one Moore owned.

When the body was first discovered it was believed it might be one of the three missing civil rights workers. The missing men are Michael Schwerner, 24 years old, of Brooklyn; Andrew Goodman, 20, of New York, both white, and James E. Chaney, 21, of Meridian, Miss., a Negro.

They were last seen near Philadelphia, Miss., where they had been arrested and held for several hours. The area where the two bodies were found in more than 100 miles southwest of Philadelphia.

In Natchez, Sheriff Odell Anders of Adams County said two rural Negro churches in the Kingston community, 18 miles south of Natchez, were burned about 3 A.M. Sunday. They were the Jerusalem Baptist and the Bethel Methodist churches.

The State Fire Marshals office found conclusive evidence of arson, Sheriff Anders said. White residents of the area, he added, had begun a drive to raise money to rebuild the churches.

Willie Washington, a 57-year-old Negro contractor, told the Natchez police a white man stopped a car in front of his home early today and tossed a fire bomb into the building, but it failed to ignite.

Kingsborough College Fills 2 Posts

Arthur Avedon

Dr. Edward K. Graham — Jack P. Hudnall

Kingsborough Community College has named Dr. Edward K. Graham dean of the faculty and Jack P. Hudnall director of administration.

Dr. Jacob I. Hartstein, president of the new two-year college in Brooklyn, said yesterday that both men had assumed their posts.

Dr. Graham, a graduate of the University of North Carolina, has for the last year been president and consultant of the College Center of the Finger Lakes, Corning, N.Y. Before that he held numerous university administration posts, including vice chancellor for academic affairs of the University of Denver, dean of the College of Liberal Arts and the Graduate School of Boston University, secretary of Cornell University and chancellor of the University of North Carolina at Greensboro. He holds a doctorate in history from Cornell.

Mr. Hudnall, who was dean of Hibbing Junior College in Minnesota from 1959 to 1963, has been a research assistant in the junior college leadership training program at Teachers College, Columbia University, while completing study for a doctorate.

M'NAMARA ORDERS SERVICE EQUALITY

Says All Commanders Must Uphold Civil Rights Law

WASHINGTON, July 13 (AP)—Secretary of Defense Robert S. McNamara told the armed forces today that every commander must "foster equal treatment for every serviceman and to support him in the lawful assertion of the rights guaranteed" by the new Civil Rights Act.

Mr. McNamara issued the instructions in the form of a memorandum to the three service Secretaries.

He said the full text of his memorandum should be sent to all commanders.

The newly enacted civil rights law, he said, has special meaning for servicemen, "all of whom have already given a personal commitment to defend freedom and justice."

Mr. McNamara declared that President Johnson expected each department of the Government to move with despatch to give full support to the Civil Rights Act.

"In the Department of Defense," the memorandum stated, "this means, primarily, the vigorous, determined, sensitive commitment by military commanders to a program of fostering and securing equal treatment for all their men, and their families, off base as well as on.

"This has been our policy Civil Rights Act creates new opportunities to win equal treatment for all servicemen, and we cannot afford to lose any opportunity to gain a goal so simple, so just and so compelling."

SEARCH IS PRESSED FOR NEGRO'S KILLER

ATHENS, Ga., July 13 (UPI) — Investigators checked on known racial extremists today in a continuing search for the men who killed Lieut. Col. Lemuel A. Penn, a Negro Army Reserve officer.

President Johnson, who ordered the Federal Bureau of Investigation into the case immediately after the shooting last Saturday, was keeping in touch with developments in the case, the White House reported.

F.B.I. Agents teamed with local authorities and agents of the Georgia Bureau of Investigation to question residents living in the sparsely populated rural areas along Routes 72 and 172. It was about 15 miles northeast of here that Colonel Penn, a 48-year-old Washington school administrator in civilian life, was killed and another Negro and his family were attacked on two consecutive nights.

The investigators, who have taken over the entire top floor of the white marble Georgian Courthouse on Main Street, refused to make any comment on the investigation.

The assassin fired two blasts from a speeding automobile that overtook Colonel Penn and two companions while they were returning to Washington from Army Reserve training at Fort Benning, Ga.

ATLANTA, July 13 (AP)—Gov. Carl E. Sanders sent a telegram of condolence today to the widow of Colonel Penn. It said:

"On behalf of the people of Georgia I extend our deepest sympathy to you and your family in your hour of bereavement.

"A representative of this state and the Georgia Department of Defense will be present at the appropriate services on Tuesday."

TWO NEW ROCKETS TO GET FLIGHT TEST

WASHINGTON, July 13 (AP)—Two rockets—forerunners of electrified - gas power plants that some day map propel astronauts through space at 100,000 miles an hour—will get their first flight test, perhaps Saturday.

The National Aeronautics and Space Administration said today that the ion electric engines will be launched from Wallops Island, Va., no earlier than Saturday on a looping ballistic flight to an altitude of 2,500 miles.

During the 50-minute flight, two different types of the engines—which spit out electrified gas as they propel — will be fired. The first engine will fire for 20 minutes.

They will be aboard a 375-pound Sert I spacecraft, and will be launched by a four-stage solid-fuel Scout rocket. Sert stands for space electric rocket test.

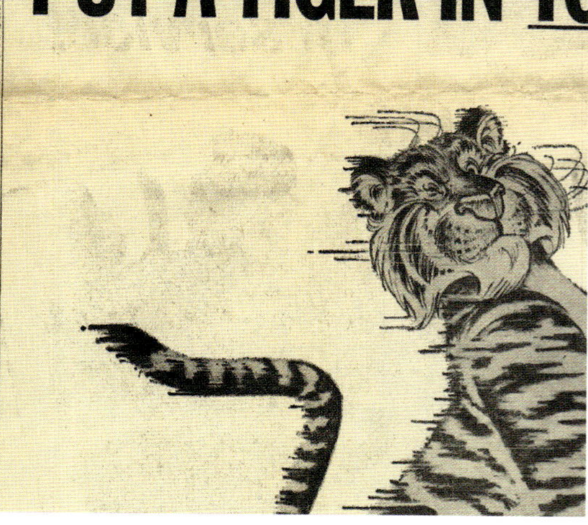

85

86. Artist unknown
Expressionist painting, *c.* 1964
Publication unknown
Tear sheet, 12.5 x 9.25 inches
Norman Rockwell Art Collection Trust,
Studio Collection

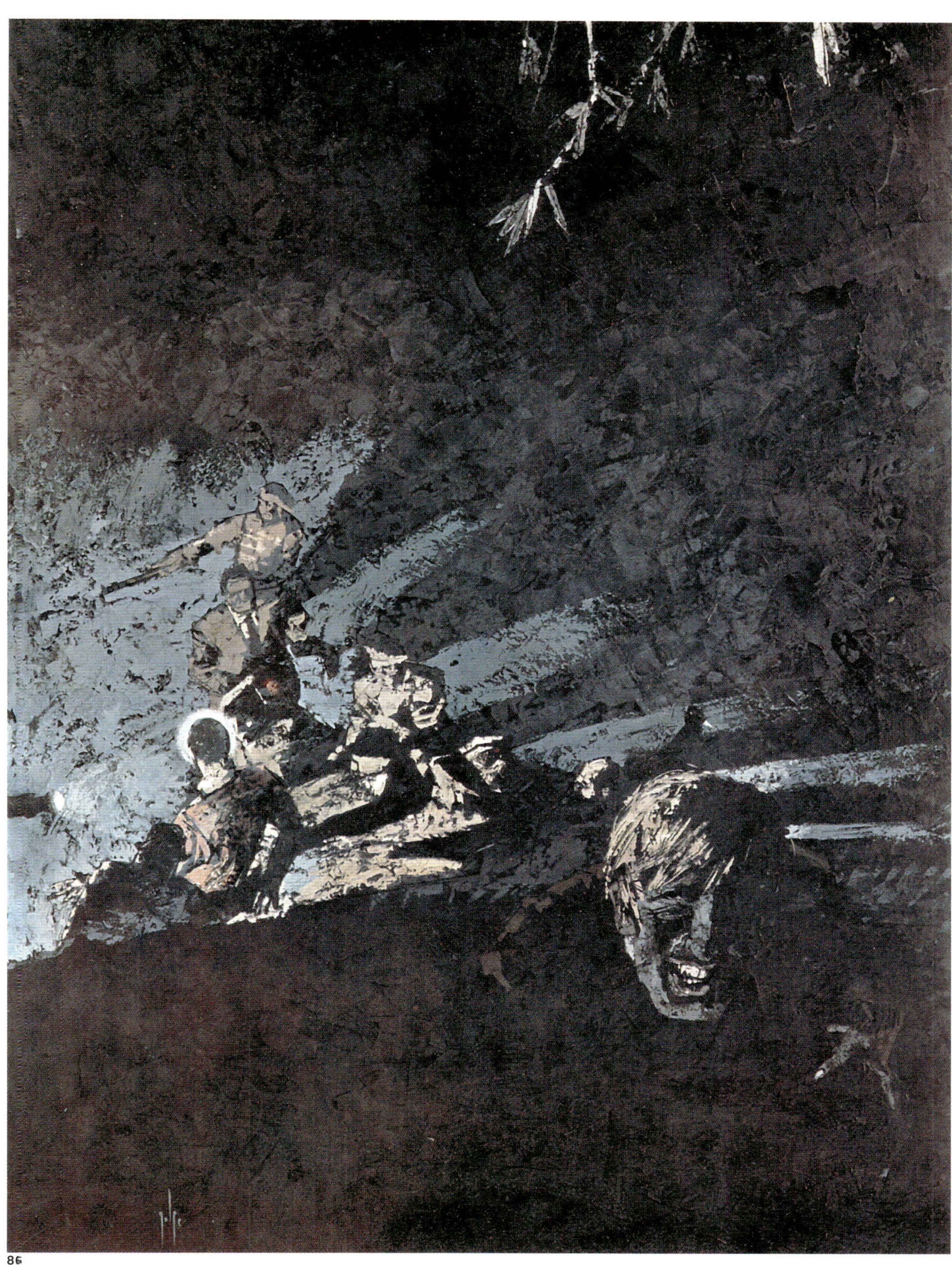

86

By all accounts, Rockwell had loved his life in Arlington, but he never looked back. He welcomed the fresh assortment of faces for his pictures and the new social opportunities. He joined in community activities that were different from his former Grange experience in Vermont. Now he gathered weekly at the Red Lion Inn with friends in the Marching and Chowder Society to discuss current events over lunch. More formal were his monthly meetings of the Monday Evening Club, a group of prominent Berkshire County citizens. On a rotating basis, each member spoke on a stimulating or provocative topical subject, and group discussion followed. In a talk titled "Extraordinary Men?" Rockwell questioned whether personality traits revealed by political leaders during posing sessions could indicate their true character. Now closer to New York, he made frequent trips to the city to meet with editors and ad agents, to give lectures at the Society of Illustrators, and for holidays at his favorite resting place, the Plaza Hotel.

Though the gregarious Rockwell on one hand enjoyed having a studio in the center of town where he could view prospective models from his second floor picture window, he was accustomed to having a much larger space laid out in the familiar manner of his former custom-built studios in New Rochelle and Arlington. Meanwhile, for Mary, the view of the cemetery from their kitchen window was an ominous landscape. In 1957, they bought an eighteenth-century home near the center of town, and that summer, they converted its carriage barn into a studio.

87. *Murder in Mississippi*, 1965
Preliminary sketch published as the final illustration for *Southern Justice* by Charles Morgan, Jr., *Look*, June 29, 1965
Oil on board, 15 x 12.75 inches
Norman Rockwell Art Collection Trust, NRACT.1973.79

Deputy Price and his stick-wielding posse were removed and represented only by menacing shadows in this quick color sketch, the left half of the original painting. Rockwell received the go-ahead to proceed with his final painting based on this sketch, but *Look* art director Allen Hurlburt, after receiving the final work, chose to publish the sketch.

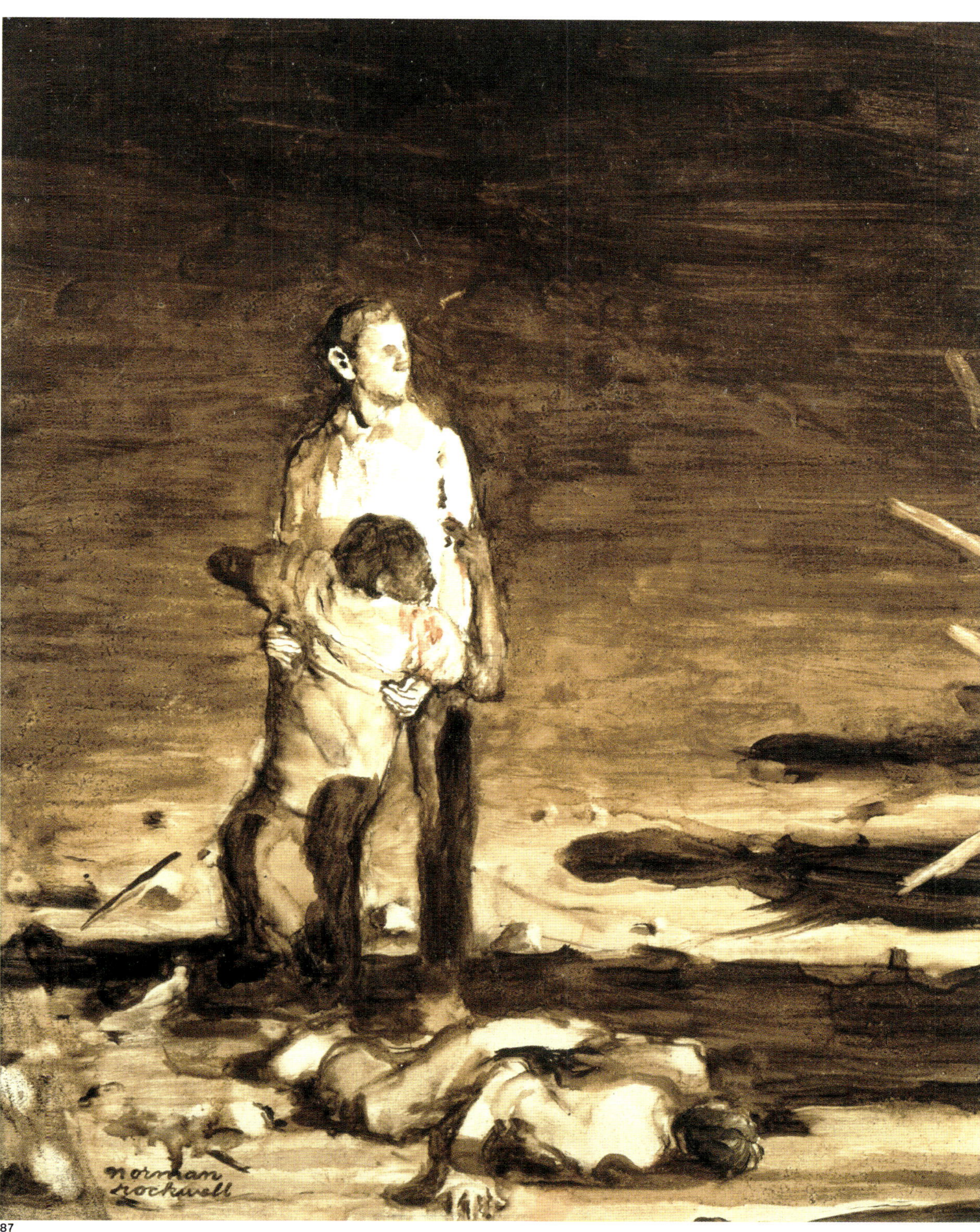

87

88. *Letter to Look art director Allen Hurlburt from Norman Rockwell,* March 17, 1965
11 x 8.5 inches
Norman Rockwell Art Collection Trust, Studio Collection

89. *Letter to Allen Hurlburt from Norman Rockwell,* April 8, 1965
11 x 8.5 inches
Norman Rockwell Art Collection Trust, Studio Collection

March 17, 1965

Dear Allen:

I am already hard at work on the Civil Rights picture.

As I told you, I am not changing the sketch which you saw and I do want to do it in the non-photographic manner which you seemed to like, and which I do. I certainly should be able to deliver it much before the deadline, which I think you said was April 15th.

Cordially yours,

88

Apr. 8, 1965

Dear Allen:

I tried in a big way (large size) to make an angry picture. If I just had a bit of Ben Shahn in me it would have helped.

Please call me and give me your reaction. I sure tried anyway.

Sincerely yours,

89

90. *Letter to Charles Morgan, Jr. from Norman Rockwell*, June 15, 1965
11 x 8.5 inches
Norman Rockwell Art Collection Trust, Studio Collection

91. *Letter to the editor from George D. Stanley*, June 16, 1965
10.5 x 8.5 inches
Norman Rockwell Art Collection Trust, Studio Collection

June 15, 1965

Mr. Charles Morgan Jr., Author
LOOK Magazine
488 Madison Avenue
New York, N.Y.

Dear Mr. Morgan:

I just can't resist writing you to tell you how much I appreciate the fine and strong words that were published on the opposite page from my Civil Rights drawing.

It was such an unanswerable indictment.

Sincerely yours,

90

June 16, 1965

Editor of Look
488 Madison Ave.
New York, N.Y. 10022

JUN 21 1965 RM

"Southern justice"

6-29-65
D

Mr. Norman Rockwell's painting which illustrated "Southern justice" was done a terrible injustice by it's use in connection with this article. Northern, Eastern or Western "justice" would have been in equally bad taste. The true picture would be – Man's justice.
Is it impossible for anyone, except a Southerner, to realize the tremendous strides being made to correct our bigoted society?
The racial problem which the present-day South inherited was created by our greedy, money-hungry ancestors; some of which it is rumored were from the North!
The South will correct it's problem while the North attempts to ridicule it and ignore the same situation at home.

George D. Stanley
210 Westridge Drive
High Point, N.C. 27260

91

92. *Letter to Norman Rockwell from Allen Hurlburt*, June 18, 1965
10.5 x 7.25 inches
Norman Rockwell Art Collection Trust, Studio Collection

93. *Letter to the editor from Bette L. Stern*, June 21, 1965
11 x 8.5 inches
Norman Rockwell Art Collection Trust, Studio Collection

LOOK

COWLES MAGAZINES AND BROADCASTING INC. 488 MADISON AVENUE NEW YORK NY 10022 MU 8-0300

ALLEN F. HURLBURT, *Art Director*

June 18, 1965

Mr. Norman Rockwell,
Stockbridge, Mass.

Dear Norman,

I'm glad things didn't go so well with those other people.

Pat sent me a goofy doll with her curlers and I presume instructions for installing them. This creature may be too big for your purpose on length, but maybe she will be of some help in putting together the voting booth picture.

I'm already getting some excited calls from people about your Southern Justice painting. Everyone thinks it's a smasher. Art Direction Magazine is doing a special piece on it; reprints are being requested by groups... etc.

I expect to be back in the office on Monday June 28th but Lee can reach me if necessary.

Sincerely,
Al
Allen F. Hurlburt
Art Director

92

4322 Lockwood Avenue
Los Angeles, Calif. 90029
June 21, 1965

Letters to the Editor
Look Magazine
488 Madison Avenue
New York, New York 10022

JUN 23 1965 RM
6/29/65 E

Gentlemen:

Thank you very much for printing the one-page article, "Southern Justice" by Charles Morgan, Jr. The illustration by Norman Rockwell accompanying it was excellent, also.

I have hung both article and illustration on my living room wall as a constant reminder of man's inhumanity to man.

I have never met Mr. Morgan in person but I have been corresponding with him for the past several months and I think he is one of the truly great men in this nation. His book, A Time to Speak, should be mandatory reading for every American.

I wonder if your readers are aware that last month Mr. Morgan received a citation on behalf of racial justice from the University of Pennsylvania Law School and an honorary fellowship in his name from the same school. I predict that Mr. Morgan will win many more honors of this nature in the years to come. It couldn't happen to a more deserving person.

Sincerely,
Bette L. Stern
(Mrs.) Bette L. Stern

93

94. *Letter to the editor from Mary Allison*, June 23, 1965
9 x 8.5 inches
Norman Rockwell Art Collection Trust,
Studio Collection

June 23, 1965

Dear Sirs, JUN 29 1965 RM

I was deeply moved by Norman Rockwells beautiful and compassionate painting of the murder of the three civil rights workers.

6/25/65
Southern Justice E

It should forever be a reminder to the conscience of mankind of the results of hate and ignorance.

Thank you for printing this fine work

Sincerely,
Mary Allison

94

95. *Event*, 1965
Typewritten notes on Norman Rockwell stationery, 10.25 x 7.25 inches
Norman Rockwell Art Collection Trust, Studio Collection

96. *Events*, 1965
Handwritten pencil notes on paper, 9.25 x 6.125 inches
Norman Rockwell Art Collection Trust, Studio Collection

STOCKBRIDGE
MASSACHUSETTS

EVENT

JUNE 21, 1964
SOMEWHERE NORTH OF PHILADELPHIA, MISS.
SOMETIME AROUND MIDNIGHT
NO MOON
SWAMPS, RED CLAY AND FLAT COUNTRY

TEMPERATURE DURING THE DAY OF JUNE 21
HAD BEEN OVER 100 DEGREES.

95

Events
100 degrees
temperature
June 21
side
scorching oppressive day
got haircuts the day before
long after dark
red clay
Price followed them to the edge of town
swamps
rattlesnakes
arrested 5 P.M. June 21 at Philadelphia Miss
moonlight 10:30 June 21 1964
rises 3:40 am June 22

96

97. *Letter to Bette L. Stern from Anne Celli*, July 6, 1965
11 x 8.5 inches
Norman Rockwell Art Collection Trust, Studio Collection

98. *Letter to Mary Allison from Anne Celli*, July 7, 1965
10 x 8.5 inches
Norman Rockwell Art Collection Trust, Studio Collection

July 6, 1965

Mrs. Bette L. Stern
4322 Lockwood Avenue
Los Angeles, California 90029

Dear Mrs. Stern:

Thank you for your letter prompted by the article, "Southern Justice," which appeared in the June 29, 1965, issue of LOOK.

The editors read with interest your kind words about this article, and the painting by Mr. Rockwell, and were indeed pleased to know that you have hung both upon your living room wall. They would also like to express their appreciation for your most complimentary comments about Mr. Charles Morgan and for your courtesy in writing as you did. They agree that the honors conferred upon Mr. Morgan were certainly deserved.

Again, thank you for your letter.

Cordially,

Anne Celli
Assistant to the Editors

AC:jb:ca

97

July 7, 1965

Mrs Eugene Allison
2809 Vanderbilt Place
Nashville, Tennessee

Dear Mrs. Allison:

Thank you for your letter prompted by the painting by Norman Rockwell which appeared in the June 29, 1965, issue of LOOK.

The editors read your comments with care, and they are appreciative of your kind words for the picture accompanying the article, "Southern Justice." Other readers, like you, told us that the painting "should be a reminder to the conscience of mankind of the results of hate and ignorance."

Again, thank you for taking the time to write and share your views with us.

Cordially,

Anne Celli
Assistant to the Editors

AC/pp/wb

98

99. *Letter to George D. Stanley from Anne Celli*, July 12, 1965
11 x 8.5 inches
Norman Rockwell Art Collection Trust, Studio Collection

100. *Victims*, 1965
Typewritten notes on Norman Rockwell stationery, 10.25 x 7.25 inches
Norman Rockwell Art Collection Trust, Studio Collection

July 12, 1965

Mr. George D. Stanley
210 Westridge Drive
High Point, North Carolina

Dear Mr. Stanley:

Thank you for your letter prompted by the article "Southern Justice" (LOOK, June 29, 1965).

The editors read your letter carefully, and considered your suggestion that Norman Rockwell's painting should have been called "Man's Justice." While this title is indeed an appropriate one for the picture, the article is entitled "Southern Justice," and the painting was used to accompany it.

Thank you again for taking the time to share your thoughts with us.

Cordially,

Anne Celli
Assistant to the Editors

AC/vr/11

99

STOCKBRIDGE
MASSACHUSETTS

VICTIMS

(I have not tried to make absolute likenesses)

MICHAEL SCHWERNER

24 YEAR OLD FROM BROOKLYN
JEWISH
RATHER HEAVY SET
BEATNIK BEARD
WHITE SNEAKERS
BLUE JEANS
KILLED WITH SINGLE BULLET IN THE HEART
WHEN BODY WAS FOUND HIS CLOTHES WERE NOT MESSED UP

JAMES CHANEY
21 YEARS OLD
NEGRO OF MERIDIAN, MISS.
TALL AND SLENDER
DARK SKIN
WORE T SHIRT
BLUE JEANS
WHITE SNEAKERS
RIGHT SHOULDER AND HAND CRUSHED BY BEATING
HE WAS SHOT THREE TIMES
CLOTHES MESSED.

ANDREW GOODMAN
20 YEARS OLD, FROM NEW YORK
WHITE
ATHEIST
DARK-HAIRED AND SLENDER
T SHIRT
BLUE JEANS
WHITE SNEAKERS
SHOT ONCE IN HEART
CLOTHES NOT MESSED UP

(They had, all three, had haircuts the day before)

100

101. *Victims*, 1965
Handwritten pencil notes on paper,
9.25 x 6.125 inches
Norman Rockwell Art Collection Trust,
Studio Collection

victims
Michael Schwerner 24
Brooklyn bearded Jewish

Andrew Goodman 20
Jew aetheist?

James Chaney 21
negro
slender
Price says he ~~[illegible]~~ them leave
10:30 Sunday night

19 men arrested
Victims in battered station wagon

drove them down a dirt
road near the preacher's
place.

101

Rockwell welcomed new friends and neighbors into his studio. He invited schoolchildren from the nearby Plain School to hear him talk about art, and later, when the Old Corner House museum was established, docents came to gain insight about his process.

In the summer of 1959, Mary, to whom Rockwell had been married for twenty-eight years, died suddenly of cardiac arrest. The following summer, to lift himself out of his depression, Rockwell joined a local sketch class. Support also came from Austen Riggs Center therapist Erik Erikson, who Rockwell had been seeing for work-related problems. In 1961, Rockwell married his third wife, Molly Punderson, who had recently retired from her post as English teacher at Milton Academy near Boston, and had returned to her hometown of Stockbridge. Rockwell's desire to shed his reputation as a painter of nostalgia for a truer image was awakened by the influence of his new wife who was resolute and vocal in her liberal political opinions.

Just as he had in New Rochelle and Arlington, Rockwell contributed often to local projects. For the anniversary of the town's library, he created a fund drive poster. When the women of St. Paul's Episcopal Church published a fundraising cookbook, he sketched a jaunty looking chef for their cover. And for the dedication ceremony of a new post office, Rockwell sketched mailman Tom Cary for the program cover. The most amazing tribute to his town, because Rockwell was least of all a painter of landscapes, was an eight-foot-long painting of the town's Main Street, published by *McCall's* to celebrate Christmas in small-town America.

In the early 1960s, having lost audience and advertisers to television, the *Post* attempted to capture readers from *Life* and *Look* by using portraits and photographs on their covers, and Rockwell was assigned to paint political figures and celebrities. He was sent to India, Cairo, and Yugoslavia to do portraits of Jawaharlal Nehru, Gamal Abdel-Nasser, and Josip Broz-Tito. Then in June 1963, he wrote to the *Post* stating new conditions for his assignments and expressing concerns for his health that would limit his future work. According to his son Thomas, "this was Pop's way of breaking-without-quite-breaking with the *Post*." There were also problems with some of the *Post*'s new staff. The art editor spent a day in Rockwell's studio trying to tell him how to do the brushstrokes in his 1963 Jackie Kennedy portrait, and managing editor Matthew J. Culligan asked him to illustrate the Bible, a project he did not want to do.

Rockwell had been approached by *McCall's* and *Look*, and he grabbed the opportunity. Almost immediately he began work for *Look*. Leaving behind his beloved story-telling scenes, Rockwell threw himself into a new genre—the documentation of social issues. He welcomed the challenge of illustrating not nostalgia but current social issues. The shackles of *Post* editorial policy had been broken and Rockwell began to voice his opinions. He had always wanted to make a difference, and as a highly marketable illustrator, he now had the opportunity to do so. Humor and pathos—traits that made his *Post* covers successful—were not needed for telling the story of life in 1960s America. The textures and colors once used to weave his lighthearted yarns were replaced by a direct, pared down, reportorial style appropriate for magazine editorials. Rockwell even experi-

102. *CHARGES These nine men—and Deputy Price—were named as members of the lynch mob*
Date unknown
Photographer unknown
Publication unknown
Digital print from archival negative, 8 x 10 inches
Norman Rockwell Museum Collection

CHARGES

These nine men— and Deputy Price— were named as members of the

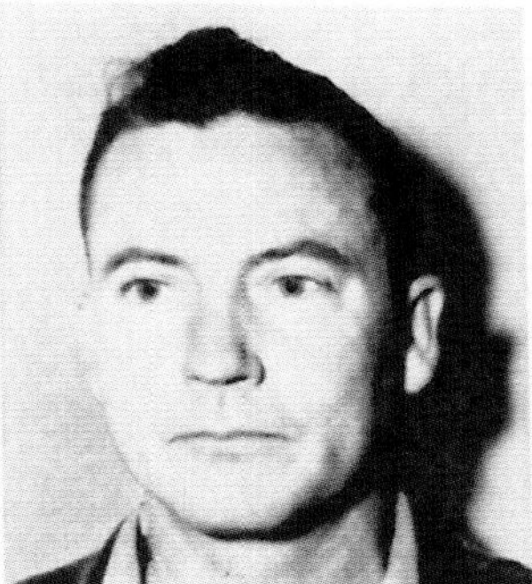

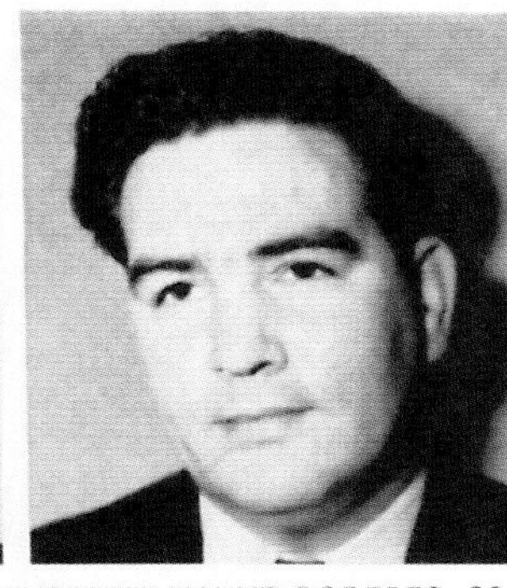

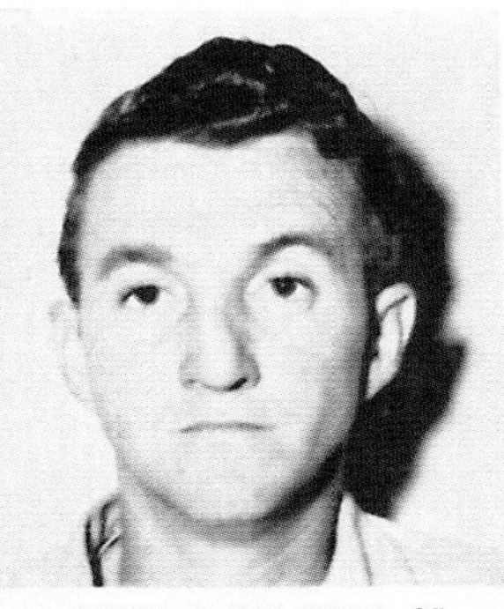

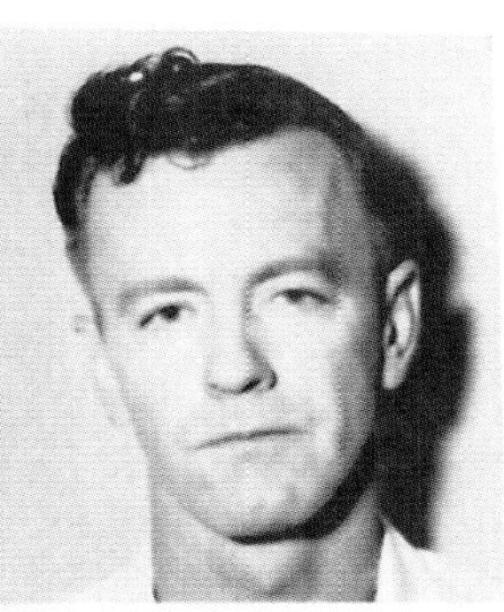

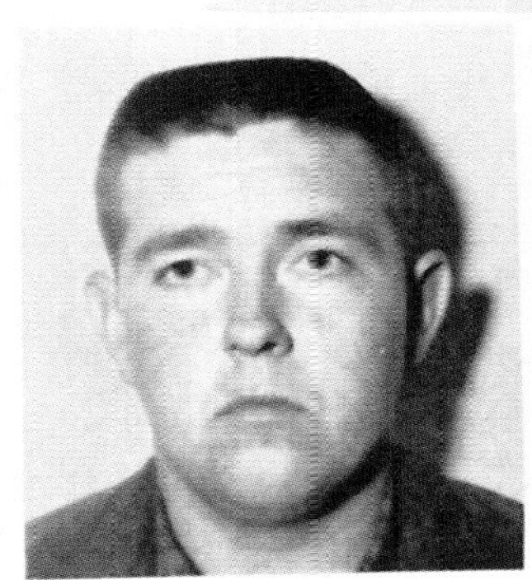

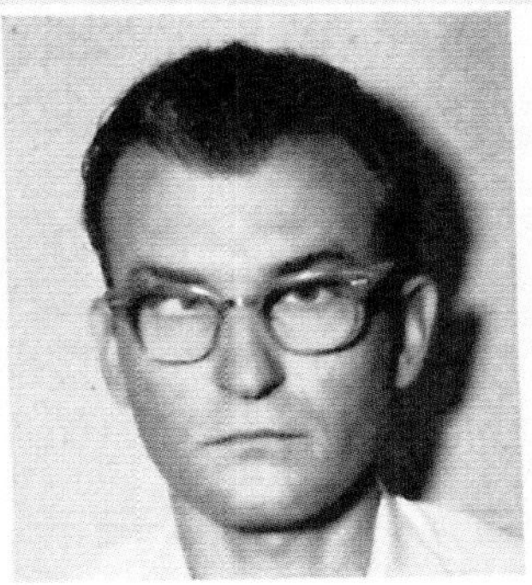

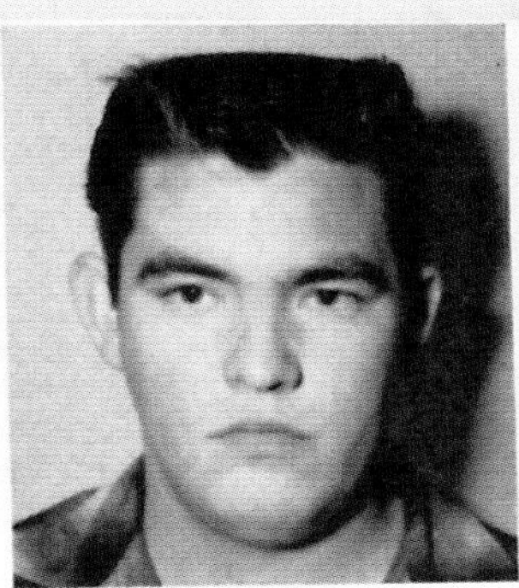

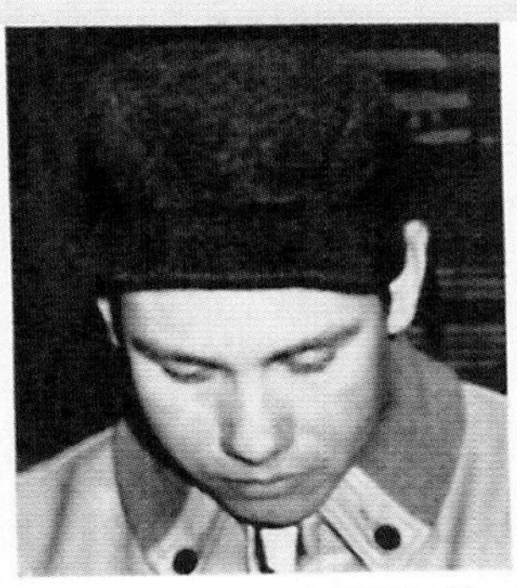

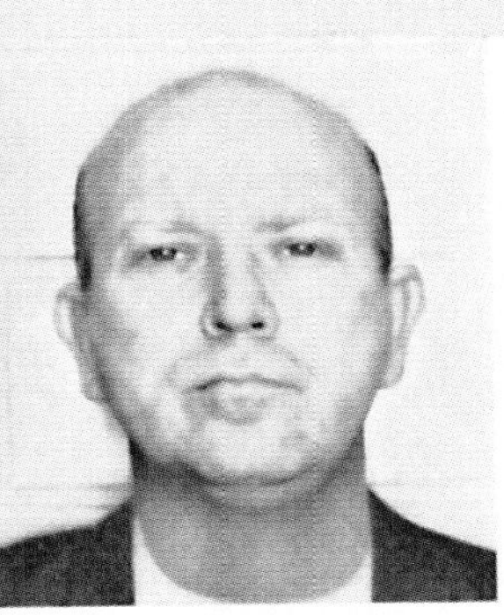

103. Jarvis Rockwell poses as Michael Schwerner; Oliver McCary poses as James Chaney, March 20, 1965
Reference photo by Louie Lamone
Gelatin silver print, 13.75 x 7.5 inches
Norman Rockwell Art Collection Trust, Studio Collection

104. Jarvis Rockwell poses as Michael Schwerner; Oliver McCary poses as James Chaney, March 22, 1965
Reference photo by Louie Lamone
Gelatin silver print,
12.75 x 8.25 inches
Norman Rockwell Art Collection Trust, Studio Collection

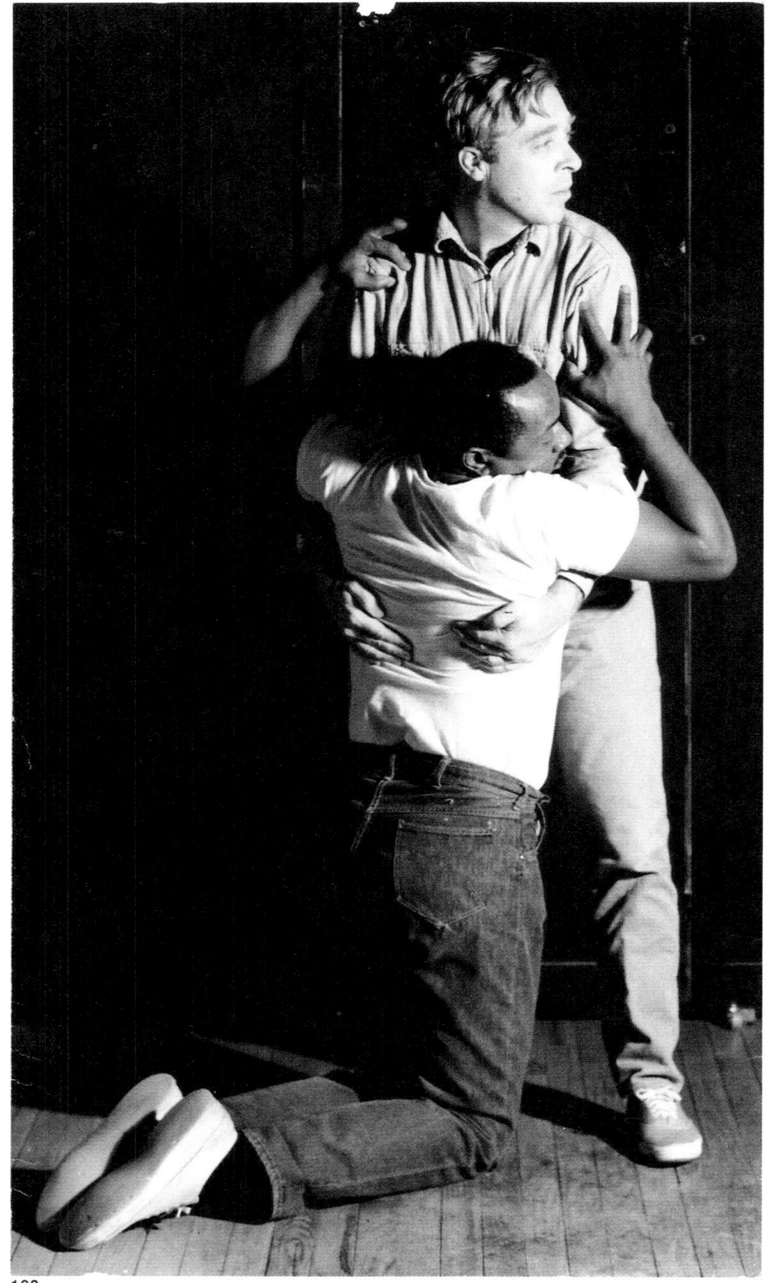

103

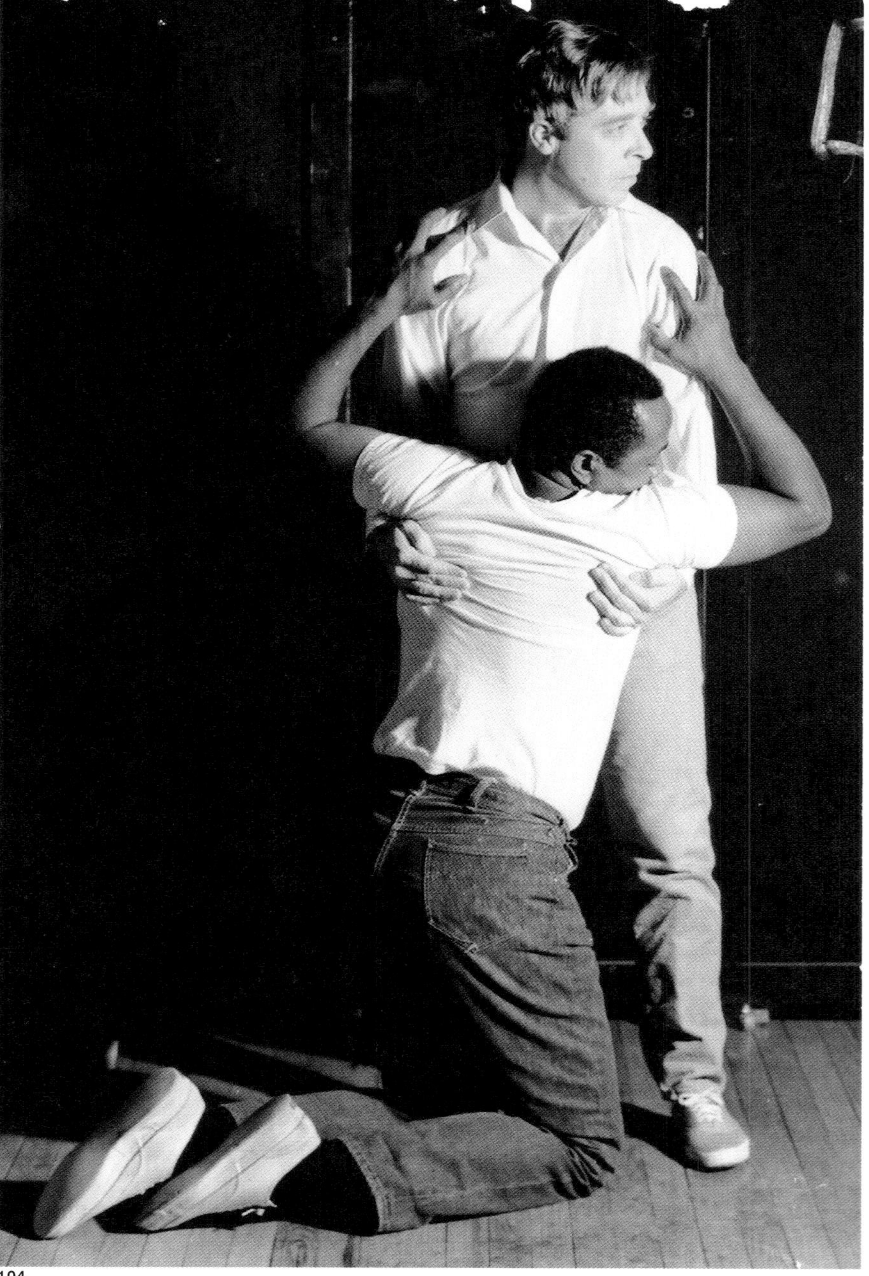

104

105. Kittridge (Kit) Hudson poses as Andrew Goodman, March 20, 1965
Reference photo by Louie Lamone
Gelatin silver print, 4.5 x 11 inches
Norman Rockwell Art Collection Trust, Studio Collection

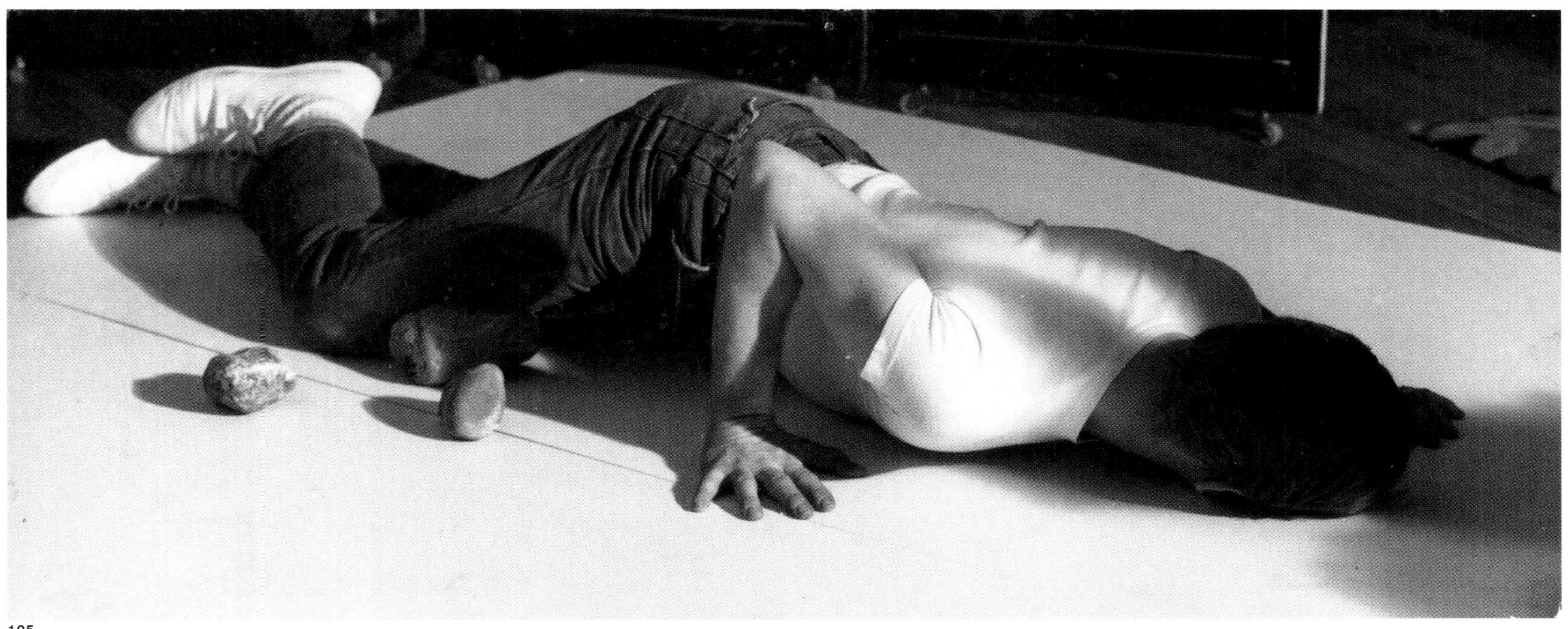

105

106. Norman Rockwell poses his hand for *Murder in Mississippi*, March 1965
Reference photo by Louie Lamone
Polaroid photo, 4.5 x 3.5 inches
Norman Rockwell Art Collection Trust, Studio Collection

107. *Moments after Saigon Bomb, a Torn Flag Flies*, 1965
Life, April 9, 1965
Double-page tear sheet, 13.25 x 21 inches
Norman Rockwell Art Collection Trust, Studio Collection

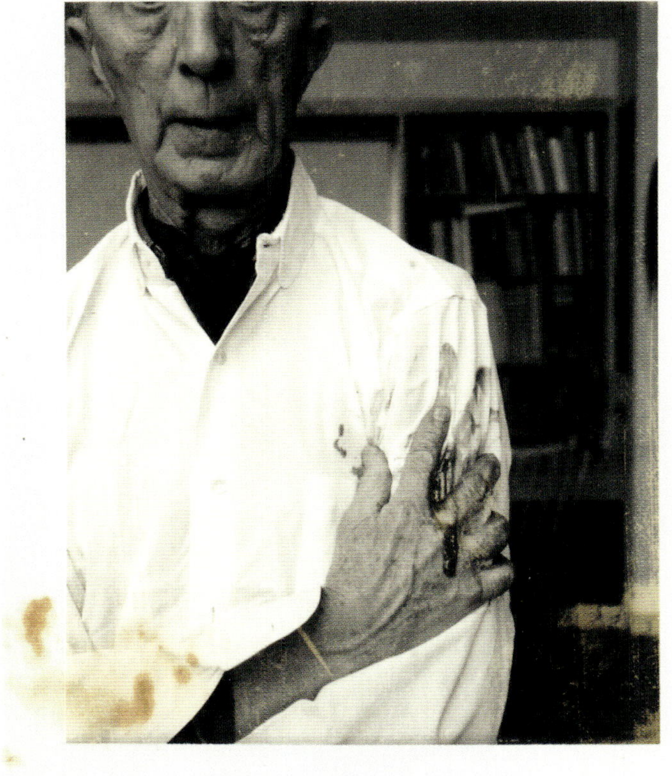

106

LIFE on the Newsfronts of the World

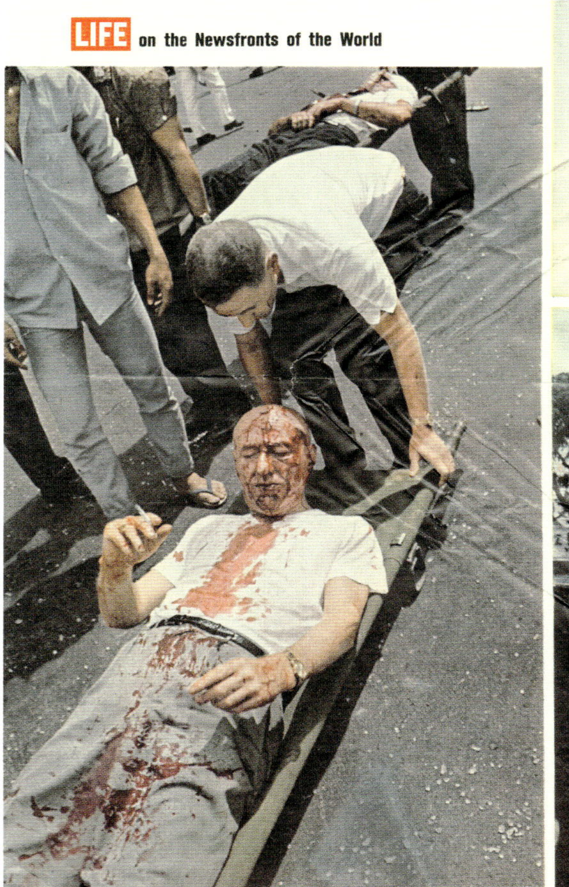

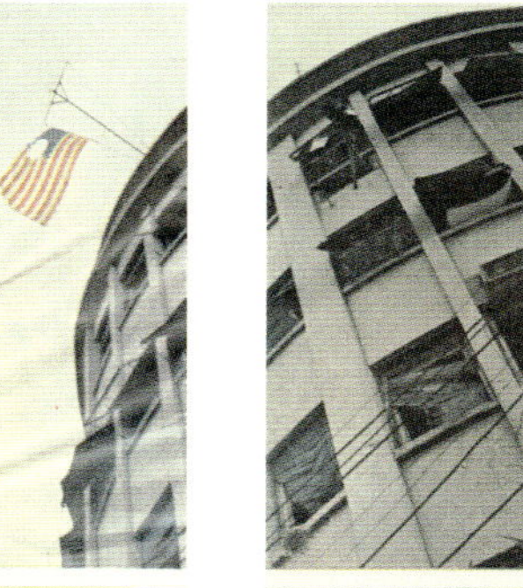

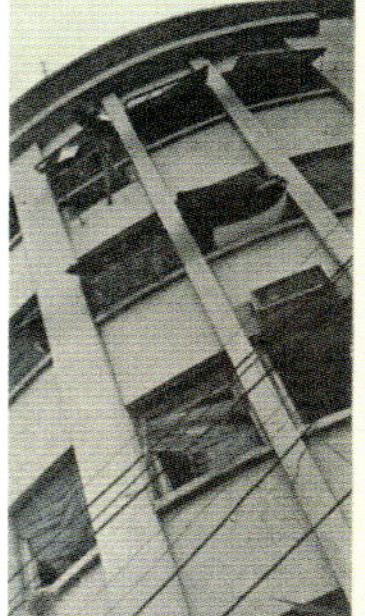

Moments after Saigon Bomb, a Torn Flag Flies

This was the horrifying scene in Saigon, minutes after the Communist Vietcong had carried out their most audacious act of terrorism against the United States. A Vietnamese drove up to the U.S. Embassy in a small French car and halted in the street. Moments later a time bomb hidden in the car, believed to have contained about 250 pounds of dynamite, exploded like a blockbuster. In the street at least 16 Vietnamese passersby and the terrorist were killed. Inside the shattered building, two Americans suffered fatal wounds, and most of the others, including Deputy Ambassador U. Alexis Johnson, were injured.

The bombing was an answer to U.S. air strikes against North Vietnam that were being mounted with ever-increasing strength. Whatever the U.S. might now do in reply, diplomacy was more than ever a dangerous activity for Americans—like the blood-soaked U.S. official at far left who calmly smoked a cigaret as rescuers carried him and other casualties from the street that was littered with the dead. Above the embassy the flag still flew (*left*)—with a hole the size of a man's chest ripped through its field of stars. And in Washington, President Johnson warned that the attack would only reinforce U.S. determination to defend South Vietnam against the Communists.

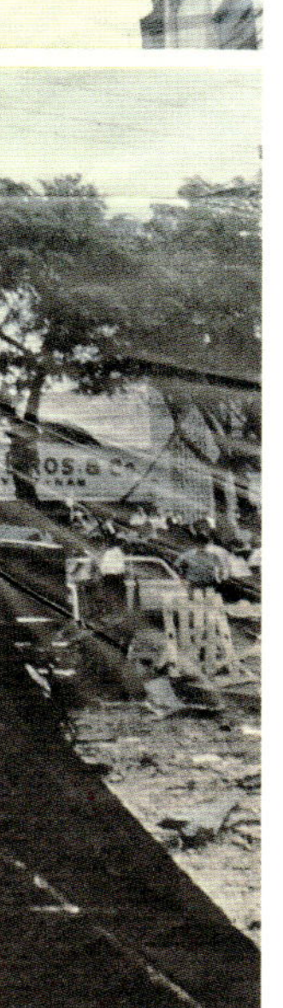

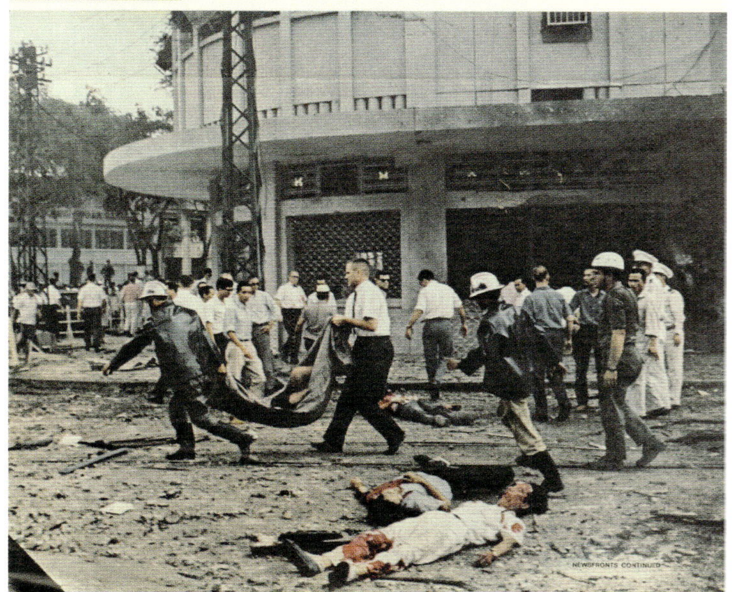

NEWSFRONTS CONTINUED

107

108. Preliminary drawing for *Murder in Mississippi*, March 24–26, 1965
Photo by Louie Lamone
Digital print from archival negative,
53 x 42 inches
Norman Rockwell Museum Collection

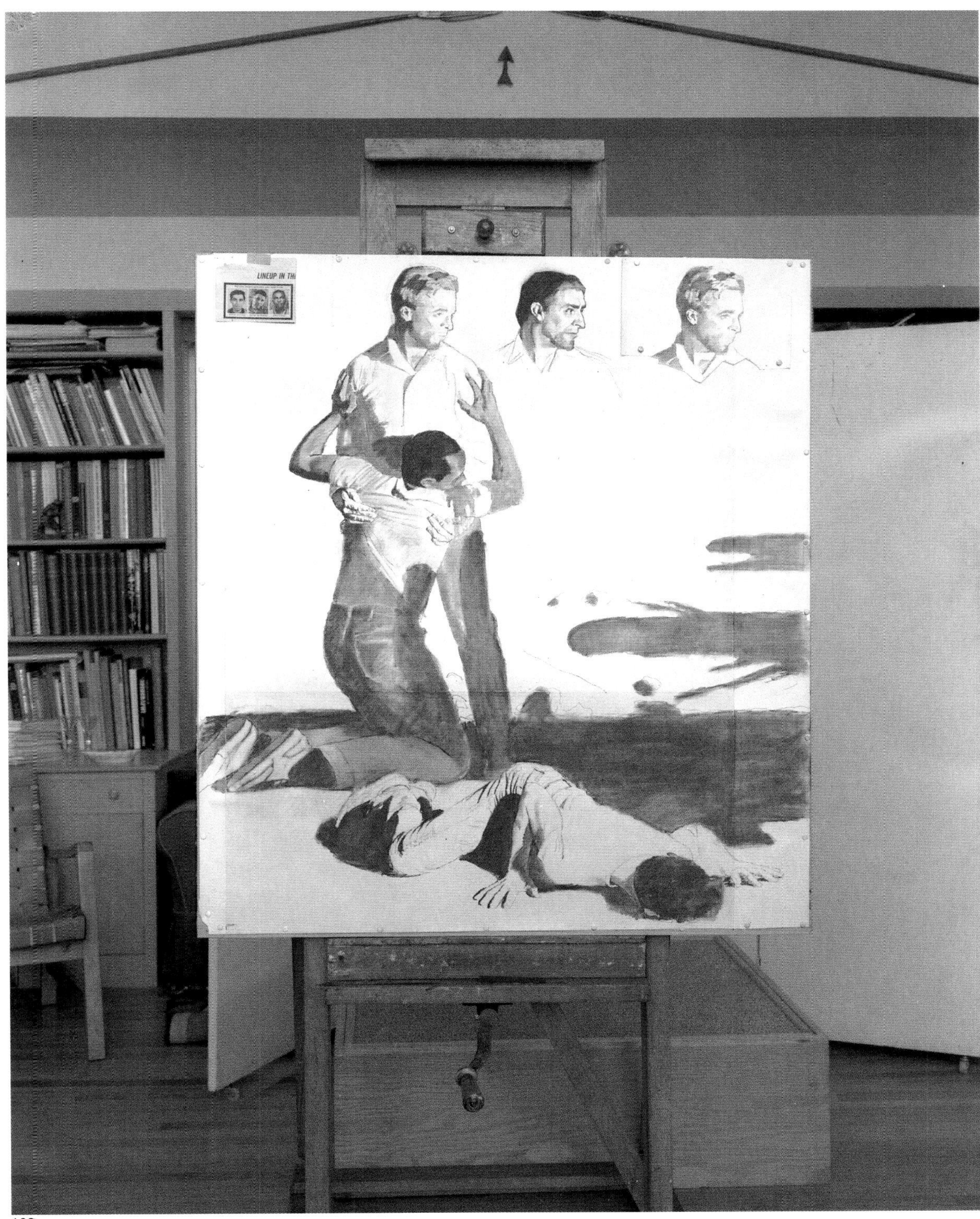

108

109. Preliminary drawing for *Murder in Mississippi*, March 28–April 5, 1965
Photo by Louie Lamone
Digital print from archival negative, 53 x 42 inches
Norman Rockwell Museum Collection

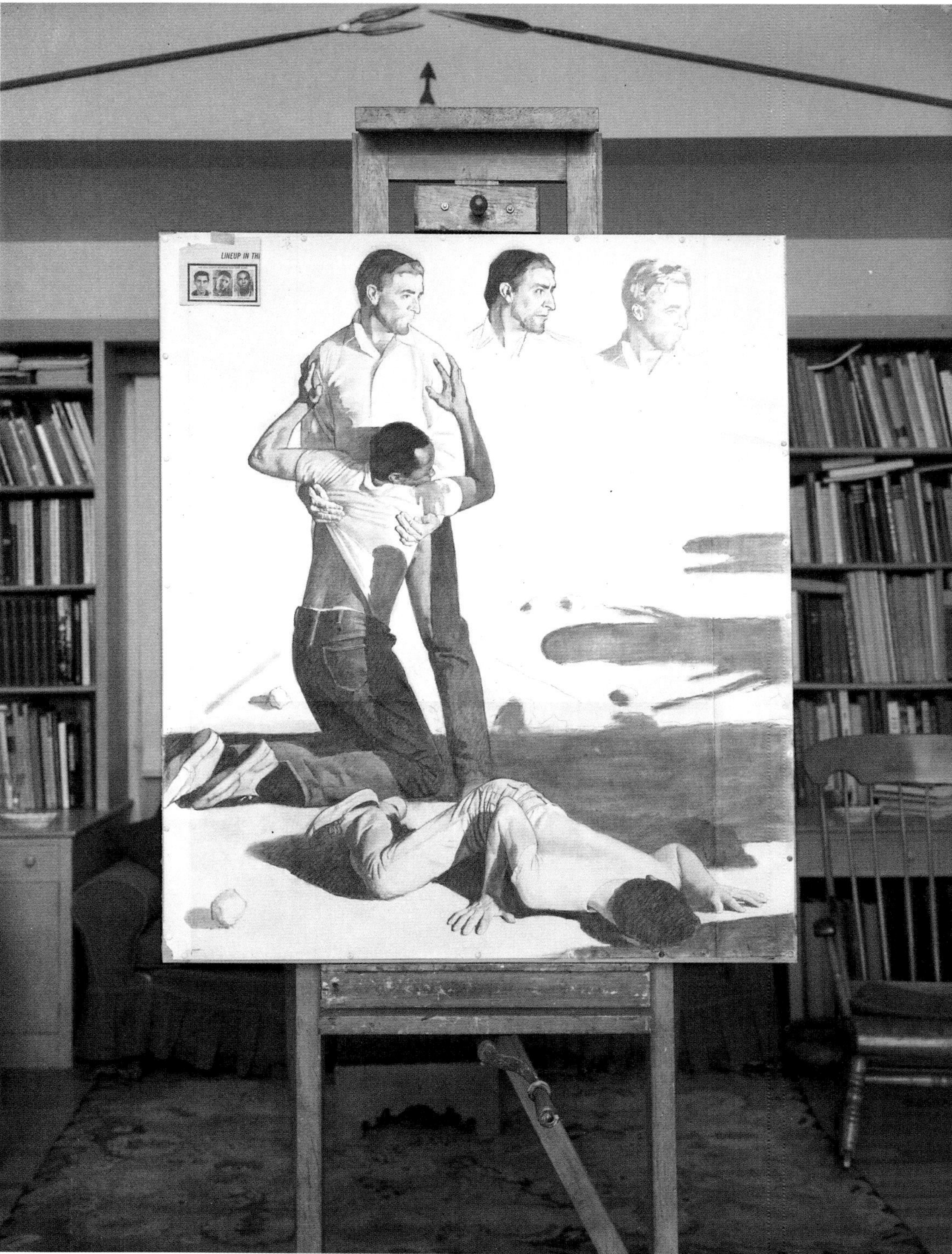

109

110. *Murder in Mississippi*, 1965
Section of pencil tracing, unpublished
Pencil on paper, 15.5 x 15 inches
Norman Rockwell Art Collection Trust,
Studio Collection, NRACT.1976.365

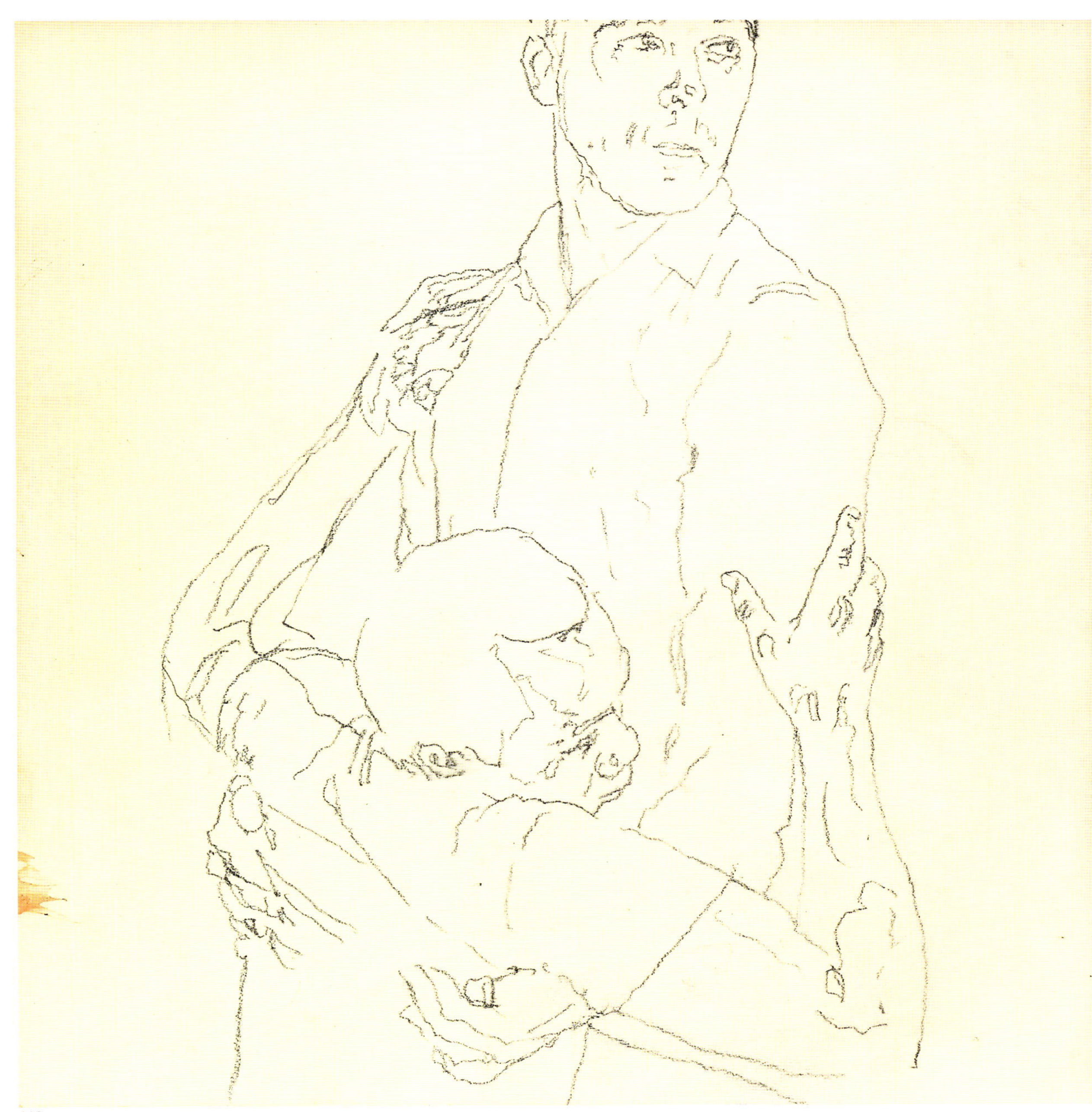

110

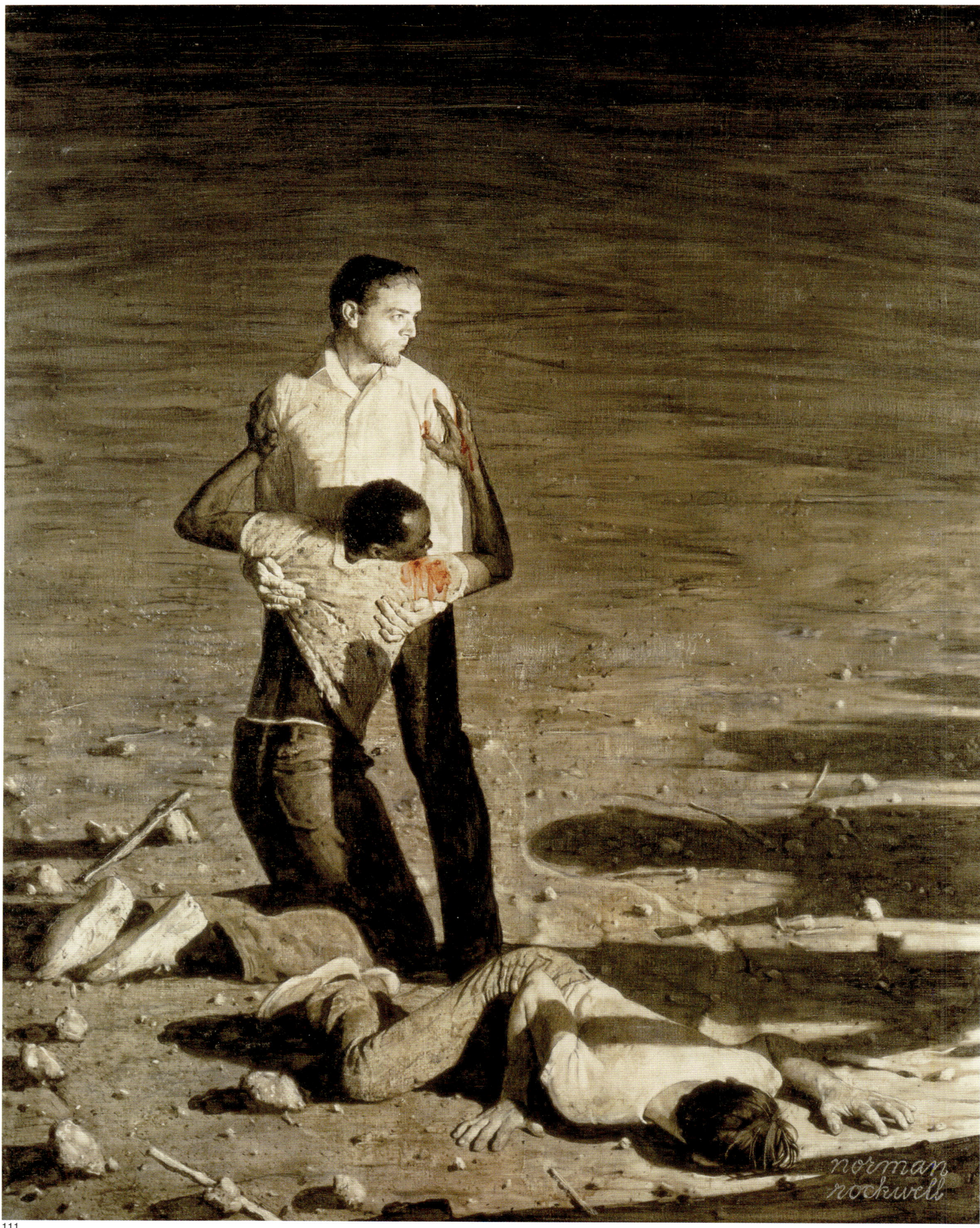

111

112. *Southern Justice*, 1965
Look, June 29, 1965
Double-page tear sheet,
13.25 x 21 inches
Norman Rockwell Museum Collection

THEY WERE an unlikely trio on an unlikely trip. Few young people go to Philadelphia, Miss., except to visit the campgrounds of the "granddaddy of county fairs." Neshoba County's people are older; most of the young folk move away.

Michael Schwerner, 24, and Andrew Goodman, 20, both Northerners and white, had hope for Neshoba County and, indeed, all of Mississippi. Their Negro comrade, James Chaney, 21, of Meridian, Miss., had hope, too—that Negroes might be free, that Negroes and whites might learn to live together. They were special young men. That is why they disappeared on a June night in 1964.

Forty-four days later, their bodies were dug out of a red-clay dam on the Old John Townsend Place, five miles from Philadelphia. They had been shot to death. Chaney's body had been mangled.

Southern justice is segregated. Judges, juries, sheriffs, police, troopers and FBI agents are white. So are jailers, bailiffs, marshals, lawyers, stenographers, clerks and coroners who command Southern courthouses and jails and electric chairs.

FEDERAL COURTS, 11 SOUTHERN STATES

	TOTAL	WHITE	NEGRO
Circuit Court Judges	12	12	0
District Court Judges	65	65	0
U.S. Commissioners	253	253	0
U.S. Clerks	28	28	0
Deputy U.S. Clerks	321	321	0
U.S. Attorneys	29	29	0
Assistant U.S. Attorneys	158	153	5
Jury Commissioners	109	109	0
U.S. Marshals	29	29	0
Deputy U.S. Marshals	165	156	9

Southern justice

In the Deep South, where Sunday-morning foot washing may precede Sunday-evening killing, justice is a weapon of repression. Lawmen are elected because they "know how to handle niggers." So do judges. Yet Negroes are told to fight their battle in white courts—courts that free white killers of Negroes, but punish Negroes harshly for minor offenses against whites. Meanwhile—

THE LIST OF DEAD IS GROWING:

William L. Moore, 35, white Baltimore postman. Shot near Attalla, Ala., April 23, 1963.

Medgar W. Evers, 37, NAACP field secretary. Ambushed in Jackson, Miss., June 12, 1963.

Denise McNair, 11, Cynthia Wesley, Carol Robertson and Addie Mae Collins, 14, Negro schoolgirls. Killed in church bombing, Birmingham, Ala., September 15, 1963.

Johnny Robinson, 16, Negro. Killed by policeman's shotgun after church bombing, Birmingham, Ala., September 15, 1963.

Lemuel A. Penn, 49, Negro school official returning to Washington, D.C., from Army Reserve training. Killed by shotgun blast on north Georgia highway, July 11, 1964.

Jimmie Lee Jackson, 26, Negro. According to witnesses, shot by state trooper while protecting his mother from beating, Marion, Ala., February 18, 1965. Died, February 26.

The Rev. James J. Reeb, 38, white Boston Unitarian minister, clubbed, Selma, Ala., March 9, 1965. Died, March 11.

Viola Gregg Liuzzo, 39, white Detroit housewife, killed on U.S. Highway 80 near Selma, Ala., March 25, 1965, following Montgomery march.

And there are forgotten casualties: Walter Bergman, Freedom Rider from Detroit, crippled in a beating on a bus near Birmingham. He will spend his life walking with canes. Little Sarah Jean Collins, 12, almost totally blinded in the bombing of the church in Birmingham, Ala.

And forgotten murders: Emmett Till, 14, Negro, murdered August 28, 1955. His killers went free. Mack Charles Parker, 23, Negro, lynched April 25, 1959. No one remembers the names of the two white men killed in the Ole Miss riot, Oxford, Miss., September 30, 1962. And no one will ever know how many more victims lie awash in the swamps and bayous of the Deep South.

The struggle in the South is not a battle for law and order. It is the struggle of law, new law, against the harsh, old order. Troopers and deputies who club demonstrators in Selma, Ala., bombings and arson across the South, the murdered, blinded and maimed are all part of a willful defiance of law.

In all the above killings, not a single conviction has been obtained.

Mickey Schwerner, James Chaney, Andrew Goodman may have cried out that night in June, 1964. We will never know. If they did, they cried for justice. *CHARLES MORGAN, JR.*

Philadelphia, Miss., June 21, 1964
Painted for LOOK by
NORMAN ROCKWELL

LOOK 6-29-65 73

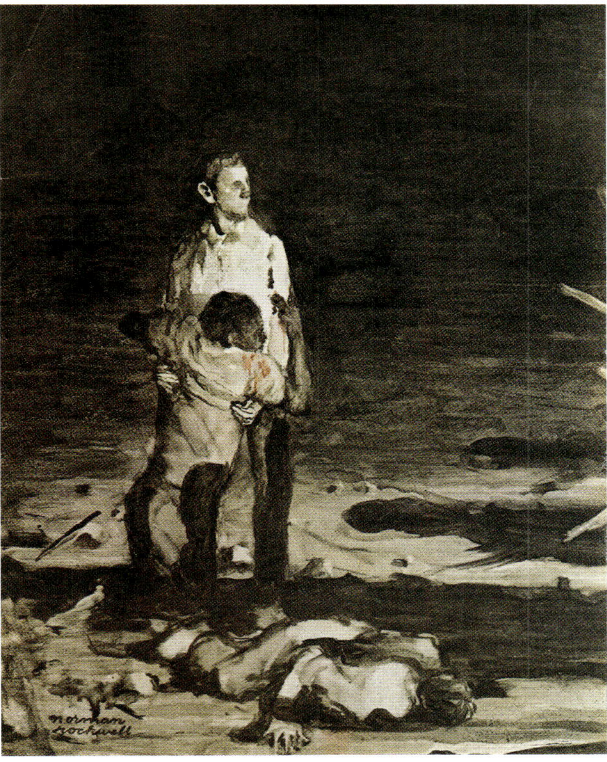

112

111. *Murder in Mississippi*,
April 6–13, 1965
Painting intended as the final
illustration for *Southern Justice*
by Charles Morgan, Jr., *Look*,
June 29, 1965, unpublished
Oil on canvas, 53 x 42 inches
Norman Rockwell Museum Collection,
NRM.1978.7

On April 14, Rockwell sent his final painting to *Look*. On the 29th, Rockwell received word that *Look* had decided to use his color study rather than the final painting. Three years later, Rockwell reflected that by the time he had finished the final painting, "all the anger that was in the sketch had gone out of it."

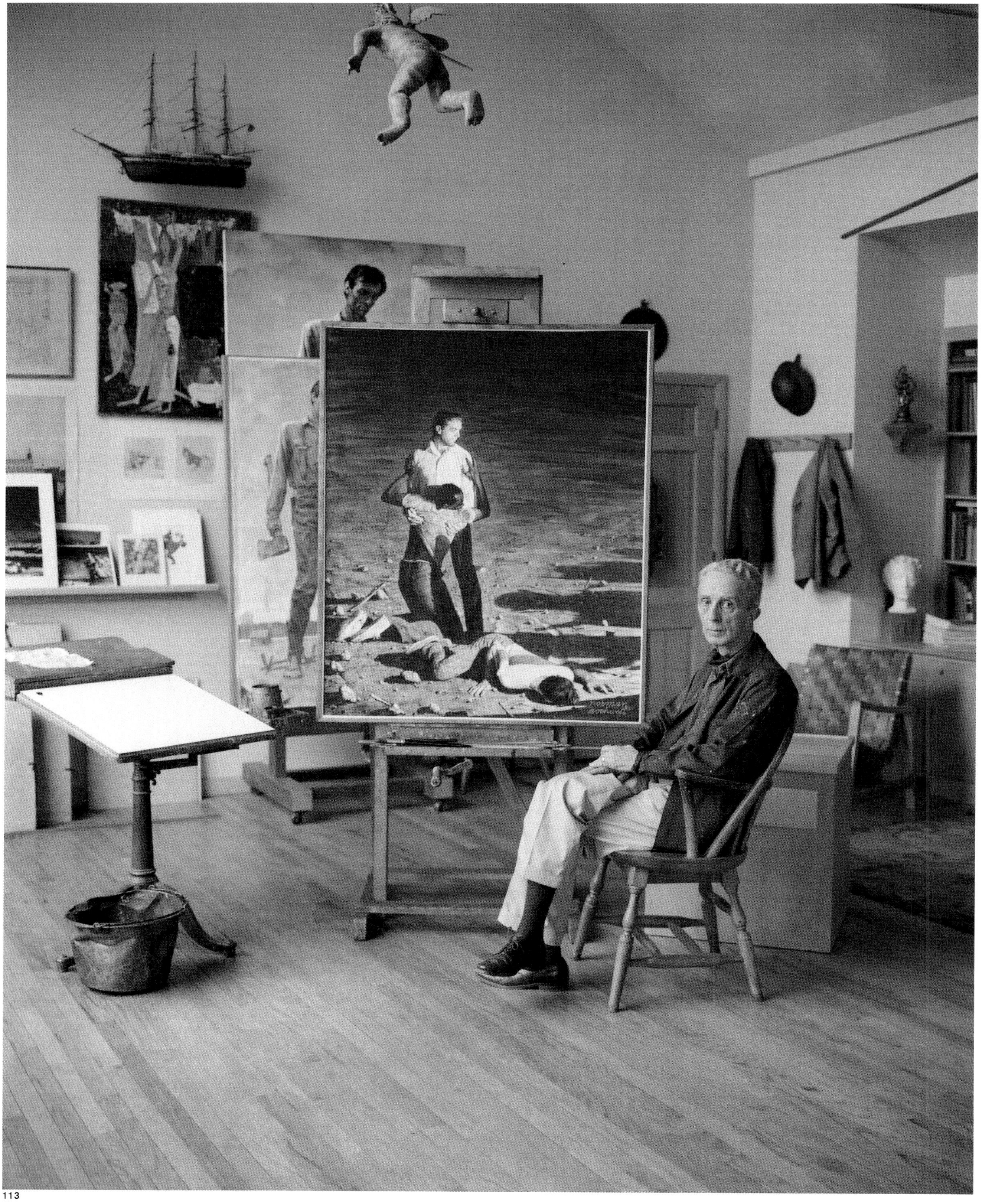

113

113. Norman Rockwell with *Murder in Mississippi*, 1965
Photo by Louie Lamone
Digital print from archival negative.
37 x 30 inches
Norman Rockwell Museum Collection

114. *Those Who Were Killed in U.S. During Civil Rights Movement*
The New York Times National,
November 4, 1989
Tear sheet, 18.5 x 9 inches
Norman Rockwell Museum Collection

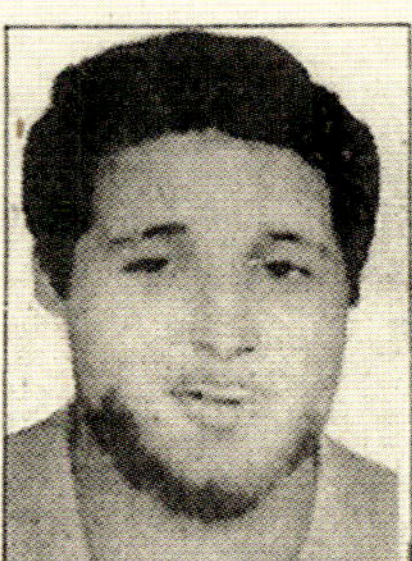

Associated Press
Michael Schwerner

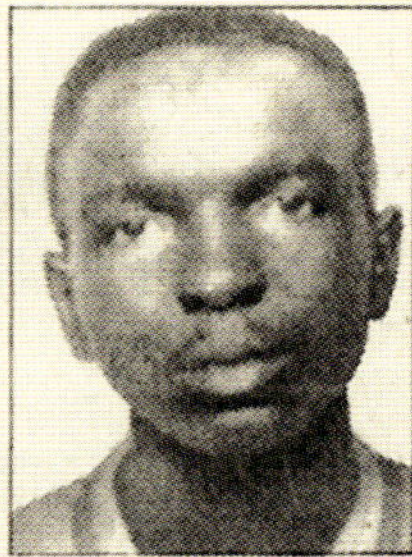

Associated Press
James Chaney

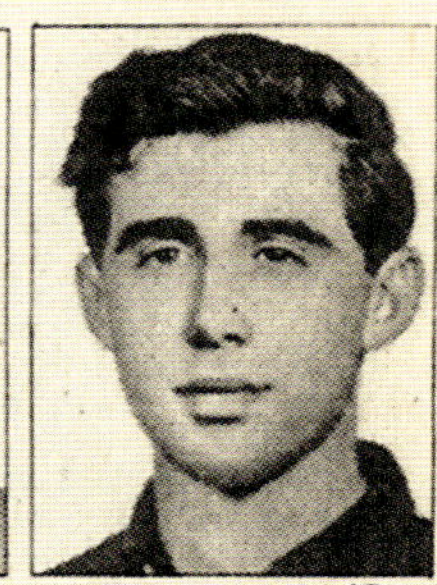

Associated Press
Andrew Goodman

Those Who Were Killed in U.S. During Civil Rights Movement

MONTGOMERY, Ala., Nov. 3 (AP) — *A civil rights memorial to be dedicated Sunday includes the names of the 40 people killed in the movement. The list, in chronological sequence, gives the date and circumstances of the person's death as described on the memorial.*

LEE, the Rev. George, killed May 7, 1955, for leading a voter registration drive in Belzoni, Miss.

SMITH, Lamar, 63 years old, slain Aug. 13, 1955, for organizing black voters in Brookhaven, Miss.

TILL, Emmett Louis, 14, slain Aug. 28, 1955, for speaking to a white woman in Money, Miss.

REESE, John Earl, 16, slain Oct. 22, 1955, by nightriders opposed to black school improvements in Mayflower, Tex.

EDWARDS, Willie Jr., killed Jan. 23, 1957, by the Ku Klux Klan in Montgomery, Ala.

PARKER, Mack Charles, 23, taken from a jail and lynched April 25, 1959, in Poplarville, Miss.

LEE, Herbert, 50, voter registration worker, killed Sept. 25, 1961, by a white legislator in Liberty, Miss.

DUCKSWORTH, Roman Jr., taken from bus and killed April 9, 1962, by the police in Taylorsville, Miss.

GUIHARD, Paul, a European reporter, killed Sept. 30, 1962, in a riot at University of Mississippi in Oxford, Miss.

MOORE, William Lewis, slain April 23, 1963, in a one-man march against segregation in Attalla, Ala.

EVERS, Medgar, 28, civil rights leader, assassinated June 12, 1963, in Jackson, Miss.

COLLINS, Addie Mae, 14, killed Sept. 15, 1963, in the bombing of the 16th Street Baptist Church in Birmingham, Ala.

MCNAIR, Denise, 11, killed Sept. 15, 1963, in the Birmingham church bombing.

ROBERTSON, Carole, 14, killed Sept. 15, 1963, in the church bombing.

WESLEY, Cynthia, 14, killed Sept. 15, 1963, in the church bombing.

WARE, Virgil Lamar, 13, killed Sept. 15, 1963, in a wave of racist violence in Birmingham, Ala.

ALLEN, Louis, witness to the killing of a civil rights worker, assassinated Jan. 31, 1964, in Liberty, Miss.

KLUNDER, the Rev. Bruce, killed April 7, 1964, protesting the construction of a segregated school in Cleveland.

DEE, Henry Hezekiah, 19, killed May 2, 1964, by the Klan in Meadville, Miss.

MOORE, Charles Eddie, 20, killed May 2, 1964, by the Klan in Meadville, Miss.

CHANEY, James, 21, civil rights worker, abducted and slain June 21, 1964, by the Klan in Philadelphia, Miss.

GOODMAN, Andrew, civil rights worker, abducted and slain June 21, 1964, by the Klan in Philadelphia, Miss.

SCHWERNER, Michael, 24, rights worker, abducted and slain June 21, 1964, by the Klan in Philadelphia, Miss.

PENN, Lemuel, 48, killed July 11, 1964, by the Klan while driving through Colbert, Ga.

JACKSON, Jimmie Lee, civil rights marcher, killed Feb. 26, 1965, by a state trooper in Marion, Ala.

REEB, the Rev. James, march volunteer, beaten to death on March 11, 1965 in Selma, Ala.

LIUZZO, Viola Gregg, 39, killed March 25, 1965, by the Ku Klux Klan while transporting marchers on a highway near Selma, Ala.

MOORE, Oneal, 34, black deputy, killed June 2, 1965, by nightriders in Varnado, La.

BREWSTER, Willie Wallace, 38, killed July 18, 1965, by nightriders in Anniston, Ala.

DANIELS, Jonathan, 26, seminary student, killed Aug. 20, 1965, by a part-time deputy in Hayneville, Ala.

YOUNGE, Samuel Jr., student civil rights worker, killed Jan. 3, 1966, in a dispute over a whites-only restroom in Tuskegee, Ala.

DAHMER, Vernon, black community leader, killed Jan. 10, 1966, in a Klan bombing in Hattiesburg, Miss.

WHITE, Ben Chester, 67, killed June 10, 1966, by the Klan in Natchez, Miss.

TRIGGS, Clarence, slain July 30, 1966, by nightriders in Bogalusa, La.

JACKSON, Wharlest, 37, civil rights leader, killed Feb. 27, 1967, after promotion to "white" job in Natchez, Miss.

BROWN, Benjamin, 22, civil rights worker, killed May 12, 1967, when the police fired on protesters in Jackson, Miss.

HAMMOND, Samuel Jr., 18, killed Feb. 8, 1968, when highway patrolmen fired on protesters in Orangeburg, S.C.

MIDDLETON, Delano, 17, killed Feb. 8, 1968, in the Orangeburg shootings.

SMITH, Henry, student killed Feb. 8, 1968, in the Orangeburg shootings.

KING, the Rev. Dr. Martin Luther Jr., 39, assassinated April 4, 1968 in Memphis.

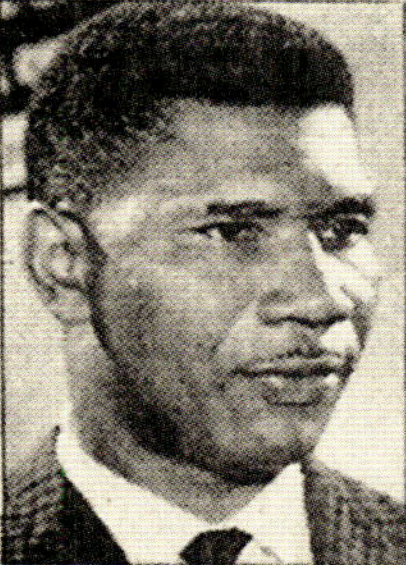

Medgar Evers

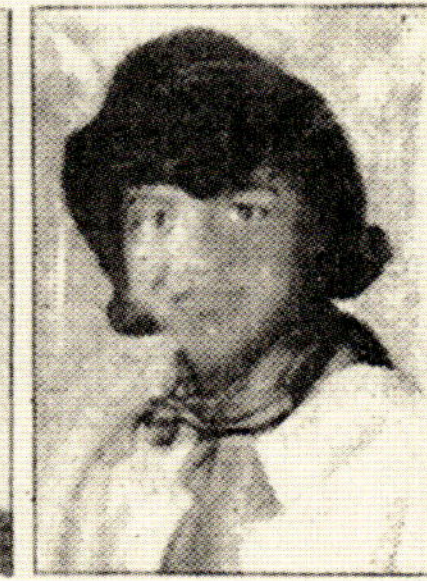

The New York Times
Cynthia Wesley

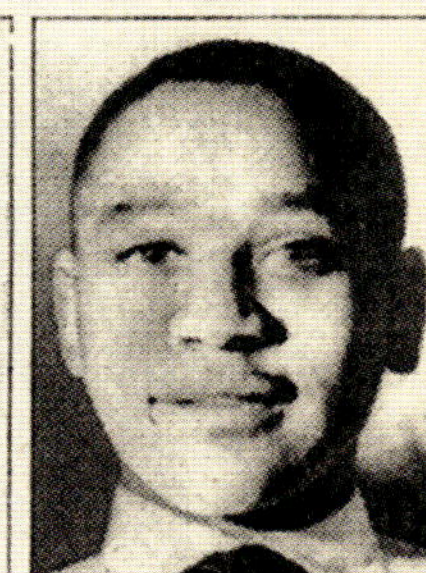

Associated Press
Emmett Louis Till

114

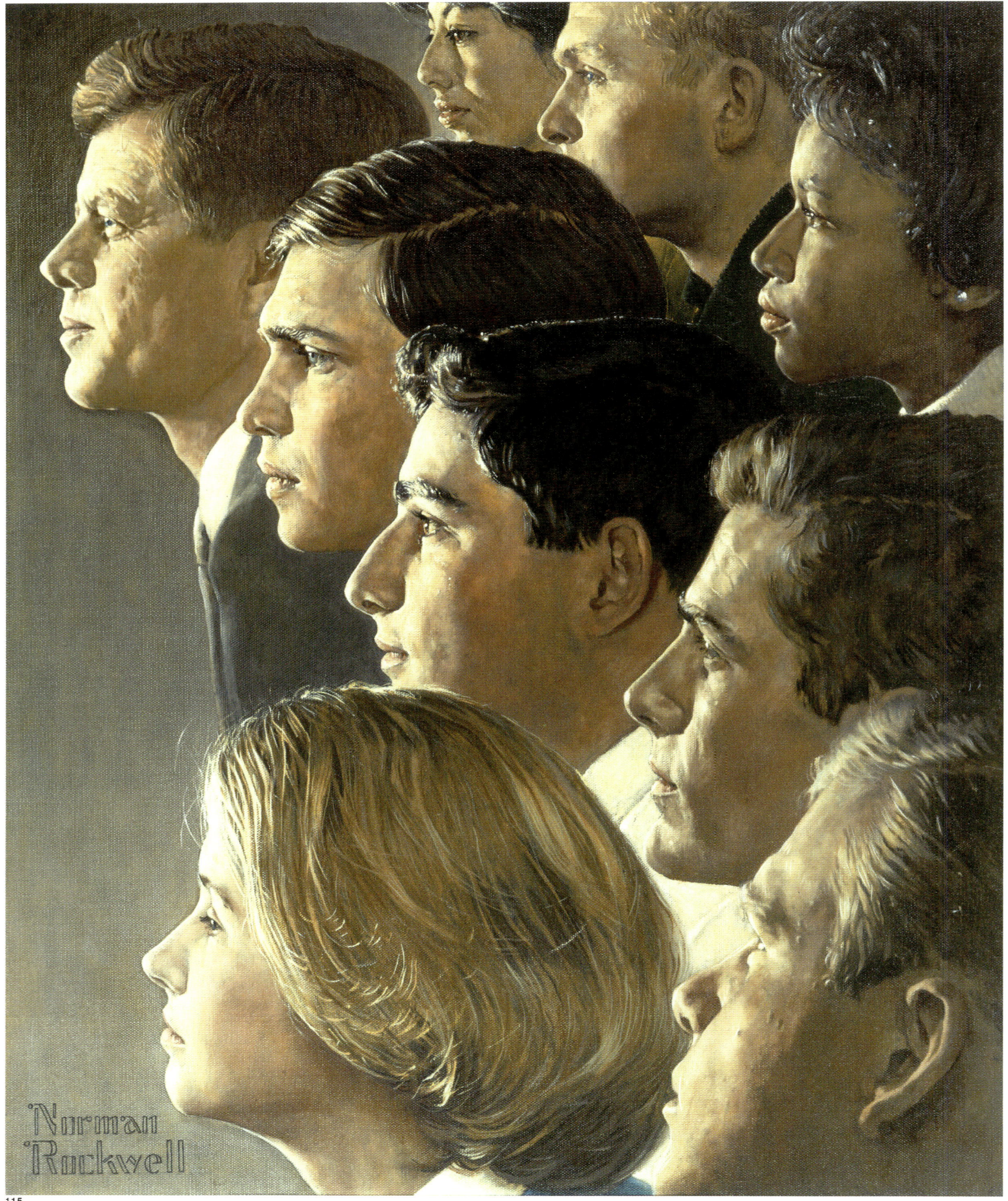
Norman
Rockwell

mented with his medium, in some cases replacing his usual oils with casein or acrylic or both.

In the years that followed, Rockwell reported on John F. Kennedy's Peace Corps program and the race to space, depicting the moon landing before and after it actually happened. In 1967, he illustrated a status report on the desegregation of our suburbs, and that fall began work on *The Right to Know*, an urgent call for government disclosure and accountability regarding Vietnam. With financial security, an adoring public and the admiration of his peers—in 1959 Rockwell was the first inductee named to the prestigious Society of Illustrators Hall of Fame—he was now free to tip the balance of his work toward the controversial subjects that concerned him: racial discrimination, poverty, and the rights of Americans to know the reasons for the choices of their government's leaders. America was at war in Vietnam and in its cities' streets, and Rockwell had the opportunity to voice his opinion. In 1971, when, after a brief hiatus, the *Post* resumed publishing under new ownership, the new editors asked Rockwell to work for them once again. When he wavered, his wife Molly interceded, saying, "Norman, you mustn't!" In 1977, President Gerald R. Ford honored Rockwell with the Presidential Medal of Freedom, the nation's highest peacetime award, for having portrayed "the American scene with unrivalled freshness and clarity," and with "insight, optimism and good humor."

115. *The Peace Corps*
(JFK's Bold Legacy), 1966
Painting for *Look* cover and story illustration, June 14, 1966
Oil on canvas, 45.5 x 36.5 inches
Norman Rockwell Art Collection Trust, NRACT.1973.83

Rockwell repeated the simple and powerful style used in *Freedom of Worship* to lend impact to this painting. Knowing his strength lay in communicating ideas and feelings through facial expressions, Rockwell chose to portray faces rather than situations to commemorate the fifth anniversary of the Corps. During his 1960 presidential campaign, John F. Kennedy proposed the idea of a volunteer organization of trained people who would be sent to developing nations in Africa and Asia to assist villagers in educational and agricultural projects. In 1961, the program, which Kennedy hoped would promote understanding between nations, was officially instated. Rockwell's portrait of Kennedy is based on a Jacques Lowe photograph from his book, *The Kennedy Years*. Former Peace Corps workers posed for most of the figures. "In this sordid world of power struggles, politics and national rivalries, the Peace Corps seems to stand almost alone," wrote Rockwell to art director Allen Hurlburt, when he sent the picture to *Look* magazine.

Odds & Ends
Rarely did Rockwell use the same model for more than one character in a painting. He once told his son Peter, "Do you know why Breughel was able to paint such beautiful trees? Because Brueghel painted each tree as an individual."

Following pages
John and Yoko's "Bed-In",
Amsterdam, March 27, 1969

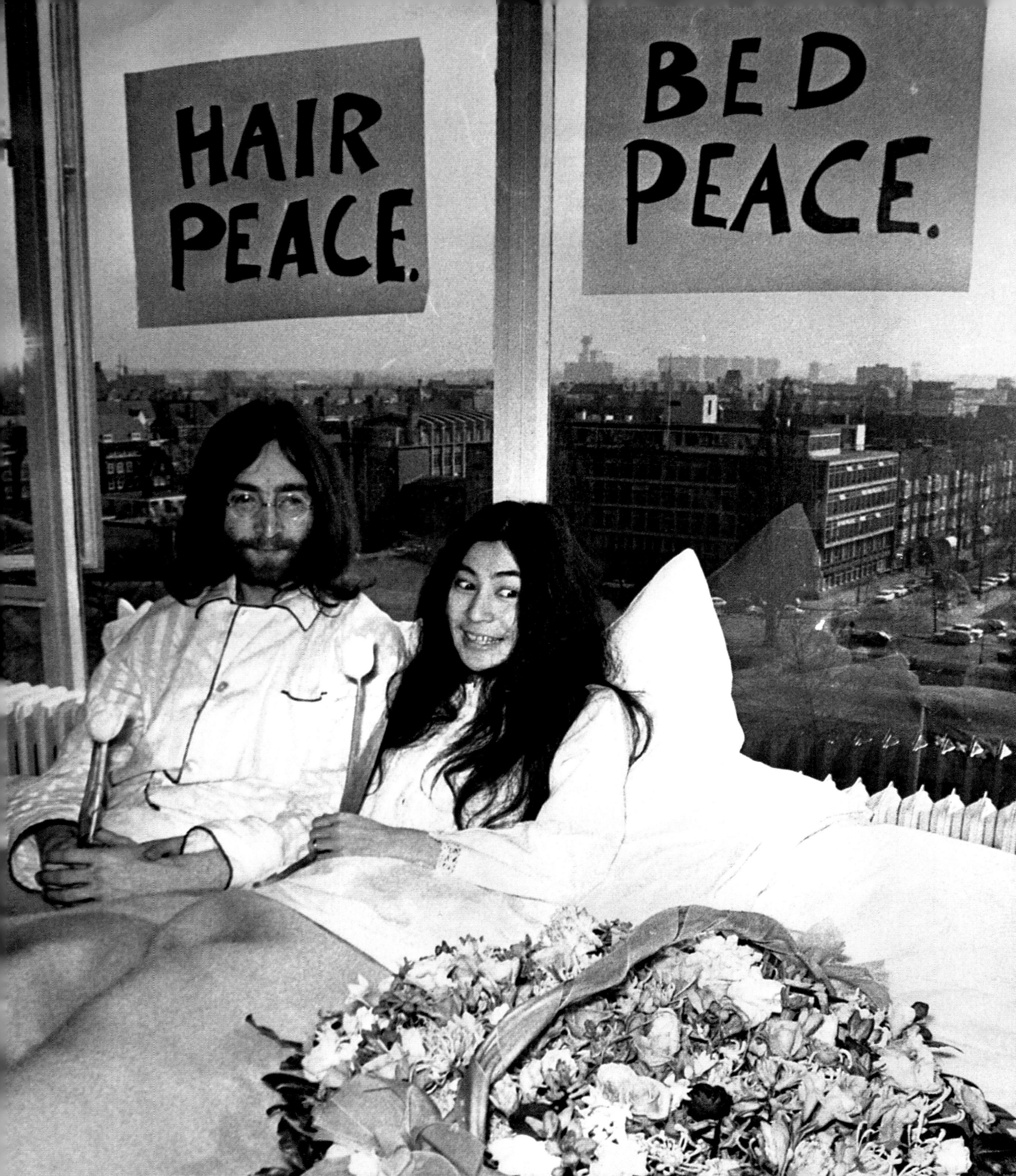
HAIR
PEACE.
BED
PEACE.

During his Stockbridge years, Rockwell produced paintings that will always resonate. *The Problem We All Live With* gently presents an aggressive assertion on moral decency. Art critics, connoisseurs, and historians continue to examine and reflect on *The Connoisseur* as they discuss "high" and "low" art and the meanings of abstract art. *Art Critic* will always intrigue us for its masterly technique and the delight we feel as we are drawn into its secret life. For five decades, Rockwell opened our hearts by lovingly portraying our foibles. When he shifted his attention to the broader picture of social ills, he faced an audience ready to receive his messages, helping us evolve into a more compassionate culture.

Despite declining health, Rockwell accepted a commission to paint the July 1976 cover of *American Artist* magazine, celebrating the country's bicentennial. That summer, in a parade and celebration, the people of Stockbridge claimed Rockwell as their own hometown hero. With the onset of dementia and the effects of emphysema resulting from years of pipe-smoking, Rockwell could no longer do the work that had so completely and passionately driven his life. In 1978, at age 84, Rockwell died at home.

116. *Christmas Eve in Bethlehem*, 1970
Painting for *Look* story illustration, "Uneasy Christmas in the Birthplace of Christ," December 29, 1970
Oil on canvas, 33 x 51 inches
Norman Rockwell Art Collection Trust, NRACT.1973.75

The Basilica of the Nativity, built between 527 and 565 AD, stands where Jesus is traditionally believed to have been born. On December 9, 1969, Rockwell decided to go to Bethlehem to paint a Christmas scene. Two weeks later, accompanied by his wife Molly and his photographer Brad Herzog, he flew to Jerusalem. On Christmas Eve, from the roof of a Bethlehem hotel, he gathered impressions for his painting and directed the photography. He was particularly impressed by the "sumptuous" presentation of the high priests, cardinals, and bishops as they proceeded to the Basilica. "The high priests carry large crucifixes and banners," he said, "and wear white and scarlet robes, some of them with their red bishop's caps.... It is indeed a tremendous spectacle and, although I am not a religious man, I was greatly impressed."
Rockwell's early version of the rooftop onlookers included "devout native Israeli, Christian, Jewish and Mohammedan." The picture was a compromise between Rockwell and *Look*'s art director, who wanted him to omit the Arab and one soldier. But Rockwell kept both soldiers, "They never seem to go singly about the streets of Bethlehem," he said. Another compromise was made when, at the art director's request, he removed the tourist family's souvenirs and guidebook from the painting.
Look wanted Rockwell to do portraits of Prime Minister Golda Meir, Jerusalem Mayor Teddy Kollek, and General Moshe Dayan during his five-day stay in Jerusalem. Rockwell met with Meir at her home and with Kollek. Dayan, however, would not meet with him. Rockwell later did a portrait of Mayor Kollek based on photos taken during the visit, but *Look* decided against the project and never published the portrait.

Odds & Ends
The entrance to the Basilica, seen in the lower left corner of the painting, is narrow and low. The most popular opinion is that the unusual design protected the church from invaders on horseback. Another is that Muslims used it during their rule to remind Christians they were guests and must bow to their hosts. A third is that it protected Christians from hostile neighbors.

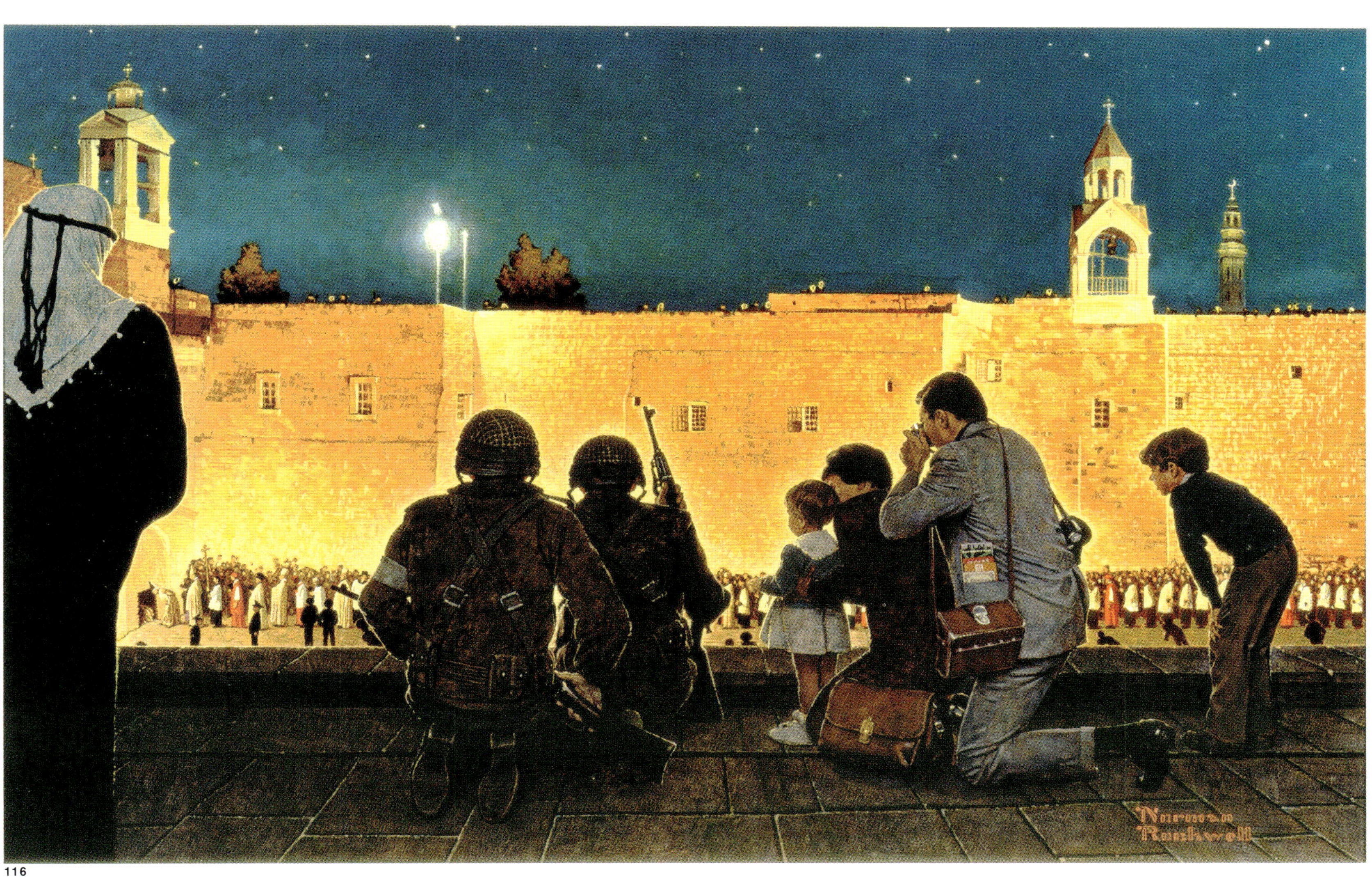
Norman
Rockwell

Appendix

Exhibitions 1914–2014

New Rochelle Art Association, May 1914, New Rochelle Public Library, New Rochelle, New York
First exhibition and debut of the Association
Group exhibition

New Rochelle Art Association, February 8, 1916 – n.d., New Rochelle Public Library, New Rochelle, New York
Artwork by Norman Rockwell, Victor C. Forsythe, and Ernest Albert, Jr.
Group exhibition

Mark Twain Museum, July 1937 – n.d., Hannibal, Missouri
Solo exhibition

Bell & Fletcher Gallery, December 1937, Boston, Massachusetts
Solo exhibition

Mark Twain Museum, February 1938 – January 1939, Hannibal, Missouri
Solo exhibition

Portrait Painters Gallery, January 30 – February 11, 1939, New York
Solo exhibition

Society of Illustrators, April 1939, New York
Thirty-Seventh Annual Exhibition
Group exhibition

Ferargil Galleries, January 6–20, 1941, New York
Solo exhibition
n.d., Detroit, Michigan
April 1941, Hackley Art Gallery, Muskegon, Michigan
May 1941, Milwaukee Art Institute, Milwaukee, Wisconsin
July–August 1941, Thayer Art Museum, Lawrence, Kansas
October 9–26, 1941, Davenport Municipal Art Gallery, Davenport, Iowa
November 1–25, 1941, Currier Gallery of Art, Manchester, New Hampshire
December 1–28, 1941, Brooks Memorial Art Gallery, Memphis, Tennessee
January 1–25, 1942, Beloit College, Beloit, Wisconsin
April 13–25, 1942, Higbee Auditorium, Cleveland, Ohio
May 3–23, 1942, Academy of Arts, Newark, New Jersey

Galleries of Associated American Artists, May 1941, New York
Twentieth Annual Exhibition of the Art Directors Club
Group exhibition

Art Students League, February 7–28, 1943, New York
Fifty Years on 57th Street
Group exhibition

Curtis Publishing Co. and U.S. Treasury
Four Freedoms War Bond Show
Group exhibition
April 27 – May 8, 1943, The Hecht Company, Washington, District of Columbia
May 15–22, 1943, Strawbridge and Clothier, Philadelphia, Pennsylvania
June 4–13, 1943, Rockefeller Center, New York
June 19–26, 1943, William Filene's Sons and Company, Boston, Massachusetts
July 14–21, 1943, The William Hengerer Company, Buffalo, New York
August 2–7, 1943, Sibley, Lindsay & Curr Company, Rochester, New York
September 8–15, 1943, Kaufmann's Department Store, Pittsburgh, Pennsylvania
September 27 – October 9, 1943, J.L. Hudson Company, Detroit, Michigan
October 25–28, 1943, May Company, Cleveland, Ohio
November 11–22, 1943, Carson Pirie Scott Company, Chicago, Illinois
December 16–23, 1943, Stix, Baer and Fuller Company, St. Louis, Missouri
January 17–21, 1944, Municipal Auditorium, New Orleans, Louisiana
January 27 – February 5, 1944, Tisch-Goettinger Company, Dallas, Texas
February 12–22, 1944, Bullock's, Los Angeles, California
March 27 – April 8, 1944, Meier & Frank Company, Portland, Oregon
May 1–6, 1944, Denver Dry Goods Company, Denver, Colorado

California Palace of the Legion of Honor, May 1945, San Francisco, California
Group exhibition

Society of Illustrators, May 3–20, 1946, International Galleries Rockefeller Center, New York
Group exhibition

Southern Vermont Artists, Inc., August 24 – September 3, 1946, Manchester, Vermont
Seventeenth Annual Exhibition
Group exhibition

The Metropolitan Museum of Art, January 7, 1947 – n.d., New York
Art in Motion Picture Advertising
Group exhibition

Curtis Publishing Company, 1947, Philadelphia, Pennsylvania
The Saturday Evening Post Art Exhibition
Group exhibition

Stevens Gross Galleries, May 20 – June 28, 1947, Chicago, Illinois
Paintings by Norman Rockwell and Mead Schaeffer
Group exhibition

Woodbury College, July 12 – August 6, 1948, Los Angeles, California
25 Original Saturday Evening Post Paintings
Group exhibition

Society of Illustrators, December 17, 1948, New York
Group exhibition

Arts and Crafts Festival, August 1–14, 1949, Skyforest, California
Group exhibition

New Rochelle Public Library, January 29 – February 15, 1951, New Rochelle, New York
Solo exhibition

Institute of Commercial Art, Inc., New York
Art America Loves
Group exhibition
March 4–18, 1951, Parthenon Museum, Nashville, Tennessee
March 1951 – n.d., New England School of Art, Boston, Massachusetts
n.d., Entwistle Galleries, Ridgewood, New Jersey
n.d., Atlanta, Georgia

The Metropolitan Museum of Art, n.d. – April 29, 1951, New York
The 75th Anniversary Exhibition of Painting & Sculpture by 75 Artists Associated with the Art Students League of New York
Group exhibition

Saint-Gaudens Memorial, August 6, 1951 – n.d., Cornish, New Hampshire
The Saturday Evening Post Art Exhibition
Group exhibition
October 1951, Cartoonists and Illustrators School, New York
November 1951, Laguna Beach, California

Curtis Publishing Company
Paintings for the *Saturday Evening Post.*
Solo exhibition
June 13, 1955, Corcoran Gallery, Washington, District of Columbia
October 1955, Asheville Art Museum, Asheville, North Carolina
June 1956, Washington County Museum of Fine Arts, Hagerstown, Maryland
n.d., Calgary Power Ltd, Calgary, Alberta, Canada
February 1957, William Filene's Sons and Company, Boston, Massachusetts

Berkshire Museum, October 1955, Pittsfield, Massachusetts
Group exhibition

Berkshire Museum, August 1–31, 1958, Pittsfield, Massachusetts
Norman Rockwell Retrospective
Solo exhibition

Virginia Beach Convention Center, January 13–25, 1960, Virginia Beach, Virginia
Solo exhibition

Berkshire Museum, February 11, 1960 – n.d., Pittsfield, Massachusetts
Original Drawings and Sketches of Local People
Solo exhibition

Seaman's Savings Bank, n.d. – February 26, 1960, New York
Solo exhibition

Southern Vermont Art Center, June 30 – July 22, 1962, Manchester, Vermont
The Saturday Evening Post Norman Rockwell Show
Solo exhibition

Cooperstown Art Association, July 29 – August 23, 1962, Cooperstown, New York
27th Annual Open Exhibition
Group exhibition
Note: between 1962 and 1974, Norman Rockwell exhibited artwork at the Annual Art Exhibition of the Cooperstown Art Association every year with the exception of 1964. In 1967 (July 30 – August 24), the Association held a solo show of his artwork

National Museum of Sport, Inc., November 1962, I.B.M. Gallery, New York
Fine Art in Sports
Group exhibition

Syracuse University/School of Art, March 6 – April 2, 1963, Syracuse, New York
15 American Illustrators
Group exhibition

Exhibit of Economic Achievements, December 13, 1963 – January 15, 1964, Moscow
American Graphics
Group exhibition

Akhenaton Gallery, January 23–27, 1964, Cairo, Egypt
Solo exhibition

Bennington Museum, June 19 – October 19, 1964, Bennington, Vermont
Paintings by Norman Rockwell
Solo exhibition

Chesterwood, July 1 – August 31, 1964, Stockbridge, Massachusetts
Exhibition of Paintings and Drawings by Norman Rockwell
Solo exhibition

City and County Savings Bank, June 1965, Albany, New York
Paintings by Norman Rockwell
Solo exhibition

Municipal Art Gallery, January 4 – February 6, 1966, Barnsdall Park, Los Angeles, California
Norman Rockwell
Solo exhibition

Bristol Art Museum, August 4–15, 1966, Bristol, Rhode Island
Paintings by Norman Rockwell
Solo exhibition

Paine Art Center and Arboretum, December 1, 1966 – January 5, 1967, Oshkosh, Wisconsin
Solo exhibition

Anchorage Gallery, January 31 – February 28, 1967, Syracuse, New York
Solo exhibition

Society of Illustrators, February 6–24, 1967, Union Carbide Exhibition Area, New York
Group exhibition

Bernard Danenberg Galleries, October 22 – November 9, 1968, New York
Major paintings by Norman Rockwell
Solo exhibition

Shaker Museum, August 2, 1969 – n.d., Old Chatham, New York
14th Annual Shaker Museum Festival
Solo exhibition

Society of Illustrators, May 8–18, 1970, New York
Artists Guild of New York, *Artist of the Year* exhibition
Solo exhibition

Lobster Pot Gallery, July 6, 1970 – n.d., Nantucket, Massachusetts
Norman Rockwell
Solo exhibition

National Air and Space Museum, Smithsonian Institution, December 1970 – April 1971, Washington, D.C.
Space Artists
Group exhibition

First Federal of Hollywood, September 27 – October 29, 1971, Los Angeles, California
Norman Rockwell
Solo exhibition

Bernard Danenberg Galleries, New York
Norman Rockwell: A Sixty Year Retrospective
Solo exhibition
February 11 – March 5, 1972, Ft. Lauderdale Museum of the Arts, Ft. Lauderdale, Florida
March 22 – May 14, 1972, Brooklyn Museum, Brooklyn, New York
May 26 – July 16, 1972, Corcoran Gallery of Art, Washington, D.C.
August 1–27, 1972, Marion Koogler McNay Art Institute, San Antonio, Texas
September 8 – November 5, 1972, M.H. De Young Memorial Museum, San Francisco, California
November 12 – December 10, 1972, Oklahoma Art Center, Oklahoma City, Oklahoma
December 18, 1972 – January 21, 1973, Indianapolis Museum of Art, Indianapolis, Indiana
January 28 – February 25, 1973, Joslyn Art Museum, Omaha, Nebraska
March 8 – April 15, 1973, Seattle Art Museum. Seattle, Washington
April 27 – May 27, 1973, Museum of the Philadelphia Civic Center, Philadelphia, Pennsylvania
April 4–9, 1975, Hankyu Department Store, Tokyo, Japan

Bamberger's, November 13 – December 30, 1972, Newark, New Jersey
Norman Rockwell
Solo exhibition

Smithsonian Institution Traveling Exhibition Service, October 6, 1973 – November 24, 1974, U.S. Department of the Interior
The American Artist and Water Reclamation: A selection of paintings from the collection of the Bureau of Reclamation
Group exhibition

Gallery 1020, May 20 – June 28, 1975, New York
Norman Rockwell
Solo exhibition

Museum of Arts and Sciences, January 15 – February 15, 1976, Daytona Beach, Florida
Norman Rockwell's America
Solo exhibition
February 19 – March 15, 1976, Norton Gallery of Art, West Palm Beach, Florida

Columbus Gallery of Fine Arts, and Allentown Art Museum, 1976–1977, Columbus, Ohio, and Allentown, Pennsylvania
Salute to Norman Rockwell
Solo exhibition

Bennington Museum, May 4 – July 28, 1978, Bennington, Vermont
Norman Rockwell Exhibition
Solo exhibition

Grand Central Art Galleries, Inc., May 8–25, 1979, New York
American Illustrators: The Twenties, Adventure, Suspense, Romance and Humor
Group exhibition

Museum of Fine Arts, June 1, 1979 – n.d., Springfield, Massachusetts
Solo exhibition

Davenport Art Gallery, 1980, Davenport, Iowa
The American Profile: Drawings by Norman Rockwell
Solo exhibition

Museum of Fine Arts, July 1 – August 3, 1980, St. Petersburg, Florida
American Illustrators: Norman Rockwell and His Contemporaries
Group exhibition

Dallas Historical Society, April – August 1981, Dallas, Texas
Norman Rockwell's World of Scouting
Solo exhibition

C.W. Post Art Gallery, Long Island University, March 19 – April 25, 1982, Greenvale, New York
The Great American Illustrators
Group exhibition

Center Art Galleries, July 1983, Honolulu, Hawaii
Norman Rockwell: Americana Collection
Solo exhibition

Judy Goffman Fine Art, December 4, 1985 – January 31, 1986, New York
Norman Rockwell: An American Tradition
Solo exhibition
March 25 – May 4, 1986, Greenville County Museum of Art, Greenville, South Carolina

Philadelphia Maritime Museum, November 7, 1986 – February 28, 1987, Philadelphia, Pennsylvania
Tales of the Mermaid
Group exhibition

June 5 – August 16, 1987,
The Mariners' Museum, Newport News, Virginia
September 8 – October 27, 1987, Explorers Hall, National Geographic Society, Washington, D.C.

Bennington Museum, 1988, Bennington, Vermont
Paintings by Norman Rockwell
Solo exhibition

Judy Goffman Fine Art, New York
Norman Rockwell: The Great American Storyteller
Solo exhibition
March 2–15, 1988, Mississippi Museum of Art, Jackson, Mississippi
June 25 – August 14, 1988, Orlando Museum of Art, Orlando, Florida
September 11 – October 30, 1988, Woods Art Gallery, University of Southern Mississippi, Hattiesburg, Mississippi
November 20, 1988 – January 9, 1989, Hunter Museum of Art, Chattanooga, Tennessee
January 30 – March 5, 1989, Center for the Arts, Vero Beach, Florida
March 26 – May 14, 1989, Lakeview Museum of Arts and Sciences, Peoria, Illinois
June 8–14, 1989, Judy Goffman Fine Art, New York

American Illustrators Gallery, New York
Norman Rockwell
Solo exhibition
August 3 – September 16, 1990, Museo "Ciasa de ra Regoles", Cortina d'Ampezzo, Italy

American Illustrators Gallery and Brain Trust, Inc., New York, and Tokyo, Japan
Norman Rockwell
Solo exhibition
February 20 – March 31, 1992, Isetan Museum of Art, Tokyo, Japan
May 7–17, 1992, Daimaru Museum, Umeda-Osaka, Osaka, Japan
July 23 – August 23, 1992, Matsuzakaya Art Museum, Nagoya, Japan

Galleria Prova, 1992, Tokyo, Japan
Heart Warming
Group exhibition

American Illustrators Gallery and Brain Trust, Inc., New York, and Tokyo, Japan
The Great American Illustrators
Group exhibition
April 21 – May 9, 1993, Odakyu Museum, Tokyo, Japan
June 12 – July 11, 1993, Fukushima Prefectural Museum of Art, Fukushima, Japan
October 20 – November 8, 1993, Daimaru Museum, Umeda-Osaka, Osaka, Japan

Norman Rockwell Museum at Stockbridge and Printemps, Stockbridge, Massachusetts, and Paris, France
Norman Rockwell's New England
Solo exhibition
November 17 – December 31, 1993, Printemps, Paris, France

Society of Illustrators and The Wagnalls Memorial Foundation, New York, and Columbus, Ohio
Ten Works from the Literary Digest Collection
Group exhibition
October 25 – November 18, 1995, Columbus College of Art & Design, Columbus, Ohio

Connecticut Valley Historical Museum, 1995, Springfield, Massachusetts
Norman Rockwell: Drawing the American Dream
Solo exhibition

Marietta/Cobb Museum of Art, Summer 1996, Marietta, Georgia
Norman Rockwell: Portrait of America
Solo exhibition

Norman Rockwell Museum and Brain Trust, Inc., Stockbridge, Massachusetts, and Tokyo, Japan
Norman Rockwell
Solo exhibition
December 4–28, 1997, Isetan Museum of Art, Tokyo, Japan
January 3–25, 1998, Matsuzakaya Art Museum, Nagoya, Japan
January 29 – March 1, 1998, Chiba Sogo Museum of Art, Chiba, Japan
March 4–17, 1998, Niigata Isetan Art Hall, Niigata, Japan
March 25 – April 13, 1998, Daimaru Museum, Umeda-Osaka, Osaka, Japan
April 18 – May 17, 1998, Hiroshima Museum of Art, Hiroshima, Japan

Norman Rockwell Museum and High Museum of Art, Stockbridge, Massachusetts, and Atlanta, Georgia
Pictures for the American People
Solo exhibition
November 6, 1999 – January 30, 2000, High Museum of Art, Atlanta, Georgia
February 26 – May 21, 2000, Chicago Historical Society, Chicago, Illinois
June 17 – September 24, 2000, Corcoran Gallery, Washington, District of Columbia
October 28 – December 31, 2000, San Diego Museum of Art, San Diego, California
January 27 – May 6, 2001, Phoenix Art Museum, Phoenix, Arizona
June 9 – October 8, 2001, Norman Rockwell Museum, Stockbridge, Massachusetts
November 16, 2001 – March 3, 2002 Solomon R. Guggenheim Museum, New York

Moi! Autoportraits du XXᵉ siècle (*Me! Self-portraits of the 20ᵗʰ Century*)
Triple Self Portrait, 1960
March 31 – July 25, 2004, Musée du Luxembourg, Paris, France
September 1, 2004 – January 2005, Palazzo Strozzi, Florence, Italy

Norman Rockwell Museum, Stockbridge, Massachusetts
Picturing Health: Norman Rockwell and the Art of Illustration
Group exhibition
July 7 – October 14, 2007, Florence Griswold Museum, Old Lyme, Connecticut

March 10 – June 2, 2008, Global Health Odyssey, Centers for Disease Control & Prevention, Atlanta, Georgia
September 20 – December 14, 2008, Kalamazoo Institute of Arts, Kalamazoo, Michigan
March 6 – May 24, 2009, Mobile Museum of Art, Mobile, Alabama
October 31, 2009 – January 31, 2010, Gari Melchers Home & Studio, Fredericksburg, Virginia
October 1, 2011 – January 1, 2012, El Paso Museum of Art, El Paso, Texas
May 5 – September 3, 2012, Heritage Museums & Gardens, Sandwich, Massachusetts

Norman Rockwell Museum, Stockbridge, Massachusetts
American Chronicles: The Art of Norman Rockwell
Solo exhibition
November 10, 2007 – February 3, 2008, Akron Art Museum, Akron, Ohio
March 1 – May 26, 2008, Orlando Museum of Art, Orlando, Florida
November 8, 2008 – February 1, 2009, Chrysler Museum of Art, Norfolk, Virginia
March 8 – May 31, 2009, Detroit Institute of Art, Detroit, Michigan
July 4 – September 7, 2009, Norman Rockwell Museum, Stockbridge, Massachusetts
November 14, 2009 – February 7, 2010, Museum of Art, Fort Lauderdale, Florida
March 6 – May 30, 2010, Wichita Art Museum, Wichita, Kansas
November 7, 2010 – January 30, 2011, North Carolina Museum of Art, Raleigh, North Carolina
February 26 – May 30, 2011, Tacoma Art Museum, Tacoma, Washington
November 12, 2011 – February 5, 2012, The Dayton Art Institute, Dayton, Ohio
March 1 – May 27, 2012 , Winnipeg Art Gallery, Winnipeg, Canada
November 10, 2012 – February 3, 2013, Crocker Art Museum, Sacramento, California
March 7 – May 28, 2013, Crystal Bridges Museum of American Art, Bentonville, Arkansas
November 1, 2013 - February 9, 2014, Frist Center for the Visual Arts, Nashville, Tennessee
February 28 – May 26, 2014, The Newark Museum, Newark, New Jersey
November 10, 2014 – February 8, 2015, Fondazione Roma Museo – Palazzo Sciarra, Rome, Italy
March 6 – May 31, 2015, Tampa Museum of Art, Tampa, Florida
November 19, 2015 – February 13, 2016, Brigham Young University Museum of Art, Provo, Utah

Norman Rockwell Museum, Stockbridge, Massachusetts
Norman Rockwell: Behind the Camera
Solo exhibition
November 7, 2009 – May 24, 2010, Norman Rockwell Museum, Stockbridge, Massachusetts
November 19, 2010 – April 10, 2011, Brooklyn Museum, Brooklyn, New York
June 25, 2011 – September 17, 2011, George Eastman House-International

Museum of Photography & Film, Rochester, New York
October 1, 2011 – January 1, 2012, El Paso Museum of Art, El Paso, Texas
May 5 – September 3, 2012 , Heritage Museums & Gardens, Sandwich, Massachusetts
October 13, 2012 – January 13, 2013, Vero Beach Museum of Art, Vero Beach, Florida
June 5 – September 1, 2013, McNay Art Museum, San Antonio, Texas
October 17, 2014- January 18, 2015, Columbia Museum of Art, Columbia, South Carolina

Telling Stories: Norman Rockwell from the Collections of George Lucas and Steven Spielberg
Solo exhibition
July 2, 2010 – January 2, 2011, Smithsonian American Art Museum, Washington, D.C.

Art and Appetite: American Painting, Culture, and Cuisine
Freedom from Want, 1943
November 12, 2013 – January 27, 2014, Art Institute of Chicago, Chicago, Illinois
February 22 – May 18, 2014, Amon Carter Museum, Fort Worth, Texas

Witness: Art and Civil Rights in the Sixties
New Kids in the Neighborhood, 1965
March 7 – July 13, 2014, Brooklyn Museum, Brooklyn, New York
August 30 – December 14, 2014, Hood Museum of Art, Dartmouth College, Dartmouth, Massachusetts
February 15 – May 10, 2015, Blanton Museum of Art, University of Texas at Austin

Intersection: Painting, Drawing and Photography
The Recruit, 1966
August 29 – October 19, 2014, Suzanne H. Arnold Art Gallery, Lebanon Valley College, Annville, Pennsylvania

Bibliography

D. Solomon, *American Mirror: The Life and Art of Norman Rockwell*, Farrar, Straus and Giroux Publishing, New York 2013.

V. Mecklenburg, T. McCarthy, *Telling Stories: Norman Rockwell from the collections of George Lucas and Steven Spielberg*, Abrams, New York 2010.

J. Edgerton, N. O'Brian, *The Unknown Rockwell: A Portrait of Two American Families*, Battenkill River Press, Essex Junction (VT) 2009.

R. Schick, *Norman Rockwell: Behind the Camera*, Little, Brown and Company, New York 2009.

L. Szekely Pero, *American Chronicles: The Art of Norman Rockwell*, Norman Rockwell Museum, Stockbridge (MA) 2007.

L. Claridge, *Norman Rockwell: A Life* (2001), "Paperback", Modern Library, New York 2003.

M.H. Hennessey, A. Knutson, *Norman Rockwell: Pictures for the American People*, Abrams, New York 1999.

S. Murray, J. McCabe, *Norman Rockwell's Four Freedoms: Images that inspire a nation*, Berkshire House/Norman Rockwell Museum, Stockbridge (MA) 1993.

L.N. Moffatt, *Norman Rockwell: A Definitive Catalogue*, 2 vols., Norman Rockwell Museum, Stockbridge (MA) 1986.

N. Rockwell, *The Norman Rockwell Album*, Doubleday, Garden City (NY) 1961.

N. Rockwell, T. Rockwell, *Norman Rockwell: My Adventures as an Illustrator* (1960), "Paperback", Abrams, New York 1995.

N. Rockwell, *How I Make a Picture* (o *Rockwell on Rockwell: How I Make a Picture*) (1948 c.), Watson-Guptill Publications, New York 1979, and Watson-Guptill Publications, in cooperation with the Famous Artists School, New York 1983.

A.L. Guptill, *Norman Rockwell Illustrator* (1946), Watson-Guptill Publications, New York 1970.

Copyrights *Saturday Evening Post* Covers
Boy with Baby Carriage
© 1916 SEPS: Licensed by Curtis Licensing, Indianapolis, IN, USA
Christmas Trio
© 1923 SEPS: Licensed by Curtis Licensing, Indianapolis, IN, USA
Parade
© 1924 SEPS: Licensed by Curtis Licensing, Indianapolis, IN, USA
Boy Making Football Tackle
© 1925 SEPS: Licensed by Curtis Licensing, Indianapolis, IN, USA
Boy and Girl Gazing at Moon (Puppy Love) (Sunset)
© 1926 SEPS: Licensed by Curtis Licensing, Indianapolis, IN, USA
Boy with Teacher (Young Scholar)
© 1926 SEPS: Licensed by Curtis Licensing, Indianapolis, IN, USA
Welcome to Elmville (*Policeman Setting Speed Trap*)
© 1929 SEPS: Licensed by Curtis Licensing, Indianapolis, IN, USA
Old Man in Fishing Boat
© 1930 SEPS: Licensed by Curtis Licensing, Indianapolis, IN, USA
Croquet
© 1931 SEPS: Licensed by Curtis Licensing, Indianapolis, IN, USA
Girl Asking Directions in French
© 1932 SEPS: Licensed by Curtis Licensing, Indianapolis, IN, USA
Brass Merchant (Bargaining with the Antiques Dealer)
© 1934 SEPS: Licensed by Curtis Licensing, Indianapolis, IN, USA
Springtime: Boy with Rabbit
© 1935 SEPS: Licensed by Curtis Licensing, Indianapolis, IN, USA
Artist Facing Blank Canvas (Deadline)
© 1938 SEPS: Licensed by Curtis Licensing, Indianapolis, IN, USA
Hundredth Year of Baseball (Baseball Player and Umpire)
© 1939 SEPS: Licensed by Curtis Licensing, Indianapolis, IN, USA
The Convention (Hat Check Girl)
© 1941 SEPS: Licensed by Curtis Licensing, Indianapolis, IN, USA
The Flirts (Girl Driving Convertible)
© 1941 SEPS: Licensed by Curtis Licensing, Indianapolis, IN, USA
Tattoo Artist
© 1944 SEPS: Licensed by Curtis Licensing, Indianapolis, IN, USA
Disabled Veteran
© 1944 SEPS: Licensed by Curtis Licensing, Indianapolis, IN, USA
Man Setting Clock
© 1945 SEPS: Licensed by Curtis Licensing, Indianapolis, IN, USA
Framed (Man Carrying Frame)
© 1946 SEPS: Licensed by Curtis Licensing, Indianapolis, IN, USA
Statue of Liberty
© 1946 SEPS: Licensed by Curtis Licensing, Indianapolis, IN, USA
Boy in Dining Car
© 1946 SEPS: Licensed by Curtis Licensing, Indianapolis, IN, USA
Boy on Highdive
© 1947 SEPS: Licensed by Curtis Licensing, Indianapolis, IN, USA
The Gossips
© 1948 SEPS: Licensed by Curtis Licensing, Indianapolis, IN, USA
The Referee (The Toss)
© 1950 SEPS: Licensed by Curtis Licensing, Indianapolis, IN, USA
The Facts of Life
© 1951 SEPS: Licensed by Curtis Licensing, Indianapolis, IN, USA
Day in the Life of a Little Boy
© 1952 SEPS: Licensed by Curtis Licensing, Indianapolis, IN, USA
Soda Jerk
© 1953 SEPS: Licensed by Curtis Licensing, Indianapolis, IN, USA
Girl at Mirror
© 1954 SEPS: Licensed by Curtis Licensing, Indianapolis, IN, USA
Art Critic
© 1955 SEPS: Licensed by Curtis Licensing, Indianapolis, IN, USA
The Discovery (Boy Discovering Santa Suit)
© 1956 SEPS: Licensed by Curtis Licensing, Indianapolis, IN, USA
Before the Shot
© 1958 SEPS: Licensed by Curtis Licensing, Indianapolis, IN, USA
Boy Graduate
© 1959 SEPS: Licensed by Curtis Licensing, Indianapolis, IN, USA
Triple Self-Portrait
© 1960 SEPS: Licensed by Curtis Licensing, Indianapolis, IN, USA
Window Washer
© 1960 SEPS: Licensed by Curtis Licensing, Indianapolis, IN, USA
Portrait of John F. Kennedy
©1960 SEPS: Licensed by Curtis Licensing, Indianapolis, IN, USA

www.curtislicensing.com
Norman Rockwell Museum Collections

Photo credits
© 2014. Foto Scala, Florence: p. 17
© 2014. Foto Austrian Archives/Scala Florence: p. 16
© Bettmann/Corbis: pp. 114–15, 199
© Colección Carmen Thyssen-Bornemisza en depósito en el Museo Thyssen-Bornemisza/Scala, Florence: p. 15 a destra
© ClassicStock/Corbis: p. 105
© Corbis: p. 25
© Hulton-Deutsch Collection/Corbis: p. 187
© Kingendai/AFLO/AFLO/Nippon News/Corbis: pp. 74–75
© Underwood & Underwood/Corbis: p. 29

Following pages
Aerial view of New York from Empire State Building

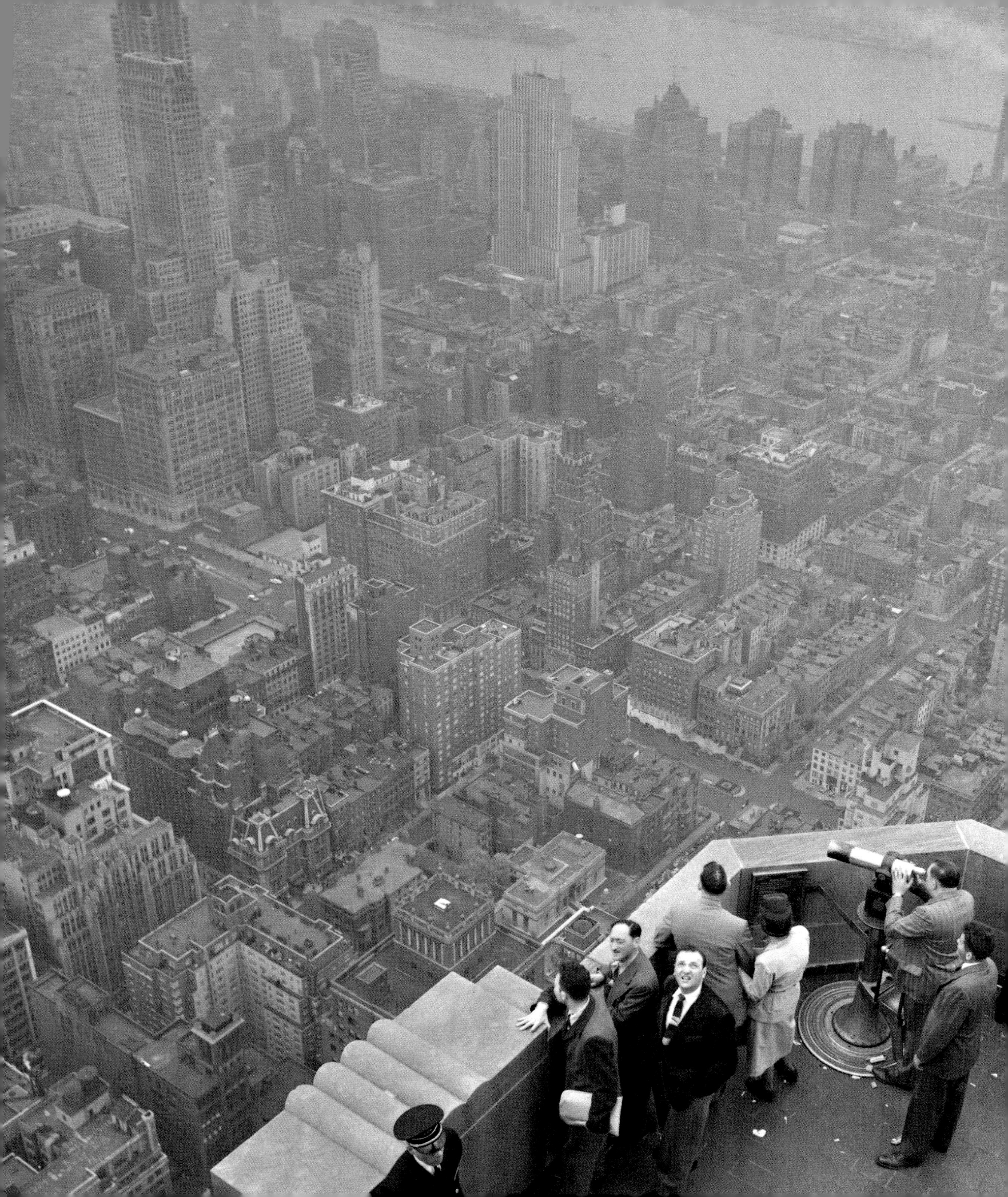

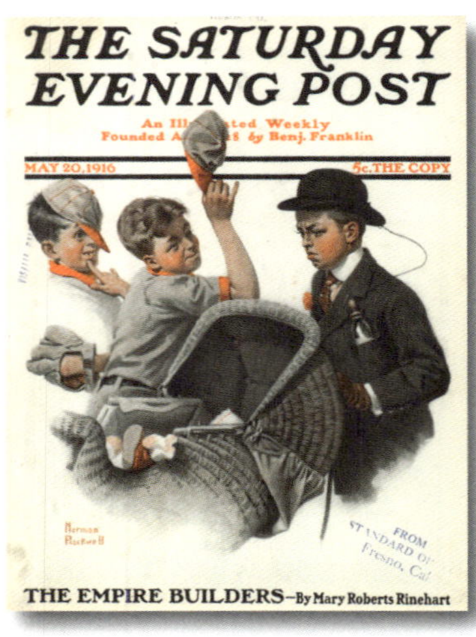
THE SATURDAY EVENING POST
MAY 20, 1916
5c. THE COPY
THE EMPIRE BUILDERS—By Mary Roberts Rinehart

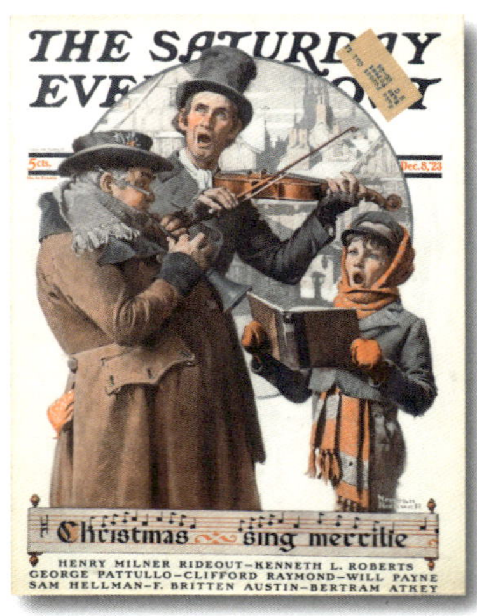
THE SATURDAY EVENING POST
Christmas sing merrilie
HENRY MILNER RIDEOUT—KENNETH L. ROBERTS
GEORGE PATTULLO—CLIFFORD RAYMOND—WILL PAYNE
SAM HELLMAN—F. BRITTEN AUSTIN—BERTRAM ATKEY

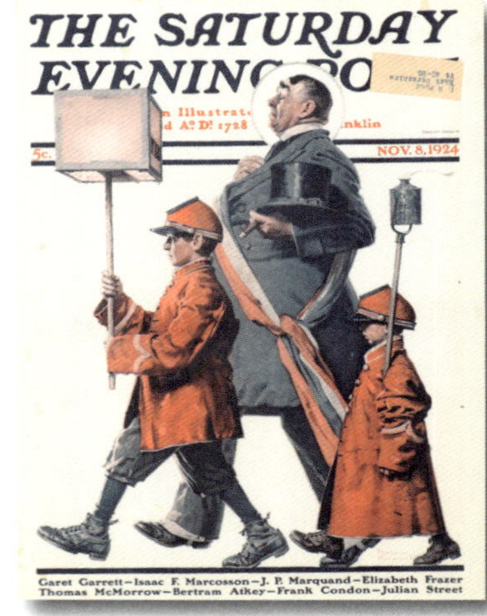
THE SATURDAY EVENING POST
NOV. 8, 1924
Garet Garrett—Isaac F. Marcosson—J. P. Marquand—Elizabeth Frazer
Thomas McMorrow—Bertram Atkey—Frank Condon—Julian Street

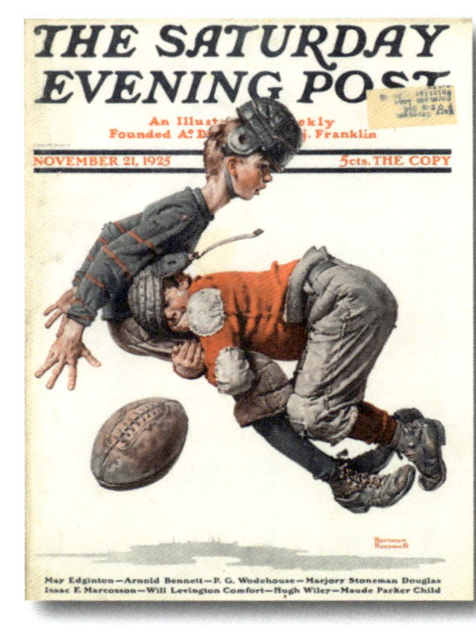
THE SATURDAY EVENING POST
NOVEMBER 21, 1925
5cts. THE COPY

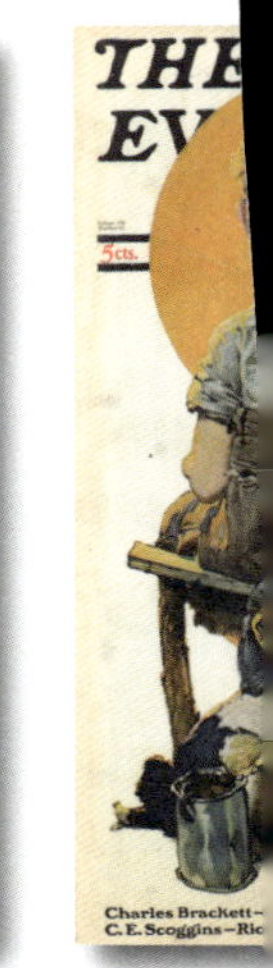

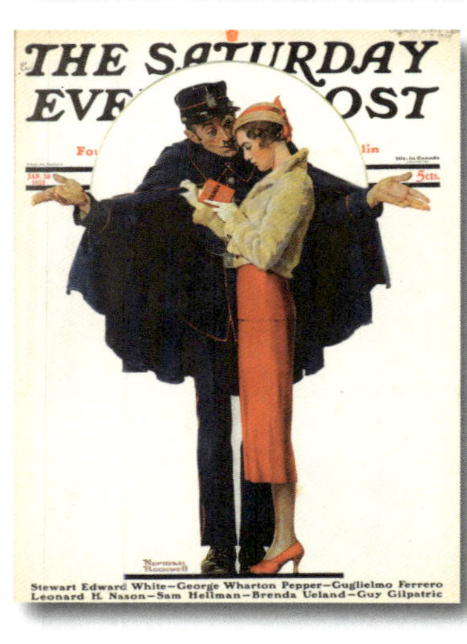
THE SATURDAY EVENING POST
Stewart Edward White—George Wharton Pepper—Guglielmo Ferrero
Leonard H. Nason—Sam Hellman—Brenda Ueland—Guy Gilpatric

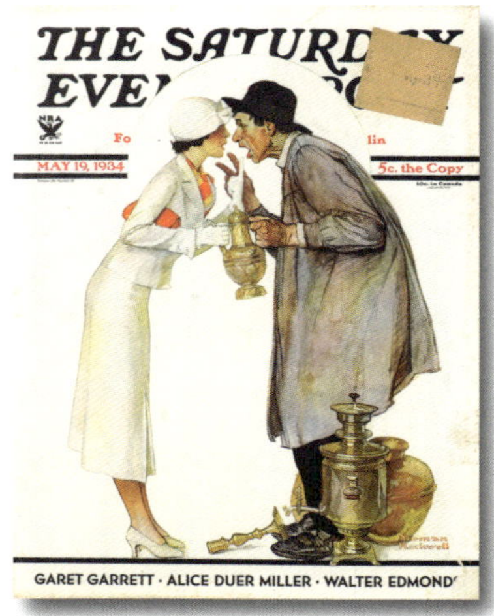
THE SATURDAY EVENING POST
MAY 19, 1934
5c. the Copy
GARET GARRETT · ALICE DUER MILLER · WALTER EDMONDS

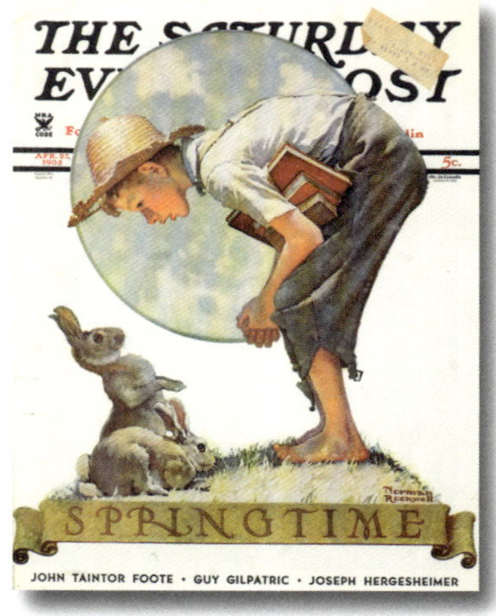
THE SATURDAY EVENING POST
SPRINGTIME
JOHN TAINTOR FOOTE · GUY GILPATRIC · JOSEPH HERGESHEIMER

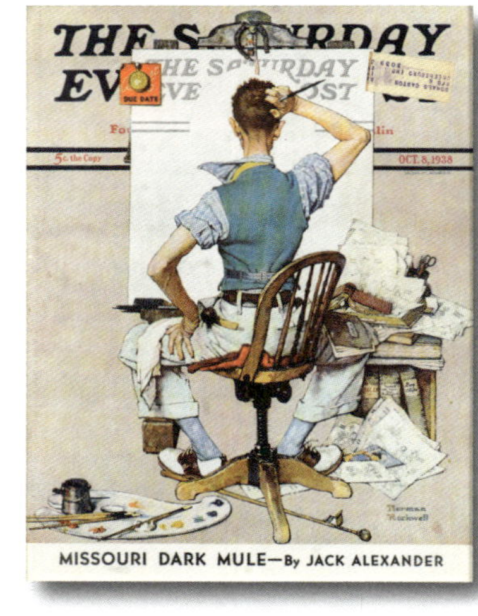
THE SATURDAY EVENING POST
OCT. 8, 1938
MISSOURI DARK MULE—By JACK ALEXANDER

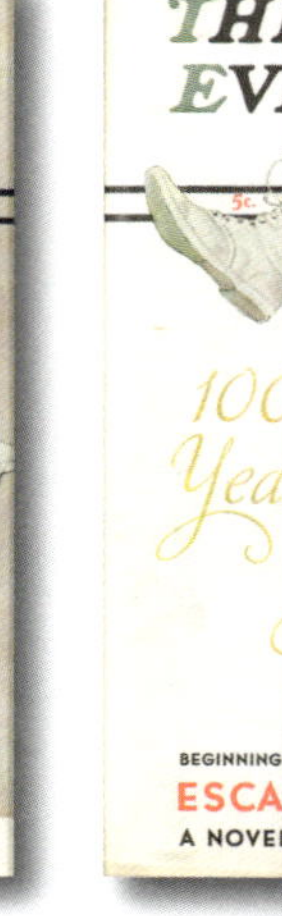

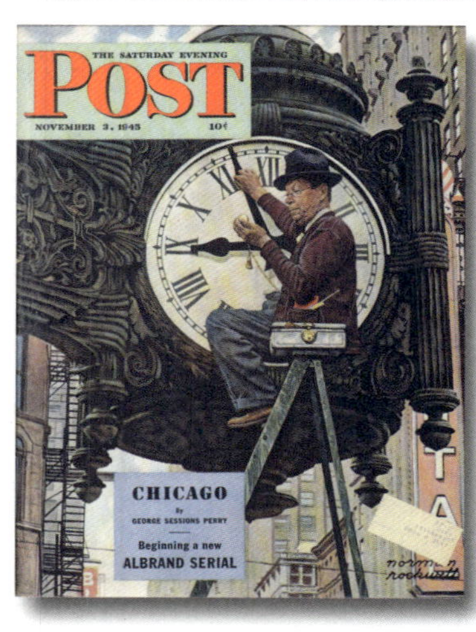
THE SATURDAY EVENING POST
NOVEMBER 3, 1945
CHICAGO
By GEORGE SESSIONS PERRY
Beginning a new ALBRAND SERIAL

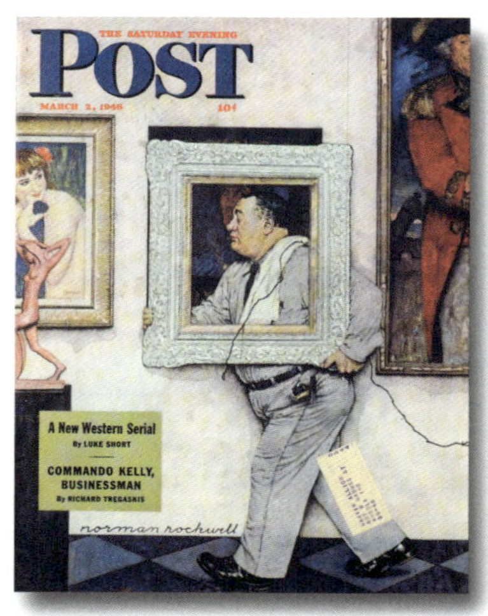
POST
A New Western Serial By LUKE SHORT
COMMANDO KELLY, BUSINESSMAN By RICHARD TREGASKIS
norman rockwell

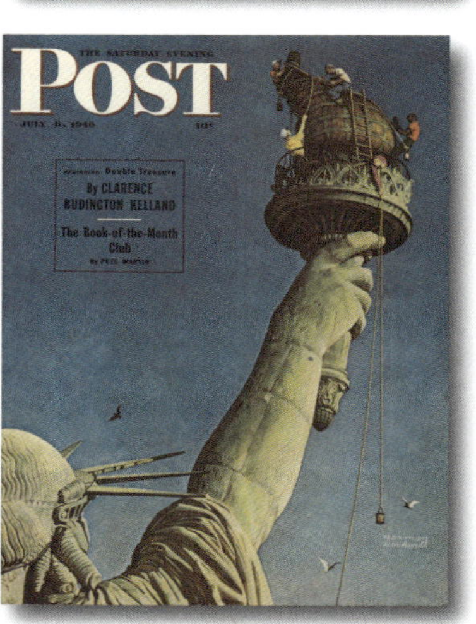
POST
By CLARENCE BUDINGTON KELLAND
The Book-of-the-Month Club

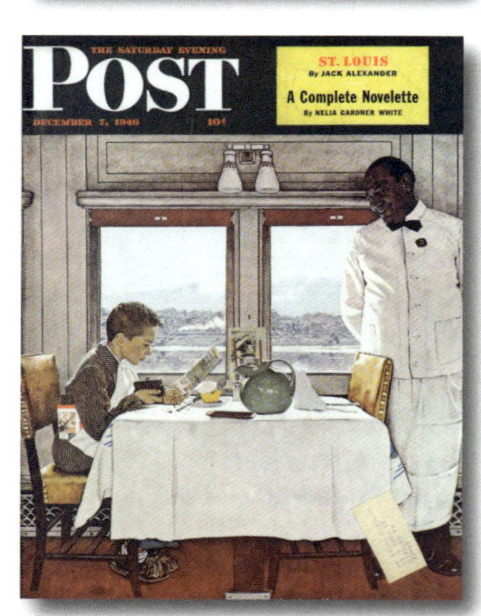
POST
ST. LOUIS By JACK ALEXANDER
A Complete Novelette By NELIA GARDNER WHITE

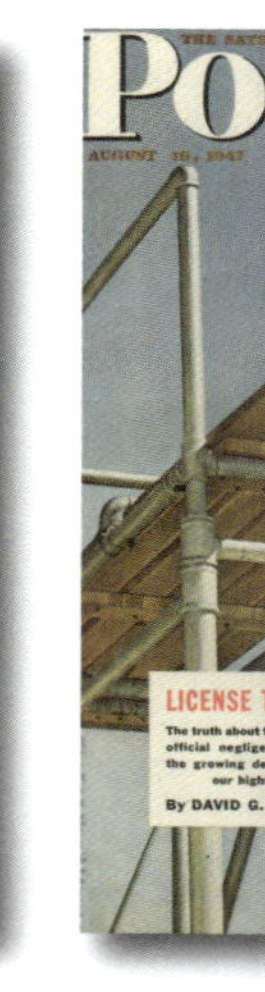

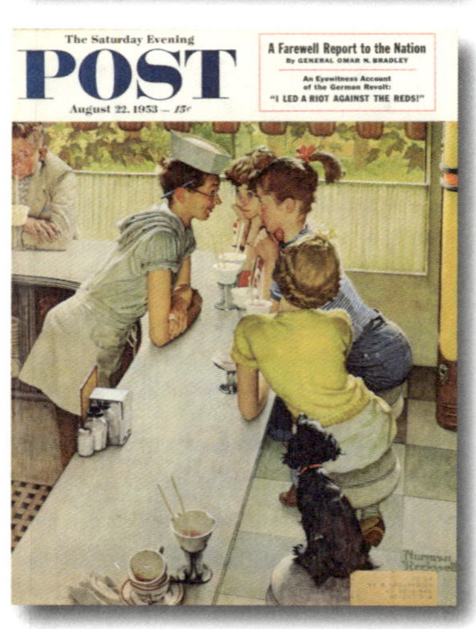
The Saturday Evening
POST
August 22, 1953 — 15¢
A Farewell Report to the Nation By GENERAL OMAR N. BRADLEY
An Eyewitness Account of the German Revolt:
"I LED A RIOT AGAINST THE REDS!"

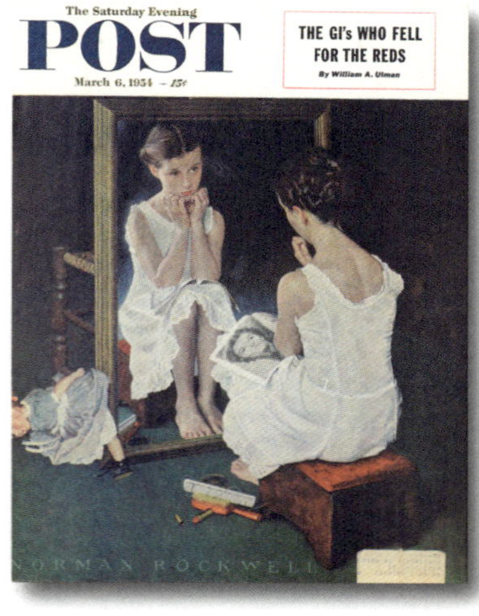
The Saturday Evening
POST
March 6, 1954 — 15¢
THE GI's WHO FELL FOR THE REDS
By William A. Ulman
NORMAN ROCKWELL

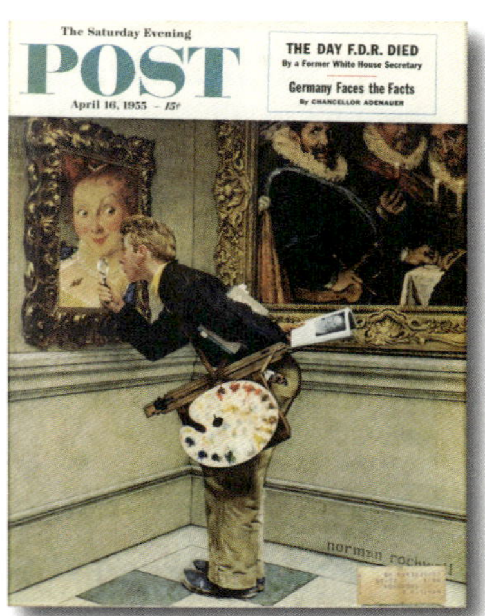
The Saturday Evening
POST
April 16, 1955 — 15¢
THE DAY F.D.R. DIED
By a Former White House Secretary
Germany Faces the Facts
By CHANCELLOR ADENAUER

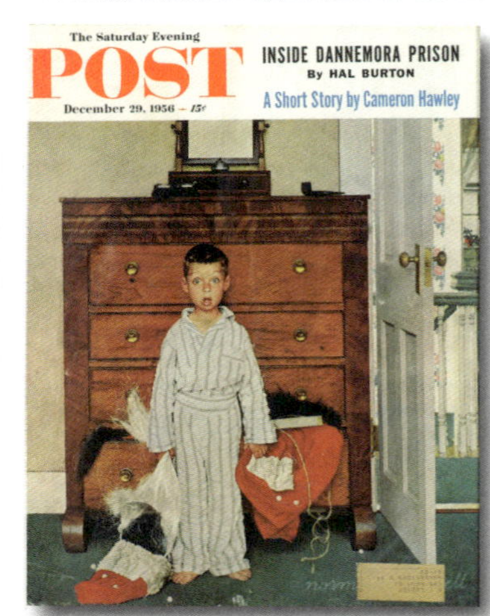
The Saturday Evening
POST
December 29, 1956 — 15¢
INSIDE DANNEMORA PRISON
By HAL BURTON
A Short Story by Cameron Hawley

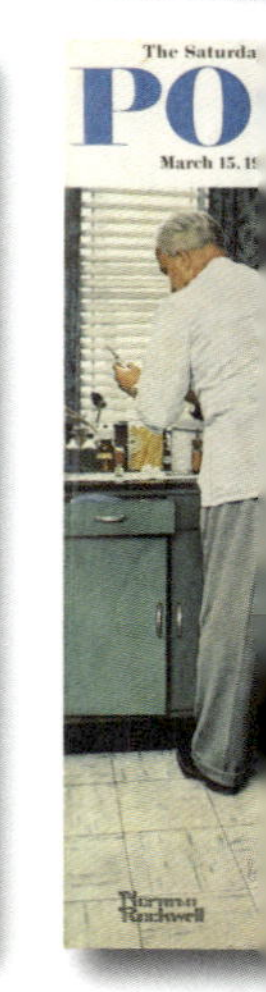